Benchmark Series

Microsoft®
PowerPoint®

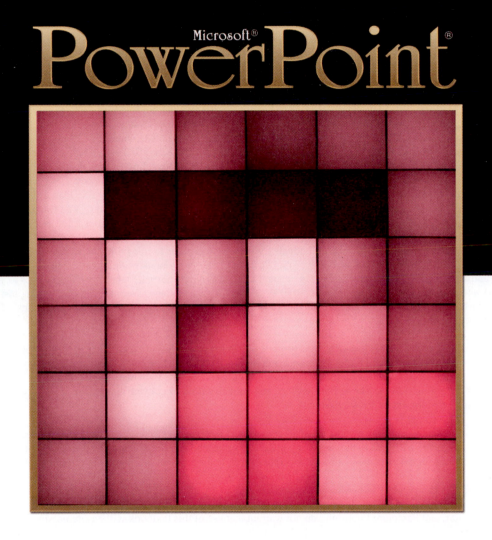

Nita Rutkosky

Pierce College at Puyallup
Puyallup, Washington

Audrey Rutkosky Roggenkamp

Pierce College at Puyallup
Puyallup, Washington

Paradigm
PUBLISHING

St. Paul • Indianapolis

Managing Editor	Sonja Brown
Senior Developmental Editor	Christine Hurney
Production Editor	Donna Mears
Copy Editor	Susan Capecchi
Cover and Text Designer	Leslie Anderson
Desktop Production	Ryan Hamner, Julie Johnston, Jack Ross
Proofreader	Laura Nelson
Indexer	Sandi Schroeder

Acknowledgements: The authors, editors, and publisher thank the following instructors for their helpful suggestions during the planning and development of the books in the Benchmark Office 2010 Series: Somasheker Akkaladevi, Virginia State University, Petersburg, VA; Ed Baker, Community College of Philadelphia, Philadelphia, PA; Lynn Baldwin, Madison Area Technical College, Madison, WI; Letty Barnes, Lake Washington Technical College, Kirkland, WA; Richard Bell, Coastal Carolina Community College, Jacksonville, NC; Perry Callas, Clatsop Community College, Astoria, OR; Carol DesJardins, St. Clair County Community College, Port Huron, MI; Stacy Gee Hollins, St. Louis Community College--Florissant Valley, St. Louis, MO Sally Haywood, Prairie State College, Chicago Heights, IL; Dr. Penny Johnson, Madison Technical College, Madison, WI; Jan Kehm, Spartanburg Community College, Spartanburg, SC; Jacqueline Larsen, Asheville Buncombe Tech, Asheville, NC; Sherry Lenhart, Terra Community College, Fremont, OH; Andrea Robinson Hinsey, Ivy Tech Community College NE, Fort Wayne, IN; Bari Siddique, University of Texas at Brownsville, Brownsville, TX; Joan Splawski, Northeast Wisconsin Technical College, Green Bay, WI; Diane Stark, Phoenix College, Phoenix, AZ; Mary Van Haute, Northeast Wisconsin Technical College, Green Bay, WI; Rosalie Westerberg, Clover Park Technical College, Lakewood, WA.

The publishing team also thanks the following individuals for their contributions to this project: checking the accuracy of the instruction and exercises—Robertt (Rob) W. Neilly, Traci Post, and Lindsay Ryan; developing lesson plans, supplemental assessments, and supplemental case studies—Jan Davidson, Lambton College, Sarina, Ontario; writing rubrics to support end-of-chapter and end-of-unit activities—Robertt (Rob) W. Neilly, Seneca College, Toronto, Ontario; writing test item banks—Jeff Johnson; writing online quiz item banks—Trudy Muller; and developing PowerPoint presentations—Janet Blum, Fanshawe College, London, Ontario.

Trademarks: Access, Excel, Internet Explorer, Microsoft, PowerPoint, and Windows are trademarks or registered trademarks of Microsoft Corporation in the United States and/or other countries. Some of the product names and company names included in this book have been used for identification purposes only and may be trademarks or registered trade names of their respective manufacturers and sellers. The authors, editors, and publisher disclaim any affiliation, association, or connection with, or sponsorship or endorsement by, such owners.

We have made every effort to trace the ownership of all copyrighted material and to secure permission from copyright holders. In the event of any question arising as to the use of any material, we will be pleased to make the necessary corrections in future printings. Thanks are due to the aforementioned authors, publishers, and agents for permission to use the materials indicated.

Paradigm Publishing is independent from Microsoft Corporation, and not affiliated with Microsoft in any manner. While this textbook may be used in assisting end users to prepare for a Microsoft Office Specialist exam, Microsoft, its designated program administrator, and Paradigm Publishing do not warrant that use of this textbook will ensure passing a Microsoft Office Specialist exam.

ISBN 978-0-76384-308-3 (Text)
ISBN 978-0-76384-309-0 (Text + CD)

© 2011 by Paradigm Publishing, Inc.
875 Montreal Way
St. Paul, MN 55102
Email: educate@emcp.com
Website: www.emcp.com

Printed in the United States of America

19 18 17 16 15 14 13 12 11 10   1 2 3 4 5 6 7 8 9 10

Contents

Microsoft PowerPoint 2010

Chapter 3 Formatting Slides 77

Chapter 4 Inserting Elements in Slides 121

Unit I Performance Assessment 177

Benchmark Microsoft PowerPoint 2010 teaches students how to build eye-catching presentations that communicate key information to audiences in business, academic, and organization settings. No prior knowledge of presentation software is required. After successfully completing a course using this textbook, students will be able to

- Plan, create, and revise presentations, including executing basic skills such as opening, editing, running, saving, and closing a file
- Format slides using design templates, slide and title masters, styles, bullets and numbering, headers and footers, and speaker notes
- Create visual appeal with images, SmartArt, charts, animation effects, and sound and video effects
- Share presentations for collaboration and review with others
- Given a workplace scenario requiring a presentation solution, assess the information requirements and then prepare the materials that achieve the goal efficiently and effectively

In addition to mastering PowerPoint skills, students will learn the essential features and functions of computer hardware, the Windows 7 operating system, and Internet Explorer 8.0. Upon completing the text, they can expect to be proficient in using PowerPoint to organize, analyze, and present information.

Achieving Proficiency in PowerPoint 2010

Since its inception several Office versions ago, the Benchmark Series has served as a standard of excellence in software instruction. Elements of the book function individually and collectively to create an inviting, comprehensive learning environment that produces successful computer users. The following visual tour highlights the text's features.

UNIT OPENERS display the unit's four chapter titles. Each unit concludes with a comprehensive unit performance assessment emphasizing the use of program features plus analytical, writing, and research skills.

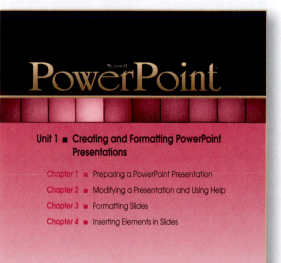

CHAPTER OPENERS present the performance objectives and an overview of the skills taught.

SNAP interactive tutorials are available to support chapter-specific skills at www.snap2010.emcp.com.

DATA FILES are provided for each chapter. A prominent note reminds students to copy the appropriate chapter data folder and make it active.

PROJECT APPROACH: Builds Skill Mastery within Realistic Context

MODEL ANSWERS provide a preview of the finished chapter projects and allow students to confirm they have created the materials accurately.

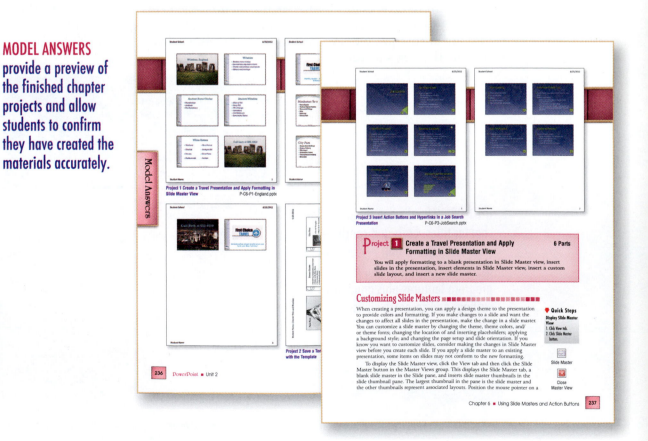

Project **2** Create and Format a Travel Photo Album — 3 Parts

You will use the photo album feature to create a presentation containing travel photographs. You will also apply formatting and insert elements in the presentation.

Creating a Photo Album

With PowerPoint's photo album feature, you can create a presentation containing personal or business pictures. You can customize and format the appearance of pictures by applying interesting layouts, frame shapes, and themes and you can also insert elements such as captions and text boxes. To create a photo album, click the Insert tab, click the Photo Album button arrow, and then click *New Photo Album* at the drop-down list. This displays the Photo Album dialog box as shown in Figure 5.14.

To insert pictures in the photo album, click the File/Disk button and the Insert New Pictures dialog box displays. At this dialog box, navigate to the desired folder and then double-click the picture you want inserted in the album. This inserts the picture name in the *Pictures in album* list box in the dialog box and also previews the picture in the *Preview* section. As you insert pictures in the photo album, the picture names display in the *Pictures in album* list box in the order in which they will appear in the presentation. When you have inserted the desired pictures in the photo album, click the Create button. This creates the photo album as a presentation and displays the first slide. The photo album feature creates the first slide with the title *Photo Album* and inserts the user's name.

▼ Quick Steps

Create Photo Album
1. Click Insert tab.
2. Click Photo Album button arrow.
3. Click *New Photo Album*.
4. Click File/Disk button.
5. Double-click desired picture.
6. Repeat steps 4 and 5 for all desired pictures.
7. Make desired changes at Photo Album dialog box.
8. Click Create button.

Photo Album

Figure 5.14 Photo Album Dialog Box

Insert a picture by clicking this button and then double-clicking the picture at the Insert New Pictures dialog box.

Choose a picture and then preview it in this Preview box.

Chapter 5 ■ Creating Tables, Charts, and Sm...

Project **2a** Creating a Travel Photo Album — Part 1 of 3

1. At a blank screen, click the Insert tab, click the Photo Album button arrow, and then click *New Photo Album* at the drop-down list.
2. At the Photo Album dialog box, click the File/Disk button.
3. At the Insert New Pictures dialog box, navigate to the PowerPoint2010C5 folder on your storage medium and then double-click *Cityscape.jpg*.
4. At the Photo Album dialog box, click the File/Disk button, and then double-click *Nightscape.jpg* at the Insert New Pictures dialog box.
5. Insert the following additional pictures: *Stonehenge.jpg, BigBen.jpg, WhiteHorse.jpg*, and *VictoriaBC.jpg*.
6. Click the Create button. (This opens a presentation with each image in a slide and the first slide containing the default text *Photo Album* followed by your name (or the user name for the computer).
7. Save the presentation and name it **P-C5-P2-Album.pptx**.
8. Run the presentation.

Step 1

Step 2

Step 6

Editing and Formatting a Photo Album

▼ Quick Steps

Edit Photo Album
1. Click Insert tab.
2. Click Photo Album button arrow.
3. Click *Edit Photo Album*.
4. Make desired changes at Edit Photo Album dialog box.
5. Click Update button.

If you want to make changes to a photo album presentation, open the presentation, click the Insert tab, click the Photo Album button arrow, and then click *Edit Photo Album* at the drop-down list. This displays the Edit Photo Album dialog box, which contains the same options as the Photo Album dialog box.

Rearrange the order of slides in the photo album presentation by clicking the desired slide in the *Pictures in album* list box and then clicking the button containing the up-pointing arrow to move the slide up in the order or clicking the button containing the down-pointing arrow to move the slide down in the order. Remove a slide by clicking the desired slide in the list box and then clicking the Remove button. With the buttons below the *Preview* box in the Edit Photo Album dialog box, you can rotate the picture in the slide, increase or decrease the contrast, and increase or decrease the brightness of the picture.

The *Picture layout* option in the *Album Layout* group has a default setting of *Fit to slide*. At this setting the picture in each slide will fill most of the slide. You can

Changing Table Layout

To further customize a table consider changing the table layout by inserting or deleting columns and rows and specifying cell alignments. Change table layout with options at the Table Tools Layout tab shown in Figure 5.2. Use options and buttons in the tab to select specific cells, delete and insert rows and columns, merge and split cells, specify cell and table height and width and text alignment in cells, and arrange elements in a slide.

HINT
If you make a mistake while formatting a table, immediately click the Undo button on the Quick Access toolbar.

Figure 5.2 Table Tools Layout Tab

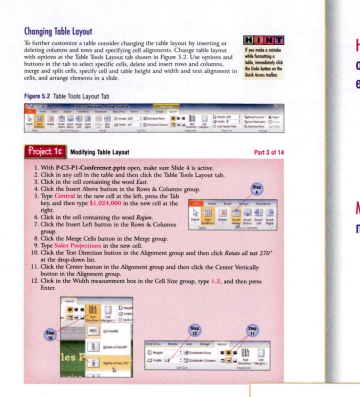

Project 1c Modifying Table Layout   Part 3 of 14

1. With **P-C5-P1-Conference.pptx** open, make sure Slide 4 is active.
2. Click in any cell in the table and then click the Table Tools Layout tab.
3. Click in the cell containing the word *East*.
4. Click the Insert Above button in the Rows & Columns group.
5. Type **Central** in the new cell at the left, press the Tab key, and then type **$1,024,000** in the new cell at the right.
6. Click in the cell containing the word *Region*.
7. Click the Insert Left button in the Rows & Columns group.
8. Click the Merge Cells button in the Merge group.
9. Type **Sales Projections** in the new cell.
10. Click the Text Direction button in the Alignment group and then click *Rotate all text 270°* at the drop-down list.
11. Click the Center button in the Alignment group and then click the Center Vertically button in the Alignment group.
12. Click in the Width measurement box in the Cell Size group, type **1.2**, and then press Enter.

---

c. Select any text that displays in the *Search for* text box in the Clip Art task pane, type **sales**, and then press Enter.
d. Scroll down the list of clip art images and then click the image shown in Figure 5.3. (If this image is not available, choose a similar clip art image related to sales.)
e. Close the Clip Art task pane.
f. With the image selected, click in the Shape Height measurement box in the Size group in the Picture Tools Format tab, type **2.8**, and then press Enter.
g. Drag the clip art image so it is positioned in the table as shown in Figure 5.3.
h. Click outside the clip art image to deselect it.
26. Save **P-C5-P1-Conference.pptx**.

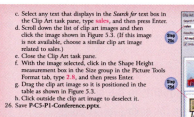

Figure 5.3 Project 1c, Slide 4

Inserting an Excel Spreadsheet

In addition to inserting a table in a slide, you can insert an Excel spreadsheet, which provides you with some Excel functions. To insert an Excel spreadsheet, click the Insert tab, click the Table button in the Tables group, and then click the *Excel Spreadsheet* option at the drop-down list. This inserts a small worksheet in the slide with two columns and two rows visible. You can increase the number of visible cells by dragging the sizing handles that display around the worksheet. Click outside the worksheet and the cells display as an object that you can format with options in the Drawing Tools Format tab. To format the worksheet with Excel options, double-click the worksheet and the ribbon displays with Excel tabs.

HINTS provide useful tips on how to use features efficiently and effectively.

MAGENTA TEXT identifies material to type.

At the end of the project, students save, print, and then close the file.

CHAPTER REVIEW ACTIVITIES: A Hierarchy of Learning Assessments

Chapter Summary

- Use the spelling feature to check spelling of slides in a presentation. Begin the spelling checker by clicking the Review tab and then clicking the Spelling button in the Proofing group.
- Click in a placeholder to select the placeholder and position the insertion point inside.
- Display the Find dialog box by clicking the Find button in the Editing group in the Home tab.
- Display the Replace dialog box by clicking the Replace button in the Editing group in the Home tab.
- With buttons in the Clipboard group or with options from a shortcut menu, you can cut and paste or copy and paste text in slides.
- You can use the mouse to move text in the Slides/Outline pane. You can select and then drag it to a new location or hold down the Ctrl key while dragging to copy text to a new location.
- Use the sizing handles that display around a selected placeholder to increase or decrease the size of the placeholder. You can use the mouse to drag a selected placeholder to a new lo...
- Use the New Slide but...
- Delete a selected slide...
- You can move or delete... pane or in Slide Sorter...
- Copy a selected slide b... the desired location.
- Use the Copy and Past... copy a slide between pr...
- Select adjacent slides i... clicking the first slide, 1... slide. Select nonadjacen... each desired slide.
- Duplicate slides in a pr... Outline pane, clicking ... *Duplicate Selected Slides*... clicking *Duplicate* at the...
- Divide a presentation i... presentation.
- You can copy slides fro... at the Reuse Slides tasl... button arrow and then ...
- Customize the Quick A... Toolbar button that dis... the desired button or o... remove buttons from th... the ribbon.

CHAPTER SUMMARY captures the purpose and execution of key features.

68   PowerPoint ▪ Unit 1

- You can type text in a slide in the Slide pane or in the Slides/Outline pane with the Outline tab selected.
- Enhance a presentation by adding transitions (how one slide is removed from the screen and replaced with the next slide) and sound. Add transitions and sound to a presentation with options in the Transitions tab.
- Advance slides automatically in a slide show by removing the check mark from the *On Mouse Click* check box in the Transitions tab, inserting a check mark in the *After* check box, and then specifying the desired time in the time option box.
- Click the Apply To All button to apply transitions, sounds, and/or time settings to all slides in a presentation.

Commands Review

FEATURE	RIBBON TAB, GROUP	BUTTON, OPTION	KEYBOARD SHORTCUT
Open dialog box	File	Open	Ctrl + O
New tab Backstage view	File	New	
Run presentation	Slide Show, Start Slide Show		F5
Close presentation	File	Close	Ctrl + F4
Slide layout	Home, Slides		
New slide	Home, Slides		
Save As dialog box	File		
Normal view	View, Presentation Views		
Slide Sorter view	View, Presentation Views		
Notes page	View, Presentation Views		
Print tab Backstage view	File		
Design theme	Design, Themes		
Transition	Transitions, Transition to		
Sound	Transitions, Timing		
Transition duration	Transitions, Timing		

COMMANDS REVIEW summarizes visually the major features and alternative methods of access.

34   PowerPoint ▪ Unit 1

Concepts Check   Test Your Knowledge

Completion: In the space provided at the right, indicate the correct term, command, or number.

1. Click this tab to display tabs and buttons for working with presentations. _____

2. This toolbar contains buttons for commonly used commands. _____

3. This area contains the tabs and commands divided into groups. _____

4. Display installed templates in this Backstage view tab. _____

5. This is the keyboard shortcut to close a presentation. _____

6. Apply a theme template to a presentation by clicking this tab and then clicking the desired theme in the Themes group. _____

7. Insert a new slide by clicking the New Slide button in this group in the Home tab. _____

8. Change to this view to view displays of all slides in the presentation in slide thumbnails. _____

9. This is the default view and displays three panes. _____

10. The Previous Slide and Next Slide buttons display in this location. _____

11. To run a presentation beginning with Slide 1, click this button in the Slide Show tab. _____

12. In Normal view, you can enter text in a slide in this pane or in the Slides/Outline pane with the Outline tab selected. _____

13. To add a transition, click a transition thumbnail in the Transition to This Slide group in this tab. _____

14. When you apply a transition to slides in a presentation, these display below the slides in the Slides/Outline pane. _____

15. To advance slides automatically, remove the check mark from the *On Mouse Click* option, insert a check mark in this option, and then insert the desired number of seconds. _____

Chapter 1 ▪ Preparing a PowerPoint Presentation   35

CONCEPTS CHECK questions assess knowledge recall.

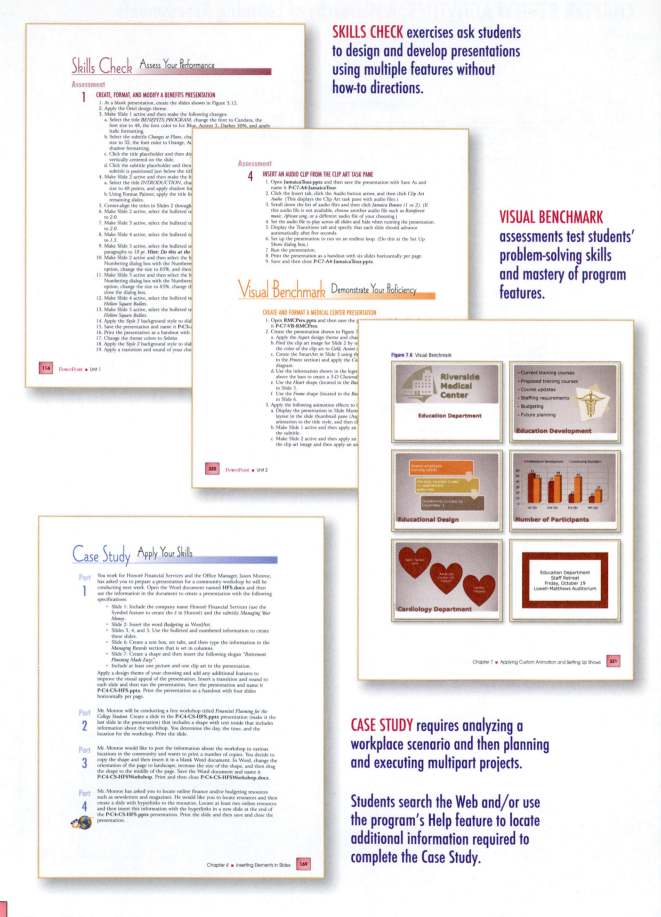

SKILLS CHECK exercises ask students to design and develop presentations using multiple features without how-to directions.

VISUAL BENCHMARK assessments test students' problem-solving skills and mastery of program features.

CASE STUDY requires analyzing a workplace scenario and then planning and executing multipart projects.

Students search the Web and/or use the program's Help feature to locate additional information required to complete the Case Study.

System Requirements ■■■■■■■■■■■■■■■■■■■■■■■■■■

This text is designed for the student to complete projects and assessments on a computer running a standard installation of Microsoft Office 2010, Professional Edition, and the Microsoft Windows 7 operating system. To effectively run this suite and operating system, your computer should be outfitted with the following:

- 1 gigahertz (GHz) processor or higher; 1 gigabyte (GB) of RAM
- DVD drive
- 15 GB of available hard-disk space
- Computer mouse or compatible pointing device

Office 2010 will also operate on computers running the Windows XP Service Pack 3 or the Windows Vista operating system.

Screen captures in this book were created using a screen resolution display setting of 1280 × 800. Refer to the *Customizing Settings* section of *Getting Started in Office 2010* following this preface for instructions on changing your monitor's resolution. Figure G.10 on page 10 shows the Microsoft Office Word ribbon at three resolutions for comparison purposes. Choose the resolution that best matches your computer; however, be aware that using a resolution other than 1280 × 800 means that your screens may not match the illustrations in this book.

About the Authors ■■■■■■■■■■■■■■■■■■■■■■■■■

Nita Rutkosky began teaching business education courses at Pierce College in Puyallup, Washington, in 1978. Since then she has taught a variety of software applications to students in postsecondary Information Technology certificate and degree programs. In addition to *Benchmark Office 2010,* she has co-authored *Marquee Series: Microsoft Office 2010, 2007,* and *2003; Signature Series: Microsoft Word 2010, 2007,* and *2003;* and *Using Computers in the Medical Office: Microsoft Word, Excel, and PowerPoint 2007* and *2003.* She has also authored textbooks on keyboarding, WordPerfect, desktop publishing, and voice recognition for Paradigm Publishing, Inc.

Audrey Rutkosky Roggenkamp has been teaching courses in the Business Information Technology department at Pierce College in Puyallup since 2005. Her courses have included keyboarding, skill building, and Microsoft Office programs. In addition to this title, she has co-authored *Marquee Series: Microsoft Office 2010* and *2007; Signature Series: Microsoft Word 2010* and *2007;* and *Using Computers in the Medical Office 2007* and *2003* for Paradigm Publishing, Inc.

What is the Microsoft® Office Specialist Program?

The Microsoft Office Specialist Program enables candidates to show that they have something exceptional to offer—proven expertise in certain Microsoft programs. Recognized by businesses and schools around the world, over 4 million certifications have been obtained in over 100 different countries. The Microsoft Office Specialist Program is the only Microsoft-approved certification program of its kind.

What is the Microsoft Office Specialist Certification?

The Microsoft Office Specialist certification validates through the use of exams that you have obtained specific skill sets within the applicable Microsoft Office programs and other Microsoft programs included in the Microsoft Office Specialist Program. Candidates can choose which exam(s) they want to take according to which skills they want to validate.

The available Microsoft Office Specialist Program exams* include:

Using Windows Vista®	Using Microsoft® Office PowerPoint® 2007
Using Microsoft® Office Word 2007	Using Microsoft® Office Access® 2007
Using Microsoft® Office Word 2007 - Expert	Using Microsoft® Office Outlook® 2007
Using Microsoft® Office Excel® 2007	Using Microsoft SharePoint® 2007
Using Microsoft® Office Excel® 2007 - Expert	

The Microsoft Office Specialist Program 2010 exams* include:

Microsoft Word 2010	Microsoft PowerPoint® 2010
Microsoft Word 2010 Expert	Microsoft Access® 2010
Microsoft Excel® 2010	Microsoft Outlook® 2010
Microsoft Excel® 2010 Expert	Microsoft SharePoint® 2010

What does the Microsoft Office Specialist Approved Courseware logo represent?

The logo indicates that this courseware has been approved by Microsoft to cover the course objectives that will be included in the relevant exam. It also means that after utilizing this courseware, you may be better prepared to pass the exams required to become a certified Microsoft Office Specialist.

For more information:

To learn more about Microsoft Office Specialist exams, visit www.microsoft.com/learning/msbc. To learn about other Microsoft approved courseware from Paradigm Publishing, Inc., visit www.ParadigmCollege.com.

*The availability of Microsoft Office Specialist certification exams varies by Microsoft program, program version, and language. Visit www.microsoft.com/learning for exam availability.

Microsoft, Access, Excel, the Office Logo, Outlook, PowerPoint, SharePoint, and Windows Vista are either registered trademarks or trademarks of Microsoft Corporation in the United States and/or other countries. The Microsoft Office Specialist logo and the Microsoft Office Specialist Approved Courseware logo are used under license from Microsoft Corporation.

Getting Started in Office 2010

In this textbook, you will learn to operate several computer application programs that combine to make an application "suite." This suite of programs is called Microsoft Office 2010. The programs you will learn to operate are the software, which includes instructions telling the computer what to do. Some of the application programs in the suite include a word processing program named Word, a spreadsheet program named Excel, a database program named Access, and a presentation program named PowerPoint.

Identifying Computer Hardware

The computer equipment you will use to operate the suite of programs is referred to as hardware. You will need access to a microcomputer system that should consist of the CPU, monitor, keyboard, printer, drives, and mouse. If you are not sure what equipment you will be operating, check with your instructor. The computer system shown in Figure G.1 consists of six components. Each component is discussed separately in the material that follows.

Figure G.1 Microcomputer System

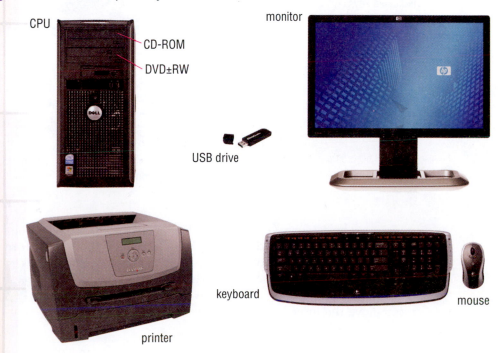

CPU

CD-ROM

DVD±RW

monitor

USB drive

printer

keyboard

mouse

CPU

CPU stands for Central Processing Unit and it is the intelligence of the computer. All the processing occurs in the CPU. Silicon chips, which contain miniaturized circuitry, are placed on boards that are plugged into slots within the CPU. Whenever an instruction is given to the computer, that instruction is processed through circuitry in the CPU.

Monitor

The monitor is a piece of equipment that looks like a television screen. It displays the information of a program and the text being input at the keyboard. The quality of display for monitors varies depending on the type of monitor and the level of resolution. Monitors can also vary in size—generally from 15-inch size up to 26-inch size or larger.

Keyboard

The keyboard is used to input information into the computer. Keyboards for microcomputers vary in the number and location of the keys. Microcomputers have the alphabetic and numeric keys in the same location as the keys on a typewriter. The symbol keys, however, may be placed in a variety of locations, depending on the manufacturer. In addition to letters, numbers, and symbols, most microcomputer keyboards contain function keys, arrow keys, and a numeric keypad. Figure G.2 shows an enhanced keyboard.

Figure G.2 Keyboard

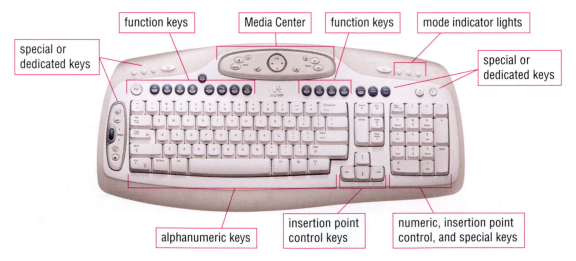

The 12 keys at the top of the keyboard, labeled with the letter F followed by a number, are called *function keys*. Use these keys to perform functions within each of the suite programs. To the right of the regular keys is a group of *special* or *dedicated keys*. These keys are labeled with specific functions that will be performed when you press the key. Below the special keys are arrow keys. Use these keys to move the insertion point in the document screen.

A keyboard generally includes three mode indicator lights. When you select certain modes, a light appears on the keyboard. For example, if you press the Caps Lock key, which disables the lowercase alphabet, a light appears next to Caps Lock. Similarly, pressing the Num Lock key will disable the special functions on the numeric keypad, which is located at the right side of the keyboard.

Disk Drives

Depending on the computer system you are using, Microsoft Office 2010 is installed on a hard drive or as part of a network system. Whether you are using Office on a hard drive or network system, you will need to have available a DVD or CD drive and a USB drive or other storage medium. You will insert the CD (compact disc) that accompanies this textbook in the DVD or CD drive and then copy folders from the CD to your storage medium. You will also save documents you complete at the computer to folders on your storage medium.

Printer

A document you create in Word is considered soft copy. If you want a hard copy of a document, you need to print it. To print documents you will need to access a printer, which will probably be either a laser printer or an ink-jet printer. A laser printer uses a laser beam combined with heat and pressure to print documents, while an ink-jet printer prints a document by spraying a fine mist of ink on the page.

Mouse

Many functions in the suite of programs are designed to operate more efficiently with a mouse. A mouse is an input device that sits on a flat surface next to the computer. You can operate a mouse with the left or the right hand. Moving the mouse on the flat surface causes a corresponding mouse pointer to move on the screen. Figure G.1 shows an illustration of a mouse.

Using the Mouse

The programs in the Microsoft Office suite can be operated with the keyboard and a mouse. The mouse may have two or three buttons on top, which are tapped to execute specific functions and commands. To use the mouse, rest it on a flat surface or a mouse pad. Put your hand over it with your palm resting on top of the mouse and your wrist resting on the table surface. As you move the mouse on the flat surface, a corresponding pointer moves on the screen.

When using the mouse, you should understand four terms — point, click, double-click, and drag. When operating the mouse, you may need to point to a specific command, button, or icon. Point means to position the mouse pointer on the desired item. With the mouse pointer positioned on the desired item, you may need to click a button on the mouse. Click means quickly tapping a button on the mouse once. To complete two steps at one time, such as choosing and then executing a function, double-click a mouse button. Double-click means to tap the left mouse button twice in quick succession. The term drag means to press and hold the left mouse button, move the mouse pointer to a specific location, and then release the button.

Using the Mouse Pointer

The mouse pointer will change appearance depending on the function being performed or where the pointer is positioned. The mouse pointer may appear as one of the following images:

- The mouse pointer appears as an I-beam (called the I-beam pointer) in the document screen and can be used to move the insertion point or select text.
- The mouse pointer appears as an arrow pointing up and to the left (called the arrow pointer) when it is moved to the Title bar, Quick Access toolbar, ribbon, or an option in a dialog box.
- The mouse pointer becomes a double-headed arrow (either pointing left and right, pointing up and down, or pointing diagonally) when performing certain functions such as changing the size of an object.
- In certain situations, such as moving an object or image, the mouse pointer displays with a four-headed arrow attached. The four-headed arrow means that you can move the object left, right, up, or down.
- When a request is being processed or when a program is being loaded, the mouse pointer may appear with a circle beside it. The moving circle means "please wait." When the process is completed, the circle is removed.
- The mouse pointer displays as a hand with a pointing index finger in certain functions such as Help and indicates that more information is available about the item. The mouse pointer also displays as a hand when you hover the mouse over a hyperlink.

Choosing Commands

Once a program is open, you can use several methods in the program to choose commands. A command is an instruction that tells the program to do something. You can choose a command using the mouse or the keyboard. When a program such as Word or PowerPoint is open, the ribbon contains buttons for completing tasks and contains tabs you click to display additional buttons. To choose a button on the Quick Access toolbar or in the ribbon, position the tip of the mouse arrow pointer on a button and then click the left mouse button.

The Office suite provides access keys you can press to use a command in a program. Press the Alt key on the keyboard to display KeyTips that identify the access key you need to press to execute a command. For example, press the Alt key in a Word document with the Home tab active and KeyTips display as shown in Figure G.3. Continue pressing access keys until you execute the desired command. For example, if you want to begin spell checking a document, you would press the Alt key, press the R key on the keyboard to display the Review tab, and then press the letter S on the keyboard.

Choosing Commands from Drop-Down Lists

To choose a command from a drop-down list with the mouse, position the mouse pointer on the desired option and then click the left mouse button. To make a selection from a drop-down list with the keyboard, type the underlined letter in the desired option.

Figure G.3 Word Home Tab KeyTips

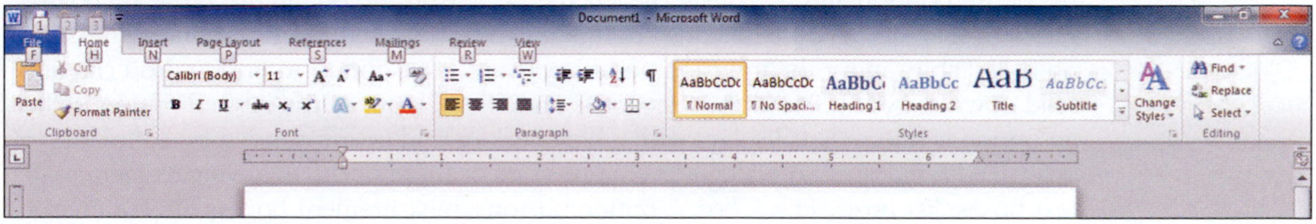

Some options at a drop-down list may be gray-shaded (dimmed), indicating that the option is currently unavailable. If an option at a drop-down list displays preceded by a check mark, that indicates that the option is currently active. If an option at a drop-down list displays followed by an ellipsis (...), a dialog box will display when that option is chosen.

Choosing Options from a Dialog Box

A dialog box contains options for applying formatting to a file or data within a file. Some dialog boxes display with tabs along the top providing additional options. For example, the Font dialog box shown in Figure G.4 contains two tabs — the Font tab and the Advanced tab. The tab that displays in the front is the active tab. To make a tab active using the mouse, position the arrow pointer on the desired tab and then click the left mouse button. If you are using the keyboard, press Ctrl + Tab or press Alt + the underlined letter on the desired tab.

Figure G.4 Word Font Dialog Box

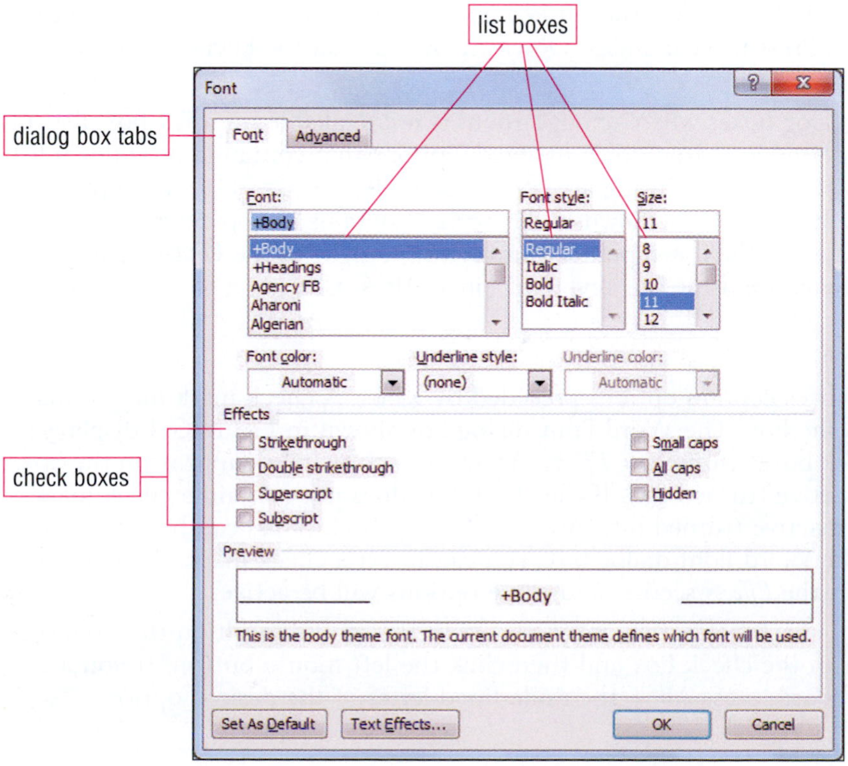

To choose options from a dialog box with the mouse, position the arrow pointer on the desired option and then click the left mouse button. If you are using the keyboard, press the Tab key to move the insertion point forward from option to option. Press Shift + Tab to move the insertion point backward from option to option. You can also hold down the Alt key and then press the underlined letter of the desired option. When an option is selected, it displays with a blue background or surrounded by a dashed box called a marquee. A dialog box contains one or more of the following elements: text boxes, list boxes, check boxes, option buttons, measurement boxes, and command buttons.

List Boxes

Some dialog boxes such as the Word Font dialog box shown in Figure G.4 may contain a list box. The list of fonts below the *Font* option is contained in a list box. To make a selection from a list box with the mouse, move the arrow pointer to the desired option and then click the left mouse button.

Some list boxes may contain a scroll bar. This scroll bar will display at the right side of the list box (a vertical scroll bar) or at the bottom of the list box (a horizontal scroll bar). You can use a vertical scroll bar or a horizontal scroll bar to move through the list if the list is longer than the box. To move down through a list on a vertical scroll bar, position the arrow pointer on the down-pointing arrow and hold down the left mouse button. To scroll up through the list in a vertical scroll bar, position the arrow pointer on the up-pointing arrow and hold down the left mouse button. You can also move the arrow pointer above the scroll box and click the left mouse button to scroll up the list or move the arrow pointer below the scroll box and click the left mouse button to move down the list. To move through a list with a horizontal scroll bar, click the left-pointing arrow to scroll to the left of the list or click the right-pointing arrow to scroll to the right of the list.

To make a selection from a list using the keyboard, move the insertion point into the box by holding down the Alt key and pressing the underlined letter of the desired option. Press the Up and/or Down Arrow keys on the keyboard to move through the list.

In some dialog boxes where enough room is not available for a list box, lists of options are inserted in a drop-down list box. Options that contain a drop-down list box display with a down-pointing arrow. For example, the *Underline style* option at the Word Font dialog box shown in Figure G.4 contains a drop-down list. To display the list, click the down-pointing arrow to the right of the *Underline style* option box. If you are using the keyboard, press Alt + U.

Check Boxes

Some dialog boxes contain options preceded by a box. A check mark may or may not appear in the box. The Word Font dialog box shown in Figure G.4 displays a variety of check boxes within the *Effects* section. If a check mark appears in the box, the option is active (turned on). If the check box does not contain a check mark, the option is inactive (turned off). Any number of check boxes can be active. For example, in the Word Font dialog box, you can insert a check mark in any or all of the boxes in the *Effects* section and these options will be active.

To make a check box active or inactive with the mouse, position the tip of the arrow pointer in the check box and then click the left mouse button. If you are using the keyboard, press Alt + the underlined letter of the desired option.

Text Boxes

Some options in a dialog box require you to enter text. For example, the boxes below the *Find what* and *Replace with* options at the Excel Find and Replace dialog box shown in Figure G.5 are text boxes. In a text box, you type text or edit existing text. Edit text in a text box in the same manner as normal text. Use the Left and Right Arrow keys on the keyboard to move the insertion point without deleting text and use the Delete key or Backspace key to delete text.

Option Buttons

The Word Insert Table dialog box shown in Figure G.6 contains options in the *AutoFit behavior* section preceded by option buttons. Only one option button can be selected at any time. When an option button is selected, a blue circle displays in the button. To select an option button with the mouse, position the tip of the arrow pointer inside the option button and then click the left mouse button. To make a selection with the keyboard, hold down the Alt key and then press the underlined letter of the desired option.

Measurement Boxes

Some options in a dialog box contain measurements or numbers you can increase or decrease. These options are generally located in a measurement box. For example, the Word Paragraph dialog box shown in Figure G.7 contains the *Left*, *Right*, *Before*, and *After* measurement boxes. To increase a number in a measurement box, position the tip of the arrow pointer on the up-pointing arrow to the right of the desired option and then click the left mouse button. To decrease the number, click the down-pointing arrow. If you are using the keyboard, press Alt + the underlined letter of the desired option and then press the Up Arrow key to increase the number or the Down Arrow key to decrease the number.

Command Buttons

In the Excel Find and Replace dialog box shown in Figure G.5, the boxes along the bottom of the dialog box are called command buttons. Use a command button to execute or cancel a command. Some command buttons display with an ellipsis (...). A command button that displays with an ellipsis will open another dialog box. To choose a command button with the mouse, position the arrow pointer on the desired button and then click the left mouse button. To choose a command button with the keyboard, press the Tab key until the desired command button contains the marquee and then press the Enter key.

Figure G.5 Excel Find and Replace Dialog Box

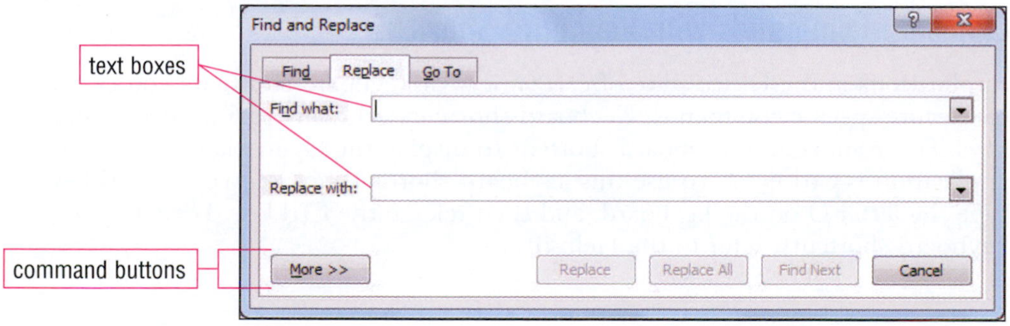

Figure G.6 Word Insert Table Dialog Box

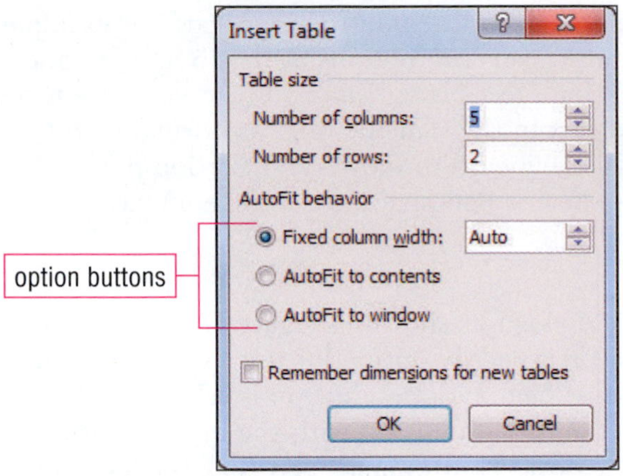

option buttons

Figure G.7 Word Paragraph Dialog Box

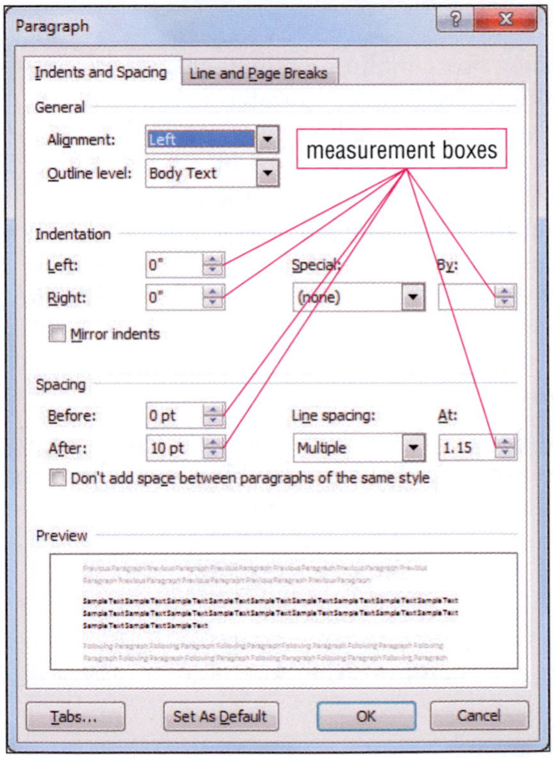

measurement boxes

Choosing Commands with Keyboard Shortcuts

Applications in the Office suite offer a variety of keyboard shortcuts you can use to execute specific commands. Keyboard shortcuts generally require two or more keys. For example, the keyboard shortcut to display the Open dialog box in an application is Ctrl + O. To use this keyboard shortcut, hold down the Ctrl key, type the letter O on the keyboard, and then release the Ctrl key. For a list of keyboard shortcuts, refer to the Help files.

Choosing Commands with Shortcut Menus

The software programs in the suite include menus that contain commands related to the item with which you are working. A shortcut menu appears in the file in the location where you are working. To display a shortcut menu, click the right mouse button or press Shift + F10. For example, if the insertion point is positioned in a paragraph of text in a Word document, clicking the right mouse button or pressing Shift + F10 will cause the shortcut menu shown in Figure G.8 to display in the document screen (along with the Mini toolbar).

To select an option from a shortcut menu with the mouse, click the desired option. If you are using the keyboard, press the Up or Down Arrow key until the desired option is selected and then press the Enter key. To close a shortcut menu without choosing an option, click anywhere outside the shortcut menu or press the Esc key.

Working with Multiple Programs ■■■■■■■■■■■■■■■■■■■■

As you learn the various programs in the Microsoft Office suite, you will notice how executing commands in each is very similar. For example, the steps to save, close, and print are virtually the same whether you are working in Word, Excel, or PowerPoint. This consistency between programs greatly enhances a user's ability to transfer knowledge learned in one program to another within the suite. Another appeal of Microsoft Office is the ability to have more than one program open at the same time. For example, you can open Word, create a document, and then open Excel, create a spreadsheet, and copy the spreadsheet into Word.

Figure G.8 Word Shortcut Menu

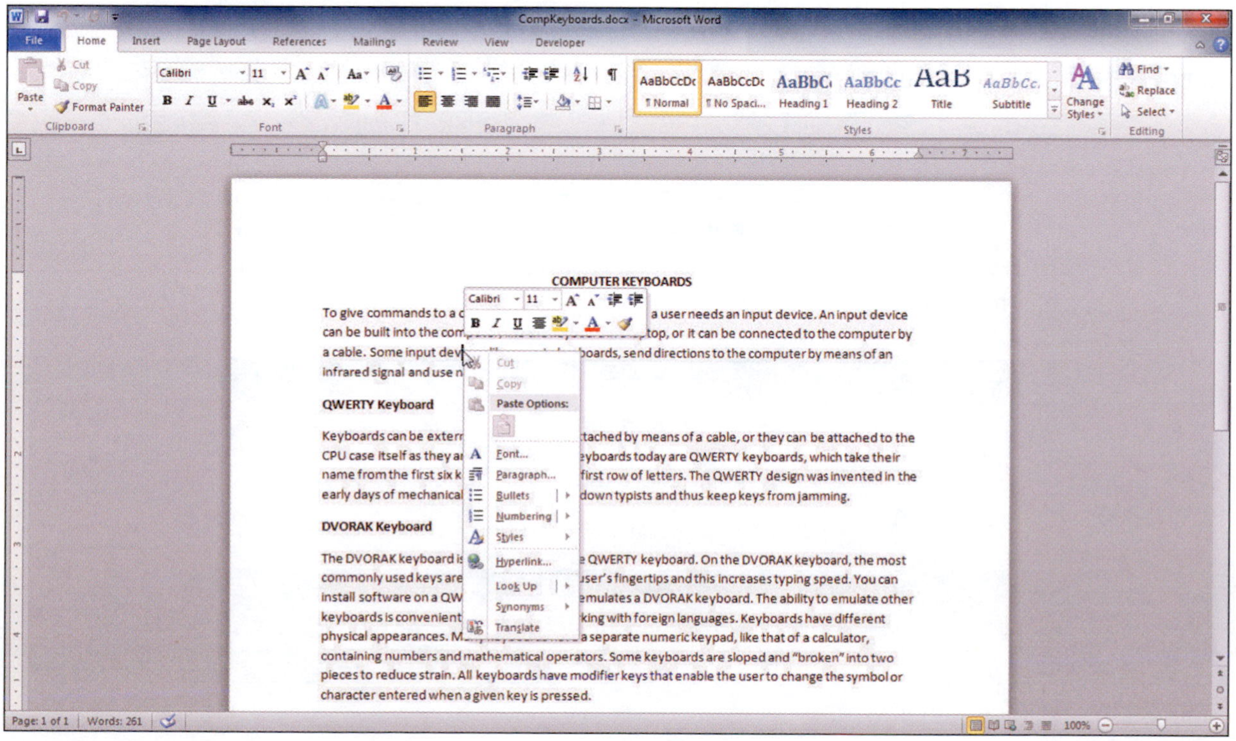

Figure G.9 Taskbar with Word, Excel, and PowerPoint Open

When you open a program, a button displays on the Taskbar containing an icon representing the program. If you open another program, a button containing an icon representing the program displays to the right of the first program button. Figure G.9 shows the Taskbar with Word, Excel, and PowerPoint open. To move from one program to another, click the button on the Taskbar representing the desired program file.

Customizing Settings

Before beginning computer projects in this textbook, you may need to customize the monitor settings and turn on the display of file extensions. Projects in the chapters in this textbook assume that the monitor display is set at 1280 by 800 pixels and that the display of file extensions is turned on.

Changing Monitor Resolutions

Before you begin learning the applications in the Microsoft Office 2010 suite, take a moment to check the display settings on the computer you are using. The ribbon in the Microsoft Office suite adjusts to the screen resolution setting of your computer monitor. Computer monitors set at a high resolution will have the ability to show more buttons in the ribbon than will a monitor set to a low resolution. The illustrations in this textbook were created with a screen resolution display set at 1280×800 pixels. In Figure G.10 the Word ribbon is shown three ways: at a lower screen resolution (1024×768 pixels), at the screen resolution featured

Figure G.10 Monitor Resolution

1024 × 768 screen resolution

1280 × 800 screen resolution

1440 × 900 screen resolution

throughout this textbook, and at a higher screen resolution (1440×900 pixels). Note the variances in the ribbon in all three examples. If possible, set your display to 1280×800 pixels to match the illustrations you will see in this textbook.

Project 1 Setting Monitor Display to 1280 by 800

1. At the Windows 7 desktop, click the Start button and then click *Control Panel*.
2. At the Control Panel dialog box, click the *Adjust screen resolution* option in the Appearance and Personalization category.
3. At the Control Panel Screen Resolution window, click the Resolution option button. (This displays a drop-down slider bar. Your drop-down slider bar may display differently than what you see in the image at the right.)
4. Drag the slider bar button on the slider bar until *1280 × 800* displays to the right of the slider button.
5. Click in the Control Panel Screen Resolution window to remove the slider bar.
6. Click the Apply button.
7. Click the Keep Changes button.
8. Click the OK button.
9. Close the Control Panel window.

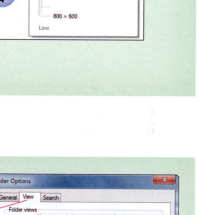

Project 2 Displaying File Extensions

1. At the Windows 7 desktop, click the Start button and then click *Computer*.
2. At the Computer window, click the Organize button on the toolbar and then click *Folder and search options* at the drop-down list.
3. At the Folder Options dialog box, click the View tab.
4. Click the *Hide extensions for known file types* check box to remove the check mark.
5. Click the Apply button.
6. Click the OK button.
7. Close the Computer window.

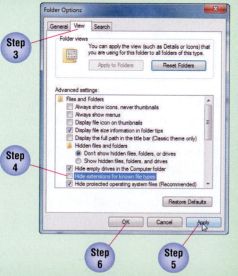

Completing Computer Projects ■■■■■■■■■■■■■■■■■■■

Some computer projects in this textbook require that you open an existing file. Project files are saved on the Student Resources CD that accompanies this textbook. The files you need for each chapter are saved in individual folders. Before beginning a chapter, copy the necessary folder from the CD to your storage medium (such as a USB flash drive) using the Computer window. If storage capacity is an issue with your storage medium, delete any previous chapter folders before copying a chapter folder onto your storage medium.

Project 3 — Copying a Folder from the Student Resources CD

1. Insert the CD that accompanies this textbook in the CD drive. At the AutoPlay window that displays, click the Close button located in the upper right corner of the window.
2. Insert your USB flash drive in an available USB port. If an AutoPlay window displays, click the Close button.
3. At the Windows desktop, open the Computer window by clicking the Start button and then clicking *Computer* at the Start menu.
4. Double-click the CD drive in the Content pane (displays with the name *BM10StudentResources* preceded by the drive letter).
5. Double-click the desired program folder name in the Content pane.
6. Click once on the desired chapter subfolder name to select it.
7. Click the Organize button on the toolbar and then click *Copy* at the drop-down list.
8. In the Computer window Content pane, click the drive containing your storage medium.
9. Click the Organize button on the toolbar and then click *Paste* at the drop-down list.
10. Close the Computer window by clicking the Close button located in the upper right corner of the window.

Project 4 — Deleting a Folder

Note: Check with your instructor before deleting a folder.

1. Insert your storage medium (such as a USB flash drive) in the USB port.
2. At the Windows desktop, open the Computer window by clicking the Start button and then clicking *Computer* at the Start menu.
3. Double-click the drive letter for your storage medium (drive containing your USB flash drive such as *Removable Disk (F:)*).
4. Click the chapter folder in the Content pane.
5. Click the Organize button on the toolbar and then click *Delete* at the drop-down list.
6. At the message asking if you want to delete the folder, click the Yes button.
7. Close the Computer window by clicking the Close button located in the upper right corner of the window.

Using Windows 7

A computer requires an operating system to provide necessary instructions on a multitude of processes including loading programs, managing data, directing the flow of information to peripheral equipment, and displaying information. Windows 7 is an operating system that provides functions of this type (along with much more) in a graphical environment. Windows is referred to as a *graphical user interface* (GUI—pronounced *gooey*) that provides a visual display of information with features such as icons (pictures) and buttons. In this introduction, you will learn these basic features of Windows 7:

- Use desktop icons and the Taskbar to launch programs and open files or folders
- Add and remove gadgets
- Organize and manage data, including copying, moving, creating, and deleting files and folders; and create a shortcut
- Explore the Control Panel and personalize the desktop
- Use the Windows Help and Support features
- Use search tools
- Customize monitor settings

Before using one of the software programs in the Microsoft Office suite, you will need to start the Windows 7 operating system. To do this, turn on the computer. Depending on your computer equipment configuration, you may also need to turn on the monitor and printer. If you are using a computer that is part of a network system or if your computer is set up for multiple users, a screen will display showing the user accounts defined for your computer system. At this screen, click your user account name and, if necessary, type your password and then press the Enter key. The Windows 7 operating system will start and, after a few moments, the desktop will display as shown in Figure W.1. (Your desktop may vary from what you see in Figure W.1.)

Exploring the Desktop ▪▪▪▪▪▪▪▪▪▪▪▪▪▪▪▪▪▪▪▪▪▪▪▪▪▪▪▪▪▪▪

When Windows is loaded, the main portion of the screen is called the *desktop*. Think of the desktop in Windows as the top of a desk in an office. A business person places necessary tools—such as pencils, pens, paper, files, calculator—on the desktop to perform functions. Like the tools that are located on a desk, the desktop contains tools for operating the computer. These tools are logically grouped and placed in dialog boxes or panels that you can display using icons on the desktop. The desktop contains a variety of features for using your computer and software programs installed on the computer. The features available on the desktop are represented by icons and buttons.

Figure W.1 Windows 7 Desktop

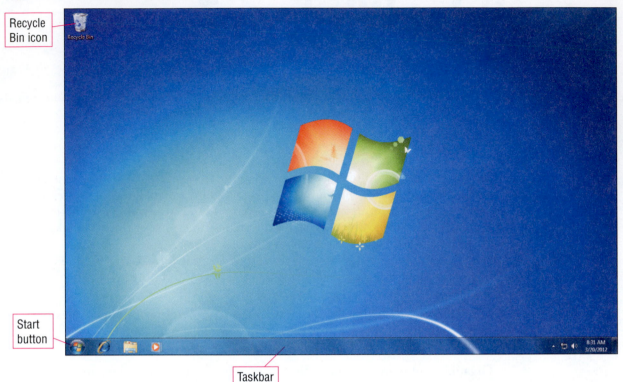

Recycle Bin icon

Start button

Taskbar

Using Icons

Icons are visual symbols that represent programs, files, or folders. Figure W.1 identifies the Recycle Bin icon located on the Windows desktop. The Windows desktop on your computer may contain additional icons. Programs that have been installed on your computer may be represented by an icon on the desktop. Also, icons may display on your desktop representing files or folders. Double-click an icon and the program, file, or folder it represents opens on the desktop.

Using the Taskbar

The bar that displays at the bottom of the desktop (see Figure W.1) is called the Taskbar. The Taskbar, shown in Figure W.2, contains the Start button, pinned items, a section that displays task buttons representing active tasks, the notification area, and the Show Desktop button.

Figure W.2 Windows 7 Taskbar

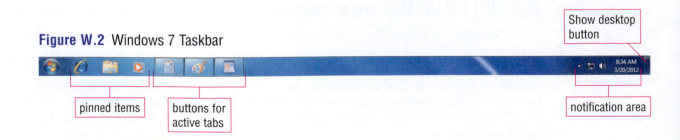

Show desktop button

pinned items

buttons for active tabs

notification area

Click the Start button, located at the left side of the Taskbar, and the Start menu displays as shown in Figure W.3 (your Start menu may vary). You can also display the Start menu by pressing the Windows key on your keyboard or by pressing Ctrl + Esc. The left side of the Start menu contains links to the most recently and frequently used programs. The name of the currently logged on user displays at the top of the darker right portion of the menu followed by the user's libraries. The two sections below the personal libraries provide links to other Windows features, such as games, the Control Panel, and Windows Help and Support. Use the Shut down button to put the system in a power-conserving state or into a locked, shut down, or sleep mode.

To choose an option from the Start menu, drag the arrow pointer to the desired option (referred to as *pointing*) and then click the left mouse button. Pointing to options at the Start menu that are followed by a right-pointing arrow will cause a side menu to display with additional options. When a program is open, a task button representing the program appears on the Taskbar. If multiple programs are open, each program will appear as a task button on the Taskbar (a few specialized tools may not).

Manipulating Windows ■■■■■■■■■ ■■■■■■■■ ■■■■■■■

When you open a program, a defined work area displays on the screen, which is referred to as a *window*. A Title bar displays at the top of a window and contains buttons at the right side for closing the window and minimizing, maximizing, and restoring the size of the window. You can open more than one window at a time and the open windows can be cascaded or stacked. Windows 7 contains a Snap feature that causes a window to "stick" to the edge of the screen when the window

Figure W.3 Start Menu

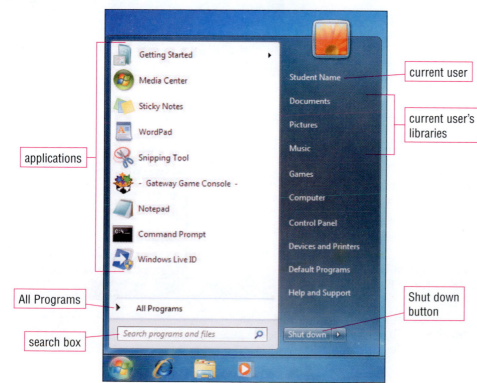

is moved to the left or right side of the screen. Move a window to the top of the screen and the window is automatically maximized. If you drag down a maximized window, the window is automatically restored down.

In addition to moving and sizing a window, you can change the display of all open windows. To do this, position the mouse pointer on the Taskbar and then click the right mouse button and a pop-up list displays with options for displaying multiple open windows. You can cascade the windows, stack the windows, and display the windows side by side.

Project 1 Opening Programs, Switching between Programs, and Manipulating Windows

1. Open Windows 7. (To do this, turn on the computer and, if necessary, turn on the monitor and/or printer. If you are using a computer that is part of a network system or if your computer is set up for multiple users, you may need to click your user account name and, if necessary, type your password and then press the Enter key. Check with your instructor to determine if you need to complete any additional steps.)

2. When the Windows 7 desktop displays, open Microsoft Word by completing the following steps:

   a. Position the arrow pointer on the Start button on the Taskbar and then click the left mouse button.

   b. At the Start menu, click *All Programs* and then click *Microsoft Office* (this displays programs in the Office suite below Microsoft Office).

   c. Drag the arrow pointer down to *Microsoft Word 2010* and then click the left mouse button.

   d. When the Microsoft Word program is open, notice that a task button representing Word displays on the Taskbar.

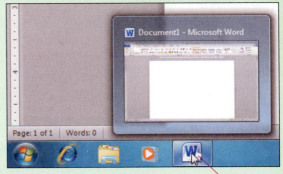

Step 2d

3. Open Microsoft Excel by completing the following steps:

   a. Position the arrow pointer on the Start button on the Taskbar and then click the left mouse button.

   b. At the Start menu, click *All Programs* and then click *Microsoft Office*.

   c. Drag the arrow pointer down to *Microsoft Excel 2010* and then click the left mouse button.

   d. When the Microsoft Excel program is open, notice that a task button representing Excel displays on the Taskbar to the right of the task button representing Word.

4. Switch to the Word program by clicking the task button on the Taskbar representing Word.

5. Switch to the Excel program by clicking the task button on the Taskbar representing Excel.

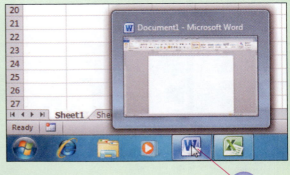

Step 4

6. Restore down the Excel window by clicking the Restore Down button that displays immediately left of the Close button in the upper right corner of the screen. (This reduces the Excel window so it displays along the bottom half of the screen.)

Step 6

7. Restore down the Word window by clicking the Restore Down button located immediately left of the Close button in the upper right corner of the screen.

8. Position the mouse pointer on the Word window Title bar, hold down the left mouse button, drag to the left side of the screen until an outline of the window displays in the left half of the screen, and then release the mouse button. (This "sticks" the window to the left side of the screen.)

9. Position the mouse pointer on the Excel window Title bar, hold down the left mouse button, drag to the right until an outline of the window displays in the right half of the screen, and then release the mouse button.

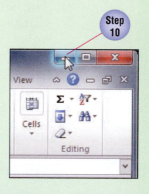

Step 10

10. Minimize the Excel window by clicking the Minimize button that displays in the upper right corner of the Excel window Title bar.

11. Hover your mouse over the Excel button on the Taskbar and notice the Excel window thumbnail that displays above the button and then click the thumbnail. (This displays the Excel window at the right side of the screen.)

12. Cascade the Word and Excel windows by positioning the arrow pointer on an empty area on the Taskbar, clicking the right mouse button, and then clicking *Cascade windows* at the pop-up list.

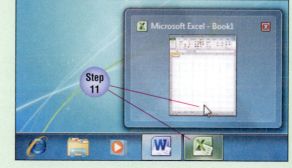

Step 11

13. After viewing the windows cascaded, display them stacked by right-clicking an empty area on the Taskbar and then clicking *Show windows stacked* at the pop-up list.

14. Display the desktop by right-clicking an empty area on the Taskbar and then clicking *Show the desktop* at the pop-up list.

15. Display the windows stacked by right-clicking an empty area on the Taskbar and then clicking *Show open windows* at the pop-up list.

16. Position the mouse pointer on the Word window Title bar, hold down the left mouse button, drag the window to the top of the screen, and then release the mouse button. This maximizes the Word window so it fills the screen.

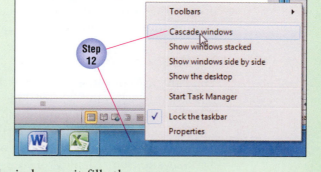

Step 12

17. Close the Word window by clicking the Close button located in the upper right corner of the window.

18. At the Excel window, click the Maximize button located immediately left of the Close button in the upper right corner of the Excel window.

19. Close the Excel window by clicking the Close button located in the upper right corner of the window.

Using the Pinned Area

The icons that display immediately right of the Start button are pinned programs. Clicking an icon opens the program associated with the icon. Click the first icon to open the Internet Explorer web browser, click the second icon to open a window containing Libraries, and click the third icon to open the Windows media player window.

Exploring the Notification Area

The notification area is located at the right side of the Taskbar and contains icons that show the status of certain system functions such as a network connection or battery power. It also contains icons you can use to manage certain programs and Windows 7 features. The notification area also contains the system clock and date. Click the time or date in the notification area and a window displays with a clock and a calendar of the current month. Click the Change date and time settings hyperlink that displays at the bottom of the window and the Date and Time dialog box displays. To change the date and/or time, click the Change date and time button and the Date and Time Settings dialog box displays similar to the dialog box shown in Figure W.4. (If a dialog box displays telling you that Windows needs your permission to continue, click the Continue button.)

Change the month and year by clicking the left-pointing or right-pointing arrow at the top of the calendar in the *Date* section. Click the left-pointing arrow to display the previous month(s) and click the right-pointing arrow to display the next month(s).

To change the day, click the desired day in the monthly calendar that displays in the dialog box. To change the time, double-click either the hour, minute, or seconds and then type the appropriate time or use the up- and down-pointing arrows in the spin boxes to adjust the time.

Some programs, when installed, will add an icon to the notification area of the Taskbar. Display the name of the icon by positioning the mouse pointer on the icon and, after approximately one second, the icon label displays. If more icons have been inserted in the notification area than can be viewed at one time, an up-pointing arrow button displays at the left side of the notification area. Click this up-pointing arrow button and the remaining icons display.

Setting Taskbar Properties

You can customize the Taskbar with options from the Taskbar shortcut menu. Display this menu by right-clicking on an empty portion of the Taskbar. The Taskbar shortcut menu contains options for turning on or off the display of specific toolbars, specifying the display of multiple windows, displaying the Start Task Manager dialog box, locking or unlocking the Taskbar, and displaying the Taskbar and Start Menu Properties dialog box.

With options in the Taskbar and Start Menu Properties dialog box shown in Figure W.5, you can change settings for the Taskbar as well as the Start menu. Display this dialog box by right-clicking on an empty area on the Taskbar and then clicking *Properties* at the shortcut menu.

Each property is controlled by a check box. Property options containing a check mark are active. Click the option to remove the check mark and make the option inactive. If an option is inactive, clicking the option will insert a check mark in the check box and turn on the option (make it active).

Figure W.4 Date and Time Settings Dialog Box

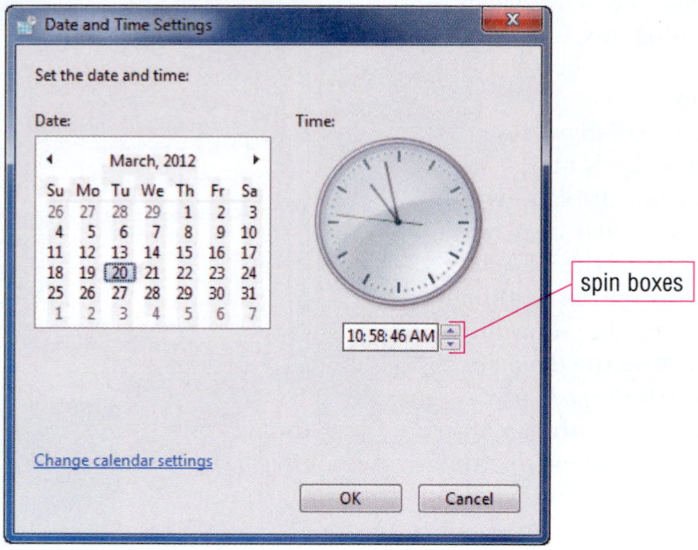

spin boxes

Figure W.5 Taskbar and Start Menu Properties Dialog Box

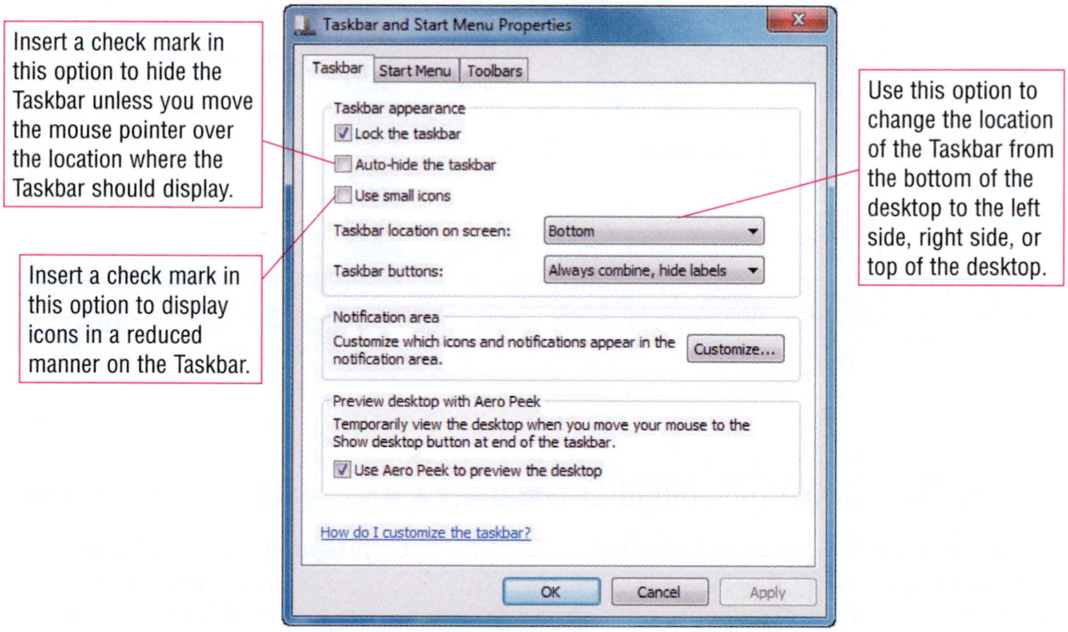

Insert a check mark in this option to hide the Taskbar unless you move the mouse pointer over the location where the Taskbar should display.

Insert a check mark in this option to display icons in a reduced manner on the Taskbar.

Use this option to change the location of the Taskbar from the bottom of the desktop to the left side, right side, or top of the desktop.

Project 2 — Changing Taskbar Properties

1. Make sure the Windows 7 desktop displays.
2. Change Taskbar properties by completing the following steps:
   a. Position the arrow pointer on any empty area on the Taskbar and then click the right mouse button.
   b. At the shortcut menu that displays, click *Properties*.

c. At the Taskbar and Start Menu Properties dialog box, click the *Auto-hide the taskbar* check box to insert a check mark.

d. Click the *Use small icons* check box to insert a check mark.

e. Click the button (displays with the word *Bottom*) that displays at the right side of the *Taskbar location on screen* option and then click *Right* at the drop-down list.

f. Click OK to close the dialog box.

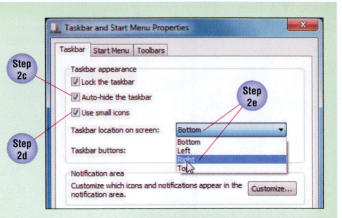

3. Since the *Auto-hide the taskbar* check box contains a check mark, the Taskbar does not display. Display the Taskbar by moving the mouse pointer to the right side of the screen. Notice that the icons on the Taskbar are smaller.

4. Return to the default settings for the Taskbar by completing the following steps:

a. Move the mouse pointer to the right side of the screen to display the Taskbar.

b. Right-click any empty area on the Taskbar and then click *Properties* at the shortcut menu.

c. Click the *Auto-hide the taskbar* check box to remove the check mark.

d. Click the *Use small icons* check box to remove the check mark.

e. Click the button (displays with the word *Right*) that displays at the right side of the *Taskbar location on screen* option and then click *Bottom* at the drop-down list.

f. Click OK to close the dialog box.

Powering Down the Computer

If you want to shut down Windows, close any open programs, click the Start button on the Taskbar, and then click the Shut down button as shown in Figure W.6. Click the button containing a right-pointing triangle that displays at the right side of the Shut down button and a drop-down list displays with options for powering down the computer.

In a multi-user environment, click the *Switch user* option to change users or click the *Log off* option to log off your computer, which shuts down your applications and files and makes system resources available to other users logged on to the system. If you need to walk away from your computer and you want to protect your work, consider locking the computer by clicking the *Lock* option. When you lock the computer, the desktop is hidden but the system is not shut down and the power is not conserved. To unlock the computer, click the icon on the desktop representing your account, type your password, and then press Enter. Click the *Restart* option to shut down and then restart the computer and click

Figure W.6 Shut Down Button and Power Options Button

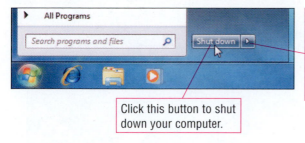

Click this button arrow to display a list of options for switching the user, logging off or locking the computer, restarting the computer, or putting the computer in sleep mode.

Click this button to shut down your computer.

the *Sleep* option to save power without having to close all files and applications. In sleep mode, Windows saves files and information about programs and then powers down the computer to a low-power state. To "wake" the computer back up, quickly press the computer's power button.

Using Gadgets

You can add gadgets to your desktop. A gadget is a mini program providing information at a glance and easy access to frequently used tools. For example, you can add a Clock gadget to your desktop that shows the current time, a Weather gadget that displays the current temperature where you live, or a Calendar gadget that displays the current date. Gadgets are added to the Sidebar, which is a location at the right side of the Windows 7 desktop.

To view available gadgets, right-click in a blank area on the desktop and then click *Gadgets* at the shortcut menu. This displays the gadget gallery similar to what you see in Figure W.7. To add a gadget to the Sidebar, double-click the desired gadget. To remove a gadget from the Sidebar, hover the mouse pointer over the gadget and then click the Close button that displays at the upper right side of the gadget. ***Note: The Gadget option on the shortcut menu may be missing if the computer you are using is located in a school setting where customization options have been disabled. If you do not see Gadget on the shortcut menu, please skip Project 3.***

Figure W.7 Gadget Gallery

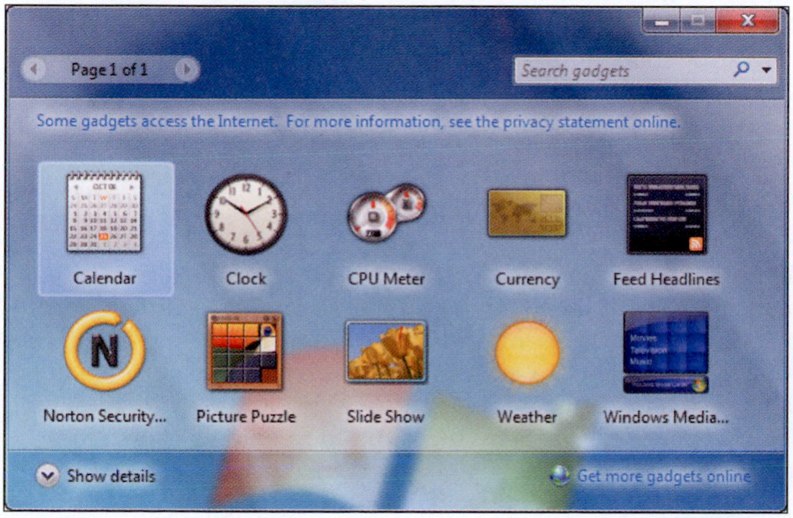

Project 3 | **Adding and Removing Gadgets**

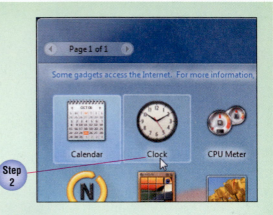

1. At the Windows 7 desktop, right-click in a blank area on the desktop and then click *Gadgets* at the shortcut menu.
2. At the Gadgets Gallery, double-click the *Clock* gadget.
3. Double-click the *Weather* gadget.
4. Double-click the *Calendar* gadget.
5. Close the Gadget Gallery by clicking the Close button located in the upper right corner of the gallery.
6. Hover your mouse over the Calendar gadget until buttons display at the right side of the gadget and then click the Larger size button. (This expands the calendar to display the days of the month.)
7. Hover your mouse over the Weather gadget and then click the Options button.
8. At the Weather dialog box that displays, type in the *Select current location* text box the name of your city followed by your state (or province) and then press Enter.
9. If a drop-down list displays with city names, scroll down the list to display your city and then click your city and state (or province).
10. Click OK to close the Weather dialog box.
11. After viewing the gadgets, remove the Clock gadget by hovering the mouse over the clock and then clicking the Close button that displays at the upper right side of the clock.
12. Close the Weather gadget by hovering the mouse over the gadget and then clicking the Close button that displays.
13. Close the Calendar gadget by hovering the mouse over the gadget and then clicking the Close button that displays.

Managing Files and Folders ■■■■■■■■■■■■■■■■■■■■■■■■

As you begin working with programs in Windows 7, you will create files in which data (information) is saved. A file might contain a Word document, an Excel workbook, or a PowerPoint presentation. As you begin creating files, consider creating folders into which those files will be stored. You can complete file management tasks such as creating a folder and copying and moving files and folders at the Computer window. To display the Computer window shown in Figure W.8, click the Start button on the Taskbar and then click *Computer*. The various components of the Computer window are identified in Figure W.8.

Figure W.8 Computer Window

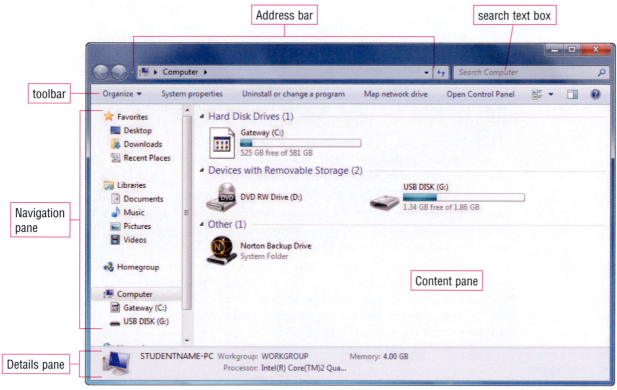

In the Content pane of the Computer window, icons display representing each hard disk drive and removable storage medium such as a CD, DVD, or USB device connected to your computer. Next to each storage device icon, Windows provides the amount of storage space available as well as a bar with the amount of used space shaded with color. This visual cue allows you to see at a glance the proportion of space available relative to the capacity of the device. Double-click a device icon in the Content pane to change the display to show the contents stored on the device. You can display contents from another device or folder using the Navigation pane or the Address bar on the Computer window.

Copying, Moving, and Deleting Files and Folders

File and folder management activities might include copying and moving files or folders from one folder or drive to another, or deleting files or folders. The Computer window offers a variety of methods for copying, moving, and deleting files and folders. This section will provide you with steps for copying, moving, and deleting files and folders using options from the Organize button on the toolbar and the shortcut menu.

To copy a file to another folder or drive, first display the file in the Content pane by identifying the location of the file. If the file is located in the Documents folder, click the *Documents* folder in the *Libraries* section in the Navigation pane and then click the file name in the Content pane that you want to copy. Click the Organize button on the toolbar and then click *Copy* at the drop-down list. In the Navigation pane, click the location where you want to copy the file. Click the Organize button and then click *Paste* at the drop-down list. You would complete similar steps to copy and paste a folder to another location.

If the desired file is located on a storage medium such as a CD, DVD, or USB device, double-click the device in the section of the Content pane labeled *Devices with Removable Storage*. (Each removable device is assigned an alphabetic drive letter by Windows, usually starting at F or G and continuing through the alphabet depending on the number of removable devices that are currently in use.) After double-clicking the storage medium in the Content pane, navigate to the desired folder and then click the file to select it. Click the Organize button on the toolbar and then click *Copy* at the drop-down list. Navigate to the desired folder, click the Organize button, and then click *Paste* at the drop-down list.

To move a file, click the desired file in the Content pane, click the Organize button on the toolbar, and then click *Cut* at the drop-down list. Navigate to the desired location, click the Organize button, and then click *Paste* at the drop-down list.

To delete a file(s) or folder(s), click the file or folder in the Content pane in the Computer window or select multiple files or folders. Click the Organize button and then click *Delete* at the drop-down list. At the message asking if you want to move the file or folder to the Recycle Bin, click the Yes button.

In Project 4, you will insert the CD that accompanies this book into the DVD or CD drive. When the CD is inserted, the drive may automatically activate and a dialog box may display telling you that the disc or device contains more than one type of content and asking what you want Windows to do. If this dialog box displays, click the Cancel button.

Project 4   Copying a File and Folder and Deleting a File

1. Insert the CD that accompanies this textbook into the appropriate drive. If a dialog box displays telling you that the disc or device contains more than one type of content and asking what you want Windows to do, click the Cancel button.
2. Insert your storage medium (such as a USB flash drive) in the USB port (or other drive). If an AutoPlay window displays, click the Close button.
3. At the Windows 7 desktop, click the Start button and then click *Computer* located at the right side of the Start menu.
4. Copy a file from the CD that accompanies this textbook to the drive containing your storage medium by completing the following steps:
   a. Double-click the CD drive in the Content pane containing the CD from the book.
   b. Double-click the *StudentDataFiles* folder in the Content pane.
   c. Double-click the *Windows7* folder in the Content pane.
   d. Click **WordDocument01.docx** in the Content pane.
   e. Click the Organize button on the toolbar and then click *Copy* at the drop-down list.

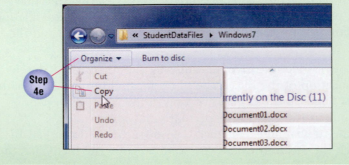

f. In the Computer section in the Navigation pane, click the drive containing your storage medium. (You may need to scroll down the Navigation pane.)

g. Click the Organize button and then click *Paste* at the drop-down list.

5. Delete ***WordDocument01.docx*** from your storage medium by completing the following steps:

   a. Make sure the contents of your storage medium display in the Content pane in the Computer window.

   b. Click ***WordDocument01.docx*** in the Content pane to select it.

   c. Click the Organize button and then click *Delete* at the drop-down list.

   d. At the message asking if you want to permanently delete the file, click the Yes button.

6. Copy the Windows7 folder from the CD to your storage medium by completing the following steps:

   a. With the Computer window open, click the drive in the *Computer* section in the Navigation pane that contains the CD that accompanies this book.

   b. Double-click *StudentDataFiles* in the Content pane.

   c. Click the *Windows7* folder in the Content pane.

   d. Click the Organize button and then click *Copy* at the drop-down list.

   e. In the *Computer* section in the Navigation pane, click the drive containing your storage medium.

   f. Click the Organize button and then click *Paste* at the drop-down list.

7. Close the Computer window by clicking the Close button located in the upper right corner of the window.

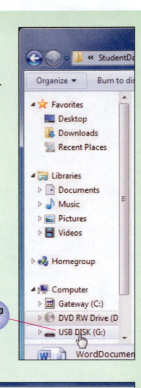

In addition to options in the Organize button drop-down list, you can use options in a shortcut menu to copy, move, and delete files or folders. To use a shortcut menu, select the desired file(s) or folder(s), position the mouse pointer on the selected item, and then click the right mouse button. At the shortcut menu that displays, click the desired option such as Copy, Cut, or Delete.

Selecting Files and Folders

You can move, copy, or delete more than one file or folder at the same time. Before moving, copying, or deleting files or folders, select the desired files or folders. To make selecting easier, consider changing the display in the Content pane to List or Details. To change the display, click the Views button arrow on the toolbar in the Computer window and then click *List* or *Details* at the drop-down list. You can also cycle through the various views by clicking the Views button. Hover your mouse over the Views button and the ScreenTip *Change your view* displays.

To select adjacent files or folders, click the first file or folder, hold down the Shift key, and then click the last file or folder. To select nonadjacent files or folders, click the first file or folder, hold down the Ctrl key, and then click any other files or folders.

Project 5   Copying and Deleting Files

1. At the Windows 7 desktop, click the Start button and then click *Computer*.
2. Copy files from the CD that accompanies this textbook to the drive containing your storage medium by completing the following steps:
   a. Make sure the CD that accompanies this textbook and your storage medium are inserted in the appropriate drives.
   b. Double-click the CD drive in the Content pane in the Computer window.
   c. Double-click the *StudentDataFiles* folder in the Content pane.
   d. Double-click the *Windows7* folder in the Content pane.
   e. Change the display to List by clicking the Views button arrow on the toolbar and then clicking *List* at the drop-down list.

   f. Click **WordDocument01.docx** in the Content pane.
   g. Hold down the Shift key, click **WordDocument05.docx**, and then release the Shift key. (This selects five documents.)
   h. Click the Organize button and then click *Copy* at the drop-down list.
   i. In the *Computer* section in the Navigation pane, click the drive containing your storage medium.
   j. Click the Organize button and then click *Paste* at the drop-down list.

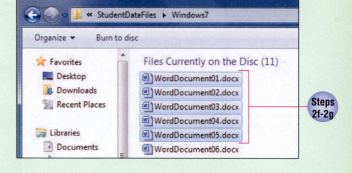

3. Delete the files from your storage medium that you just copied by completing the following steps:
   a. Change the view by clicking the Views button arrow bar and then clicking *List* at the drop-down list.
   b. Click **WordDocument01.docx** in the Content pane.
   c. Hold down the Shift key, click **WordDocument05.docx**, and then release the Shift key.
   d. Position the mouse pointer on any selected file, click the right mouse button, and then click *Delete* at the shortcut menu.
   e. At the message asking if you are sure you want to permanently delete the files, click Yes.
4. Close the Computer window by clicking the Close button located in the upper right corner of the window.

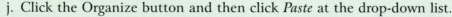
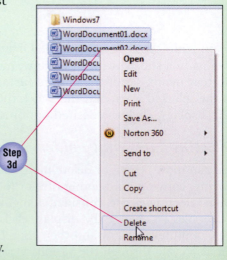

Manipulating and Creating Folders

As you begin working with and creating a number of files, consider creating folders in which you can logically group the files. To create a folder, display the Computer window and then display in the Content pane the drive or folder where you want to create the folder. Position the mouse pointer in a blank area in the Content pane, click the right mouse button, point to *New* in the shortcut menu, and then click *Folder* at the side menu. This inserts a folder icon in the Content pane and names the folder *New folder*. Type the desired name for the new folder and then press Enter.

Project 6   Creating a New Folder

1. At the Windows 7 desktop, open the Computer window.
2. Create a new folder by completing the following steps:
   a. Double-click in the Content pane the drive that contains your storage medium.
   b. Double-click the *Windows7* folder in the Content pane. (This opens the folder.)
   c. Click the Views button arrow and then click *List* at the drop-down list.
   d. Position the mouse pointer in a blank area in the Content pane and then click the right mouse button.
   e. Point to *New* in the shortcut menu and then click *Folder* at the side menu.

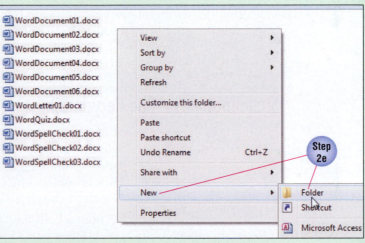

   f. Type **SpellCheckFiles** and then press Enter. (This changes the name from *New folder* to *SpellCheckFiles*.)
3. Copy **WordSpellCheck01.docx**, **WordSpellCheck02.docx**, and **WordSpellCheck03.docx** into the SpellCheckFiles folder you just created by completing the following steps:
   a. Click the Views button arrow and then click *List* at the drop-down list. (Skip this step if *List* is already selected.)
   b. Click once on the file named **WordSpellCheck01.docx** located in the Content pane.
   c. Hold down the Shift key, click once on the file named **WordSpellCheck03.docx**, and then release the Shift key. (This selects three documents.)
   d. Click the Organize button and then click *Copy* at the drop-down list.
   e. Double-click the *SpellCheckFiles* folder in the Content pane.
   f. Click the Organize button and then click *Paste* at the drop-down list.

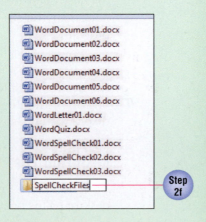

4. Delete the SpellCheckFiles folder and its contents by completing the following steps:

a. Click the Back button (contains a left-pointing arrow) located at the left side of the Address bar.

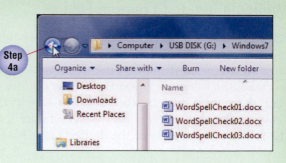

Step 4a

b. With the SpellCheckFiles folder selected in the Content pane, click the Organize button and then click *Delete* at the drop-down list.

c. At the message asking you to confirm the deletion, click Yes.

5. Close the window by clicking the Close button located in the upper right corner of the window.

Using the Recycle Bin ■■■■■■■■■■■■■■■■■■■■■■■■■■■■■■■

Deleting the wrong file can be a disaster but Windows 7 helps protect your work with the Recycle Bin. The Recycle Bin acts just like an office wastepaper basket; you can "throw away" (delete) unwanted files, but you can "reach in" to the Recycle Bin and take out (restore) a file if you threw it away by accident.

Deleting Files to the Recycle Bin

A file or folder or selected files or folders you delete from the hard drive are sent automatically to the Recycle Bin. If you want to permanently delete files or folders from the hard drive without first sending them to the Recycle Bin, select the desired file(s) or folder(s), right click on one of the selected files or folders, hold down the Shift key, and then click *Delete* at the shortcut menu.

Files and folders deleted from a USB flash drive or disc are deleted permanently. (Recovery programs are available, however, that will help you recover deleted files or folders. If you accidentally delete a file or folder from a USB flash drive or disc, do not do anything more with the USB flash drive or disc until you can run a recovery program.)

You can delete files in the manner described earlier in this section and you can also delete a file by dragging the file icon to the Recycle Bin. To do this, click the desired file in the Content pane in the Computer window, drag the file icon on top of the Recycle Bin icon on the desktop until the text *Move to Recycle Bin* displays, and then release the mouse button.

Restoring Files from the Recycle Bin

To restore a file from the Recycle Bin, double-click the Recycle Bin icon on the desktop. This opens the Recycle Bin window shown in Figure W.9. (The contents of the Recycle Bin will vary.) To restore a file, click the file you want restored and then click the Restore this item button on the toolbar. This removes the file from the Recycle Bin and returns it to its original location. You can also restore a file by positioning the mouse pointer on the file, clicking the right mouse button, and then clicking *Restore* at the shortcut menu.

Figure W.9 Recycle Bin Window

toolbar
Navigation pane
Content pane
Details pane

Organize ▾	Empty the Recycle Bin Restore all items

WordSpellCheck01.docx
Microsoft Word Document
15.8 KB

WordSpellCheck02.docx
Microsoft Word Document
15.7 KB

WordSpellCheck03.docx
Microsoft Word Document
17.6 KB

Favorites
Desktop
Downloads
Recent Places

Libraries
Documents
Music
Pictures
Videos

Homegroup

Computer
Gateway (C:)
DVD RW Drive (D
USB DISK (G:)

3 items

Project 7   Deleting Files to and Restoring Files from the Recycle Bin

Before beginning this project, check with your instructor to determine if you can copy files to the hard drive.

1. At the Windows 7 desktop, open the Computer window.
2. Copy files from your storage medium to the Documents folder on your hard drive by completing the following steps:
   a. Double-click in the Content pane the drive containing your storage medium.
   b. Double-click the *Windows7* folder in the Content pane.
   c. Click the Views button arrow and then click *List* at the drop-down list. (Skip this step if *List* is already selected.)
   d. Click *WordSpellCheck01.docx* in the Content pane.
   e. Hold down the Shift key, click *WordSpellCheck03.docx*, and then release the Shift key.
   f. Click the Organize button and then click *Copy* at the drop-down list.
   g. Click the *Documents* folder in the *Libraries* section in the Navigation pane.
   h. Click the Organize button and then click *Paste* at the drop-down list.

Step 2g

Organize ▾	W Open Print Burn New folder

Recent Places

Libraries
Documents
Music
Pictures
Videos

Homegroup

Computer
Gateway (C:)

WordDocument01.docx
WordDocument02.docx
WordDocument03.docx
WordDocument04.docx
WordDocument05.docx
WordDocument06.docx
WordLetter01.docx
WordQuiz.docx
WordSpellCheck01.docx
WordSpellCheck02.docx
WordSpellCheck03.docx

Computer ▸ USB DISK (G:) ▸ Windows7

3. Delete to the Recycle Bin the files you just copied by completing the following steps:
   a. With **WordSpellCheck01.docx** through **WordSpellCheck03.docx** selected in the Content pane, click the Organize button and then click *Delete* at the drop-down list.
   b. At the message asking you if you are sure you want to move the items to the Recycle Bin, click Yes.
4. Close the Computer window.
5. At the Windows 7 desktop, display the contents of the Recycle Bin by double-clicking the Recycle Bin icon.
6. Restore the files you just deleted by completing the following steps:
   a. Select **WordSpellCheck01.docx** through **WordSpellCheck03.docx** in the Recycle Bin Content pane. (If these files are not visible, you will need to scroll down the list of files in the Content pane.)
   b. Click the Restore the selected items button on the toolbar.

7. Close the Recycle Bin by clicking the Close button located in the upper right corner of the window.
8. Display the Computer window.
9. Click the *Documents* folder in the *Libraries* section in the Navigation pane.
10. Delete the files you restored.
11. Close the Computer window.

Emptying the Recycle Bin

Just like a wastepaper basket, the Recycle Bin can get full. To empty the Recycle Bin, position the arrow pointer on the Recycle Bin icon on the desktop and then click the right mouse button. At the shortcut menu that displays, click the *Empty Recycle Bin* option. At the message asking if you want to permanently delete the items, click Yes. You can also empty the Recycle Bin by displaying the Recycle Bin window and then clicking the Empty the Recycle Bin button on the toolbar. At the message asking if you want to permanently delete the items, click Yes. To delete a specific file from the Recycle Bin window, click the desired file in the Recycle Bin window, click the Organize button, and then *Delete* at the drop-down list. At the message asking if you want to permanently delete the file, click Yes. When you empty the Recycle Bin, the files cannot be recovered by the Recycle Bin or by Windows 7. If you have to recover a file, you will need to use a file recovery program.

Project 8   Emptying the Recycle Bin

Before beginning this project, check with your instructor to determine if you can delete files/folders from the Recycle Bin.

1. At the Windows 7 desktop, double-click the Recycle Bin icon.
2. At the Recycle Bin window, empty the contents by clicking the Empty the Recycle Bin button on the toolbar.
3. At the message asking you if you want to permanently delete the items, click Yes.
4. Close the Recycle Bin by clicking the Close button located in the upper right corner of the window.

Step 2

Creating a Shortcut ■■■■■■■■■■■■■■■■■■■■■■■■■■■■■

If you use a file or program on a consistent basis, consider creating a shortcut to the file or program. A shortcut is a specialized icon that represents very small files that point the operating system to the actual item, whether it is a file, a folder, or an application. If you create a shortcut to a Word document, the shortcut icon is not the actual document but a path to the document. Double-click the shortcut icon and Windows 7 opens the document in Word.

One method for creating a shortcut is to display the Computer window and then make active the drive or folder where the file is located. Right-click the desired file, point to *Send To*, and then click *Desktop (create shortcut)*. You can easily delete a shortcut icon from the desktop by dragging the shortcut icon to the Recycle Bin icon. This deletes the shortcut icon but does not delete the file to which the shortcut pointed.

Project 9   Creating a Shortcut

1. At the Windows 7 desktop, display the Computer window.
2. Double-click the drive containing your storage medium.
3. Double-click the *Windows7* folder in the Content pane.
4. Change the display of files to a list by clicking the Views button arrow and then clicking *List* at the drop-down list. (Skip this step if *List* is already selected.)
5. Create a shortcut to the file named **WordLetter01.docx** by right-clicking **WordLetter01.docx**, pointing to *Send to*, and then clicking *Desktop (create shortcut)*.

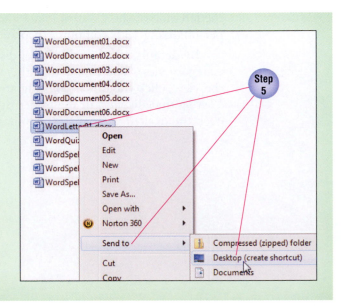

6. Close the Computer window.
7. Open Word and the file named **WordLetter01.docx** by double-clicking the *WordLetter01.docx* shortcut icon on the desktop.
8. After viewing the file in Word, exit Word by clicking the Close button that displays in the upper right corner of the window.
9. Delete the *WordLetter01.docx* shortcut icon by completing the following steps:
    a. At the desktop, position the mouse pointer on the *WordLetter01.docx* shortcut icon.
    b. Hold down the left mouse button, drag the icon on top of the Recycle Bin icon, and then release the mouse button.

Step 7

Exploring the Control Panel

The Control Panel, shown in Figure W.10, contains a variety of icons you can use to customize the appearance and functionality of your computer as well as access and change system settings. Display the Control Panel by clicking the Start button on the Taskbar and then clicking *Control Panel* at the Start menu. The Control Panel organizes settings into categories to make them easier to find. Click a category icon and the Control Panel displays lower-level categories and tasks within each of them.

Hover your mouse over a category icon in the Control Panel and a ScreenTip displays with an explanation of what options are available. For example, if you hover the mouse over the Appearance and Personalization icon, a ScreenTip displays with information about the tasks available in the category such as changing the appearance of desktop items, applying a theme or screen saver to your computer, or customizing the Start menu and Taskbar.

If you click a category icon in the Control Panel, the Control Panel displays all of the available subcategories and tasks in the category. Also, the categories display in text form at the left side of the Control Panel. For example, if you click the Appearance and Personalization category icon, the Control Panel displays as shown in Figure W.11. Notice how the Control Panel categories display at the left side of the Control Panel and options for changing the appearance and personalizing your computer display in the middle of the Control Panel.

By default, the Control Panel displays categories of tasks in what is called Category view. You can change this view to *Large icons* or *Small icons*. To change the view, click the down-pointing arrow that displays at the right side of the text *View by* that displays in the upper right corner of the Control Panel, and then click the desired view at the drop-down list (see Figure W.10).

Figure W.10 The Control Panel

Click a category icon or hyperlink to display all of the category's options.

Use this option to change views.

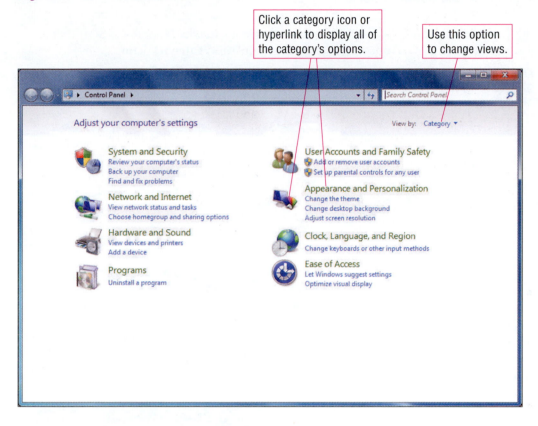

Figure W.11 Appearance and Personalization Window

lower-level categories

task hyperlinks

Click this option to return to the main Control Panel.

Click a category to display category options.

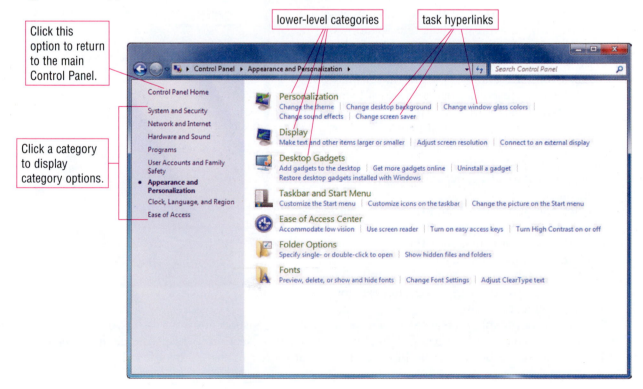

1. At the Windows 7 desktop, click the Start button and then click *Control Panel* at the Start menu.
2. At the Control Panel, click the Appearance and Personalization category icon.

Step 2

3. Click the <u>Change the theme</u> hyperlink that displays below the Personalization category in the panel at the right in the Control Panel.
4. At the window that displays with options for changing visuals and sounds on your computer, click the *Landscapes* theme.

Step 3

5. Click the <u>Desktop Background</u> hyperlink that displays in the lower left corner of the panel at the right.
6. Click the button that displays below the text *Change picture every* and then click *10 Seconds* at the drop-down list. (This tells Windows to change the picture on your desktop every 10 seconds.)
7. Click the Save changes button that displays in the lower right corner of the Control Panel.
8. Click the Close button located in the upper right corner to close the Control Panel.
9. Look at the picture that displays as the background at the desktop. Wait for 10 seconds and then look at the second picture that displays.
10. Click the Start button and then click *Control Panel* at the Start menu.
11. At the Control Panel, click the Appearance and Personalization category icon.
12. Click the <u>Change the theme</u> hyperlink that displays below the Personalization category in the panel at the right.
13. At the window that displays with options for changing visuals and sounds on your computer, click the *Windows 7* theme in the *Aero Themes* section. (This is the default theme.)
14. Click the Close button located in the upper right corner of the Control Panel.

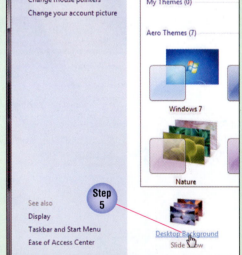

Step 5

Searching in the Control Panel

The Control Panel contains a large number of options for customizing the appearance and functionality of your computer. If you want to customize a feature and are not sure where the options for the feature are located, search for the feature. To do this, display the Control Panel and then type the name of the desired feature. By default, the insertion point is positioned in the *Search Control Panel* text box. When you type the feature name in the Search Control Panel, options related to the feature display in the Control Panel.

 Project 11 — **Customizing the Mouse**

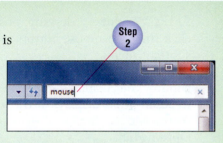

1. Click the Start button and then click *Control Panel*.
2. At the Control Panel, type **mouse**. (The insertion point is automatically located in the *Search Control Panel* text box when you open the Control Panel. When you type *mouse*, features for customizing the mouse display in the Control Panel.)
3. Click the Mouse icon that displays in the Control Panel.
4. At the Mouse Properties dialog box, notice the options that display. (The *Switch primary and secondary buttons* option might be useful, for example, if you are left-handed and want to switch the buttons on the mouse.)
5. Click the Cancel button to remove the dialog box.
6. At the Control Panel, click the <u>Change the mouse pointer display or speed</u> hyperlink.

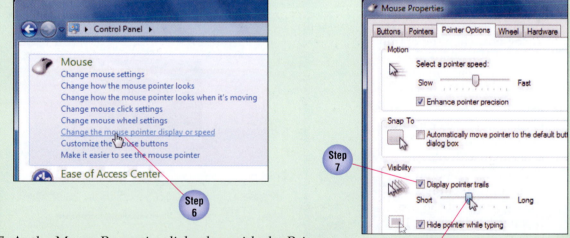

7. At the Mouse Properties dialog box with the Pointer Options tab selected, click the *Display pointer trails* check box in the *Visibility* section to insert a check mark.
8. Drag the button on the slider bar (located below the *Display pointer trails* check box) approximately to the middle of the bar.
9. Click OK to close the dialog box.
10. Close the Control Panel.
11. Move the mouse pointer around the screen to see the pointer trails as well as the speed at which the mouse moves.

Displaying Personalize Options with a Shortcut Command

In addition to the Control Panel, you can display customization options with a command from a shortcut menu. Display a shortcut menu by positioning the mouse pointer in the desired position and then clicking the right mouse button. For example, display a shortcut menu with options for customizing the desktop by positioning the mouse pointer in an empty area on the desktop and then clicking the right mouse button. At the shortcut menu that displays, click the desired shortcut command.

Project 12 | Customizing with a Shortcut Command

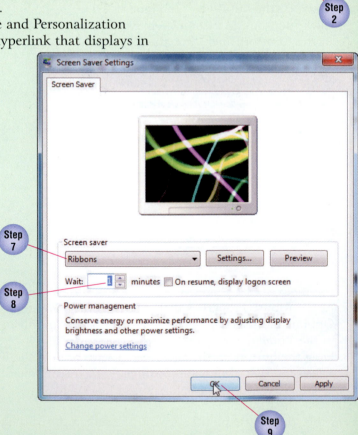

1. At the Windows 7 desktop, position the mouse pointer in an empty area on the desktop, click the right mouse button, and then click *Personalize* at the shortcut menu.
2. At the Control Panel Appearance and Personalization window that displays, click the <u>Change mouse pointers</u> hyperlink that displays at the left side of the window.
3. At the Mouse Properties dialog box, click the Pointer Options tab.
4. Click in the *Display pointer trails* check box to remove the check mark.
5. Click OK to close the dialog box.
6. At the Control Panel Appearance and Personalization window, click the <u>Screen Saver</u> hyperlink that displays in the lower right corner of the window.
7. At the Screen Saver Settings dialog box, click the option button below the *Screen saver* option and then click *Ribbons* at the drop-down list.
8. Check the number in the *Wait* text box. If a number other than *1* displays, click the down-pointing arrow in the spin box at the right side of the text box until *1* displays. (This tells Windows to display the screen saver after one minute of inactivity.)
9. Click OK to close the dialog box.
10. Close the Control Panel by clicking the Close button located in the upper right corner of the window.

11. Do not touch the mouse or keyboard and wait over one minute for the screen saver to display. After watching the screen saver, move the mouse. (This redisplays the desktop.)
12. Right-click in an empty area on the desktop and then click *Personalize* at the shortcut menu.
13. At the Control Panel Appearance and Personalization window, click the <u>Screen Saver</u> hyperlink.
14. At the Screen Saver Settings dialog box, click the option button below the *Screen saver* option and then click *(None)* at the drop-down list.
15. Click OK to close the dialog box.
16. Close the Control Panel Appearance and Personalization window.

Exploring Windows Help and Support

Windows 7 includes an on-screen reference guide providing information, explanations, and interactive help on learning Windows features. Get help at the Windows Help and Support window shown in Figure W.12. Display this window by clicking the Start button and then clicking *Help and Support* at the Start menu. Use buttons in the window toolbar to display the opening Windows Help and Support window, print the current information, display a list of contents, get customer support or other types of services, and display a list of Help options.

Figure W.12 Windows Help and Support Window

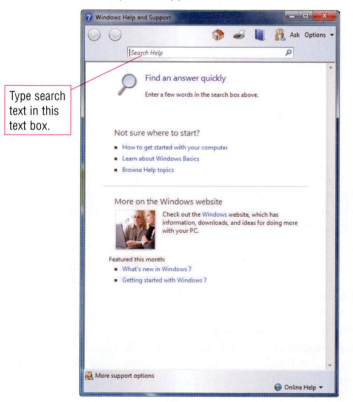

Type search text in this text box.

1. At the Windows 7 desktop, click the Start button and then click *Help and Support* at the Start menu.
2. At the Windows Help and Support window, click the <u>Learn about Windows Basics</u> hyperlink.
3. Click a hyperlink that interests you, read the information, and then click the Back button on the Windows Help and Support window toolbar. (The Back button is located in the upper left corner of the window.)
4. Click another hyperlink that interests you and then read the information.
5. Click the Help and Support home button that displays on the window toolbar. (This returns you to the opening Windows Help and Support window.)
6. Click in the *Search Help* text box, type **delete files**, and then press Enter.
7. Click the <u>Delete a file or folder</u> hyperlink that displays in the window.
8. Read the information that displays about deleting files or folders and then click the Print button on the window toolbar.
9. At the Print dialog box, click the Print button.
10. Click the Close button to close the Windows Help and Support window.

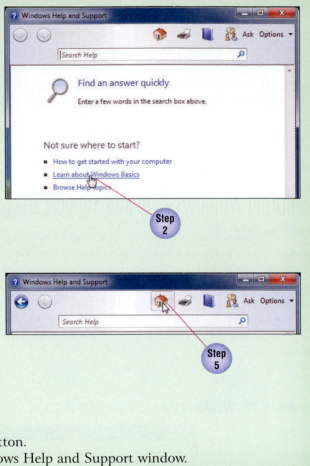

Using Search Tools ■■■■■■■■■ ■■■■■■■■ ■■■■■

The Start menu contains a search tool you can use to quickly find a program or file on your computer. To use the search tool, click the Start button and then type the first few characters of the program or file for which you are searching in the *Search programs and files* text box. As you type characters in the text box, a pop-up list displays with program names or file names that begin with the characters. As you continue typing characters, the search tool refines the list.

You can also search for programs or files with the search text box in the Computer window. The search text box displays in the upper right corner of the Computer window at the right side of the Address bar. If you want to search a specific folder, make that folder active in the Content pane and then type the search text in the text box.

When conducting a search, you can use the asterisk (*) as a wildcard character in place of any letters, numbers, or symbols within a file name. For example, in the following project you will search for file names containing *check* by typing ***check** in the search text box. The asterisk indicates that the file name can start with any letter but it must contain the letters *check* somewhere in the file name.

Project 14 — Searching for Programs and Files

1. At the Windows 7 desktop, click the Start button.
2. With the insertion point positioned in the *Search programs and files* text box, type **paint**. (Notice as you type the letters that Windows displays programs and/or files that begin with the same letters you are typing or that are associated with the same letters in a keyword. Notice that the Paint program displays below the heading *Programs* at the top of the list. Depending on the contents stored in the computer you are using, additional items may display below Paint.)

Step 2

Step 1

3. Click *Paint* that displays below the *Programs* heading.
4. Close the Paint window.
5. Click the Start button and then click *Computer*.
6. At the Computer window, double-click the icon representing your storage medium.
7. Double-click the *Windows7* folder.
8. Click in the search text box located at the right of the Address bar and then type **document**. (As you begin typing the letters, Windows filters the list of files in the Content pane to those that contain the letters you type. Notice that the Address bar displays *Search Results in Windows7* to indicate that the files that display matching your criteria were limited to the current folder.)

Step 8

9. Select the text *document* that displays in the search text box and then type ***check**. (Notice that the Content pane displays file names containing the letters *check* no matter how the file name begins.)
10. Double-click *WordSpellCheck02.docx* to open the document in Word.

Step 9

11. Close the document and exit Word by clicking the Close button located in the upper right corner of the window.
12. Close the Computer window.

Step 10

Browsing the Internet Using Internet Explorer 8.0

Microsoft Internet Explorer 8.0 is a web browser program with options and features for displaying sites as well as navigating and searching for information on the Internet. The **Internet** is a network of computers connected around the world. Users access the Internet for several purposes: to communicate using instant messaging and/or email, to subscribe to newsgroups, to transfer files, to socialize with other users around the globe in chat rooms, and also to access virtually any kind of information imaginable.

Using the Internet, people can find a phenomenal amount of information for private or public use. To use the Internet, three things are generally required: an Internet Service Provider (ISP), a program to browse the Web (called a **web browser**), and a **search engine**. In this section, you will learn how to:

- Navigate the Internet using URLs and hyperlinks
- Use search engines to locate information
- Download web pages and images

You will use the Microsoft Internet Explorer web browser to locate information on the Internet. Uniform Resource Locators, referred to as URLs, are the method used to identify locations on the Internet. The steps for browsing the Internet vary but generally include: opening Internet Explorer, typing the URL for the desired site, navigating the various pages of the site, navigating to other sites using links, and then closing Internet Explorer.

To launch Internet Explorer 8.0, click the Internet Explorer icon on the Taskbar at the Windows desktop. Figure IE.1 identifies the elements of the Internet Explorer, version 8.0, window. The web page that displays in your Internet Explorer window may vary from what you see in Figure IE.1.

If you know the URL for the desired website, click in the Address bar, type the URL, and then press Enter. The website's home page displays in a tab within the Internet Explorer window. URLs (Uniform Resource Locators) are the method used to identify locations on the Internet. The format of a URL is *http://server-name.path*. The first part of the URL, *http*, stands for HyperText Transfer Protocol, which is the protocol or language used to transfer data within the World Wide Web. The colon and slashes separate the protocol from the server name. The server name is the second component of the URL. For example, in the URL http://www.microsoft.com, the server name is *microsoft*. The last part of the URL specifies the domain to which the server belongs. For example, *.com* refers to "commercial" and establishes that the URL is a commercial company. Examples of other domains include *.edu* for "educational," *.gov* for "government," and *.mil* for "military."

Figure IE.1 Internet Explorer Window

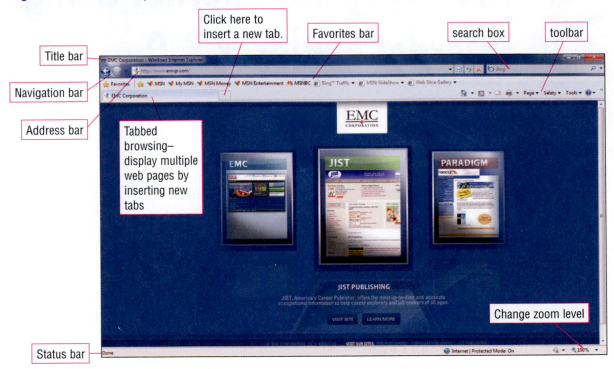

Title bar

Navigation bar

Address bar

Click here to insert a new tab.

Favorites bar

search box

toolbar

Tabbed browsing–display multiple web pages by inserting new tabs

Change zoom level

Status bar

Project 1   Browsing the Internet Using URLs

1. Make sure you are connected to the Internet through an Internet Service Provider and that the Windows desktop displays. (Check with your instructor to determine if you need to complete steps for accessing the Internet such as typing a user name and password to log on.)
2. Launch Microsoft Internet Explorer by clicking the Internet Explorer icon located on the Taskbar located at the bottom of the Windows desktop.
3. At the Internet Explorer window, explore the website for Yosemite National Park by completing the following steps:
   a. Click in the Address bar, type **www.nps.gov/yose**, and then press Enter.
   b. Scroll down the home page for Yosemite National Park by clicking the down-pointing arrow on the vertical scroll bar located at the right side of the Internet Explorer window.
   c. Print the home page by clicking the Print button located on the Internet Explorer toolbar. (Some websites have a printer friendly button you can click to print the page.)

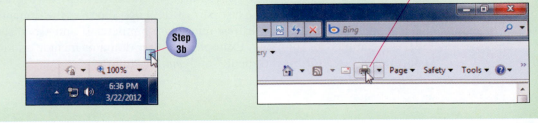

Step 3a

Step 3b

Step 3c

4. Explore the website for Glacier National Park by completing the following steps:
   a. Click in the Address bar, type **www.nps.gov/glac**, and then press Enter.
   b. Print the home page by clicking the Print button located on the Internet Explorer toolbar.
5. Close Internet Explorer by clicking the Close button (contains an X) located in the upper right corner of the Internet Explorer window.

Step
4a

Navigating Using Hyperlinks ▪▪▪▪▪▪▪▪▪▪▪▪▪▪▪▪▪▪▪▪▪▪▪▪▪▪

Most web pages contain "hyperlinks" that you click to connect to another page within the website or to another site on the Internet. Hyperlinks may display in a web page as underlined text in a specific color or as images or icons. To use a hyperlink, position the mouse pointer on the desired hyperlink until the mouse pointer turns into a hand, and then click the left mouse button. Use hyperlinks to navigate within and between sites on the Internet. The navigation bar in the Internet Explorer window contains a Back button that, when clicked, takes you to the previous web page viewed. If you click the Back button and then want to return to the previous page, click the Forward button. You can continue clicking the Back button to back your way out of several linked pages in reverse order since Internet Explorer maintains a history of the websites you visit.

Project 2 Navigating Using Hyperlinks

1. Make sure you are connected to the Internet and then click the Internet Explorer icon on the Taskbar.
2. At the Internet Explorer window, display the White House web page and navigate in the page by completing the following steps:
   a. Click in the Address bar, type **whitehouse.gov**, and then press Enter.
   b. At the White House home page, position the mouse pointer on a hyperlink that interests you until the pointer turns into a hand, and then click the left mouse button.
   c. At the linked web page, click the Back button. (This returns you to the White House home page.)
   d. At the White House home page, click the Forward button to return to the previous web page viewed.
   e. Print the web page by clicking the Print button on the Internet Explorer toolbar.

Step
2c

3. Display the website for Amazon.com and navigate in the site by completing the following steps:
   a. Click in the Address bar, type **www.amazon.com**, and then press Enter.

Step
3a

b. At the Amazon.com home page, click a hyperlink related to books.

c. When a book web page displays, click the Print button on the Internet Explorer toolbar.

4. Close Internet Explorer by clicking the Close button (contains an X) located in the upper right corner of the Internet Explorer window.

Searching for Specific Sites

If you do not know the URL for a specific site or you want to find information on the Internet but do not know what site to visit, complete a search with a search engine. A search engine is a software program created to search quickly and easily for desired information. A variety of search engines are available on the Internet, each offering the opportunity to search for specific information. One method for searching for information is to click in the search box located to the right of the Address bar, type a keyword or phrase related to your search, and then click the Search button or press Enter. Another method for completing a search is to visit the website for a search engine and use options at the site.

Bing is Microsoft's online search portal and is the default search engine used by Internet Explorer. Bing organizes search results by topic category and provides related search suggestions.

Project 3   Searching for Information by Topic

1. Start Internet Explorer.
2. At the Internet Explorer window, search for sites on bluegrass music by completing the following steps:
   a. Click in the search box (may display *Bing*) located at the right side of the Address bar.
   b. Type **bluegrass music** and then press Enter.
   c. When a list of sites displays in the Bing results window, click a site that interests you.
   d. When the page displays, click the Print button.

3. Use the Yahoo! search engine to find sites on bluegrass music by completing the following steps:
   a. Click in the Address bar, type **www.yahoo.com**, and then press Enter.
   b. At the Yahoo! website, with the insertion point positioned in the search text box, type **bluegrass music** and then press Enter. (Notice that the sites displayed vary from sites displayed in the earlier search.)
   c. Click hyperlinks until a website displays that interests you.
   d. Print the page.

4. Use the Google search engine to find sites on jazz music by completing the following steps:
   a. Click in the Address bar, type **www.google.com**, and then press Enter.
   b. At the Google website, with the insertion point positioned in the search text box, type **jazz music** and then press Enter.
   c. Click a site that interests you.
   d. Print the page.
5. Close Internet Explorer.

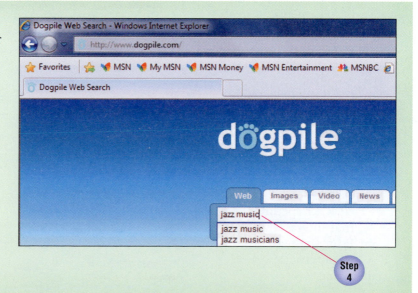

Using a Metasearch Engine

Bing, Yahoo!, and Google are search engines that search the Web for content and display search results. In addition to individual search engines, you can use a metasearch engine, such as Dogpile, that sends your search text to other search engines and then compiles the results in one list. With a metasearch engine, you type the search text once and then access results from a wider group of search engines. The Dogpile metasearch engine provides search results from Google, Yahoo!, Bing, and Ask.

Project 4   **Searching with a Metasearch Search Engine**

1. At the Windows desktop, click the Internet Explorer icon on the Taskbar.
2. Click in the Address bar.
3. Type **www.dogpile.com** and then press Enter.
4. At the Dogpile website, type **jazz music** in the search text box and then press Enter.
5. Click a hyperlink that interests you.
6. Close the Internet Explorer window.

Completing Advanced Searches for Specific Sites ■■■■■■■■■■

Web Search

The Internet contains an enormous amount of information. Depending on what you are searching for on the Internet and the search engine you use, some searches can result in several thousand "hits" (sites). Wading through a large number of sites can be very time-consuming and counterproductive. Narrowing a search to very specific criteria can greatly reduce the number of hits for a search. To narrow a search, use the advanced search options offered by the search engine.

Project 5 Narrowing a Search

1. Start Internet Explorer.
2. Search for sites on skydiving in Oregon by completing the following steps:
   a. Click in the Address bar, type **www.yahoo.com**, and then press Enter.
   b. At the Yahoo! home page, click the Web Search button next to the search text box.
   c. Click the <u>more</u> hyperlink located above the search text box and then click Advanced Search at the drop-down list.
   d. At the Advanced Web Search page, click in the search text box next to *all of these words*.
   e. Type **skydiving Oregon tandem static line**. (This limits the search to web pages containing all of the words typed in the search text box.)
   f. Click the Yahoo! Search button.
   g. When the list of websites displays, click a hyperlink that interests you.
   h. Click the Back button until the Yahoo! Advanced Web Search page displays.
   i. Click in the *the exact phrase* text box and then type **skydiving in Oregon**.
   j. Click the *Only .com domains* in the *Site/Domain* section.
   k. Click the Yahoo! Search button.
   l. When the list of websites displays, click a hyperlink that interests you.
   m. Print the page.
3. Close Internet Explorer.

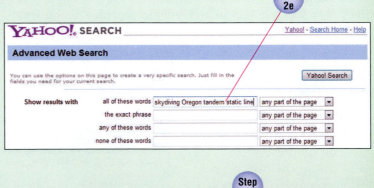

Step 2c

Step 2e

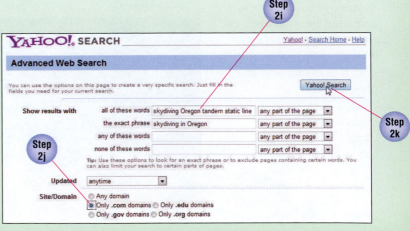

Step 2i

Step 2j

Step 2k

Downloading Images, Text, and Web Pages from the Internet ▪■■■

The image(s) and/or text that display when you open a web page as well as the web page itself can be saved as a separate file. This separate file can be viewed, printed, or inserted in another file. The information you want to save in a separate file is downloaded from the Internet by Internet Explorer and saved in a folder of your choosing with the name you specify. Copyright laws protect much of the information on the Internet. Before using information downloaded from the Internet, check the site for restrictions. If you do use information, make sure you properly cite the source.

Project 6   Downloading Images and Web Pages

1. Start Internet Explorer.
2. Download a web page and image from Banff National Park by completing the following steps:
   a. Search for sites on the Internet for Banff National Park.
   b. From the list of sites that displays, choose a site that contains information about Banff National Park and at least one image of the park.
   c. Save the web page as a separate file by clicking the Page button on the Internet Explorer toolbar and then clicking *Save As* at the drop-down list.
   d. At the Save Webpage dialog box, type **BanffWebPage**.
   e. Navigate to the drive containing your storage medium and then click the Save button.

3. Save an image file by completing the following steps:
   a. Right-click an image that displays at the website. (The image that displays may vary from what you see below.)
   b. At the shortcut menu that displays, click *Save Picture As*.
   c. At the Save Picture dialog box, type **BanffImage** in the *File name* text box.

   d. Navigate to the drive containing your storage medium and then click the Save button.
4. Close Internet Explorer.

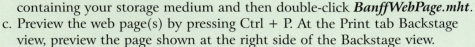

Project 7   **Opening the Saved Web Page and Image in a Word Document**

1. Open Microsoft Word by clicking the Start button on the Taskbar, clicking *All Programs*, clicking *Microsoft Office*, and then clicking *Microsoft Word 2010*.
2. With Microsoft Word open, insert the image in a document by completing the following steps:
   a. Click the Insert tab and then click the Picture button in the Illustrations group.
   b. At the Insert Picture dialog box, navigate to the drive containing your storage medium and then double-click *BanffImage.jpg*.
   c. When the image displays in the Word document, print the document by pressing Ctrl + P and then clicking the Print button.
   d. Close the document by clicking the File tab and then clicking the Close button. At the message asking if you want to save the changes, click *Don't Save*.
3. Open the **BanffWebPage.mht** file by completing the following steps:
   a. Click the File tab and then click the Open button.
   b. At the Open dialog box, navigate to the drive containing your storage medium and then double-click *BanffWebPage.mht*.
   c. Preview the web page(s) by pressing Ctrl + P. At the Print tab Backstage view, preview the page shown at the right side of the Backstage view.
4. Close Word by clicking the Close button (contains an X) that displays in the upper right corner of the screen.

Microsoft PowerPoint®

Unit 1 ■ Creating and Formatting PowerPoint Presentations

Microsoft® PowerPoint®

Preparing a PowerPoint Presentation

PERFORMANCE OBJECTIVES

Upon successful completion of Chapter 1, you will be able to:

- Create a PowerPoint presentation with an installed template
- Open, save, run, print, close, and delete a presentation
- Plan a presentation
- Create a presentation using a theme template
- Insert slides, insert text in slides, and choose slide layouts
- Change presentation views
- Navigate and edit slides
- Preview and print a presentation
- Create a presentation from an existing presentation
- Apply a design theme to slides in a presentation
- Prepare a presentation from a blank presentation
- Prepare a presentation in the Slides/Outline pane
- Add transitions and sounds to a presentation

Tutorials

1.1 Creating and Saving a Presentation
1.2 Opening, Organizing, and Viewing a Presentation
1.3 Printing a Presentation
1.4 Previewing Slides
1.5 Completing the Presentation Cycle
1.6 Adding Transition Effects and Sound
1.7 Setting Timings for Slides

During a presentation, the person doing the presenting may use visual aids to strengthen the impact of the message as well as help organize the information. Visual aids may include transparencies, slides, photographs, or an on-screen presentation. With Microsoft's PowerPoint program, you can easily create visual aids for a presentation and then print copies of the aids as well as run the presentation. PowerPoint is a presentation graphics program that you can use to organize and present information. Model answers for this chapter's projects appear on the following page.

PowerPoint2010C1

Note: Before beginning the projects, copy to your storage medium the PowerPoint2010C1 subfolder from the PowerPoint2010 folder on the CD that accompanies this textbook. Steps on how to copy a folder are presented on the inside of the back cover of this textbook. Do this every time you start a chapter's projects.

Project 2 Create an Internet Presentation Using a Theme Template
P-C1-P2-Internet.pptx

Project 3 Create a Planning Presentation from an Existing Presentation
P-C1-P3-PlanningPres.pptx

Project 4 Create a Technology Presentation in the Slides/Outline Pane
P-C1-P4-Computers.pptx

Project **1** **Open and Run a Template Presentation** **1 Part**

You will open an installed template presentation, run the presentation, and then close the presentation.

Creating a PowerPoint Presentation ■■■■■■■■■■■■■

PowerPoint provides several methods for creating a presentation. You can create a presentation using an installed template or using a theme template and prepare a presentation from a blank presentation or from an existing presentation. The steps you follow to create a presentation will vary depending on the method you choose, but will probably follow these basic steps:

1. Open PowerPoint.
2. Choose the desired installed template or theme or open an existing presentation or start with a blank presentation.
3. Type the text for each slide, adding additional elements as needed such as graphic images.
4. If necessary, apply a design theme.
5. Save the presentation.
6. Print the presentation as slides, handouts, notes pages, or an outline.
7. Run the presentation.
8. Close the presentation.
9. Exit PowerPoint.

When you choose the specific type of presentation you want to create, you are presented with the PowerPoint window in the Normal view. What displays in the window will vary depending on the type of presentation you are creating. However, the PowerPoint window contains some consistent elements as shown in Figure 1.1. The PowerPoint window contains many elements that are similar to other Microsoft Office programs such as Word and Excel. For example, the PowerPoint window, like the Word window, contains a File tab, Quick Access toolbar, tabs, ribbon, vertical and horizontal scroll bars, and a Status bar. The PowerPoint window elements are described in Table 1.1.

PowerPoint, like other Microsoft Office programs, provides enhanced ScreenTips for buttons and options. Hover the mouse pointer on a button or option and, after approximately one second, an enhanced ScreenTip displays near the button or option. The enhanced ScreenTip displays the name of the button or option, any shortcut command if one is available, and a description of the button or option.

Figure 1.1 PowerPoint Window

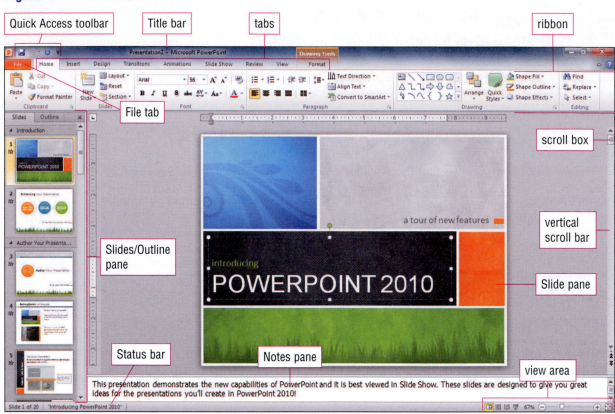

Table 1.1 PowerPoint Window Elements

Feature	Description
Quick Access toolbar	Contains buttons for commonly used commands.
File tab	Click the File tab and the Backstage view displays containing tabs and buttons for working with and managing presentations.
Title bar	Displays presentation name followed by the program name.
Tabs	Contains commands and features organized into groups.
Ribbon	Area containing the tabs and commands divided into groups.
Slides/Outline pane	Displays at the left side of the window with two tabs — Slides and Outline. With the Slides tab selected, slide miniatures (thumbnails) display in the pane; with the Outline tab selected, presentation contents display in the pane.
Slide pane	Displays the slide and slide contents.
Notes pane	Add notes to a presentation in this pane.
Vertical scroll bar	Display specific slides using this scroll bar.
I-beam pointer	Used to move the insertion point or to select text.
Insertion point	Indicates the location of the next character entered at the keyboard.
View area	Located toward the right side of the Status bar and contains buttons for changing the presentation view.
Status bar	Displays the slide number and number of slides, name of the applied design theme, view buttons, and the Zoom slider bar.

Opening a Presentation ■■■■■■■■■■■■■■■■■■■■■■■

When you create and then save a presentation, you can open the presentation at the Open dialog box. Display this dialog box by clicking the File tab and then clicking the Open button at the Backstage view. You can also display the Open dialog box by using the keyboard shortcut, Ctrl + O, or by inserting an Open button on the Quick Access toolbar. To insert the button, click the Customize Quick Access toolbar button that displays at the right side of the toolbar and then click *Open* at the drop-down list. At the Open dialog box, navigate to the desired folder and then double-click the desired presentation in the Content pane.

By default, PowerPoint displays the recently opened presentations in the Recent Presentations list. To open one of these presentations, click the File tab, click the Recent tab, and then click the desired presentation in the *Recent Presentations* list. If you want a presentation to remain in the list, "pin" the presentation to the list by clicking the pin button that displays at the right side of the presentation name. This changes the dimmed gray stick pin to a blue stick pin. To "unpin" the presentation, click the pin button to change it from a blue pin to a gray pin.

Microsoft provides a number of predesigned presentation templates you can view and also use as a basis for preparing your own presentation. To display the installed templates, click the File tab and then click the New tab. This displays the New tab Backstage view as shown in Figure 1.2. In this view, available templates and themes display as well as online templates. To display available templates, click the *Sample templates* option in the Available Templates and Themes category of the Backstage view. To open a template presentation, double-click the desired presentation.

▼ **Quick Steps**

Open a Presentation
1. Click File tab, Open button.
2. Navigate to desired folder or drive.
3. Double-click presentation.

Open an Installed Template
1. Click File tab, New tab.
2. Click *Sample templates* option.
3. Double-click desired presentation.

Figure 1.2 New Tab Backstage View

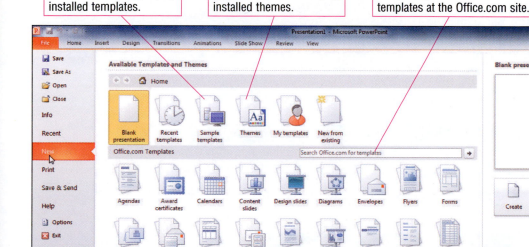

Click this option to display installed templates.

Click this option to display installed themes.

Use this option to search for templates at the Office.com site.

Starting a Presentation ▪■■■■■■■■■■■■■■■■■■■■■

▼ Quick Steps

Run a Presentation
1. Click Slide Show button in view area on Status bar.
2. Click left mouse button to advance slides.

Close a Presentation
1. Click File tab.
2. Click Close button.
OR
Press Ctrl + F4.

When you open a presentation, the presentation displays in Normal view. In this view, you can edit and customize the presentation. To run the presentation, click the Slide Show button in the view area on the Status bar or click the Slide Show tab and then click the From Beginning button in the Start Slide Show group. Navigate through slides in the presentation by clicking the left mouse button.

Closing a Presentation ■■■■■■■■■■■■■■■■■■■■■

To remove a presentation from the screen, close the presentation. You can close a presentation by clicking the File tab and then clicking the Close button. You can also close a presentation with the keyboard shortcut Ctrl + F4. To use this shortcut, hold down the Ctrl key on the keyboard, press the F4 function key located toward the top of the keyboard, and then release the Ctrl key. If you made any changes to the presentation, you will be asked if you want to save the presentation.

Project 1   Opening, Running, and Closing a Template Presentation   Part 1 of 1

1. Open PowerPoint by clicking the Start button on the Taskbar, pointing to *All Programs*, clicking *Microsoft Office*, and then clicking *Microsoft PowerPoint 2010*. (Depending on your operating system, these steps may vary.)
2. Click the File tab and then click the New tab.
3. At the New tab Backstage view, click the *Sample templates* option in the Available Templates and Themes category.
4. Double-click the *Introducing PowerPoint 2010* template.

5. Run the presentation by completing the following steps:
   a. Click the Slide Show button in the view area on the Status bar.
   b. Read the information in the first slide in the presentation and then click the left mouse button.
   c. Continue reading information in slides and clicking the left mouse button to advance slides.
   d. At the black screen with the message *End of slide show, click to exit*, click the left mouse button. (This returns the presentation to Normal view.)
6. Close the presentation by clicking the File tab and then clicking the Close button.

Step 5a

Project 2 — Create an Internet Presentation Using a Theme Template

3 Parts

You will use a theme template to create a presentation, insert text in slides in the presentation, choose a slide layout, insert new slides, change views, navigate through the presentation, edit text in slides, and then print the presentation.

Planning a Presentation ■■■■■■■■■■■■■■■■■■■■■■■■■■

With PowerPoint, you can create slides for an on-screen presentation and you can print handouts of the presentation, print an outline, or print the entire presentation. When planning a presentation, first define the purpose of the presentation. Is the intent to inform? educate? sell? motivate? and/ or entertain? Additionally, consider the audience who will be listening to and watching the presentation. Determine the content of the presentation and also the medium that will be used to convey the message. Will a computer be used to display the slides of a presentation or will the presentation be projected onto a screen? Some basic guidelines to consider when preparing the content of the presentation include:

- **Determine the main purpose of the presentation.** Do not try to cover too many topics — this may strain the audience's attention or cause confusion. Identifying the main point of the presentation will help you stay focused and convey a clear message to the audience.

- **Determine the output.** Is the presentation going to be presented on a computer or will the slides be projected? To help decide the type of output needed, consider the availability of equipment, the size of the room where the presentation will be made, and the number of people who will be attending the presentation.

- **Show one idea per slide.** Each slide in a presentation should convey only one main idea. Too many thoughts or ideas on a slide may confuse the audience and cause you to stray from the purpose of the slide. Determine the specific message you want to convey to the audience and then outline the message to organize ideas.

- **Maintain a consistent layout.** A consistent layout and color scheme for slides in a presentation will create continuity and cohesiveness. Do not get carried away by using too many colors and too many pictures or other graphic elements.

- **Keep slides easy to read and uncluttered.** Keep slides simple and easy for the audience to read. Keep words and other items such as bullets to a minimum.
- **Determine the output needed.** Will you be providing audience members with handouts? If so, will these handouts consist of a printing of each slide? an outline of the presentation? a printing of each slide with space for taking notes?

Creating a Presentation Using a Theme Template ■■■■■

▼ **Quick Steps**

Create Presentation Using a Theme Template
1. Click File tab.
2. Click New tab.
3. Click *Themes* option.
4. Double-click desired theme template.

PowerPoint provides a variety of predesigned theme templates you can use when creating slides for a presentation. These *theme templates* include formatting such as color, background, fonts, and so on. You can choose a theme template in the Available Templates and Themes category in the New tab Backstage view. Display these options by clicking the File tab and then clicking the New tab. In the Available Templates and Themes category, click *Themes* and then double-click the desired theme template.

Inserting Text in Slides ■■■■■■■■■■■■■■■■■■■■■■

When you choose a theme template at the New tab Backstage view or start with a blank presentation, click the Design tab and then click the desired theme in the Themes group, a slide displays in the Slide pane in Normal view. The slide displays with a default Title Slide layout. This layout contains placeholders for entering the slide title and the slide subtitle. To insert text in a placeholder, click the placeholder text. This moves the insertion point inside the placeholder, removes the default placeholder text, and selects the placeholder. A selected placeholder displays surrounded by a dashed border with sizing handles and a green rotation handle. Figure 1.3 displays a selected placeholder.

With the insertion point positioned in a placeholder, type the desired text. Edit text in a placeholder in the same manner as editing text in a Word document. Press the Backspace key to delete the character immediately left of the insertion point and press the Delete key to delete the character immediately right of the insertion point. Use the arrow keys on the keyboard to move the insertion point in the desired direction.

Figure 1.3 Selected Placeholder

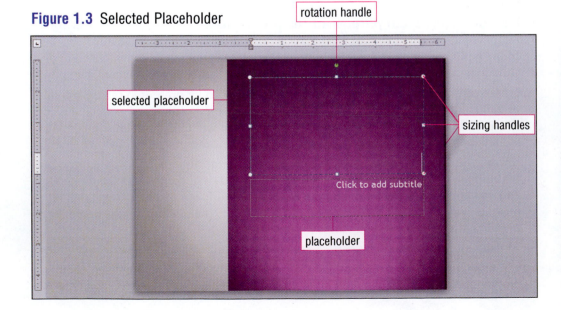

Choosing a Slide Layout ■■■■■■■■■■■■■■■■■■■

When you choose a theme template or a theme in a blank presentation, the slide displays in the Title Slide layout. This layout provides two placeholders for text — title text and subtitle text. You can change the slide layout with the Layout button in the Slides group in the Home tab. Click the Layout button and a drop-down list of layouts displays. Click the desired layout at the drop-down list and the layout is applied to the current slide.

Inserting a New Slide ■■■■■■■■■■■■■■■■■■■

Create a new slide in a presentation by clicking the New Slide button in the Slides group in the Home tab. By default, PowerPoint inserts a new slide with the Title and Content layout. You can choose a different slide layout for a new slide by clicking the New Slide button arrow and then clicking the desired layout at the drop-down list. You can also change the slide layout by clicking the Layout button in the Slides group in the Home tab and then clicking the desired layout at the drop-down list.

Saving a Presentation ■■■■■■■■■■■■■■■■■■■

After creating a presentation, save it by clicking the Save button on the Quick Access toolbar or by clicking the File tab and then the Save As button. This displays the Save As dialog box. At the Save As dialog box, type a name for the presentation in the *File name* text box, navigate to the desired folder, and then click the Save button.

▼ **Quick Steps**

Choose a Slide Layout
1. Click Layout button.
2. Click desired layout option in drop-down list.

Insert a New Slide
Click New Slide button.

Save a Presentation
1. Click Save button.
2. Type presentation name in *File name* text box.
3. Navigate to desired folder.
4. Click Save button.

H I N T

PowerPoint includes nine built-in standard layouts.

Layout   New   Save
          Slide

Project 2a   **Creating a Presentation Using a Theme Template**   **Part 1 of 3**

1. With PowerPoint open, click the File tab and then click the New tab.
2. At the New tab Backstage view, click the *Themes* option.
3. Scroll down the *Themes* list box and then double-click *Opulent*.
4. Click in the placeholder text *CLICK TO ADD TITLE* and then type **the internet**. (The design theme changes the text to uppercase letters.)
5. Click in the placeholder text *Click to add subtitle* and then type **A Global Network**.

6. Click the New Slide button in the Slides group in the Home tab (this inserts a slide with the Title and Content layout).

7. Click the placeholder text *CLICK TO ADD TITLE* and then type **communications**. (The design theme changes the text to uppercase letters.)

8. Click the placeholder text *Click to add text* and then type **Email**.

9. Press the Enter key (this moves the insertion point to the next line and inserts a bullet) and then type **Chat Rooms**.

10. Press the Enter key and then type **Instant Messaging**.

11. Press the Enter key and then type **Blogs**.

12. Press the Enter key and then type **Electronic Bulletin Boards**.

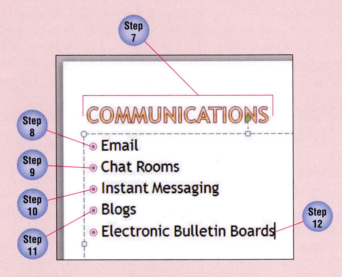

13. Click the New Slide button in the Slides group in the Home tab.

14. Click the placeholder text *CLICK TO ADD TITLE* and then type **entertainment**.

15. Click the placeholder text *Click to add text* and then type **Online Games**.

16. Press the Enter key and then type **Online Gambling**.

17. Press the Enter key and then type **Music**.

18. Press the Enter key and then type **Video**.

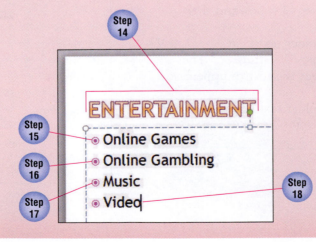

19. Click the New Slide button arrow and then click the *Title Slide* layout.
20. Click the placeholder text *CLICK TO ADD TITLE* and then type internet issues.
21. Click the placeholder text *Click to add subtitle* and then type Community and Policy Issues.
22. Click the New Slide button.
23. Click the placeholder text *CLICK TO ADD TITLE* and then type community issues.
24. Click the placeholder text *Click to add text* and then type Flaming.
25. Press the Enter key and then type Netiquette.
26. Press the Enter key and then type Moderated Environments.
27. Click the New Slide button in the Slides group in the Home tab.
28. Click the placeholder text *CLICK TO ADD TITLE* and then type policy issues.
29. Click the placeholder text *Click to add text* and then type Privacy Issues.
30. Press the Enter key and then type Security Protection.
31. Press the Enter key and then type Viruses.
32. Press the Enter key and then type Copyright Infringement.
33. Click in the Slide pane but outside the slide. (This deselects the placeholder.)
34. Save the presentation by completing the following steps:
    a. Click the Save button on the Quick Access toolbar.
    b. At the Save As dialog box type P-C1-P2-Internet (for PowerPoint, Chapter 1, Project 2, and the topic of the presentation).
    c. Navigate to the PowerPoint2010C1 folder on your storage medium.
    d. Click the Save button.

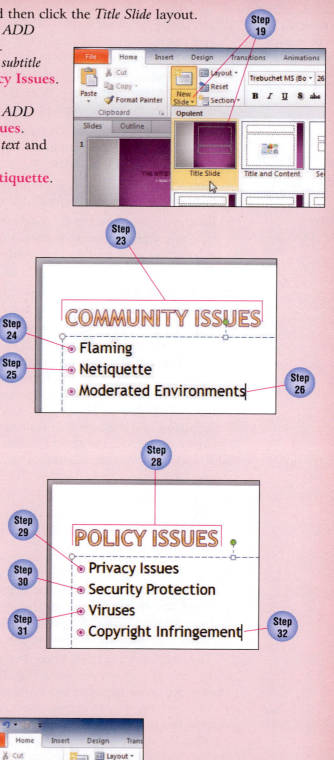

Changing Views

PowerPoint provides a variety of viewing options for a presentation. You can change the view with buttons in the view area on the Status bar or with options in the Presentation Views group in the View tab. The viewing choices include:

- **Normal view:** This is the default view and displays three panes — Slides/Outline, Slide, and Notes. With these three panes, you can work with all features in one place and write and design your presentation.

- **Slide Sorter view:** Choosing the Slide Sorter view displays all slides in the presentation in slide thumbnails. In this view, you can easily add, move, rearrange, and delete slides.

- **Notes Page view:** Change to the Notes Page view and an individual slide displays on a page with any added notes displayed below the slide.

- **Reading view:** Use the Reading view when you deliver your presentation to someone viewing the presentation on his or her own computer. Or, use this view to view the presentation in a window with controls that make the presentation easy to view.

- **Slide Show view:** Use the Slide Show view to run a presentation. When you choose this view, the slide fills the entire screen.

The view area on the Status bar contains four buttons for changing the view — Normal, Slide Sorter, Reading View, and Slide Show with the active button displaying with a light orange background. You can also change views with buttons in the View tab. The Presentation Views group in the View tab contains a number of buttons for changing views. Four buttons in the group include the Normal, Slide Sorter, Notes Page, and Reading View button. Click the Notes Page button and the active slide displays along with a space below the slide for inserting text. Click the text *Click to add text* that displays in the box below the slide and then type the desired note. When running the presentation, you can display any note attached to the slide.

View tab · Status bar

Normal · Normal

Slide Sorter · Slide Sorter

Page Notes · Slide Show

Reading View · Reading View

Navigating in a Presentation

In the Normal view, change slides by clicking the Previous Slide or Next Slide buttons located at the bottom of the vertical scroll bar. You can also change to a different slide using the mouse pointer on the vertical scroll bar. To do this, position the mouse pointer on the scroll box on the vertical scroll bar, hold down the left mouse button, drag up or down until a box displays with the desired slide number, and then release the button.

Previous Slide

Next Slide

You can also use the keyboard to display slides in a presentation. In Normal view, press the Down Arrow or Page Down key to display the next slide or press the Up Arrow or Page Up key to display the previous slide in the presentation. Press the Home key to display the first slide in the presentation and press End to display the last slide in the presentation. Navigate in the Slides/Outline pane by clicking the desired slide thumbnail. Navigate in the Slide Sorter view by clicking the desired slide or using the arrow keys on the keyboard.

1. With **P-C1-P2-Internet.pptx** open, navigate in the presentation by completing the following steps:

   a. Make sure that a placeholder in the slide is not selected.

   b. Press the Home key to display Slide 1 in the Slide pane.

   c. Click the Next Slide button located toward the bottom of the vertical scroll bar.

   d. Press the End key to display the last slide in the Slide pane.

   e. Click the Slide Sorter button in the view area on the Status bar.

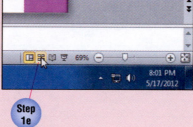

   f. Click Slide 1. (Notice that the active slide displays with an orange border.)

   g. Double-click Slide 5. (This closes Slide Sorter view and displays the presentation in Normal view with Slide 5 active.)

2. Insert text in slides by completing the following steps:

   a. Click on any character in the bulleted text. (This selects the placeholder.)

   b. Move the insertion point so it is positioned immediately right of *Flaming*.

   c. Press the Enter key and then type Email Pointers.

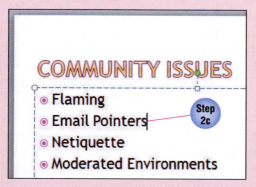

   d. Click Slide 3 in the Slides/Outline pane. (This displays Slide 3 in the Slide pane.)

   e. Click on any character in the bulleted text.

   f. Move the insertion point so it is positioned immediately right of *Video*.

   g. Press the Enter key and then type Travel.

3. Type a note in the Notes pane by completing the following steps:

   a. Click Slide 6 in the Slides/Outline pane.

   b. Click the text *Click to add notes* that displays in the Notes pane.

c. Type **Discuss the Digital Millennium Copyright Act of 1998.**

d. Display the slide in Notes Page view by clicking the View tab and then clicking the Notes Page button in the Presentation Views group. (Notice the note you typed displays below the slide in this view.)

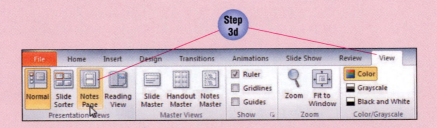

e. Return to Normal view by clicking the Normal button in the view area on the Status bar.

f. Press the Home key to make Slide 1 the active slide.

4. Save the presentation by clicking the Save button on the Quick Access toolbar.

Printing and Previewing a Presentation ■■■■■■■■■■

You can print a PowerPoint presentation in a variety of formats. You can print each slide on a separate piece of paper; print each slide at the top of the page, leaving the bottom of the page for notes; print a specific number of slides (up to nine slides) on a single piece of paper; or print the slide titles and topics in outline form. Use options in the Print tab in the Backstage view, shown in Figure 1.4, to specify what you want printed. To display options in the Print tab, click the File tab and then click the Print tab. You can also press Ctrl + P, which is the keyboard shortcut to display the Print tab Backstage view.

The left side of the Print tab Backstage view displays three categories—Print, Printer, and Settings. Click the Print button in the Print category to send the presentation to the printer and specify the number of copies you want printed with the *Copies* option. The two other categories contain galleries. For example, use the gallery in the Printer category to specify the desired printer. Click the first gallery in the Settings category and options display for specifying what you want printed such as all of the presentation or specific slides in the presentation. The Settings category also contains a number of galleries that describe how the slides will print.

In the Settings category, you can print a range of slides using the hyphen and print specific slides using a comma. For example, to print Slides 2 through 6, you would type *2-6* in the *Slides* text box. To print Slides 1, 3, and 7, you would type *1,3,7*. You can combine a hyphen and comma. For example, to print Slides 1 through 5 and Slide 8, you would type *1-5,8* in the *Slides* text box.

Figure 1.4 Print Tab Backstage View

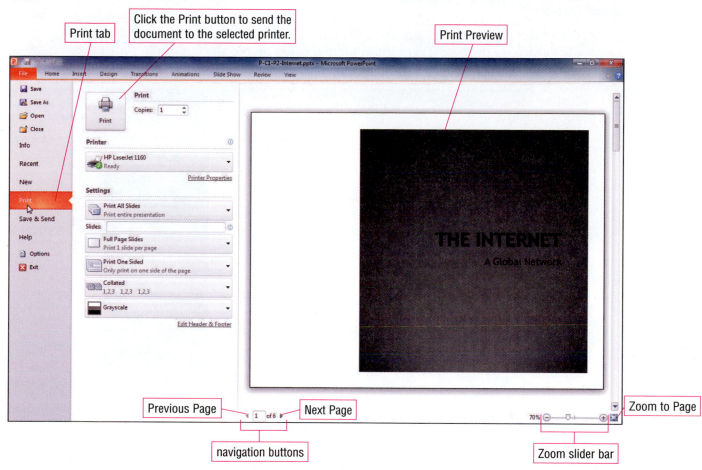

A preview of how a slide or slides will print displays at the right side of the Print tab Backstage view. If you have a color printer selected, the slide or slides that display at the right side of the Print tab Backstage view display in color, and if you have a black and white printer selected, the slide or slides will display in grayscale. Use the Next Page button (right-pointing arrow) located below and to the left of the page to view the next slide in the presentation, click the Previous Page button (left-pointing arrow) to display the previous slide in the presentation, use the Zoom slider bar to increase/decrease the size of the slide, and click the Zoom to Page button to fit the slide in the viewing area in the Print tab Backstage view.

You can choose to print a presentation as individual slides, handouts, notes pages, or an outline. If you print a presentation as handouts or an outline, PowerPoint will automatically print the current date in the upper right corner of the page and the page number in the lower right corner. If you print the presentation as notes pages, PowerPoint will automatically print the page number in the lower right corner. PowerPoint does not insert the date or page number when you print individual slides.

1. With **P-C1-P2-Internet.pptx** open, click the File tab and then click the Print tab.
2. Click twice on the Next Page button located below and to the left of the slide in the previewing area to display Slide 3 in the presentation.

Step 1

Step 2

3. Click twice on the Previous Page button to display Slide 1.
4. Increase and decrease the zoom by completing the following steps:
   a. Position the mouse pointer on the Zoom slider bar button (located at the bottom right of the Print tab Backstage view), drag the button to the right to increase the size of the slide in the viewing area of the Print tab Backstage view, and then drag the slider bar to the left to decrease the size of the slide.
   b. Click the percentage number that displays at the left side of the Zoom slider bar. (This displays the Zoom dialog box.)
   c. Click the *50%* option in the Zoom dialog box and then click OK.
   d. Click the Zoom to Page button located to the right of the Zoom slider bar. (This increases the size of the slide to fill the viewing area in the Print tab Backstage view.)

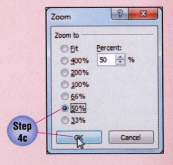

Step 4c

Step 4d

5. Print the presentation as a handout with six slides per page by completing the following steps:
   a. At the Print tab Backstage view, click the *Full Page Slides* option (the second gallery) in the Settings category and then click *6 Slides Horizontal* in the *Handouts* section.
   b. Click the Print button.

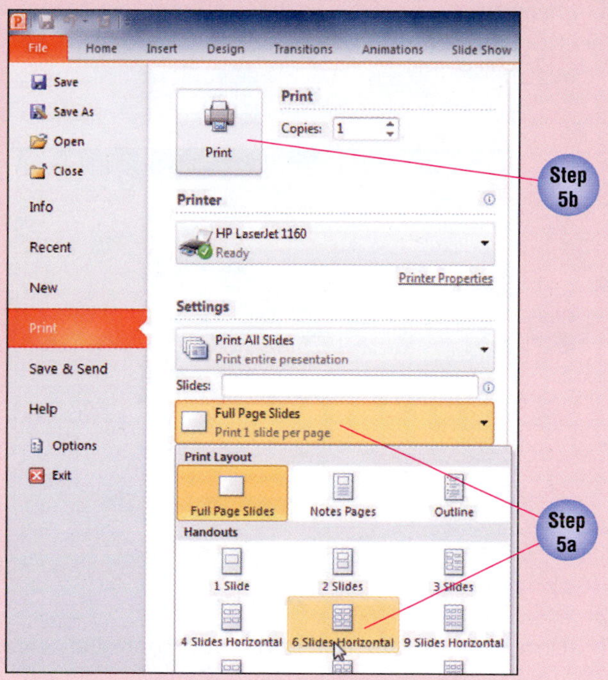

Step
5b

Step
5a

6. Print Slide 6 as a notes page by completing the following steps:
   a. Click the File tab and then click the Print tab at the Backstage view.
   b. At the Print tab Backstage view, click in the *Slides* text box located in the Settings category, and then type 6.
   c. Click the *6 Slides Horizontal* option in the Settings category and then click *Notes Pages* in the *Print Layout* section.
   d. Click the Print button.

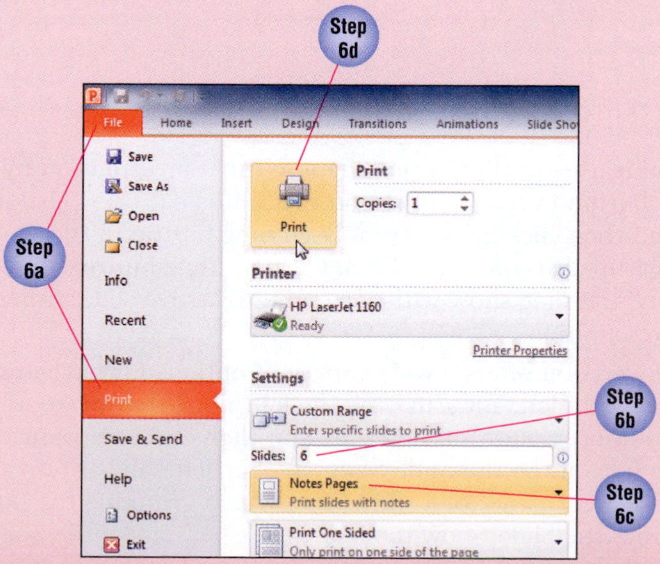

Step
6d

Step
6a

Step
6b

Step
6c

7. Print Slides 1 through 3 and Slide 5 by completing the following steps:
   a. Click the File tab and then click the Print tab.
   b. At the Print tab Backstage view, click in the *Slides* text box located in the Settings category, and then type 1-3,5.
   c. Click the *Notes Pages* option in the Settings category and then click *4 Slides Horizontal* in the *Handouts* section.
   d. Click the Print button.

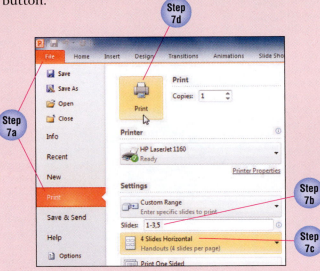

8. Close the presentation by clicking the File tab and then clicking the Close button.

Project 3   Create a Planning Presentation from an Existing Presentation   3 Parts

You will create a presentation from an existing presentation, apply a design theme to the presentation, run the presentation, and then delete the presentation.

Running a Slide Show ■■■■■■■■■■■■■■■■■■■■■■■■

From Beginning

From Current Slide

As you learned earlier in this chapter, run a presentation by clicking the Slide Show button in the view area on the Status bar or by clicking the Slide Show tab and then clicking the From Beginning button in the Start Slide Show group. This group also contains a From Current Slide button. Use this button to begin running the slide show with the currently active slide rather than the first slide in the presentation.

PowerPoint offers a wide variety of options for navigating through slides in a presentation. You can click the left mouse button to advance slides in a presentation, right-click in a slide and then choose options from a shortcut menu, or use buttons on the Slide Show toolbar. The Slide Show toolbar displays in the lower left corner of a slide when you are running the presentation. Figure 1.5 identifies the Slide Show toolbar.

Figure 1.5 Slide Show Toolbar

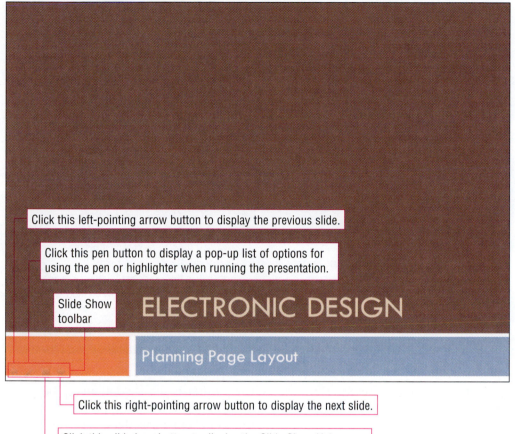

Click this left-pointing arrow button to display the previous slide.

Click this pen button to display a pop-up list of options for using the pen or highlighter when running the presentation.

Slide Show toolbar

ELECTRONIC DESIGN

Planning Page Layout

Click this right-pointing arrow button to display the next slide.

Click this slide icon button to display the Slide Show Help menu containing a list of options for navigating in the presentation.

To display this toolbar, run the presentation and then move the mouse pointer over the buttons. Click the right arrow button on the toolbar to display the next slide and click the left arrow button to display the previous slide. Click the slide icon button and a pop-up list displays with the following options: *Next, Previous, Last Viewed, Go to Slide, Go to Section, Custom Show, Screen, Help, Pause,* and *End Show*. Use these options to navigate to a particular slide in the presentation, display the Slide Show Help window, and pause or end the show. If you click the *Help* option at the pop-up list, the Slide Show Help window displays as shown in Figure 1.6. This helpful window describes the various keyboard options available when running a presentation.

The Slide Show toolbar also contains a pen button. Click this button and a pop-up list displays with the following options: *Arrow, Pen, Highlighter, Ink Color, Eraser, Erase All Ink on Slide,* and *Arrow Options*. Click the desired option and then drag with the mouse in the slide to draw or erase content on the slide. For example, to draw in a slide with the mouse, click the pen button on the Slide Show toolbar and then click the *Pen* option at the pop-up list. This turns the arrow pointer into a small dot. Draw in the slide by dragging with the mouse. If you draw in slides when running a slide show, you will be asked if you want to keep the ink annotations when the slide show is finished.

▼ **Quick Steps**

Use Pen/Highlighter during Presentation
1. Run presentation.
2. Display desired slide.
3. Click pen button on Slide Show toolbar.
4. Click pen or highlighter option.
5. Drag to draw line or highlight text.

HINT

If you use the pen or highlighter on a slide when running a presentation, choose an ink color that the audience can see easily.

Figure 1.6 Slide Show Help Menu

Slide Show Help	?	X

General | Rehearse/Record | Media | Ink

Slide show navigation shortcuts

'N', left click, space, right or down arrow, enter, or page down	Advance to the next slide
'P', backspace, left or up arrow, or page up	Return to the previous slide
Right mouse click	Popup menu/Previous slide
Number followed by Enter	Go to that slide
Esc, Ctrl+Break, or '-'	End slide show
Ctrl+S	All Slides dialog
'B' or '.'	Blacks/Unblacks the screen
'W' or ','	Whites/Unwhites the screen
'S' or '+'	Stop/Restart automatic show
'H'	Go to next slide if hidden
Hold both the Right and Left Mouse buttons down for 2 seconds	Return to first slide
Ctrl+T	View task bar
Ctrl+H/U	Hide/Show arrow on mouse move

OK

When running a presentation, the mouse pointer is set, by default, to be hidden automatically after three seconds of inactivity. The mouse pointer will appear again when you move the mouse. You can change this default setting by clicking the pen button on the Slide Show toolbar, pointing to *Arrow Options*, and then clicking *Visible* if you want the mouse pointer always visible or *Hidden* if you do not want the mouse to display at all as you run the presentation. The *Automatic* option is the default setting.

Creating a Presentation from an Existing Presentation ■■■■■■■■■■■■■■■■■■■■

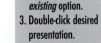

▼ Quick Steps

Create Presentation from an Existing Presentation
1. Click File tab, New tab.
2. Click *New from existing* option.
3. Double-click desired presentation.
4. Edit presentation.
5. Save presentation with new name.

You can create a presentation from an installed template, an installed theme, a blank presentation, or from an existing presentation. To create a presentation from an existing presentation, click the File tab and then click the New tab. At the New tab Backstage view, click the *New from existing* option in the Available Templates and Themes category. This displays the New from Existing Presentation dialog box with options similar to the Open dialog box. Double-click the desired presentation in the dialog box Content pane. This opens a new presentation based on the existing presentation and the Title bar displays *Presentation* followed by a number. Edit the presentation and then save the presentation with a new name.

1. Click the File tab and then click the New tab.
2. At the New tab Backstage view, click the *New from existing* option in the Available Templates and Themes category.
3. At the New from Existing Presentation dialog box, navigate to the PowerPoint2010C1 folder on your storage medium and then double-click *PlanningPres.pptx*.
4. Save the presentation by completing the following steps:
   a. Click the Save button on the Quick Access toolbar.
   b. At the Save As dialog box, make sure the PowerPoint2010C1 folder on your storage medium is active and then type **P-C1-P3-PlanningPres** in the *File name* text box.
   c. Press Enter or click the Save button.
5. Run the presentation by completing the following steps:
   a. Click the Slide Show button in the view area on the Status bar.
   b. When Slide 1 fills the screen, move the mouse to display the Slide Show toolbar. (This toolbar displays in a dimmed manner in the lower left corner of the slide.)
   c. Click the button containing the right arrow. (This displays the next slide.)
   d. Continue clicking the button containing the right arrow until a black screen displays.
   e. Click the left mouse button. (This displays the presentation in Normal view.)

   Step 5c

6. Run the presentation from the current slide and use the pen and highlighter to emphasize specific words by completing the following steps:
   a. Click Slide 2 in the Slides/Outline pane. (This makes Slide 2 active.)
   b. Click the Slide Show tab.
   c. Click the From Current Slide button in the Start Slide Show group.

   Step 6b

   Step 6c

   d. With Slide 2 active, use the pen to underline a word by completing the following steps:
      1) Move the mouse to display the Slide Show toolbar.
      2) Click the pen button on the Slide Show toolbar and then click *Pen* at the pop-up list. (This changes the mouse pointer to a small circle.)

   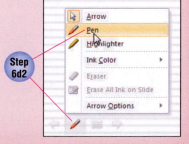

   Step 6d2

3) Using the mouse, draw a circle around the text *STEP 1*.
4) Draw a line below the word *identify*.
5) Click the pen button on the Slide Show toolbar and then click *Arrow* at the pop-up list. (This returns the mouse pointer to an arrow.)

e. Erase the pen markings by clicking the pen button on the Slide Show toolbar and then clicking *Erase All Ink on Slide* at the pop-up list.

f. Change the color of the pen ink by clicking the pen button, pointing to *Ink Color*, and then clicking the purple color (first option from the right in the bottom row).

g. Draw a circle around *STEP 1*.

h. Click the pen button on the Slide Show toolbar and then click *Arrow* at the pop-up list.

i. Discard the pen markings by pressing the Esc key to end the slide show and at the message that displays asking if you want to keep or discard the ink annotations, click the Discard button.

j. With Slide 2 active, click the Slide Show button in the Status bar to start the slide show and then click the left mouse button to display the next slide (Slide 3).

k. Click the pen button in the Slide Show toolbar and then click *Highlighter* at the pop-up list.

l. Drag through the word *target* to highlight it.

m. Click the button in the Slide Show toolbar containing the right arrow. (This displays Slide 4.)

n. Turn on the highlighter and then drag through the words *best format* to highlight them.

o. Click the pen button on the Slide Show toolbar and then click *Arrow* at the pop-up list.

7. Continue clicking the left mouse button to run the presentation.

8. At the black screen, click the left mouse button.

9. At the message asking if you want to keep your ink annotations, click the Keep button.

10. Save the presentation with a new name by completing the following steps:

    a. Click the File tab and then click the Save As button.

    b. At the Save As dialog box, make sure the PowerPoint2010C1 folder on your storage medium is the active folder, type **P-C1-P3-PlanningPres-Ink** in the *File name* text box, and then press Enter.

11. Print Slides 2, 3, and 4 as handouts. (For help, refer to Project 2c, Step 7.)

12. Close **P-C1-P3-PlanningPres-Ink.pptx**.

13. Open **P-C1-P3-PlanningPres.pptx**.

Applying a Design Theme ▪▪▪▪▪▪▪▪▪▪▪▪▪▪▪▪▪▪▪▪▪

As you learned, PowerPoint provides a variety of predesigned theme templates you can use when creating slides for a presentation. You can choose a theme template at the New tab Backstage view or with options in the Themes group in the Design tab. Click the Design tab and theme thumbnails display in the Themes group. Click one of these themes to apply it to the current presentation. To display additional themes, click the More button that displays at the right side of the visible theme thumbnails. You can also click the up-pointing or down-pointing arrow at the right side of the theme thumbnails to scroll through the list. Hover your mouse pointer over a theme and the active slide in the presentation displays with the theme formatting applied. This is an example of the *live preview* feature, which allows you to see how theme formatting affects your presentation.

Themes similar to the ones available in PowerPoint are also available in Word, Excel, Access, and Outlook. When you hover the mouse pointer over a theme thumbnail, a ScreenTip displays (after approximately a second) containing the theme name. Theme names in PowerPoint are similar in Word, Excel, Access, and Outlook and apply similar formatting. With the availability of the themes across these applications, you can "brand" your business files such as documents, workbooks, and presentations with a consistent and uniform appearance.

▼ **Quick Steps**

Apply a Design Theme
1. Click Design tab.
2. Click desired theme in Themes group.

H I N T

Design themes were designed by professional graphic artists who understand the use of color, space, and design.

More

Project 3b **Applying Design Themes**   **Part 2 of 3**

1. With **P-C1-P3-PlanningPres.pptx** open, make Slide 1 active, and make sure the presentation displays in Normal view.
2. Apply a different design theme to the presentation by completing the following steps:
   a. Click the Design tab.
   b. Hover the mouse pointer over the third theme thumbnail in the Themes group and notice the theme formatting applied to the slide in the Slide pane.
   c. Click the More button located to the right of the theme thumbnails, hover the mouse pointer over the remaining visible theme thumbnails, and notice the formatting applied to the active slide.
   d. Click the *Civic* theme.

3. Run the presentation and notice the formatting applied by the theme.
4. With the presentation in Normal view, apply a different design theme by completing the following steps:
   a. Click the More button that displays at the right side of the theme thumbnails.
   b. Click *Verve* at the drop-down gallery.

5. Run the presentation.
6. Print the presentation as a handout by completing the following steps:
    a. Click the File tab and then click the Print tab.
    b. At the Print tab Backstage view, click the *Full Page Slides* option in the Settings category and then click *6 Slides Horizontal* in the *Handouts* section.
    c. Click the Print button.
7. Save and then close **P-C1-P3-PlanningPres.pptx**.

▼ **Quick Steps**

Delete Presentation
1. Click File tab.
2. Click Open button.
3. Navigate to desired folder or drive.
4. Click the presentation.
5. Click Organize button, *Delete*.
6. Click Yes.

Deleting a Presentation ■■■■■■■■■■■■■■■■■■■■

File management tasks in PowerPoint can be performed at the Open or Save As dialog box. To delete a PowerPoint presentation, display the Open dialog box, click the presentation you want deleted, click the Organize button on the toolbar, and then click *Delete* at the drop-down list. At the message asking if you are sure you want to delete the presentation, click the Yes button. The presentation file must be closed to delete the file.

Project 3c **Deleting a PowerPoint Presentation**   **Part 3 of 3**

1. Click the File tab and then click the Open button.
2. At the Open dialog box, make sure the PowerPoint2010C1 folder on your storage medium is the active folder, and then click **PlanningPres.pptx** in the Content pane.
3. Click the Organize button on the toolbar and then click *Delete* at the drop-down list.

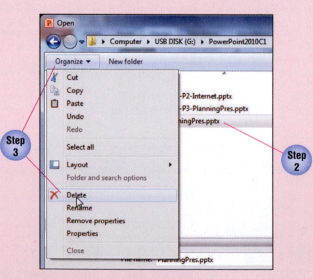

4. At the message asking if you are sure you want to delete the presentation, click Yes.
5. Click the Cancel button to close the Open dialog box.

Project **4**   **Create a Technology Presentation in the**   **3 Parts**
                 Slides/Outline Pane

You will create a computer technology presentation in the Slides/Outline pane
with the Outline tab selected, add and remove transitions and sounds to the
presentation, and set up the presentation to advance slides automatically after a
specified amount of time.

Preparing a Presentation from a Blank Presentation ■■■

When you first open PowerPoint, a blank presentation displays in which you can
enter text in slides. You can also display a blank presentation by clicking the File
tab and clicking the New tab. At the New tab Backstage view, click the *Blank
presentation* option in the Available Templates and Themes category and then click
the Create button that displays at the right side of the New tab Backstage view.
You can also double-click *Blank presentation*.

▼ **Quick Steps**

**Prepare a
Presentation from a
Blank Presentation**
1. Click File tab.
2. Click New tab.
3. Click *Blank
   presentation* option.
4. Click Create button.

Create

Preparing a Presentation in the Slides/Outline Pane ■■■

In Normal view, you can enter text in a slide in the Slide pane and you can
also enter text in a presentation in the Slides/Outline pane with the Outline tab
selected. To create a slide in the Slides/Outline pane, click the Outline tab, click in
the pane, and then type the text. Press the Tab key to move the insertion point to
the next tab stop. This moves the insertion point and also changes the formatting.
The formatting will vary depending on the theme you chose. Press Shift + Tab
to move the insertion point to the previous tab stop and change the formatting.
Moving the insertion point back to the left margin will begin another slide. Slides
are numbered at the left side of the screen and are followed by a slide icon.

Project 4a   **Preparing a Presentation in the Slides/Outline Pane**   **Part 1 of 3**

1. At a blank screen, click the File tab and then click the New tab.
2. At the New tab Backstage view, double-click the *Blank presentation* option in the Available
   Templates and Themes category.
3. At the blank presentation, click the Outline tab in the Slides/Outline pane.

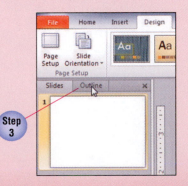

4. Click immediately right of the Slide 1 icon in the Slides/Outline pane, type the first slide title shown in Figure 1.7 *(Computer Technology)*, and then press Enter.
5. Type the second slide title shown in Figure 1.7 *(The Motherboard)* and then press Enter.
6. Press the Tab key, type the text after the first bullet in Figure 1.7 *(Buses)*, and then press Enter.
7. Continue typing the text as it displays in Figure 1.7. Press the Tab key to move the insertion point to the next tab stop or press Shift + Tab to move the insertion point back to a previous tab stop.

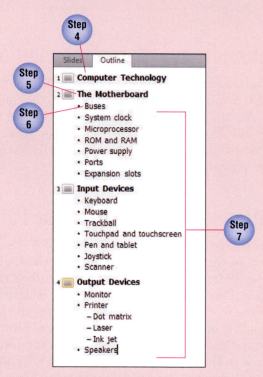

8. After typing all of the information as shown in Figure 1.7, click the Slides tab in the Slides/Outline tab.
9. Click Slide 1 in the Slides/Outline pane. (This displays Slide 1 in the Slide pane.)
10. Apply a design theme by completing the following steps:
    a. Click the Design tab.
    b. Click the More button that displays at the right side of the design theme thumbnails.
    c. Click *Hardcover* at the drop-down gallery.
11. Save the presentation and name it **P-C1-P4-Computers**.
12. Run the presentation.

Figure 1.7 Project 4a

1 Computer Technology
2 The Motherboard
- Buses
- System clock
- Microprocessor
- ROM and RAM
- Power supply
- Ports
- Expansion slots
3 Input Devices
- Keyboard
- Mouse
- Trackball
- Touchpad and touchscreen
- Pen and tablet
- Joystick
- Scanner
4 Output Devices
- Monitor
- Printer
  - Dot matrix
  - Laser
  - Ink jet
- Speakers

Adding Transitions and Sound Effects ∎∎∎∎∎∎∎∎∎∎∎

You can apply interesting transitions and sounds to a presentation. A ***transition*** is how one slide is removed from the screen during a presentation and the next slide is displayed. You can apply transitions such as cut, fade, push, wipe, split, reveal, and random bars. To add transitions and sounds, open a presentation, and then click the Transitions tab. This displays transition buttons and options as shown in Figure 1.8.

Transitions and sounds apply by default to the active slide. If you want transitions and sound to affect all slides, click the Apply To All button in the Timing group. In Slide Sorter view, you can select all slides by pressing Ctrl + A (or by clicking the Home tab, clicking the Select button, and then clicking *Select All* at the drop-down list) and then apply the desired transition and/or sound.

Apply To All

Figure 1.8 Transitions Tab

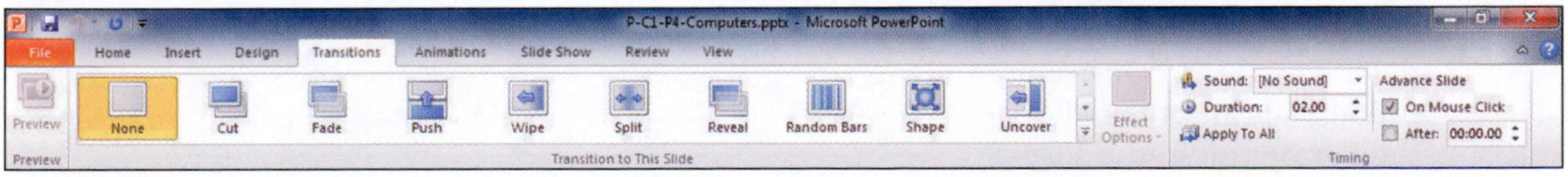

Adding Transitions

▼ **Quick Steps**

Apply Transition to Slides
1. Click Transitions tab.
2. Click desired transition in Transition to This Slide group.
3. Click Apply To All button.

Apply Sound to Slides
1. Click Transitions tab.
2. Click down-pointing arrow at right of *Sound* option.
3. Click desired sound.
4. Click Apply To All button.

Make a presentation more appealing by adding effects such as transitions and sounds.

To add a transition, click a transition thumbnail in the Transition to This Slide group in the Transitions tab. When you click a transition thumbnail, the transition displays in the slide in the Slide pane. Use the down-pointing and up-pointing arrows at the right side of the transition thumbnails to display additional transitions. Click the More button that displays at the right side of the visible transition thumbnails and a drop-down gallery displays with additional transition options. Use the *Duration* option to specify the duration slides transition when running the presentation. Click the up- or down-pointing arrow at the right side of the *Duration* option box to apply a duration time to slides. You can also select the current time in the text box and then type the desired time.

When you apply a transition to slides in a presentation, animation icons display below the slides in the Slides/Outline pane and in Slide Sorter view. Click an animation icon for a particular slide and the slide will display the transition effect.

Adding Sounds

As a slide is removed from the screen and another slide is displayed, you can add a sound. To add a sound, click the down-pointing arrow at the right side of the *Sound* option box and then click the desired sound at the drop-down gallery. If you have applied a transition to slides, you can hover your mouse pointer over a sound in the list box to hear the sound.

Removing Transitions and Sounds

You can remove a transition and sound from specific slides or from all slides in a presentation. To remove a transition, click the *None* transition thumbnail in the Transition to This Slide group. To remove transitions from all slides, click the Apply To All button in the Timing group. To remove sound from a slide, click the down-pointing arrow at the right side of the *Sound* option and then click *[No Sound]* at the drop-down gallery. To remove sound from all slides, click the Apply To All button.

Project 4b **Adding Transitions and Sounds to a Presentation** **Part 2 of 3**

1. With **P-C1-P4-Computers.pptx** open, click the Transitions tab.
2. Hover the mouse pointer over each of the transition thumbnails (except the first one) and notice how the transition displays in the slide in the Slide pane.
3. Apply transitions and sound to all slides in the presentation by completing the following steps:
   a. Click the More button at the right side of the transition thumbnails and then click the *Box* option in the *Exciting* section.

b. Click the Effect Options button in the Transition to This Slide group and then click *From Top* at the drop-down list.

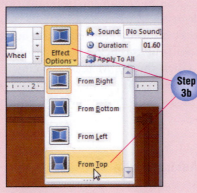

Step 3b

c. Click in the *Duration* option box in the Timing group, type 3, and then press Enter.
d. Click the down-pointing arrow at the right side of the *Sound* option box in the Timing group and then click *Chime* at the drop-down gallery.
e. Click the Apply To All button in the Timing group.

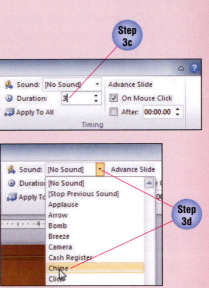

Step 3c

Step 3d

4. Run the presentation. (Notice the transitions and sounds as you move from slide to slide.)
5. With the presentation in Normal view and the Transitions tab active, remove the transitions and sound by completing the following steps:
   a. Click the More button at the right side of the transition thumbnails and then click the *None* option in the *Subtle* section.
   b. Click the down-pointing arrow at the right side of the *Sound* option box and then click *[No Sound]* at the drop-down gallery.
   c. Click the Apply To All button.
6. Apply transitions and sounds to specific slides by completing the following steps:
   a. Make sure the presentation displays in Normal view.
   b. Click Slide 1 in the Slides/Outline pane.
   c. Hold down the Shift key and then click Slide 2. (Slides 1 and 2 will display with orange backgrounds.)
   d. Click the More button at the right side of the transition thumbnails and then click a transition of your choosing.
   e. Click the down-pointing arrow at the right side of the *Sound* option box and then click a sound of your choosing.
   f. Click Slide 3 in the Slides/Outline pane.
   g. Hold down the Shift key and then click Slide 4.
   h. Click the More button at the right side of the transition thumbnails and then click a transition of your choosing.
   i. Click the down-pointing arrow at the right side of the *Sound* option box and then click a sound of your choosing.
7. Run the presentation from the beginning.
8. Remove the transitions and sounds from all slides. (Refer to Step 5.)
9. Save **P-C1-P4-Computers.pptx**.

▼ **Quick Steps**

Advance Slides Automatically
1. Click Transitions tab.
2. Click *After* check box.
3. Insert desired number of seconds in text box.
4. Click *On Mouse Click* check box.
5. Click Apply To All button.

Advancing Slides Automatically

You can advance slides in a slide show after a specific number of seconds with options in the Timing group in the Transitions tab. To advance slides automatically, click in the *After* check box and then insert the desired number of seconds in the text box. You can select the current time in the text box and then type the desired time or click the up- or down-pointing arrow to increase or decrease the time. Click the *On Mouse Click* check box to remove the check mark. If you want the transition time to affect all slides in the presentation, click the Apply To All button. In Slide Sorter view, the transition time displays below each affected slide.

Project 4c **Advancing Slides Automatically**   **Part 3 of 3**

1. With **P-C1-P4-Computers.pptx** open, make sure the Transitions tab is active.
2. Click in the *After* check box in the Timing group to insert a check mark.
3. Click in the *On Mouse Click* check box to remove the check mark.
4. Click the up-pointing arrow at the right side of the *After* option box until *00:04.00* displays in the box.
5. Click the Apply To All button.
6. Run the presentation from the beginning. (Each slide will advance automatically after four seconds.)
7. At the black screen, click the left mouse button.
8. Print the presentation as an outline by completing the following steps:
   a. Click the File tab and then click the Print tab.
   b. At the Print tab Backstage view, click the *Full Page Slides* option in the Settings category and then click *Outline* in the *Print Layout* section.
   c. Click the Print button.
9. Save and then close **P-C1-P4-Computers.pptx**.

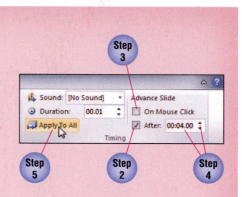

Step 3

Step 5 Step 2 Step 4

Chapter Summary

- PowerPoint is a software program you can use to create slides for an on-screen presentation.

- Open a presentation at the Open dialog box. Display this dialog box by clicking the File tab and then clicking the Open button.

- Predesigned presentation templates are available at the New tab Backstage view. Display this Backstage view by clicking the File tab and then clicking the New tab.

- Start running a presentation by clicking the Slide Show button in the view area on the Status bar or by clicking the View tab and then clicking the From Beginning button.

- Close a presentation by clicking the File tab and then clicking the Close button or with the keyboard shortcut, Ctrl + F4.

- Before creating a presentation in PowerPoint, plan the presentation by defining the purpose and determining the content and medium.

- You can use a predesigned theme template to create a presentation. A theme template provides slides with formatting such as color, background elements, and fonts.

- To insert text in a slide, click the desired placeholder and then type text.

- A slide layout provides placeholders for specific data in a slide. Choose a slide layout by clicking the Layout button in the Slides group in the Home tab.

- Insert a new slide in a presentation with the Title and Content layout by clicking the New Slide button in the Slides group in the Home tab. Insert a new slide with a specific layout by clicking the New Slide button arrow and then clicking the desired layout at the drop-down list.

- Save a presentation by clicking the Save button on the Quick Access toolbar or clicking the File tab and then clicking the Save As button. At the Save As dialog box, type a name for the presentation.

- View a presentation in one of the following five views: Normal view, which is the default and displays three panes — Slides/Outline, Slide, and Notes; Slide Sorter view, which displays all slides in the presentation in slide miniatures; Reading view when delivering a presentation to someone viewing it on his or her own computer; Notes Page view, which displays an individual slide with any added notes displayed below the slide; and Slide Show view, which runs the presentation.

- Navigate to various slides in a presentation using the mouse and/or keyboard. You can use the Previous Slide and Next Slide buttons located at the bottom of the vertical scroll bar, the scroll box on the vertical scroll bar, arrow keys on the keyboard, or the Page Up and Page Down buttons on the keyboard.

- Click the File tab and the Backstage view displays containing tabs and buttons for working with and managing presentations.

- With options at the Print tab Backstage view, you can print presentations with each slide on a separate piece of paper; each slide at the top of the page, leaving room for notes; all or a specific number of slides on a single piece of paper; or slide titles and topics in outline form.

- When running a presentation, the Slide Show toolbar displays in the lower left corner of the slide. This toolbar contains buttons and options for running a presentation. You can navigate to slides, make ink notations on slides, and display a Help menu. Click the slide show icon on the toolbar and then click *Help* and the Slide Show Help menu displays with options for using the keyboard to navigate in a presentation.

- Apply a design theme to a presentation by clicking the Design tab and then clicking the desired theme in the Themes group. Click the More button to display additional themes.

- Delete a presentation at the Open dialog box by clicking the presentation file name, clicking the Organize button on the toolbar, and then clicking *Delete* at the drop-down list.

- At the New tab Backstage view you can choose to prepare a presentation from an existing presentation or a blank presentation.

- You can type text in a slide in the Slide pane or in the Slides/Outline pane with the Outline tab selected.
- Enhance a presentation by adding transitions (how one slide is removed from the screen and replaced with the next slide) and sound. Add transitions and sound to a presentation with options in the Transitions tab.
- Advance slides automatically in a slide show by removing the check mark from the *On Mouse Click* check box in the Transitions tab, inserting a check mark in the *After* check box, and then specifying the desired time in the time option box.
- Click the Apply To All button to apply transitions, sounds, and/or time settings to all slides in a presentation.

Commands Review

FEATURE	RIBBON TAB, GROUP	BUTTON, OPTION	KEYBOARD SHORTCUT
Open dialog box	File	Open	Ctrl + O
New tab Backstage view	File	New	
Run presentation	Slide Show, Start Slide Show		F5
Close presentation	File	Close	Ctrl + F4
Slide layout	Home, Slides		
New slide	Home, Slides		Ctrl + M
Save As dialog box	File		Ctrl + S
Normal view	View, Presentation Views		
Slide Sorter view	View, Presentation Views		
Notes page	View, Presentation Views		
Print tab Backstage view	File	Print	Ctrl + P
Design theme	Design, Themes		
Transition	Transitions, Transition to This Slide		
Sound	Transitions, Timing		
Transition duration	Transitions, Timing		

Concepts Check Test Your Knowledge

Completion: In the space provided at the right, indicate the correct term, command, or number.

1. Click this tab to display tabs and buttons for working with presentations. _____

2. This toolbar contains buttons for commonly used commands. _____

3. This area contains the tabs and commands divided into groups. _____

4. Display installed templates in this Backstage view tab. _____

5. This is the keyboard shortcut to close a presentation. _____

6. Apply a theme template to a presentation by clicking this tab and then clicking the desired theme in the Themes group. _____

7. Insert a new slide by clicking the New Slide button in this group in the Home tab. _____

8. Change to this view to view displays of all slides in the presentation in slide thumbnails. _____

9. This is the default view and displays three panes. _____

10. The Previous Slide and Next Slide buttons display in this location. _____

11. To run a presentation beginning with Slide 1, click this button in the Slide Show tab. _____

12. In Normal view, you can enter text in a slide in this pane or in the Slides/Outline pane with the Outline tab selected. _____

13. To add a transition, click a transition thumbnail in the Transition to This Slide group in this tab. _____

14. When you apply a transition to slides in a presentation, these display below the slides in the Slides/Outline pane. _____

15. To advance slides automatically, remove the check mark from the *On Mouse Click* option, insert a check mark in this option, and then insert the desired number of seconds. _____

Skills Check Assess Your Performance

Assessment

1 CREATE A DEDUCTIBLE INCOME EXCEPTIONS PRESENTATION

1. Create a presentation with the text shown in Figure 1.9 by completing the following steps:
   a. With PowerPoint open, click the File tab and then click the New tab.
   b. At the New tab Backstage view, click the *Themes* option, and then double-click *Waveform* in the list box. (You may need to scroll down the list to display this theme.)
   c. Create slides with the text shown in Figure 1.9. Choose the *Title Slide* layout when inserting new slides.
2. Save the completed presentation in the PowerPoint2010C1 folder on your storage medium and name the presentation **P-C1-A1-Income**.
3. Apply the *Blinds* transition with a *Vertical* effect to all slides in the presentation.
4. Change the transition speed to *02.00*.
5. Apply the *Laser* sound to all slides in the presentation.
6. Run the presentation.
7. Print the presentation as a handout with six slides horizontally per page.
8. Save and then close **P-C1-A1-Income.pptx**.

Figure 1.9 Assessment 1

Slide 1	Title	=	DEDUCTIBLE INCOME
	Subtitle	=	Exceptions to Deductible Income
Slide 2	Title	=	EXCEPTION 1
	Subtitle	=	Any cost of living increase if increase becomes effective while disabled
Slide 3	Title	=	EXCEPTION 2
	Subtitle	=	Reimbursement for hospital, medical, or surgical expense
Slide 4	Title	=	EXCEPTION 3
	Subtitle	=	Reasonable attorney's fees incurred in connection with a claim for deductible income
Slide 5	Title	=	EXCEPTION 4
	Subtitle	=	Benefits from any individual disability insurance policy
Slide 6	Title	=	EXCEPTION 5
	Subtitle	=	Group credit or mortgage disability insurance benefits

Assessment

2 CREATE A PRESENTATION ON PREPARING A COMPANY NEWSLETTER

1. At the blank screen, click the File tab and then click the New tab.
2. At the New tab Backstage view, double-click the *Blank presentation* option in the Available Templates and Themes category.
3. Create slides with the text shown in Figure 1.10.
4. Apply a design theme of your choosing.
5. Run the presentation.
6. Print the presentation as a handout with six slides horizontally per page.
7. Make the following changes to the presentation:
   a. Apply a different design theme.
   b. Add a transition of your choosing to all slides.
   c. Add a sound of your choosing to all slides.
   d. Specify that all slides advance automatically after five seconds.
8. Run the presentation.
9. Save the presentation and name it **P-C1-A2-Newsletter**.
10. Close **P-C1-A2-Newsletter.pptx**.

Visual Benchmark Demonstrate Your Proficiency

CREATE A PRESENTATION ON PREPARING A NEWSLETTER

1. Create the presentation shown in Figure 1.11 with the following specifications:
   a. At a blank presentation, apply the *Austin* theme.
   b. Create the slides as shown in the figure (reading from left to right).
   c. Apply a transition, sound, and transition duration time of your choosing to each slide in the presentation.
2. Save the completed presentation and name it **P-C1-VB-Interview**.
3. Run the presentation.
4. Print the presentation as a handout with all six slides printed horizontally on the page.
5. Close the presentation.

Figure 1.10 Assessment 2

Slide 1	Title	=	PREPARING A COMPANY NEWSLETTER
	Subtitle	=	Planning and Designing the Layout

Slide 2	Title	=	Planning a Newsletter
	Bullets	=	• If a scanner is available, use pictures of different people from your organization in each issue.
			• Distribute contributor sheets soliciting information from employees.
			• Keep the focus of the newsletter on issues of interest to employees.

Slide 3	Title	=	Planning a Newsletter
	Bullets	=	• Make sure the focus is on various levels of employment; do not focus on top management only.
			• Conduct regular surveys to see if your newsletter provides a needed source of information.

Slide 4	Title	=	Designing a Newsletter
	Bulllets	=	• Maintain consistent elements from issue to issue such as:
			- Column layout
			- Nameplate formatting and location
			- Formatting of headlines
			- Use of color

Slide 5	Title	=	Designing a Newsletter
	Bullets	=	• Consider the following elements when designing a newsletter:
			- Focus
			- Balance
			- White space
			- Directional flow

Slide 6	Title	=	Creating a Newsletter Layout
	Bullets	=	• Choose paper size
			• Choose paper weight
			• Determine margins
			• Specify column layout

Figure 1.11 Visual Benchmark

Case Study Apply Your Skills

Part 1

You work for Citizens for Consumer Safety, a nonprofit organization providing information on household safety. Your supervisor, Melinda Johansson, will be presenting information on smoke detectors at a community meeting and has asked you to prepare a PowerPoint presentation. Open the Word document named **PPSmokeDetectors.docx**. Read over the information and then use the information to prepare a presentation. Consider the information in the *Planning a Presentation* section of this chapter and then prepare at least five slides. Apply an appropriate design theme and add a transition and sound to all slides. Save the presentation and name it **P-C1-CS-PPSmokeDetectors**. Run the presentation and then print the presentation as a handout with all slides on one page.

Part 2

Ms. Johansson has looked at the printout of the presentation and has asked you to print the presentation with two slides per page and in grayscale. Use the Help feature to learn about printing in grayscale and then print the presentation in grayscale with two slides per page.

Part 3

Ms. Johansson would like to provide information to participants at the presentation on online companies that sell smoke detectors. Using the Internet, locate at least three online stores that sell smoke detectors. Insert a new slide in the presentation that includes the names of the stores, web addresses, and any additional information you feel is important. Save the presentation and then print the presentation in Outline view. Close the presentation.

CHAPTER 2

Modifying a Presentation and Using Help

PERFORMANCE OBJECTIVES

Upon successful completion of Chapter 2, you will be able to:

- **Check spelling**
- **Insert and delete text in slides**
- **Find and replace text in slides**
- **Cut, copy, and paste text in slides**
- **Rearrange text in the Slides/Outline pane**
- **Size and rearrange placeholders**
- **Insert, delete, move, and copy slides**
- **Copy slides between presentations**
- **Duplicate slides**
- **Reuse slides**
- **Customize the Quick Access toolbar**
- **Use the Help feature**

Tutorials

2.1 Using the Spelling and Thesaurus Feature
2.2 Editing Text within Slides and Modifying Placeholders
2.3 Using the Clipboard and Finding, Replacing, and Moving Text
2.4 Cutting, Copying, Pasting, and Aligning Text
2.5 Rearranging, Deleting, and Hiding Slides
2.6 Duplicating and Reusing Slides
2.7 Using Help
2.8 Creating Sections
2.9 Customizing the Quick Access Toolbar

When preparing a presentation, you may need to modify a presentation by inserting and deleting text in slides or finding and replacing specific text. Improve the quality of your presentation by completing a spelling check to ensure that the words in your presentation are spelled correctly. Additional modifications you may need to make to a presentation include sizing and rearranging placeholders and rearranging, inserting, deleting, or copying slides. In this chapter, you will learn how to make these modifications to a presentation as well as how to preview a presentation and use the Help feature. Model answers for this chapter's projects appear on the following pages.

PowerPoint2010C2

Note: Before beginning the projects, copy to your storage medium the PowerPoint2010C2 subfolder from the PowerPoint2010 folder on the CD that accompanies this textbook and then make PowerPoint2010C2 the active folder.

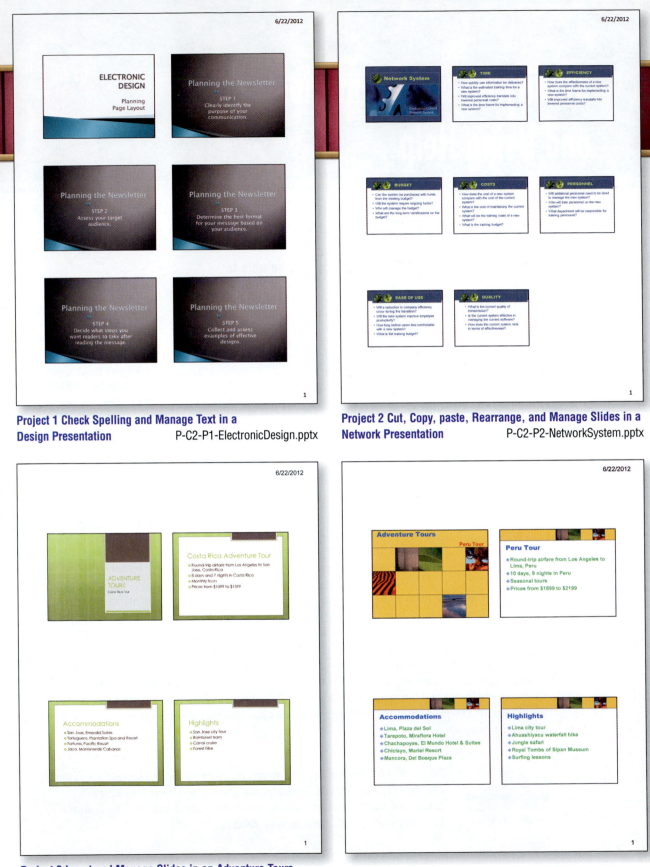

Project 1 Check Spelling and Manage Text in a Design Presentation
P-C2-P1-ElectronicDesign.pptx

Project 2 Cut, Copy, paste, Rearrange, and Manage Slides in a Network Presentation
P-C2-P2-NetworkSystem.pptx

Project 3 Insert and Manage Slides in an Adventure Tours Presentation
P-C2-P3-AdvTours.pptx

Model Answers

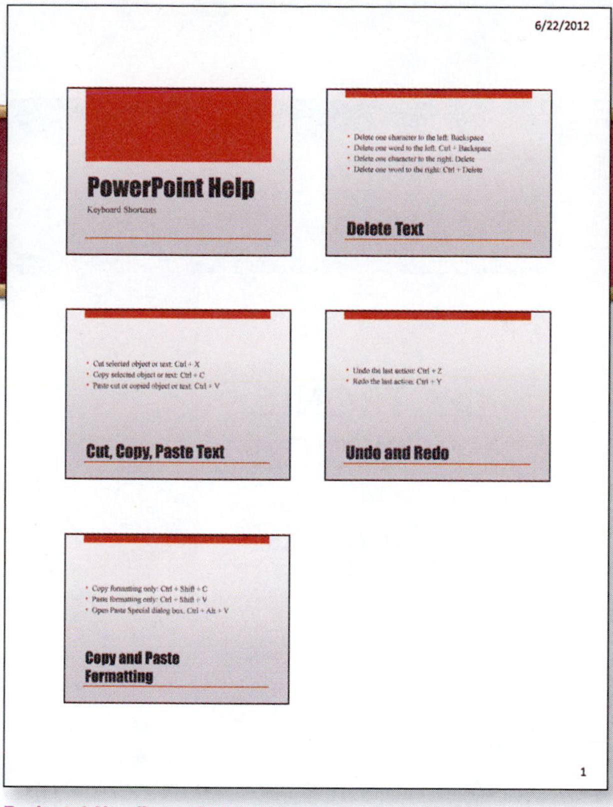

Project 4 Use PowerPoint Help Feature and Create a Presentation

P-C2-P4-Shortcuts.pptx

Project **1** **Check Spelling and Manage Text in a Design Presentation** **3 Parts**

You will open a presentation on steps for planning a design publication, complete a spelling check on the text in the presentation, and find and replace specific text in slides.

Checking Spelling ▪▪▪▪▪▪▪▪▪▪▪▪▪▪▪▪▪▪▪▪▪▪

When preparing a presentation, perform a spelling check on text in slides using PowerPoint's spelling feature. The spelling feature compares words in slides in a presentation with words in its dictionary. If a match is found, the word is passed over. If a match is not found, the spelling checker selects the word and offers replacement suggestions. To perform a spelling check on a PowerPoint presentation, click the Review tab and then click the Spelling button in the Proofing group. You can also start the spelling checker by pressing the F7 function key on the keyboard.

When you begin spell checking text in a presentation in Project 1a, the spelling checker will stop at the misspelled word *Layuot* and display the Spelling dialog box as shown in Figure 2.1. The options available in the Spelling dialog box are described in Table 2.1.

▼ Quick Steps

Complete a Spelling Check
1. Click Review tab.
2. Click Spelling button.
3. Change or ignore errors.
4. Click OK.

ABC ✓

Spelling

Figure 2.1 Spelling Dialog Box

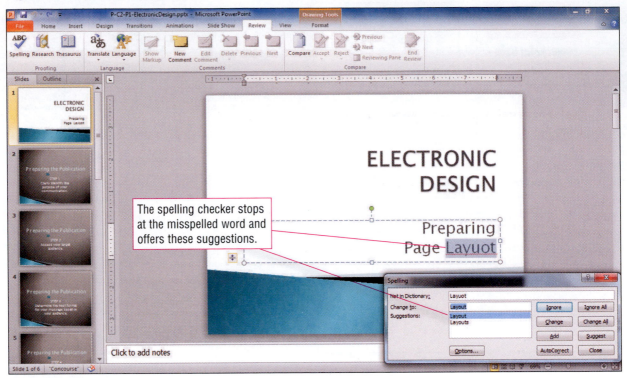

The spelling checker stops at the misspelled word and offers these suggestions.

Table 2.1 Spelling Dialog Box Options

Button	Function
Ignore	Skips that occurrence of the word.
Ignore All	Skips that occurrence of the word and all other occurrences of the word in slides.
Change	Replaces selected word in slide with selected word in *Suggestions* list box.
Change All	Replaces selected word in slide with selected word in *Suggestions* list box and all other occurrences of the word.
Add	Adds selected word to the main spelling check dictionary.
Suggest	Makes active the first suggestion in the *Suggestions* list box.
AutoCorrect	Inserts selected word and correct spelling of word in AutoCorrect dialog box.
Close	Closes the Spelling dialog box.
Options	Displays PowerPoint Options dialog box with *Proofing* selected that contains options for customizing a spelling check.

1. Open **ElectronicDesign.pptx** and then save the presentation with Save As and name it **P-C2-P1-ElectronicDesign**.

2. With the presentation in Normal view, complete a spelling check by completing the following steps:

    a. Click the Review tab.

    b. Click the Spelling button in the Proofing group.

    c. When the spelling checker selects the misspelled word *Layuot* and displays the correct spelling (*Layout*) in the *Change to* text box, click the Change button (or Change All button).

    d. When the spelling checker selects the misspelled word *Clerly* and displays the correct spelling (*Clearly*) in the *Change to* text box, click the Change button (or Change All button).

    e. When the spelling checker selects the misspelled word *massege*, click *message* in the *Suggestions* list box and then click the Change button (or Change All button).

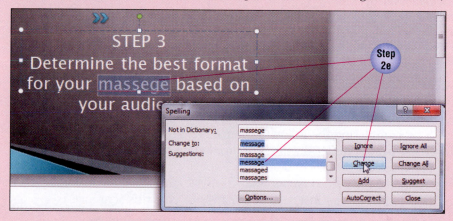

    f. When the spelling checker selects the misspelled word *fo* and displays the correct spelling (*of*) in the *Change to* text box, click the Change button.

    g. At the message telling you that the spelling check is complete, click the OK button.

3. Save **P-C2-P1-ElectronicDesign.pptx**.

Managing Text in Slides ■■■■■■■■■■■■■■■■■■■■

As you enter text in slides or as you manage existing slides, you may need to edit, move, copy, or delete text from slides. You may also want to find specific text in slides and replace it with other text. Text is generally inserted in a slide placeholder and this placeholder can be moved, sized, and/or deleted.

Inserting and Deleting Text in Slides

To insert or delete text in an individual slide, open the presentation, edit the text as needed, and then save the presentation again. If you want to delete more than an individual character, consider selecting the text first. Several methods can be used for selecting text as shown in Table 2.2.

Text in a slide is positioned inside of a placeholder. Slide layouts provide placeholders for text and generally display with a message suggesting the type of text to be entered in the slide. For example, the Title and Content slide layout contains a placeholder with the text *Click to add title* and another with the text *Click to add text*. Click placeholder text and the insertion point is positioned inside the placeholder, the default text is removed, and the placeholder is selected.

Table 2.2 Selecting Text

To do this	Perform this action
Select text mouse pointer passes through	Click and drag mouse
Select entire word	Double-click word
Select entire paragraph	Triple-click anywhere in paragraph
Select entire sentence	Ctrl + click anywhere in sentence
Select all text in selected placeholder	Click Select, Select All or press Ctrl + A

Project 1b   **Inserting and Deleting Text in Slides**   **Part 2 of 3**

1. With **P-C2-P1-ElectronicDesign.pptx** open and the presentation in Normal view, click the Previous Slide button (or Next Slide button) located at the bottom of the vertical scroll bar until Slide 5 displays.
2. Edit Slide 5 by completing the following steps:
   a. Position the I-beam pointer on the sentence below *STEP 4* and then click the left mouse button. (This selects the placeholder.)
   b. Edit the sentence so it reads *Decide what steps you want readers to take after reading the message.* (Use deleting and inserting commands to edit this sentence.)

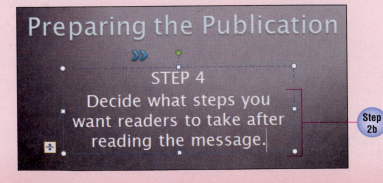

3. Click the Next Slide button to display Slide 6 and then edit Slide 6 in the Slides/Outline pane by completing the following steps:
   a. Click the Outline tab in the Slides/Outline pane.
   b. Click in the sentence below *STEP 5* and then edit the sentence so it reads *Collect and assess examples of effective designs*.
   c. Click the Slides tab.
4. Save **P-C2-P1-ElectronicDesign.pptx**.

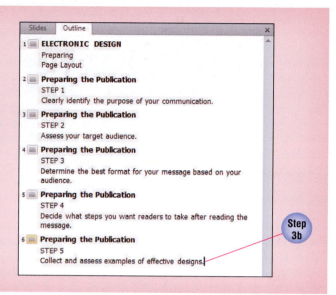

Step 3b

Finding and Replacing Text in Slides

Use the find feature to look for specific text in slides in a presentation and use the find and replace feature to look for specific text in slides in a presentation and replace with other text. Begin a find by clicking the Find button in the Editing group in the Home tab. This displays the Find dialog box shown in Figure 2.2. In the *Find what* text box, type the text you want to find and then click the Find Next button. Continue clicking this button until a message displays telling you that the search is complete. At this message, click OK.

Use options at the Replace dialog box shown in Figure 2.3 to search for text and replace it with other text. Display this dialog box by clicking the Replace button in the Home tab. Type the text you want to find in the *Find what* text box, press the Tab key, and then type the replacement text in the *Replace with* text box. Click the Find Next button to find the next occurrence of the text or click the Replace All button to replace all occurrences in the presentation.

Both the Find and Replace dialog boxes contain two additional options for conducting a find and a find and replace. Insert a check mark in the *Match case* check box to specify that the text should exactly match the case of the text entered in the *Find what* text box. For example, if you search for *Planning*, PowerPoint will stop at *Planning* but not *planning* or *PLANNING*. Insert a check mark in the *Find whole words only* check box to specify that the text is a whole word and not part of a word. For example, if you search for *plan*, and did not check the *Find whole words only* option, PowerPoint would stop at ex*plan*ation, *plan*ned, *plan*et, and so on.

▼ Quick Steps

Find Text
1. Click Find button.
2. Type text for which you are searching.
3. Click Find Next button.

Replace Text
1. Click Replace button.
2. Type text for which you are searching.
3. Press Tab key.
4. Type replacement text.
5. Click Replace All button.

Find

Replace

Figure 2.2 Find Dialog Box

In this text box, type the text for which you are searching.

Find	? ✕
Fi**n**d what:	[▾] Find Next
☐ Match case	Close
☐ Find whole words only	Replace...

Figure 2.3 Replace Dialog Box

In this text box, type the text for which you are searching.

In this text box, type the replacement text.

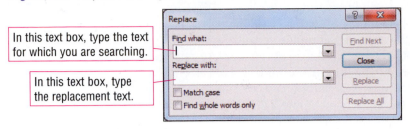

Project 1c   **Finding and Replacing Text**   **Part 3 of 3**

1. With **P-C2-P1-ElectronicDesign.pptx** open, make Slide 1 active.
2. Find all occurrences of *Preparing* in the presentation and replace with *Planning* by completing the following steps:
   a. With Slide 1 active, click the Replace button in the Editing group in the Home tab.
   b. At the Replace dialog box, type **Preparing** in the *Find what* text box.
   c. Press the Tab key.
   d. Type **Planning** in the *Replace with* text box.
   e. Click the Replace All button.
   f. At the message telling you that 6 replacements were made, click OK.
   g. Click the Close button to close the Replace dialog box.
3. Find all occurrences of *Publication* and replace with *Newsletter* by completing steps similar to those in Step 2.
4. Save the presentation.
5. Apply a transition and sound of your choosing to all slides in the presentation.
6. Run the presentation.
7. Print Slide 1 by completing the following steps:
   a. Click the File tab and then click the Print tab.
   b. At the Print tab Backstage view, click in the *Slides* text box in the Settings category and then type 1.
   c. Click the Print button.
8. Print the presentation as a handout with 6 slides horizontally per page. (Change the second gallery in the Settings category to *6 Slides Horizontal* and delete the *1* in the *Slides* text box.)
9. Save and then close **P-C2-P1-ElectronicDesign.pptx**.

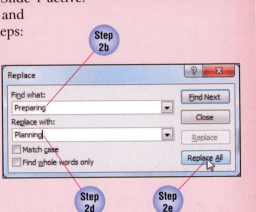

Step 2b

Step 2d

Step 2e

Project 2   **Cut, Copy, Paste, Rearrange, and Manage**   **5 Parts**
                 Slides in a Network Presentation

You will open a network evaluation presentation and then cut, copy, and paste text in slides; rearrange text in the Slides/Outline pane; size and rearrange placeholders in slides; and manage slides by inserting, deleting, moving, and copying slides. You will also create sections within a presentation and copy slides between presentations.

Cutting, Copying, and Pasting Text in Slides

With buttons in the Clipboard group in the Home tab and also with shortcut menu options, you can cut, copy, and/or paste text in slides. For example, to move text in a slide, click once in the placeholder containing the text to be moved, select the text, and then click the Cut button in the Clipboard group. Position the insertion point where you want the text inserted and then click the Paste button in the Clipboard group. To cut and paste with the shortcut menu, select the text you want to move, right-click the text, and then click *Cut* at the shortcut menu. Position the insertion point where you want the text inserted, right-click the location, and then click *Paste* at the shortcut menu. Complete similar steps to copy and paste text except click the Copy button instead of the Cut button or click the *Copy* option at the shortcut menu instead of the *Cut* option.

 HINT
Ctrl + X is the keyboard shortcut to cut selected text, Ctrl + C is the keyboard shortcut to copy selected text, and Ctrl + V is the keyboard shortcut to paste cut or copied text.

Cut

Copy

Paste

Project 2a **Cutting, Copying, and Pasting Text in Slides** **Part 1 of 5**

1. Open **NetworkSystem.pptx** located in the PowerPoint2010C2 folder on your storage medium and then save the presentation with Save As and name it **P-C2-P2-NetworkSystem**.
2. Insert a new slide by completing the following steps:
   a. Make Slide 4 active.
   b. Click the New Slide button in the Slides group in the Home tab.
   c. Click in the *Click to add title* placeholder and then type TIME.
3. Cut text from Slide 3 and paste it into Slide 5 by completing the following steps:
   a. Make Slide 3 active.
   b. Click on any character in the bulleted text (in the Slide pane).
   c. Using the mouse, select the text following the bottom three bullets. (The bullets will not be selected.)
   d. With the text selected, click the Cut button in the Clipboard group in the Home tab.

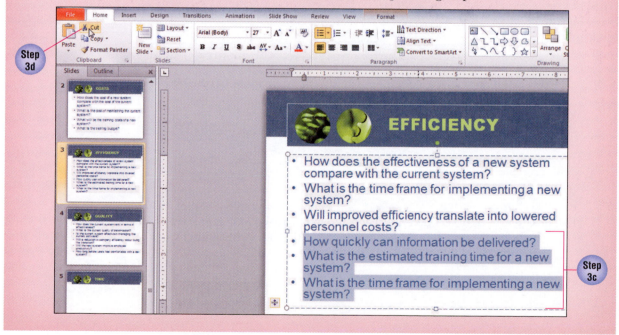

e. Make Slide 5 the active slide (contains the title *TIME*).

f. Click in the *Click to add text* placeholder.

g. Click the Paste button in the Clipboard group.

h. If the insertion point is positioned below the third bulleted item following a bullet, press the Backspace key twice. (This removes the bullet and deletes the blank line below the bullet.)

4. Insert a new slide by completing the following steps:

a. With Slide 5 the active slide, click the New Slide button in the Slides group in the Home tab.

b. Click in the *Click to add title* placeholder and then type **EASE OF USE**.

5. Cut text from Slide 4 and paste it into Slide 6 by completing the following steps:

a. Make Slide 4 active.

b. Click on any character in the bulleted text.

c. Select the text following the bottom three bullets.

d. Click the Cut button in the Clipboard group in the Home tab.

e. Make Slide 6 active (contains the title *EASE OF USE*).

f. Click in the *Click to add text* placeholder.

g. Click the Paste button in the Clipboard group.

h. If the insertion point is positioned below the third bulleted item following a bullet, press the Backspace key twice.

6. Copy text from Slide 3 to Slide 5 by completing the following steps:

a. Make Slide 3 active.

b. Click on any character in the bulleted text.

c. Position the mouse pointer on the last bullet until the pointer turns into a four-headed arrow and then click the left mouse button. (This selects the text following the bullet.)

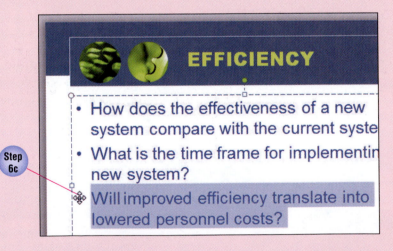

d. Click the Copy button in the Clipboard group.

e. Make Slide 5 active.

f. Click in the bulleted text and then move the insertion point so it is positioned immediately right of the question mark in the second bulleted item.

g. Press the Enter key. (This moves the insertion point down to the next line and inserts another bullet.)

h. Click the Paste button in the Clipboard group.

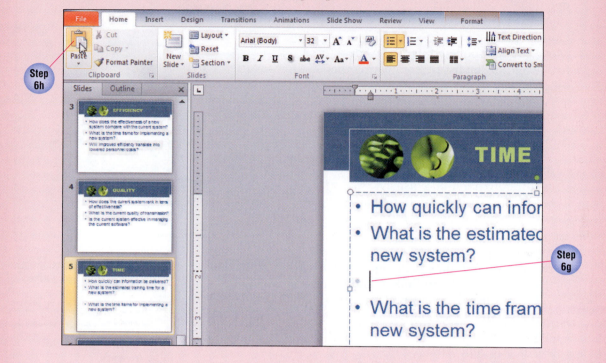

i. If a blank line is inserted between the third and fourth bullets, press the Backspace key twice.

7. Save **P-C2-P2-NetworkSystem.pptx**.

Rearranging Text in the Slides/Outline Pane

You can use the mouse to move text in the Slides/Outline pane with the Outline tab selected. To do this, position the mouse pointer on the slide icon or bullet at the left side of the text until the arrow pointer turns into a four-headed arrow. Hold down the left mouse button, drag the arrow pointer (a thin horizontal line displays) to the desired location, and then release the mouse button.

If you position the arrow pointer on the slide icon and then hold down the left mouse button, all of the text in the slide is selected. If you position the arrow pointer on the bullet and then hold down the left mouse button, all text following that bullet is selected.

Dragging selected text with the mouse moves the selected text to a new location in the presentation. You can also copy selected text. To do this, click the slide icon or click the bullet to select the desired text. Position the arrow pointer in the selected text, hold down the Ctrl key, and then the left mouse button. Drag the arrow pointer (displays with a light gray box and a plus sign attached) to the desired location, release the mouse button, and then release the Ctrl key.

HINT
Press Ctrl + Shift + Tab to switch between the Slides and Outline tabs in the Slides/Outline pane.

1. With **P-C2-P2-NetworkSystem.pptx** open, make Slide 1 active.
2. Click the Outline tab in the Slides/ Outline pane.
3. Move the first bulleted item in Slide 4 to the end of the list by completing the following steps:
   a. Position the mouse pointer on the first bullet below *QUALITY* until it turns into a four-headed arrow.
   b. Hold down the left mouse button, drag the arrow pointer down until a thin horizontal line displays below the last bulleted item, and then release the mouse button.
4. Copy and paste text by completing the following steps:
   a. In the Slides/Outline pane, move the insertion point to the end of the text in Slide 6 and then press the Enter key. (This inserts a new bullet in the slide.)
   b. Scroll up the Slides/Outline pane until the last bulleted item in Slide 2 is visible in the Slides/Outline pane as well as the last bullet in Slide 6.
   c. Position the mouse pointer on the fourth bullet below *COSTS* until it turns into a four-headed arrow and then click the left mouse button. (This selects the text.)
   d. Position the mouse pointer in the selected text, hold down the left mouse button, hold down the Ctrl key, and then drag down until the arrow pointer and light blue vertical line display on the blank line below the text in Slide 6.
   e. Release the mouse button and then release the Ctrl key.
5. Click the Slides tab in the Slides/Outline pane.
6. Save **P-C2-P2-NetworkSystem.pptx**.

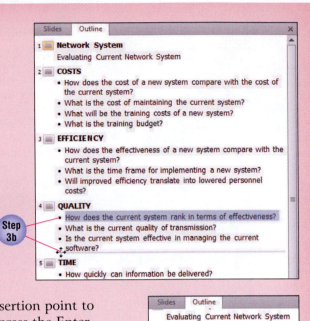

Sizing and Rearranging Placeholders in a Slide

Click inside a placeholder to select it and white sizing handles and a green rotation handle display around the placeholder border. With the sizing handles, you can increase or decrease the size of the placeholder. You can also move a placeholder by dragging it with the mouse. Increase or decrease the size of a placeholder by positioning the arrow pointer on a sizing handle until the pointer turns into a double-headed arrow and then dragging the placeholder border to the desired size. To move a placeholder, position the arrow pointer on the placeholder border until the arrow pointer displays with a four-headed arrow attached. Hold down the left mouse button, drag the outline of the placeholder to the desired position, and then release the mouse button.

Dragging a selected placeholder with the mouse moves the placeholder. If you want to copy a placeholder, hold down the Ctrl key while dragging the placeholder. When the outline of the placeholder is in the desired position, release the mouse button, and then release the Ctrl key. If you make a change to the size and/or location of a placeholder, click the Reset button in the Slides group in the Home tab to return the formatting of the placeholder back to the default.

Project 2c   Sizing and Rearranging Placeholders   Part 3 of 5

1. With **P-C2-P2-NetworkSystem.pptx** open, make Slide 1 active.
2. Size and move a placeholder by completing the following steps:
   a. Click on any character in the subtitle *Evaluating Current Network System*.
   b. Position the arrow pointer on the sizing handle that displays in the middle of the right border until the pointer turns into a left- and right-pointing arrow.
   c. Hold down the left mouse button, drag to the left until the right border displays just to the right of the text in the placeholder, and then release the mouse button (see image at the top right).
   d. Position the arrow pointer on the border of the placeholder until the pointer turns into a four-headed arrow.
   e. Hold down the left mouse button, drag the placeholder to the right so the placeholder is positioned as shown at the right, and then release the mouse button.
3. Make Slide 4 active.
4. Size and move a placeholder by completing the following steps:
   a. Click on any character in the bulleted text.
   b. Position the arrow pointer on the sizing handle that displays in the middle of the right border until the pointer turns into a left- and right-pointing arrow.
   c. Hold down the left mouse button and then drag to the left until the right border displays just to the right of the word *in* in the third bulleted text (see image above).

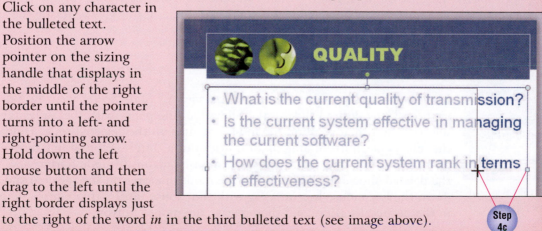

d. Drag the middle sizing handle on the bottom border up until the bottom border of the placeholder displays just below the last bulleted text.

e. Position the arrow pointer on the border of the placeholder until the pointer turns into a four-headed arrow.

f. Hold down the left mouse button and then drag the placeholder to the right so the placeholder is positioned approximately in the middle of the white portion of the slide.

5. Save **P-C2-P2-NetworkSystem.pptx**.

Step 4f

QUALITY

• What is the current quality of transmission?

• Is the current system effective in managing the current software?

• How does the current system rank in terms of effectiveness?

Managing Slides ▪▪▪▪▪▪▪▪▪▪▪▪▪▪▪▪▪▪▪▪▪▪▪▪▪▪▪

As you edit a presentation, you may need to reorganize slides and insert a new slide or delete an existing slide. You can manage slides in the Slides/Outline pane or in Slide Sorter view. Switch to Slide Sorter view by clicking the Slide Sorter button in the view area on the Status bar or by clicking the View tab and then clicking Slide Sorter in the Presentation Views group.

Inserting and Deleting Slides

As you learned in Chapter 1, click the New Slide button in the Slides group in the Home tab to insert a new slide in the presentation immediately following the currently active slide. You can also insert a new slide in Slide Sorter view. To do this, click the slide that will immediately precede the new slide and then click the New Slide button in the Slides group. Delete a slide in Normal view by clicking the slide miniature in the Slides/Outline pane and then pressing the Delete key. You can also delete a slide by switching to Slide Sorter view, clicking the slide miniature, and then pressing the Delete key.

Moving Slides

Move slides in a presentation in Normal view or Slide Sorter view. In Normal view, click the desired slide in the Slides/Outline pane (with the Slides tab selected) and then position the mouse pointer on the selected slide. Hold down the left mouse button, drag up or down until a thin horizontal line displays in the desired location, and then release the mouse button. In Slide Sorter view, click the desired slide and then position the mouse pointer on the selected slide. Hold down the left mouse button, drag with the mouse until a thin vertical line displays in the desired location, and then release the mouse button.

▼ **Quick Steps**

Insert Slide
Click New Slide button.
OR
1. Click Slide Sorter button in view area of Status bar.
2. Click slide that will immediately precede new slide.
3. Click New Slide button.

Delete Slide
1. Click slide miniature in Slides/Outline pane.
2. Press Delete key.
OR
1. Click Slide Sorter button in view area of Status bar.
2. Click desired slide.
3. Press Delete key.

Press Ctrl + M to insert a new slide.

Copying a Slide

Slides in some presentations may contain similar text, objects, and formatting. Rather than create a new slide, consider copying a slide. To do this, display the presentation in either Slide Sorter view or in Normal view with the Slides tab selected in the Slides/Outline pane. Position the arrow pointer in the slide, hold down the Ctrl key and then the left mouse button. Drag to the location where you want the slide copied, then release the mouse button and then the Ctrl key.

HINT
Press Ctrl + X to cut the selected slide and then press Ctrl + V to insert the cut slide.

HINT
Press Ctrl + C to copy the selected slide and then press Ctrl + V to insert the copied slide.

Project 2d **Moving and Copying Slides** **Part 4 of 5**

1. With **P-C2-P2-NetworkSystem.pptx** open in Normal view, move slides by completing the following steps:
   a. Make sure the Slides tab is selected in the Slides/Outline pane.
   b. Click Slide 3 (*EFFICIENCY*) in the Slides/Outline pane.
   c. Position the mouse pointer on Slide 3, hold down the left mouse button, drag up until a thin horizontal line displays between Slides 1 and 2, and then release the mouse button.
   d. Click Slide 4 (*QUALITY*) in the Slides/Outline pane.
   e. Position the mouse pointer on Slide 4, hold down the left mouse button, drag down until a thin horizontal line displays below Slide 6, and then release the mouse button.
2. Move and copy slides in Slide Sorter view by completing the following steps:
   a. Click the Slide Sorter button in the view area on the Status bar.
   b. Click Slide 4 to make it the active slide. (The slide displays with an orange border.)
   c. Position the mouse pointer on Slide 4, hold down the left mouse button, drag to the left until the thin vertical line displays between Slides 1 and 2, and then release the mouse button.

Step 1c

Step 2c

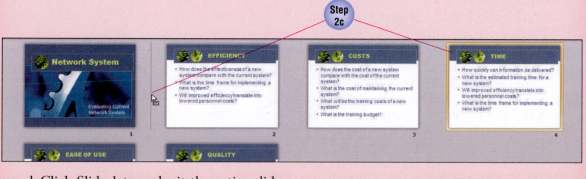

   d. Click Slide 1 to make it the active slide.

e. Position the mouse pointer on Slide 1, hold down the left mouse button, and then hold down the Ctrl key.

f. Drag down and to the right until the thin vertical line displays immediately right of Slide 6.

g. Release the mouse button and then the Ctrl key.

3. Click the Normal button in the view area on the Status bar.

4. Save **P-C2-P2-NetworkSystem.pptx**.

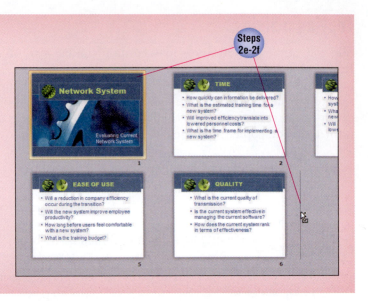

Steps
2e–2f

Copying a Slide between Presentations

You can copy slides within a presentation as well as between presentations. To copy a slide, click the slide you want to copy (either in Slide Sorter view or in Normal view with the Slides tab selected in the Slides/Outline pane) and then click the Copy button in the Clipboard group in the Home tab. Open the presentation into which the slide is to be copied (in either Slide Sorter view or Normal view with the Slides tab selected in the Slides/Outline pane). Click in the location where you want the slide positioned and then click the Paste button. The copied slide will take on the design theme of the presentation into which it is copied.

Project 2e **Copying Slides between Presentations** **Part 5 of 5**

1. With **P-C2-P2-NetworkSystem.pptx** open, open the presentation named **EvalNetwork.pptx** located in the PowerPoint2010C2 folder on your storage medium.

2. Copy Slide 2 to the **P-C2-P2-NetworkSystem.pptx** presentation by completing the following steps:
   a. Click Slide 2 in the Slides/Outline pane to make it the active slide.
   b. Click the Copy button in the Clipboard group in the Home tab.
   c. Click the PowerPoint button on the Taskbar and then click the **P-C2-P2-NetworkSystem.pptx** presentation thumbnail.
   d. Click Slide 4 (*COSTS*) in the Slides/Outline pane.
   e. Click the Paste button in the Clipboard group.
   f. Click the PowerPoint button on the Taskbar and then click the **EvalNetwork.pptx** presentation thumbnail.

3. Copy Slide 3 to the **P-C2-P2-NetworkSystem.pptx** by completing the following steps:
   a. Click Slide 3 in the Slides/Outline pane.
   b. Position the mouse pointer on Slide 3 and then click the right mouse button. (This displays a shortcut menu.)

c. Click *Copy* at the shortcut menu.

d. Click the PowerPoint button on the Taskbar and then click the **P-C2-P2-NetworkSystem.pptx** thumbnail.

e. Right-click Slide 3 in the Slides/Outline pane.

f. Click the Use Destination Theme button that displays in the *Paste Options* section.

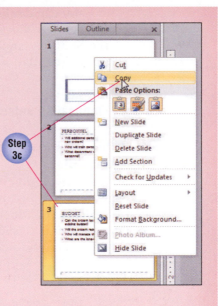

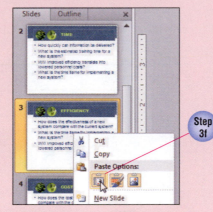

4. Click the PowerPoint button on the Taskbar and then click the **EvalNetwork.pptx** thumbnail.
5. Close the presentation.
6. With **P-C2-P2-NetworkSystem.pptx** open, delete Slide 9 by completing the following steps:
   a. If necessary, scroll down the Slides/Outline pane until Slide 9 is visible.
   b. Click Slide 9 to select it.
   c. Press the Delete key.
7. Save the presentation.
8. Print the presentation as a handout with nine slides horizontally per page.
9. Close **P-C2-P2-NetworkSystem.pptx**.

Project 3 Insert and Manage Slides in an Adventure Tours Presentation   4 Parts

You will open a presentation on Adventure Tours and then insert additional slides in the presentation by duplicating existing slides in the presentation and reusing slides from another presentation. You will also divide the presentation into sections and print a section.

Duplicating Slides

In Project 2, you used the Copy and Paste buttons in the Clipboard group and also options from a shortcut menu to copy slides in a presentation. You can also copy slides in a presentation using the *Duplicate Selected Slides* option from the New Slide button drop-down list or by clicking the Copy button arrow and then clicking *Duplicate* at the drop-down list. In addition to duplicating slides, you can use the *Duplicate* option from the Copy button drop-down list to duplicate a selected object such as a placeholder in a slide.

▼ **Quick Steps**

Duplicate Slides
1. Select desired slides in Slides/Outline pane.
2. Click New Slide button arrow.
3. Click *Duplicate Selected Slides* at drop-down list.

You can duplicate a single slide or selected slides. To select adjacent (sequential) slides, click the first slide in the Slides/Outline pane, hold down the Shift key, and then click the last in the sequence. To select nonadjacent (nonsequential) slides, hold down the Ctrl key while clicking each desired slide.

Project 3a   **Duplicating Selected Slides**   **Part 1 of 4**

1. Open **AdvTours.pptx** and then save the presentation with Save As and name it **P-C2-P3-AdvTours**.
2. Make sure the presentation displays in Normal view and that the Slides tab is active in the Slides/Outline pane.
3. Select and then duplicate slides by completing the following steps:
   a. Click Slide 1 in the Slides/Outline pane.
   b. Hold down the Ctrl key.
   c. Click Slide 3, Slide 4, and Slide 5.
   d. Release the Ctrl key.
   e. Click the New Slide button arrow in the Slides group in the Home tab and then click *Duplicate Selected Slides* at the drop-down list.

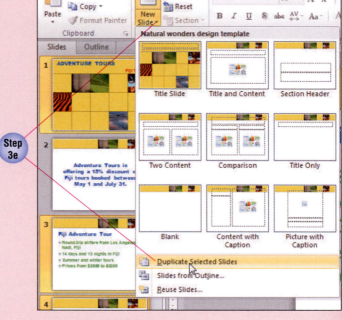

4. With Slide 6 active in the Slide pane, change *Fiji Tour* to *Costa Rica Tour*.
5. Make Slide 7 active, select *Fiji* and then type **Costa Rica**. Select and delete the bulleted text, and then type the following bulleted text:
   • Round-trip airfare from Los Angeles to San Jose, Costa Rica
   • 8 days and 7 nights in Costa Rica
   • Monthly tours
   • Prices from $1099 to $1599
6. Make Slide 8 active, select and delete the bulleted text, and then type the following bulleted text:
   • San Jose, Emerald Suites
   • Tortuguero, Plantation Spa and Resort
   • Fortuna, Pacific Resort
   • Jaco, Monteverde Cabanas
7. Make Slide 9 active, select and delete the bulleted text, and then type the following bulleted text:
   • San Jose city tour
   • Rainforest tram
   • Canal cruise
   • Forest hike
8. Save **P-C2-P3-AdvTours.pptx**.

Reusing Slides

PowerPoint provides another method for copying slides from one presentation to another. Click the New Slide button arrow and then click the *Reuse Slides* option at the drop-down list and the Reuse Slides task pane displays at the right side of the screen as shown in Figure 2.4. At this task pane, click the Browse button, click *Browse File* at the drop-down list, and the Browse dialog box displays. At this dialog box, navigate to the desired folder and then double-click the desired presentation. This inserts the presentation slides in the Reuse Slides task pane. Click a slide in the Reuse Slides task pane to insert it in the currently open presentation.

You can also share and reuse slides from a Slide Library on a server running Office SharePoint Server 2007 or Microsoft SharePoint Server 2010. You can add slides to a Slide Library and insert slides from a Slide Library into a presentation. Before reusing slides from a Slide Library, the Slide Library must be created. Refer to the SharePoint help files to learn how to create a Slide Library. To reuse slides in a presentation from a Slide Library, click the Open a Slide Library hyperlink located in the Reuse Slides task pane. You can also click the Browse button in the Reuse Slides task pane and then click *Browse Slide Library* at the drop-down list. This displays the Select a Slide Library dialog box. At this dialog box, navigate to the location of the desired library, and then double-click the library.

By default, the slides you insert from the Reuse Slides task pane into the currently open presentation take on the formatting of the current presentation. If you want the slides to retain their original formatting when inserted in the presentation, insert a check mark in the *Keep source formatting* check box located toward the bottom of the Reuse Slides task pane.

▼ **Quick Steps**

Reuse Slides
1. Click New Slide button arrow.
2. Click *Reuse Slides*.
3. Click Browse button, *Browse File*.
4. Navigate to desired folder.
5. Double-click desired presentation.
6. Click desired slide in Reuse Slides task pane.

Figure 2.4 Reuse Slides Task Pane

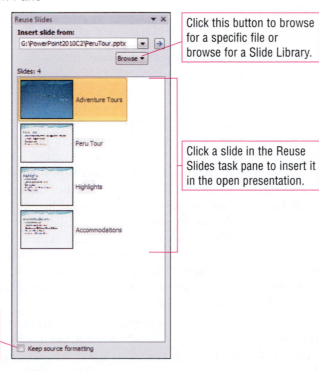

Click this button to browse for a specific file or browse for a Slide Library.

Click a slide in the Reuse Slides task pane to insert it in the open presentation.

Insert a check mark in this check box if you want the inserted slide to maintain source formatting.

1. With **P-C2-P3-AdvTours.pptx** open, click the New Slide button arrow in the Slides group in the Home tab and then click *Reuse Slides* at the drop-down list. (This displays the Reuse Slides task pane at the right side of the screen.)

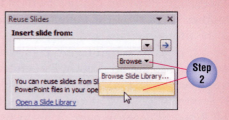

Step 2

2. Click the Browse button in the Reuse Slides task pane and then click *Browse File* at the drop-down list.
3. At the Browse dialog box, navigate to the PowerPoint2010C2 folder on your storage medium and then double-click *PeruTour.pptx*.
4. In the Slides/Outline pane, scroll down the slide thumbnails until Slide 9 displays and then click below Slide 9. (This inserts a thin, horizontal line below the Slide 9 thumbnail in the Slides/Outline pane.)
5. Click the first slide thumbnail (*Adventure Tours*) in the Reuse Slides task pane. (This inserts the slide in the open presentation immediately below Slide 9.)

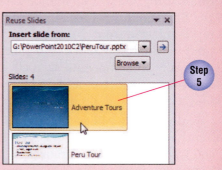

Step 5

6. Click the second slide thumbnail (*Peru Tour*) in the Reuse Slides task pane.
7. Click the fourth slide thumbnail (*Accommodations*) in the Reuse Slides task pane.
8. Click the third slide thumbnail (*Highlights*) in the Reuse Slides task pane.
9. Close the Reuse Slides task pane by clicking the Close button (contains an X) located in the upper right corner of the task pane.
10. Save **P-C2-P3-AdvTours.pptx**.

Creating Sections within a Presentation ■■■■■■■■■■

If you are working on a presentation with others in a group, or you are working in a presentation containing numerous slides, consider dividing related slides in the presentation into sections. Dividing a presentation into sections allows you to easily navigate and edit slides within a presentation. Create a section by selecting the first slide in the desired section in the Slides/Outline pane, clicking the Section button in the Slides group in the Home tab, and then clicking *Add Section* at the drop-down list. A section title bar displays in the Slides/Outline pane with the Slides tab selected. By default, the section title name is *Untitled Section*. Rename a section by clicking the Section button in the Slides group in the Home tab and then clicking *Rename Section* at the drop-down list. You can also rename a section by right-clicking the section title bar in the Slides/Outline pane and then clicking *Rename Section* at the shortcut menu. You can remove, move, collapse, and expand sections with options in the Section button drop-down list or by right-clicking the section title bar and then clicking the desired option. You can also apply different formatting to an individual section by clicking the section title bar to select the section and then applying the desired formatting.

When you create sections within a presentation, you can print only desired sections within the presentation. To print a section in a presentation, click the File tab, click the Print tab, click the first gallery in the Settings category, click the desired section in the drop-down list, and then click the Print button.

1. With **P-C2-P3-AdvTours.pptx** open, create a section for slides about Fiji by completing the following steps:
   a. Click Slide 1 in the Slides/Outline pane.
   b. Click the Section button in the Slides group in the Home tab and then click *Add Section* at the drop-down list.

2. Rename the new section by completing the following steps:
   a. Click the Section button and then click *Rename Section* at the drop-down list.
   b. At the Rename Section dialog box, type **Fiji Tour** and then click the Rename button.

3. Create a section for slides about Costa Rica by completing the following steps:
   a. Click Slide 6 in the Slides/Outline pane.
   b. Click the Section button in the Slides group and then click *Add Section* at the drop-down list.
   c. Right-click on the section title bar (contains the text *Untitled Section*) and then click *Rename Section* at the shortcut menu.
   d. At the Rename Section dialog box, type **Costa Rica Tour** and then press Enter.

4. Complete steps similar to those in Step 3 to create a section beginning with Slide 10 and then rename the section *Peru Tour*.

5. Change the design theme of a section by completing the following steps:
   a. Click the *Fiji Tour* section Title bar located at the top of the Slides/Outline pane.
   b. Click the Design tab.
   c. Click the More button located to the right of the themes thumbnails and then click *Flow* at the drop-down gallery.
   d. Display Slide 2 in the Slides pane and move the placeholder down so it is positioned attractively on the slide.

6. Complete steps similar to those in Steps 5a through 5c to apply the Austin design theme to the *Costa Rica Tour* section.

7. Display only slides in the *Costa Rica Tour* section by completing the following steps:
   a. Click the Home Tab, click the Section button in the Slides group, and then click *Collapse All* at the drop-down list.

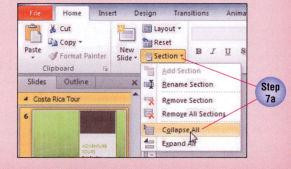

b. Double-click the *Costa Rica Tour* section bar in the Slides/Outline pane. (Notice that only Slides 6 through 9 display in the Slides/Outline pane and the slides in the *Fiji Tour* and *Peru Tour* sections are hidden.)

8. Redisplay the *Fiji Tour* section slides by double-clicking the *Fiji Tour* section title bar in the Slides/Outline pane.

9. Display all sections by clicking the Section button in the Slides group and then clicking *Expand All* at the drop-down list.

10. Print only the *Costa Rica Tour* section by completing the following steps:
   a. Click the File tab and then click the Print tab.
   b. At the Print tab Backstage view, click the first gallery in the Settings category and then click *Costa Rica Tour* in the *Sections* section (located toward the bottom of the drop-down list).
   c. Click the *Full Page Slides* option in the Settings category and then click *4 Slides Horizontal* in the *Handouts* section.
   d. Click the Print button.

11. Complete steps similar to those in Step 8 to print only the *Peru Tour* section.

12. Save **P-C2-P3-AdvTours.pptx**.

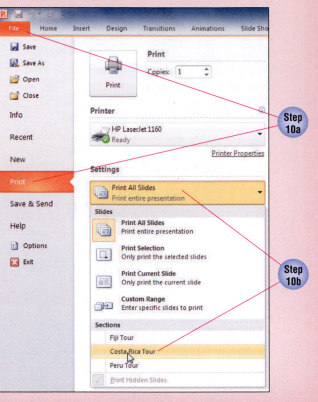

Customizing the Quick Access Toolbar ■■■■■■■■■■■

The Quick Access toolbar contains buttons for some of the most commonly performed tasks. By default, the toolbar contains the Save, Undo, and Redo buttons. You can easily add buttons to the Quick Access toolbar or delete buttons from the toolbar. To add a button to or delete a button from the Quick Access toolbar, click the Customize Quick Access Toolbar button that displays at the right side of the toolbar. At the drop-down list that displays, insert a check mark before those buttons you want to display on the toolbar and remove the check mark from those you do not want to appear.

Click the *More Commands* option at the drop-down list and the PowerPoint Options dialog box displays with *Customize* selected in the left panel. With options at this dialog box, you can choose to add a button from a list of PowerPoint commands. You can also click the Reset button at the dialog box to reset the Quick Access toolbar back to the default.

By default, the Quick Access toolbar displays above the ribbon tabs. You can display the Quick Access toolbar below the ribbon by clicking the Customize Quick Access Toolbar button that displays at the right side of the toolbar and then clicking the *Show Below the Ribbon* option at the drop-down list.

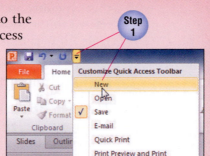

Step
1

1. With **P-C2-P3-AdvTours.pptx** open, add a New button to the Quick Access toolbar by clicking the Customize Quick Access Toolbar button that displays at the right side of the Quick Access toolbar and then clicking *New* at the drop-down list.
2. Add an Open button to the Quick Access toolbar by clicking the Customize Quick Access Toolbar button and then clicking *Open* at the drop-down list.
3. Add a Print Preview and Print button to the Quick Access toolbar by clicking the Customize Quick Access Toolbar button and then clicking *Print Preview and Print* at the drop-down list.
4. Move the Quick Access toolbar below the ribbon by clicking the Customize Quick Access Toolbar button and then clicking the *Show Below the Ribbon* option at the drop-down list.
5. Click the Print Preview and Print button on the Quick Access toolbar. (This displays the Print tab Backstage view.)
6. Click the File tab to close the Print tab Backstage view.
7. Close **P-C2-P3-AdvTours.pptx**.
8. Click the New button to open a new blank document.
9. Click the Open button to display the Open dialog box.
10. Close the Open dialog box and then close the blank presentation.
11. Move the Quick Access toolbar back to the original position and remove buttons by completing the following steps:
    a. Click the Customize Quick Access Toolbar button at the right side of the Quick Access toolbar and then click the *Show Above the Ribbon* option at the drop-down list.
    b. Click the Customize Quick Access Toolbar button and then click *New* at the drop-down list.
    c. Click the Customize Quick Access Toolbar button and then click *Open* at the drop-down list.
    d. Click the Customize Quick Access Toolbar button and then click *Print Preview and Print* at the drop-down list.

Project   **4**   **Use PowerPoint Help Feature and Create a Presentation**   **2 Parts**

You will use the Help feature to learn more about PowerPoint features. You will also use the Help feature to find information on keyboard shortcuts and then use the information to create a presentation.

Using Help

Microsoft PowerPoint includes a Help feature that contains information about PowerPoint features and commands. This on-screen reference manual is similar to Windows Help and the Help features in Word, Excel, and Access. Click the Microsoft PowerPoint Help button (the circle with the question mark) located in the upper right corner of the screen or press the keyboard shortcut F1 to display the PowerPoint Help window. In this window, type a topic, feature, or question in the Search text box and then press the Enter key. Topics related to the search

Help

text display in the PowerPoint Help window. Click a topic that interests you. If the topic window contains a Show All hyperlink in the upper right corner, click this hyperlink and the topic options expand to show additional help information related to the topic. When you click the Show All hyperlink, it becomes the Hide All hyperlink.

Getting Help at the Help Tab Backstage View

▼ **Quick Steps**

Use the Help Feature
1. Click Microsoft PowerPoint Help button.
2. Type topic or feature.
3. Press Enter.
4. Click desired topic.

Display Help Tab Backstage View
1. Click File tab.
2. Click Help tab.

The Help tab Backstage view, shown in Figure 2.5, contains an option for displaying the PowerPoint Help window as well as other options. Display this view by clicking the File tab and then clicking the Help tab. Click the Microsoft Office Help button in the Support category to display the PowerPoint Help window and click the Getting Started button to access the Microsoft website that displays information about getting started with PowerPoint 2010. Click the Contact Us button in the Support category and the Microsoft Support website displays. Click the Options button in the Tools for Working With Office category and the PowerPoint Options dialog box displays with options for customizing PowerPoint. Click the Check for Updates button and the Microsoft Update website displays with information on available updates. The right side of the Help tab Backstage view displays information about Office and PowerPoint.

Figure 2.5 Help Tab Backstage View

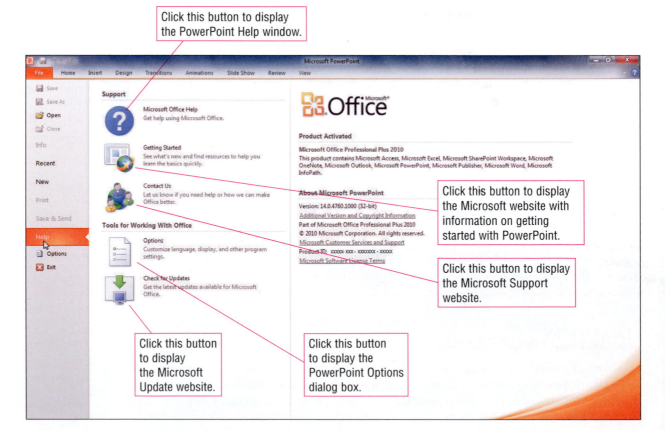

Getting Help on a Button

When you position the mouse pointer on a button, a ScreenTip displays with information about the button. Some button ScreenTips display with the message "Press F1 for more help." that is preceded by an image of the Help button. With the ScreenTip visible, press the F1 function key on your keyboard and the PowerPoint Help window opens and displays information about the specific button.

Project 4a **Using the Help Feature** **Part 1 of 2**

1. At the blank screen, press Ctrl + N to display a blank presentation. (Ctrl + N is the keyboard shortcut to open a blank presentation.)
2. Click the Microsoft PowerPoint Help button located in the upper right corner of the screen.
3. At the PowerPoint Help window, type **create a presentation** in the Search text box and then press the Enter key.
4. When the list of topics displays, click the <u>Create a basic PowerPoint presentation</u> hyperlink. (If your PowerPoint Help window does not display the online options, check the lower right corner of the window. If the word *Offline* displays, click *Offline* and then click the *Show content from Office.com* option at the drop-down list.)
5. Scroll down the PowerPoint Help window and then click a hyperlink to an article that interests you.
6. Read the information in the article. (If you want a printing of the information, you can click the Print button located toward the top of the PowerPoint Help window and then click the Print button at the Print dialog box.)
7. Close the PowerPoint Help window by clicking the Close button located in the upper right corner of the window.
8. Click the File tab and then click the Help tab.
9. At the Help tab Backstage view, click the Getting Started button in the Support category. (You must be connected to the Internet to display the web page.)
10. Look at the information that displays at the website and then click the Close button located in the upper right corner of the web page.

11. Click the File tab and then click the Help tab.
12. Click the Contact Us button, look at the information that displays at the website, and then close the web page.
13. At the blank presentation, click the text *Click to add title* and then type **PowerPoint Help**.
14. Click the text *Click to add subtitle* and then type **Keyboard Shortcuts**.
15. Hover the mouse pointer over the Font Color button in the Font group in the Home tab until the ScreenTip displays and then press F1.
16. At the PowerPoint Help window, read the information that displays and then close the window.

Getting Help in a Dialog Box or Backstage View

Some dialog boxes, as well as the Backstage view, contain a Help button you can click to display a help window with specific information about the dialog box or Backstage view. After reading and/or printing the information, close a dialog box by clicking the Close button located in the upper right corner of the dialog box or close the Backstage view by clicking the File tab or clicking any other tab in the ribbon.

Project 4b Getting Help in a Dialog Box and Backstage View and Creating a Presentation

Part 2 of 2

1. At the presentation, click the File tab and then click the Save As button.
2. At the Save As dialog box, click the Help button located near the upper right corner of the dialog box.
3. Read the information about saving files that displays in the Windows Help and Support window.
4. Close the window by clicking the Close button located in the upper right corner of the window.
5. At the Save As dialog box, select the text that displays in the *File name* text box, type **P-C2-P4-Shortcuts**, and then press Enter.
6. Click the File tab.
7. At the Backstage view, click the Help button located in the upper right corner of the window.
8. At the PowerPoint Help window, click a hyperlink that interests you.

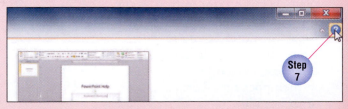

9. Read the information and then close the PowerPoint Help window by clicking the Close button located in the upper right corner of the window.
10. Click the File tab to return to the presentation.
11. Click the PowerPoint Help button.
12. At the Help window, type **keyboard shortcuts** in the Search text box and then press the Enter key.
13. When the list of topics displays, scroll down the list and then click the <u>Keyboard shortcuts for use while creating a presentation in PowerPoint 2010</u>. (Not all of the hyperlink text will be visible.)

14. Scroll down the list of topics, display the *Common tasks in Microsoft Office PowerPoint* section, and then click the <u>Delete and copy text and objects</u> hyperlink. (This displays a list of keyboard shortcuts.)

15. Select the list of keyboard shortcuts by positioning the mouse pointer at the left side of the heading *TO DO THIS*, hold down the left mouse button, drag down to the lower right corner of the list of keyboard shortcuts, and then release the mouse button. (See image at right.)

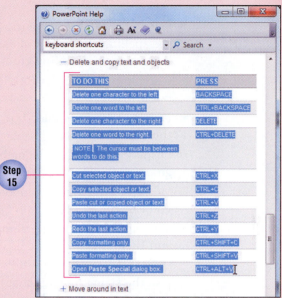

16. With the information selected, click the Print button that displays on the PowerPoint Help window toolbar.

17. At the Print dialog box, click the *Selection* option in the *Page Range* section and then click the Print button.

18. Close the PowerPoint Help window.

19. Using the information you printed, create slides with the following information:
    - Slide 2: Insert the text **Delete Text** as the title and then insert the four delete keyboard shortcuts as bulleted text. (For each keyboard shortcut, type the description followed by a colon and then the keyboard shortcut. For example, type **Delete one character to the left: Backspace** as the first bulleted item in the slide.)
    - Slide 3: Insert the text **Cut, Copy, Paste Text** as the title and then insert the three cut, copy, and paste keyboard shortcuts as bulleted text.
    - Slide 4: Insert the text **Undo and Redo** as the title and then insert the two undo and redo keyboard shortcuts as bulleted text.
    - Slide 5: Insert the text **Copy and Paste Formatting** as the title and then insert the three copy and paste formatting keyboard shortcuts as bulleted text.

20. Apply the Newsprint design theme to the presentation.
21. Apply a transition and sound of your choosing to all slides in the presentation.
22. Print the presentation as a handout with six slides printed horizontally per page.
23. Save and then close **P-C2-P4-Shortcuts.pptx**.

Chapter Summary

- Use the spelling feature to check spelling of slides in a presentation. Begin the spelling checker by clicking the Review tab and then clicking the Spelling button in the Proofing group.

- Click in a placeholder to select the placeholder and position the insertion point inside.

- Display the Find dialog box by clicking the Find button in the Editing group in the Home tab.

- Display the Replace dialog box by clicking the Replace button in the Editing group in the Home tab.

- With buttons in the Clipboard group or with options from a shortcut menu, you can cut and paste or copy and paste text in slides.

- You can use the mouse to move text in the Slides/Outline pane. You can select and then drag it to a new location or hold down the Ctrl key while dragging to copy text to a new location.

- Use the sizing handles that display around a selected placeholder to increase or decrease the size of the placeholder. You can use the mouse to drag a selected placeholder to a new location in the slide.

- Use the New Slide button in the Home tab to insert a slide in a presentation.

- Delete a selected slide by pressing the Delete key.

- You can move or delete a selected slide in Normal view in the Slides/Outline pane or in Slide Sorter view.

- Copy a selected slide by holding down the Ctrl key while dragging the slide to the desired location.

- Use the Copy and Paste buttons in the Clipboard group in the Home tab to copy a slide between presentations.

- Select adjacent slides in the Slides/Outline pane or in Slide Sorter view by clicking the first slide, holding down the Shift key, and then clicking the last slide. Select nonadjacent slides by holding down the Ctrl key while clicking each desired slide.

- Duplicate slides in a presentation by selecting the desired slides in the Slides/Outline pane, clicking the New Slide button arrow, and then clicking the *Duplicate Selected Slides* option or clicking the Copy button arrow and then clicking *Duplicate* at the drop-down list.

- Divide a presentation into sections to easily navigate and edit slides in a presentation.

- You can copy slides from a presentation into the open presentation with options at the Reuse Slides task pane. Display this task pane by clicking the New Slide button arrow and then clicking *Reuse Slides* at the drop-down list.

- Customize the Quick Access toolbar by clicking the Customize Quick Access Toolbar button that displays at the right side of the toolbar and then clicking the desired button or option at the drop-down list. You can add buttons to or remove buttons from the Quick Access toolbar and display the toolbar below the ribbon.

- Click the Microsoft PowerPoint Help button or press F1 to display the PowerPoint Help window.
- Click the File tab and then the Help tab to display the Help tab Backstage view.
- Some dialog boxes, as well as the Backstage view, contain a Help button you can click to display information specific to the dialog box or Backstage view.

Commands Review

FEATURE	RIBBON TAB, GROUP	BUTTON, OPTION	KEYBOARD SHORTCUT
Spelling check	Review, Proofing	ABC✓	F7
Find dialog box	Home, Editing	🔍	Ctrl + F
Replace dialog box	Home, Editing	ab↻ac	Ctrl + H
Cut text or slide	Home, Clipboard	✂	Ctrl + X
Copy text or slide	Home, Clipboard	📋	Ctrl + C
Paste text or slide	Home, Clipboard	📋	Ctrl + V
Duplicate slide	Home, Slides	, Duplicate Selected Slides	
Section	Home, Slides	Section ▾	
Reuse Slides task pane	Home, Slides	, Reuse Slides	
PowerPoint Help window		❓	F1

Concepts Check Test Your Knowledge

Completion: In the space provided at the right, indicate the correct term, symbol, or command.

1. The Spelling button is located in the Proofing group in this tab. _____

2. This is the keyboard shortcut to select all text in a placeholder. _____

3. The Find button is located in this group in the Home tab. _____

4. To copy text to a new location in the Slides/Outline pane with the Outline tab selected, hold down this key while dragging text. _____

5. The border of a selected placeholder displays these handles as well as a green rotation handle.

_____

6. You can reorganize slides in a presentation in the Slides/Outline pane or in this view.

_____

7. You can copy selected slides in a presentation using this option from the New Slide button drop-down list.

_____

8. To select adjacent slides, click the first slide, hold down this key, and then click the last slide.

_____

9. Click the New Slide button arrow and then click the *Reuse Slides* option at the drop-down list and this displays.

_____

10. Divide a presentation into these to easily navigate and edit slides in a presentation.

_____

11. Display the Quick Access toolbar below the ribbon by clicking this button located at the right side of the toolbar and then clicking the *Show Below the Ribbon* option at the drop-down list.

_____

12. This is the keyboard shortcut to display the PowerPoint Help window.

_____

Skills Check   Assess Your Performance

Assessment

1 CREATE AN ELECTRONIC DESIGN PRESENTATION

1. Create the presentation shown in Figure 2.6 using a design theme of your choosing. (When typing bulleted text, press the Tab key to move the insertion point to the desired tab level.)
2. After creating the slides, complete a spelling check on the text in the slides.
3. Save the presentation into the PowerPoint2010C2 folder on your storage medium and name the presentation **P-C2-A1-ElecDesign**.
4. Run the presentation.
5. Print the presentation as a handout with four slides horizontally per page.
6. Make the following changes to the presentation:
   a. Change to Slide Sorter view and then move Slide 3 between Slides 1 and 2.
   b. Move Slide 4 between Slides 2 and 3.
   c. Change to Normal view.
   d. Search for the word *document* and replace it with the word *brochure*. (After the replacements, make Slide 1 active and, if necessary, capitalize the "b" in "brochure.")
   e. Add a transition and sound of your choosing to each slide.
7. Save the presentation.

Figure 2.6 Assessment 1

Slide 1	Title	=	Electronic Design and Production
	Subtitle	=	Designing a Document
Slide 2	Title	=	Creating Balance
	Bullets	=	• Symmetrical balance: Balancing similar elements equally on a page (centered alignment) of the document
			• Asymmetrical balance: Balancing contrasting elements on a page of the document
Slide 3	Title	=	Creating Focus
	Bullets	=	• Creating focus with titles, headings, and subheads in a document
			• Creating focus with graphic elements in a document
			○ Clip art
			○ Watermarks
			○ Illustrations
			○ Photographs
			○ Charts
			○ Graphs
Slide 4	Title	=	Providing Proportion
	Bullets	=	• Evaluating proportions in a document
			• Sizing graphic elements in a document
			• Using white space in a document

8. Display the Reuse Slides task pane, browse to the PowerPoint2010C2 folder on your storage medium, and then double-click *LayoutTips.pptx*.
9. Insert the *Layout Punctuation Tips* slide below Slide 4.
10. Insert the *Layout Tips* slide below Slide 5.
11. Close the Reuse Slides task pane.
12. Find all occurrences of *Layout* and replace with *Design*. (Insert a check mark in the *Match case* check box.)
13. Move Slide 5 between Slides 1 and 2.
14. Move Slide 6 between Slides 2 and 3.
15. Change to Normal view and then save the presentation.
16. Print the presentation as a handout with six slides horizontally per page.
17. Beginning with Slide 2, create a section named *Design Tips*.
18. Beginning with Slide 4, create a section named *Design Features*.
19. Print only the Design Features section as a handout with four slides horizontally per page.
20. Save and then close **P-C2-A1-ElecDesign.pptx**.

Assessment

2 CREATE A NETIQUETTE PRESENTATION

1. Create a presentation with the text shown in Figure 2.7. You determine the slide layout. Apply the Pushpin design theme.
2. If necessary, size and move placeholders so the text is positioned attractively on the slide.
3. Select Slides 4 through 6 and then duplicate the slides.
4. Type the following text in place of the existing text in the identified slides:
   a. Slide 7: Select the placeholder netiquette rule text and then type **Do not plagiarize.**
   b. Slide 8: Select the netiquette rule text in the placeholder and then type **Respect and accept people's differences.**
   c. Slide 9: Select the netiquette rule text in the placeholder and then type **Respect others' time.**
5. Complete a spelling check on text in the presentation.
6. Save the presentation and name it **P-C2-A2-InternetApps**.
7. Print the presentation as a handout with nine slides horizontally per page.
8. Make the following edits to the presentation:
   a. Display the presentation in Slide Sorter view.
   b. Move Slide 3 between Slide 5 and Slide 6.
   c. Move Slide 7 between Slide 3 and Slide 4.
9. Add a transition and sound of your choosing to all slides in the presentation.
10. Save the presentation.

Figure 2.7 Assessment 2

Slide I	Title	=	INTERNET APPLICATIONS
	Subtitle	=	Internet Community
Slide 2	Title	=	Community Issues
	Bullets	=	• Flaming
			• Email
			• Moderated environments
			• Netiquette
Slide 3	Title	=	Netiquette Rule
	Subtitle	=	Remember you are dealing with people.
Slide 4	Title	=	Netiquette Rule
	Subtitle	=	Adhere to the same standards of behavior online that you follow in real life.
Slide 5	Title	=	Netiquette Rule
	Subtitle	=	Respect the privacy of others.
Slide 6	Title	=	Netiquette Rule
	Subtitle	=	Share expert knowledge.

11. Run the presentation.

12. Print the presentation as a handout with nine slides horizontally per page.

13. Close **P-C2-A2-InternetApps.pptx**.

Assessment

3 **DOWNLOAD A DESIGN THEME**

1. If your computer is connected to the Internet, Office.com provides a number of design themes you can download to your computer. Display the New tab Backstage view, click in the search text box located to the right of the *Office.com Templates* heading, type computer, and then press Enter.

2. In the Office.com Templates section, click the *Computer monitor design template* option and then click the Download button that displays at the right.

3. When the design theme is downloaded and a presentation is opened with the design theme applied, open **P-C2-A2-InternetApps.pptx**.

4. Select the nine slides in the **P-C2-A2-InternetApps.pptx** presentation and then click the Copy button.

5. Click the PowerPoint button on the Taskbar and then click the thumbnail representing the presentation with the downloaded design theme applied.

6. Click the Paste button to paste the nine slides in the current presentation.

7. Delete Slide 1.

8. Scroll through and look at each slide and make any changes required so the text is positioned attractively on each slide.

9. Save the presentation and name it **P-C2-A3-InternetApps**.

10. Run the presentation.

11. Print the presentation as a handout with nine slides horizontally per page.

12. Close **P-C2-A3-InternetApps.pptx** and then close **P-C2-A2-InternetApps.pptx**.

Visual Benchmark Demonstrate Your Proficiency

FORMATTING A PRESENTATION ON ONLINE LEARNING

1. Open **OnlineLearning.pptx** in the PowerPoint2010C2 folder and then save the presentation with Save As and name it **P-C2-VB-OnlineLearning**.

2. Format the presentation so it appears as shown in Figure 2.8 with the following specifications:
   a. Apply the Newsprint design theme.
   b. Use the *Reuse Slides* option from the New Slide button drop-down list to insert the last two additional slides from the **Learning.pptx** presentation.
   c. Arrange the slides to match what you see in Figure 2.8. (Read the slides from left to right.)
   d. Size and/or move placeholders so text displays in each slide as shown in Figure 2.8.

3. Add a transition and sound of your choosing to each slide.

4. Run the presentation.

5. Print the presentation as a handout with six slides horizontally per page.

6. Save and then close **P-C2-VB-OnlineLearning.pptx**.

Figure 2.8 Visual Benchmark

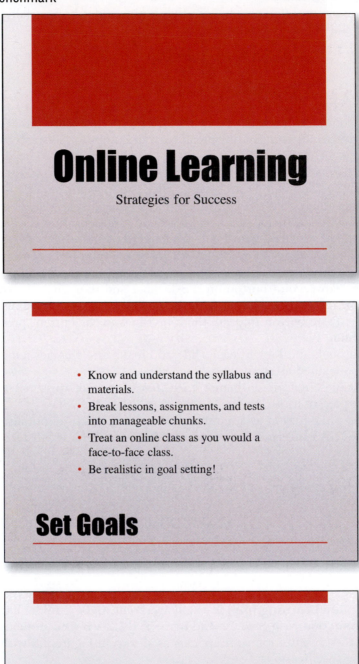

Figure 2.8 Visual Benchmark—*continued*

- Determine if you are a visual, auditory, or kinesthetic learner.
- Look for real-life situations that you can apply to your learning.
- Put learning into practice as soon as possible.

Know Your Learning Style

- Work with others who are experiencing the same learning.
- Join groups or clubs outside of the classroom setting for more practice in learning.
- Utilize online bulletin boards and chat rooms for peer discussion.
  - Be considerate in your comments and emails.
  - Be patient with classmates in their response times.

Join a Study Group

- Don't be afraid to ask for help.
- Utilize instructor help.
- Be persistent until you receive the necessary answers.

Ask Questions

Case Study — Apply Your Skills

Part 1

You are the office manager at the Company Connections agency. One of your responsibilities is to conduct workshops for preparing individuals for the job search process. A coworker has given you a presentation for the workshop but the presentation needs some editing and modifying. Open **JobAnalysis.pptx** and then save the presentation with Save As and name it **P-C2-CS-JobAnalysis**. Check each slide in the presentation and then make modifications to maintain consistency in the size and location of placeholders (consider using the Reset button to reset the formatting and size of the placeholders), maintain consistency in heading text, move text from an overcrowded slide to a new slide, complete a spelling check, apply a design theme, and make any other modifications to improve the presentation. Save **P-C2-CS-JobAnalysis.pptx**.

Part 2

After reviewing the presentation, you realize that you need to include slides on resumes. Open the **ResumePres.pptx** presentation and then copy Slides 2 and 3 into the **P-C2-CS-JobAnalysis.pptx** presentation (at the end of the presentation). You want to add additional information on resume writing tips and decide to use the Internet to find information. Locate information on the Internet with tips on writing a resume and then create a slide (or two) with the information you find. Add a transition and sound to all slides in the presentation. Save the **P-C2-CS-JobAnalysis.pptx** presentation.

Part 3

You know that Microsoft Word offers a number of resume templates you can download from the Office.com website. You decide to include information in the presentation on how to find and download resumes. Open Microsoft Word, click the File tab, and then click the New tab. At the New tab Backstage view, click in the search box that displays to the right of the *Office.com Templates* heading, type **resume**, and then press Enter. Scroll through the list of resume templates that displays and then experiment with downloading a template. With the **P-C2-CS-JobAnalysis.pptx** presentation open, add an additional slide to the end of the presentation that provides steps on how to download a resume in Microsoft Word. Print the presentation as a handout with nine slides horizontally per page. Save, run, and then close the presentation.

Microsoft® *PowerPoint*®

Formatting Slides

PERFORMANCE OBJECTIVES

Upon successful completion of Chapter 3, you will be able to:

- Apply font and paragraph formatting to text in slides
- Apply formatting with the Mini toolbar and Format Painter
- Customize bullets and numbers
- Modify theme colors and fonts
- Change slide background
- Change page setup
- Create custom themes including custom theme colors and theme fonts
- Delete custom themes

Tutorials

3.1 Changing Font Attributes
3.2 Changing Paragraph Formatting
3.3 Customizing Bullets and Numbering
3.4 Changing the Design Theme, Theme Color, and Background Style
3.5 Changing the Page Setup
3.6 Changing the Background Style
3.7 Creating and Deleting Custom Themes

The Font and Paragraph groups in the Home tab contain a number of buttons and options you can use to format text in slides. PowerPoint also provides a Mini toolbar and the Format Painter feature to help you format text. You can modify the design theme colors and fonts provided by PowerPoint and you can create your own custom themes. You will learn to use these features in this chapter along with how to change page setup options. Model answers for this chapter's projects appear on the following pages.

PowerPoint2010C3

Note: Before beginning the projects, copy to your storage medium the PowerPoint2010C3 subfolder from the PowerPoint2010 folder on the CD that accompanies this textbook and then make PowerPoint2010C3 the active folder.

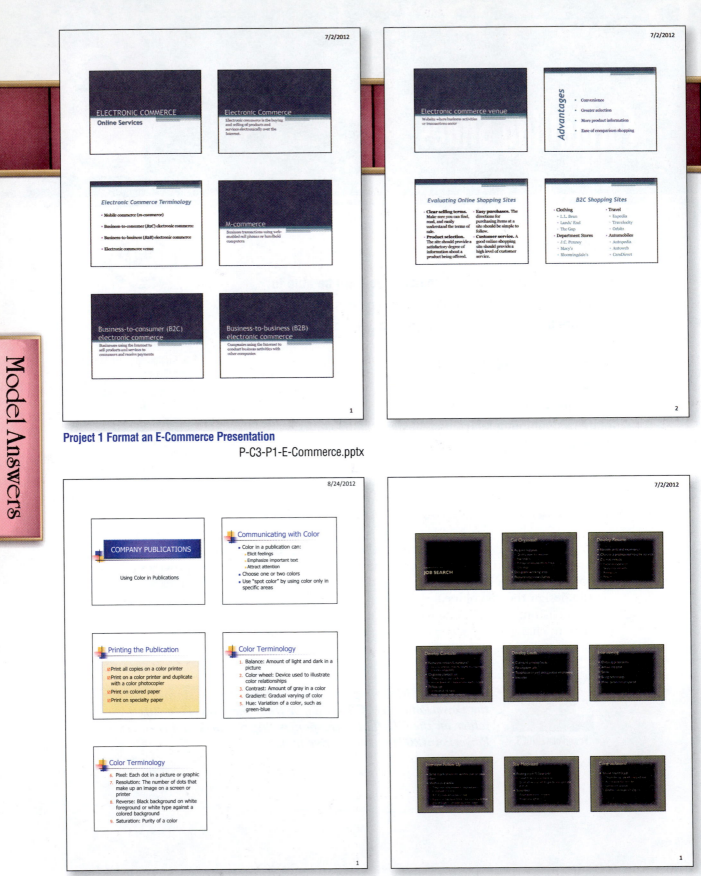

Project 1 Format an E-Commerce Presentation

P-C3-P1-E-Commerce.pptx

Project 2 Customize Bullets and Numbers in a Network Presentation

P-C3-P2-ColorPres.pptx

Project 3 Modify the Theme and Slide Background of a Job Search Presentation

P-C3-P3-JobSearch.pptx

Project 4 Create and Apply Custom Themes to Presentations

P-C3-P4-JobSearch.pptx

P-C3-P4-ResumePres.pptx

Project **1** **Format an E-Commerce Presentation**   **5 Parts**

You will open an e-commerce presentation, apply font and paragraph formatting, apply formatting with Format Painter, apply column formatting to text in placeholders, and rotate and vertically align text in placeholders.

Formatting a Presentation ▪▪▪▪▪▪▪▪▪▪▪▪▪▪▪▪▪▪▪▪▪

PowerPoint provides a variety of design themes you can apply to a presentation. These themes contain formatting such as font, color, and graphics. In some situations, the formatting provided by the theme is appropriate; in other situations, you may want to change or enhance the formatting of a slide.

Applying Font Formatting

The Font group in the Home tab contains a number of buttons for applying font formatting to text in a slide such as changing the font, font size, color, and applying font effects. Table 3.1 describes the buttons in the Font group along with any keyboard shortcuts to apply font formatting.

Changing Fonts

Design themes apply a font to text in slides. You may want to change this default to some other font for such reasons as changing the mood of a presentation, enhancing the visual appeal of slides, and increasing the readability of the text in slides. Change the font with the Font and Font Size buttons in the Font group in the Home tab.

When you select text and then click the Font button arrow, a drop-down gallery displays with font options. Hover your mouse pointer over a font option and the selected text in the slide displays with the font applied. You can continue hovering your mouse pointer over different font options to see how the selected text displays in the specified font. The Font button drop-down gallery

Consider using a sans serif typeface for titles and headings and a serif typeface for body text.

is an example of the *live preview* feature, which allows you to see how the font formatting affects your text without having to return to the presentation. The live preview feature is also available when you click the Font Size button arrow.

Fonts may be decorative or plain and generally fall into one of two categories: *serif fonts* or *sans serif fonts*. A serif is a small line at the end of a character stroke. A serif font is easier to read and is generally used for large amounts of text. A sans serif font does not have serifs (*sans* is French for *without*) and is generally used for titles and headings.

Use options at the Font dialog box with the Character Spacing tab selected to increase or decrease spacing between characters and to apply kerning to text.

In addition to buttons in the Font group in the Home tab, you can use options at the Font dialog box shown in Figure 3.1 to apply character formatting to text. Display the Font dialog box by clicking the Font group dialog box launcher or with the keyboard shortcut Ctrl + Shift + F. (The dialog box launcher is the small button containing a diagonal arrow that displays in the lower right corner of the group.) Use options at the Font dialog box to choose a font, font style, font size, and to apply special effects to text in slides such as superscript, subscript, and double strikethrough.

Table 3.1 PowerPoint Home Tab Font Group Buttons

Button	Name	Function	Keyboard Shortcut
Calibri	Font	Changes selected text to a different font.	
32	Font Size	Changes selected text to a different font size.	
A^	Increase Font Size	Increases font size of selected text to next available larger size.	Ctrl + Shift + >
A˅	Decrease Font Size	Decreases font size of selected text to next available smaller size.	Ctrl + Shift + <
	Clear All Formatting	Clears all character formatting from selected text.	Ctrl + Spacebar
B	Bold	Adds or removes bold formatting to or from selected text.	Ctrl + B
I	Italic	Adds or removes italic formatting to or from selected text.	Ctrl + I
U	Underline	Adds or removes underline formatting to or from selected text.	Ctrl + U
S	Text Shadow	Adds or removes shadow formatting to or from selected text.	
abc	Strikethrough	Inserts or removes a line through the middle of selected text.	
AV	Character Spacing	Adjusts spacing between characters.	
Aa	Change Case	Changes the case of selected text.	Shift + F3
A	Font Color	Changes the font color for selected text.	

Figure 3.1 Font Dialog Box

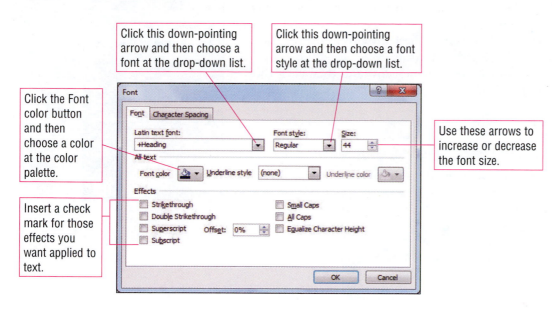

Click this down-pointing arrow and then choose a font at the drop-down list.

Click this down-pointing arrow and then choose a font style at the drop-down list.

Click the Font color button and then choose a color at the color palette.

Use these arrows to increase or decrease the font size.

Insert a check mark for those effects you want applied to text.

Formatting with the Mini Toolbar

When you select text, the Mini toolbar displays in a dimmed fashion above the selected text. Hover the mouse pointer over the Mini toolbar and it becomes active. Click a button on the Mini toolbar to apply formatting to selected text. If you do not want the Mini toolbar to display when you select text, you can turn it off. To do this, click the File tab and then click the Options button that displays below the Help tab. At the PowerPoint Options dialog box with the *General* option selected in the left panel, click the *Show Mini Toolbar on selection* check box to remove the check mark.

Project 1a **Applying Font Formatting to Text** **Part 1 of 5**

1. Open **E-Commerce.pptx** and then save the presentation with Save As and name it **P-C3-P1-E-Commerce**.
2. Apply the Urban design theme to the presentation by completing the following steps:
   a. Click the Design tab.
   b. Click the More button located to the right of the theme thumbnails.
   c. Scroll down the drop-down gallery of design themes (the list is alphabetized) and then click the *Urban* theme.
3. Change the font formatting of the Slide 1 subtitle by completing the following steps:
   a. With Slide 1 active, click any character in the subtitle *Online Services*.
   b. Select *Online Services*.
   c. Click the Home tab.
   d. Click the Font button arrow, scroll down the drop-down gallery, and then click *Trebuchet MS*.

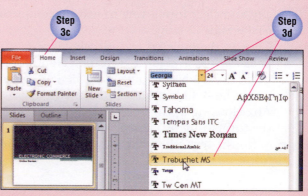

Step 3c

Step 3d

e. Click the Font Size button arrow and then click *40* at the drop-down gallery.

f. Click the Bold button in the Font Group.

g. Click the Text Shadow button.

h. Click the Font Color button arrow and then click the *Blue-Gray, Accent 6, Darker 25%* option as shown below.

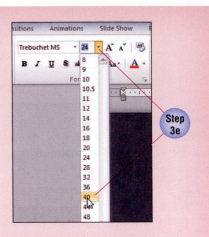

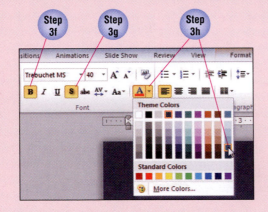

4. Change the size of the title text by completing the following steps:
   a. Click any character in the title *ELECTRONIC COMMERCE* and then select the title.
   b. Click the Increase Font Size button in the Font group.

5. Change the case of text by completing the following steps:
   a. Make Slide 2 active.
   b. Click in the title *ELECTRONIC COMMERCE* and then select the title.
   c. Click the Change Case button in the Font group and then click *Capitalize Each Word* at the drop-down list.

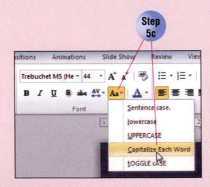

6. Apply and clear formatting to text by completing the following steps:
   a. Make Slide 3 active.
   b. Click in the bulleted text placeholder.
   c. Select *m-commerce* located in the parentheses.
   d. Click the Underline button in the Font group in the Home tab.
   e. Click the Bold button in the Font group.
   f. After looking at the text set with underlining and bold formatting, you decide to remove the formatting by clicking the Clear All Formatting button in the Font group.
   g. With the text still selected, click the Italic button in the Font group in the Home tab.

7. Apply italic formatting with the Mini toolbar by completing the following steps:

a. Select *B2C*, hover the mouse pointer over the Mini toolbar to make it active, and then click the Italic button.

Step 7a

b. Select *B2B*, hover the mouse pointer over the Mini toolbar to make it active, and then click the Italic button.

8. Save **P-C3-P1-E-Commerce.pptx**.

Formatting with Format Painter

If you apply character and/or paragraph formatting to text in a slide and want to apply the same formatting to text in the slide or other slides, use the Format Painter. With Format Painter, you can apply the same formatting in more than one location in a slide or slides. To use the Format Painter, apply the desired formatting to text, position the insertion point anywhere in the formatted text, and then double-click the Format Painter button in the Clipboard group in the Home tab. Using the mouse, select the additional text to which you want the formatting applied. After applying the formatting in the desired locations, click the Format Painter button to deactivate it. If you need to apply formatting in only one other location, click the Format Painter button once. The first time you select text, the formatting is applied and the Format Painter is deactivated.

Project 1b   **Applying Formatting with Format Painter**   **Part 2 of 5**

1. With **P-C3-P1-E-Commerce.pptx** open, make sure Slide 3 is active.
2. Apply formatting to the title by completing the following steps:

a. Click in the title text and then select the title *Electronic Commerce Terminology*.

b. Click the Font group dialog box launcher.

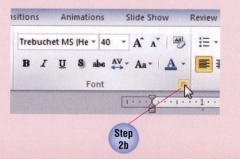

Step 2b

c. At the Font dialog box, click the down-pointing arrow at the right side of the *Font style* option box and then click *Bold Italic* at the drop-down list.

d. Select the current number in the *Size* text box and then type **36**.

e. Click the Font color button and then click the *Blue-Gray, Accent 6, Darker 25%* option.

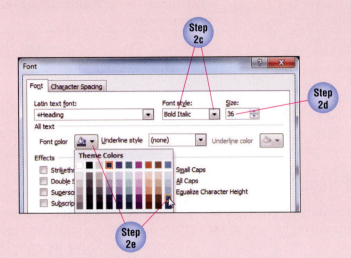

f. Click OK to close the dialog box.

3. Click on any character in the title.

4. Double-click the Format Painter button in the Clipboard group.

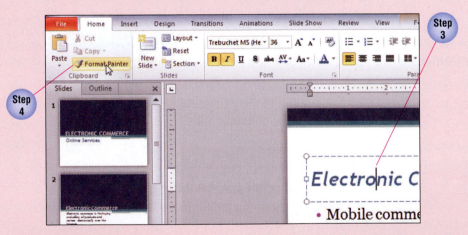

5. Make Slide 8 active.

6. Using the mouse, select the title *Advantages of Online Shopping*. (The mouse pointer displays as an I-beam with a paintbrush attached. You can also click each word in the title to apply the formatting.)

7. Make Slide 9 active and then select the title (or click each word in the title).

8. Make Slide 10 active and then select the title (or click each word in the title).

9. Click the Format Painter button to deactivate it.

10. If necessary, deselect the text.

11. Save **P-C3-P1-E-Commerce.pptx**.

Formatting Paragraphs

The Paragraph group in the Home tab contains a number of buttons for applying paragraph formatting to text in a slide such as applying bullets and numbers, increasing and decreasing list levels, changing the horizontal and vertical alignment of text, changing line spacing, and rotating text in a placeholder. Table 3.2 describes the buttons in the Paragraph group along with any keyboard shortcuts.

Table 3.2 PowerPoint Home Tab Paragraph Group Buttons

Button	Name	Function	Keyboard Shortcut
	Bullets	Adds or removes bullets to or from selected text.	
	Numbering	Adds or removes numbers to or from selected text.	
	Decrease List Level	Moves text to the previous tab stop (level).	Shift + Tab
	Increase List Level	Moves text to the next tab stop (level).	Tab
	Line Spacing	Increases or reduces spacing between lines of text.	
	Align Text Left	Left-aligns text.	Ctrl + L
	Center	Center-aligns text.	Ctrl + E
	Align Text Right	Right-aligns text.	Ctrl + R
	Justify	Justifies text.	
	Columns	Splits text into two or more columns.	
	Text Direction	Rotates or stacks text.	
	Align Text	Changes the alignment of text within a text box.	
	Convert to SmartArt Graphic	Converts selected text to a SmartArt graphic.	

1. With **P-C3-P1-E-Commerce.pptx** open, change bullets by completing the following steps:
   a. Make Slide 3 active.
   b. Click on any character in the bulleted text.
   c. Select the bulleted text.
   d. Click the Bullets button arrow in the Paragraph group in the Home tab and then click the *Filled Square Bullets* option at the drop-down gallery.

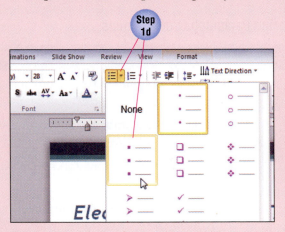

2. Change bullets to numbers by completing the following steps:
   a. Make Slide 8 active.
   b. Click on any character in the bulleted text.
   c. Select the bulleted text.
   d. Click the Numbering button arrow in the Paragraph group in the Home tab and then click the *A. B. C.* option at the drop-down gallery.

   e. After looking at the numbering, you decide to change to numbers by clicking the Numbering button arrow and then clicking the *1. 2. 3.* option at the drop-down gallery.
3. Decrease and increase list levels by completing the following steps:
   a. With Slide 8 active and the numbered text selected, click the Increase List Level button in the Paragraph group in the Home tab.
   b. With the text still selected, click the Font Color button arrow in the Font group in the Home tab and then click the Dark Blue color (second color from the right in the bottom row).

c. Make Slide 10 active.

d. Click on any character in the bulleted text.

e. Move the insertion point so it is positioned immediately left of the *J.* in *J.C. Penney*.

f. Click the Decrease List Level button in the Paragraph group in the Home tab.

g. Move the insertion point so it is positioned immediately left of the *M* in *Macy's*.

h. Press Shift + Tab.

i. Move the insertion point so it is positioned immediately left of the first *L.* in *L.L. Bean*.

j. Click the Increase List Level button in the Paragraph group.

k. Move the insertion point so it is positioned immediately left of the *T* in *The Gap*.

l. Press the Tab key.

m. Complete similar steps to those in 3j or 3l to indent the following text to the next level: *Bloomingdale's, Expedia, Travelocity,* and *Orbitz*.

4. Change text line spacing by completing the following steps:

a. Make Slide 3 active.

b. Click in the bulleted text and then select the bulleted text.

c. Click the Line Spacing button in the Paragraph group in the Home tab and then click *1.5* at the drop-down list.

d. Make Slide 8 active.

e. Click in the numbered text and then select the numbered text.

f. Click the Line Spacing button and then click *2.0* at the drop-down list.

5. Change paragraph alignment by completing the following steps:

a. Make Slide 3 active, click on any character in the title, and then click the Center button in the Paragraph group.

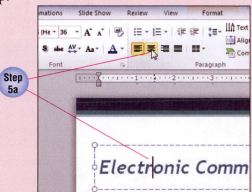

b. Make Slide 8 active, click on any character in the title, and then click the Center button.

c. Make Slide 9 active, click on any character in the title, and then click the Center button.

d. Make Slide 10 active, click on any character in the title, and then click the Center button.

6. Split text into two columns by completing the following steps:
   a. Make Slide 9 active.
   b. Click in the bulleted text and then select the bulleted text.
   c. Click the Columns button in the Paragraph group and then click *Two Columns* at the drop-down list.

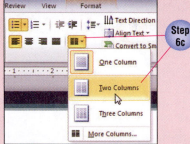

d. Select the first sentence in the first bulleted paragraph (the sentence *Clear selling terms.*) and then click the Bold button.
e. Select and then bold the first sentence in the remaining bulleted paragraphs of text in Slide 9.
7. Save **P-C3-P1-E-Commerce.pptx**.

Customizing Paragraphs

Line Spacing

If you want more control over paragraph alignment, indenting, and spacing, click the Paragraph group dialog box launcher. This displays the Paragraph dialog box as shown in Figure 3.2. You can also display this dialog box by clicking the Line Spacing button in the Paragraph group and then clicking *Line Spacing Options* at the drop-down list. Use options at this dialog box to specify text alignment, paragraph indentation, spacing before and after paragraphs, and line spacing.

Figure 3.2 Paragraph Dialog Box

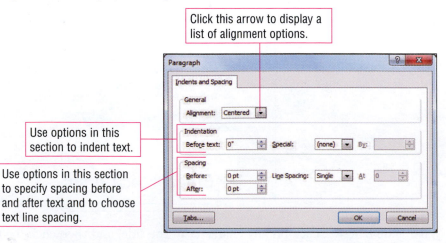

Customizing Columns

Click the Columns button in the Paragraph group and you can choose one, two, or three columns. If you want to choose a number for columns other than the three choices or if you want to control spacing between columns, click the *More Columns* option at the drop-down list. This displays the Columns dialog box shown in Figure 3.3. With options in this dialog box, you can specify the number of columns and the spacing measurement between columns.

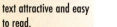

Columns

Figure 3.3 Columns Dialog Box

Specify the number of columns and spacing between columns in this dialog box.

Project 1d   **Customizing Paragraph and Column Formatting**   **Part 4 of 5**

1. With **P-C3-P1-E-Commerce.pptx** open, change line and paragraph spacing by completing the following steps:
   a. Make Slide 3 active.
   b. Click in the bulleted text and then select the bulleted text.
   c. Click the Paragraph group dialog box launcher.
   d. At the Paragraph dialog box, click twice on the up-pointing arrow at the right side of the *Before text* measurement box. (This inserts *0.6"* in the measurement box.)
   e. Click twice on the up-pointing arrow at the right side of the *After* measurement box in the *Spacing* section. (This inserts *12 pt* in the box.)
   f. Click the down-pointing arrow at the right side of the *Line Spacing* option box and then click *Multiple* at the drop-down list.
   g. Select the current measurement in the *At* text box and then type 1.8.
   h. Click OK.

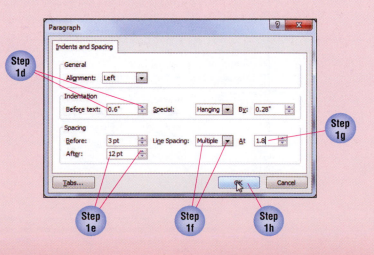

2. Format text in columns by completing the following steps:
   a. Make Slide 10 active.
   b. Click in the bulleted text and then select the text.
   c. Click the Columns button in the Paragraph group and then click *More Columns*.
   d. At the Columns dialog box, click once on the up-pointing arrow at the right side of the *Number* option. (This inserts a *2* in the text box.)
   e. Click the up-pointing arrow at the right side of the *Spacing* measurement box until *0.5″* displays in the box.
   f. Click OK.
   g. With the text still selected, click the Paragraph group dialog box launcher.
   h. At the Paragraph dialog box, click once on the up-pointing arrow at the right side of the *After* measurement box in the *Spacing* section. (This inserts *6 pt* in the box.)
   i. Click OK.
3. Save **P-C3-P1-E-Commerce.pptx**.

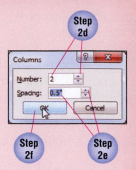

Step 2d

Step 2f

Step 2e

Rotating and Vertically Aligning Text

Text Direction

Align Text

If you click the Text Direction button in the Paragraph group, a drop-down list displays with options for rotating and stacking text. Click *More Options* at the drop-down list and the Format Text Effects dialog box with *Text Box* selected in the left panel displays as shown in Figure 3.4. Use options in this dialog box to specify vertical alignment and text direction, autofit contents, and change internal margins. Click the Align Text button in the Paragraph group and a drop-down list displays with options for changing the alignment to top, middle, or bottom of the placeholder.

Figure 3.4 Format Text Effects Dialog Box with *Text Box* Selected

Use options in this section to specify internal margins for text in a placeholder.

1. With **P-C3-P1-E-Commerce.pptx** open, change vertical alignment by completing the following steps:
   a. Make Slide 9 active.
   b. Click on any character in the bulleted text.
   c. Click the Align Text button in the Paragraph group in the Home tab and then click *Middle* at the drop-down list.

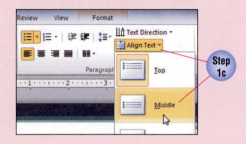

2. Make Slide 8 active and then modify the slide so it displays as shown in Figure 3.5 by completing the following steps:
   a. Click in the numbered text and then select the numbered text.
   b. Click the Bullets button arrow and then click the *Filled Square Bullets* option.
   c. Decrease the size of the bulleted text placeholder so the placeholder borders display just outside the text.
   d. Drag the placeholder so the bulleted text is positioned as shown in Figure 3.5.
   e. Click on any character in the title *Advantages of Online Shopping*.
   f. Delete *of Online Shopping*.
   g. Select *Advantages* and then change the font size to 60.
   h. Drag in the right border of the placeholder to the left so it is positioned just outside the text.
   i. Click the Text Direction button in the Paragraph group and then click *Rotate all text 270°*.

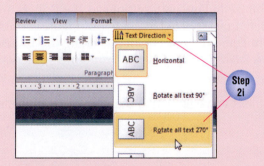

   j. Using the sizing handles that display around the title placeholder, increase the height and decrease the width of the placeholder and then drag the placeholder so the title displays as shown in Figure 3.5.
3. Apply a transition and sound to all slides in the presentation.
4. Print the presentation as a handout with six slides horizontally per page.
5. Save and then close **P-C3-P1-E-Commerce.pptx**.

Figure 3.5 Project 1e, Slide 8

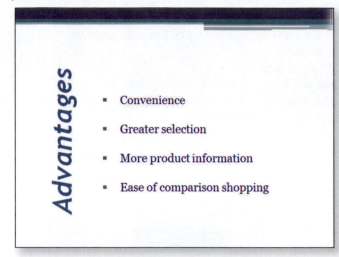

Project 2   Customize Bullets and Numbers in a Network Presentation   3 Parts

You will open a presentation on using colors in publications and then create and apply custom bullets and numbering.

Customizing Bullets

Quick Steps

Customize Bullets
1. Click in bulleted text.
2. Click Bullets button arrow.
3. Click *Bullets and Numbering* at drop-down gallery.
4. Make desired changes.
5. Click OK.

Each design theme contains a Title and Content slide layout containing bullets. The appearance and formatting of the bullets varies with each design theme. You can choose to use the bullet provided by the design theme or create custom bullets. Customize bullets with options at the Bullets and Numbering dialog box with the Bulleted tab selected as shown in Figure 3.6. Display this dialog box by clicking in a bulleted list placeholder, clicking the Bullets button arrow, and then clicking *Bullets and Numbering* at the drop-down gallery.

Figure 3.6 Bullets and Numbering Dialog Box with Bulleted Tab Selected

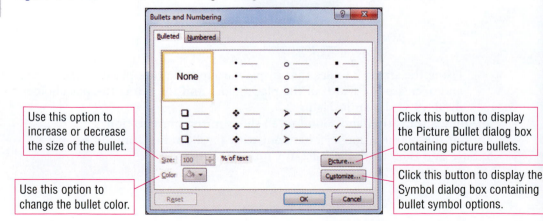

Use this option to increase or decrease the size of the bullet.

Use this option to change the bullet color.

Click this button to display the Picture Bullet dialog box containing picture bullets.

Click this button to display the Symbol dialog box containing bullet symbol options.

At the Bullets and Numbering dialog box, choose one of the predesigned bullets from the list box, change the size of the bullets by percentage in relation to the text size, change the bullet color, and display bullet pictures and characters. Click the Picture button located toward the bottom of the dialog box and the Picture Bullet dialog box displays. Click the desired bullet in the list box and then click OK. Click the Customize button located toward the bottom of the Bullets and Numbering dialog box and the Symbol dialog box displays. Choose a symbol bullet option at the Symbol dialog box and then click OK. Picture or symbol bullets are particularly effective in adding visual interest.

If you want to move the insertion point down to the next line without inserting a bullet, press Shift + Enter. This inserts a line break without inserting a bullet. If you press the Enter key, bulleting is turned back on.

Choose a custom bullet that matches the theme or mood of the presentation.

Picture

Project 2a   **Customizing Bullets and Numbers**   **Part 1 of 3**

1. Open **ColorPres.pptx** and then save the presentation with Save As and name it **P-C3-P2-ColorPres**.
2. Increase list level and create custom bullets by completing the following steps:
   a. Make Slide 2 active.
   b. Select the second, third, and fourth bulleted paragraphs.
   c. Click the Increase List Level button in the Paragraph group in the Home tab.
   d. With the three bulleted paragraphs still selected, click the Bullets button arrow and then click *Bullets and Numbering* at the drop-down list.
   e. At the Bullets and Numbering dialog box with the Bulleted tab selected, click the up-pointing arrow at the right side of the *Size* option until *75* displays in the text box.
   f. Click the Picture button located toward the bottom right corner of the dialog box.
   g. At the Picture Bullet dialog box, click a yellow square bullet option like the one shown below.
   h. Click OK to close the Picture Bullet dialog box and the Bullets and Numbering dialog box.

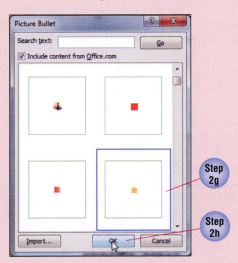

3. Insert symbol bullets by completing the following steps:
   a. Make Slide 3 active.
   b. Select all of the bulleted text.
   c. Click the Bullets button arrow and then click *Bullets and Numbering* at the drop-down list.
   d. At the Bullets and Numbering dialog box with the Bulleted tab selected, click the up-pointing arrow at the right side of the *Size* option until *80* displays in the text box.

e. Click the Customize button located toward the bottom right corner of the dialog box.

f. At the Symbol dialog box, click the down-pointing arrow at the right side of the *Font* option box, scroll down the drop-down list, and then click *Wingdings*. (This option is located toward the bottom of the list.)

g. Scroll to the bottom of the Symbol dialog box list box until the last row of symbols displays and then click the second symbol from the right in the bottom row (check mark inside of a square).

h. Click OK.

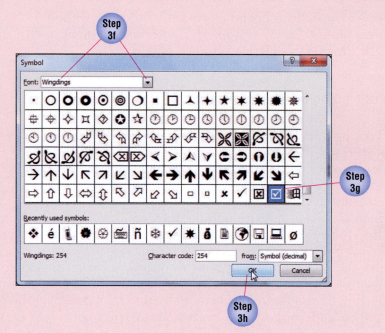

i. At the Bullets and Numbering dialog box, click the Font Color button and then click the Red color (second color from the left in the *Standard Colors* section).

j. Click OK to close the Bullets and Numbering dialog box. (This applies the red check mark symbol bullets to the selected text.)

4. Save **P-C3-P2-ColorPres.pptx**.

Customizing Numbering

▼ **Quick Steps**

Customize Numbering

1. Click in numbered text.
2. Click Numbering button arrow.
3. Click *Bullets and Numbering* at drop-down gallery.
4. Make desired changes.
5. Click OK.

Click the Numbering button arrow in the Paragraph group and several numbering options display in a drop-down gallery. You can customize numbering with options at the Bullets and Numbering dialog box with the Numbered tab selected as shown in Figure 3.7. Display this dialog box by clicking the Numbering button arrow and then clicking *Bullets and Numbering* at the drop-down gallery. Use options at this dialog box to change the size and color of numbers as well as the starting number.

If you want to move the insertion point down to the next line without inserting a number, press Shift + Enter. If you press Enter, numbering is turned back on.

Numbering

Figure 3.7 Bullets and Numbering Dialog Box with Numbered Tab Selected

Use this option to increase or decrease the size of the number.

Use this option to change the number color.

Change the starting number with this option.

Project 2b   **Customizing Numbers**   **Part 2 of 3**

1. With **P-C3-P2-ColorPres.pptx** open, make sure the presentation displays in Normal view.
2. Customize and insert numbers by completing the following steps:
   a. Make Slide 4 active.
   b. Select the bulleted text in the slide.
   c. Click the Numbering button arrow in the Paragraph group in the Home tab and then click the *Bullets and Numbering* option at the drop-down list.
   d. At the Bullets and Numbering dialog box with the Numbered tab selected, click the *1. 2. 3.* option (second option from the left in the top row).
   e. Click the up-pointing arrow at the right side of the *Size* option until *80* displays in the text box.
   f. Click the Font Color button and then the Dark Red color (first color option from the left in the *Standard Colors* row).
   g. Click OK.

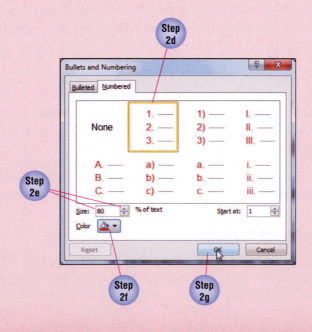

Step 2d

Step 2e

Step 2f

Step 2g

h. Make Slide 5 active.
i. Select the bulleted text in the slide.
j. Click the Numbering button arrow and then click the *Bullets and Numbering* option at the drop-down list.
k. At the Bullets and Numbering dialog box with the Numbered tab selected, click the *1. 2. 3.* option (second option from the left in the top row).
l. Click the up-pointing arrow at the right side of the *Size* option until *80* displays in the text box.
m. Click the Font Color button and then click the Dark Red color (first color option from the left in the *Standard Colors* row).
n. Click the up-pointing arrow at the right of the *Start at* option until *6* displays in the text box.
o. Click OK.
3. Add a transition and sound of your choosing to all slides in the presentation.
4. Run the presentation.
5. Save **P-C3-P2-ColorPres.pptx**.

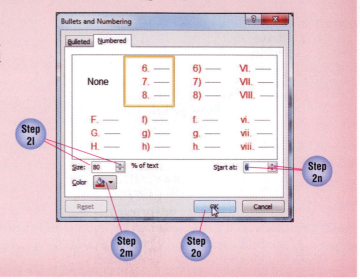

Customizing Placeholders

Quick Styles

Shape Fill

Shape Outline

Shape Effects

You can customize a placeholder in a slide with buttons in the Drawing group in the Home tab. For example, you can apply a fill color, an outline, and an effect to a placeholder. You can also customize a placeholder by applying a *Quick Style*. To customize a placeholder, click in the placeholder to select it and then click the desired button in the Drawing group. Apply a Quick Style to the selected placeholder by clicking the Quick Styles button and then clicking the desired style at the drop-down gallery. Click the *Other Theme Fills* option that displays at the bottom of the drop-down gallery and a side menu displays with additional fills.

In addition to the Quick Styles button, you can use the Shape Fill, Shape Outline, and Shape Effects buttons in the Drawing group in the Home tab to customize a placeholder. Click the Shape Fill button arrow and a drop-down gallery displays with options for applying a color, picture, gradient, or texture to the placeholder. Use the Shape Outline button to apply an outline to a placeholder and specify the outline color, weight, and style. With the Shape Effects button, you can choose from a variety of effects such as shadow, reflection, glow, and soft edges.

Changing Internal Margins

When you apply formatting to a placeholder, you may need to move text within the placeholder. You can do this with the internal margins measurements in the Format Text Effects dialog box with the *Text Box* option selected in the left panel (shown in Figure 3.4). Use the *Left*, *Right*, *Top*, and *Bottom* measurements boxes to specify internal margins for text inside the placeholder.

1. With **P-C3-P2-ColorPres.pptx** open, customize the title placeholder in Slide 1 by completing the following steps:

    a. If necessary, make Slide 1 active.

    b. Click in the title to select the placeholder.

    c. If necessary, click the Home tab.

    d. Click the Quick Styles button in the Drawing group.

    e. Click the *Moderate Effect - Green, Accent 1* option at the drop-down gallery (second option from the left in the fifth row).

    f. Click the Shape Outline button arrow in the Drawing group and then click *Blue* in the *Standard Colors* section.

    g. Click the Shape Outline button arrow, point to *Weight,* and then click *3 pt* at the side menu.

    h. Click the Shape Effects button, point to *Bevel,* and then click *Cool Slant* at the side menu (last option in the top row in the *Bevel* section).

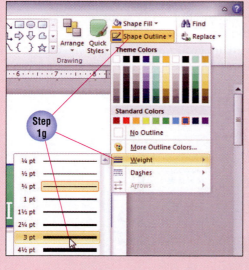

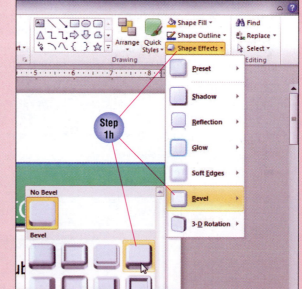

    i. After looking at the fill color, you decide to change it by clicking the Quick Styles button in the Drawing group, pointing to *Other Theme Fills* that displays at the bottom of the drop-down gallery, and then clicking *Style 11* at the side menu (third option from the left in the bottom row).

2. Change the internal margins for the text in the title placeholder by completing the following steps:

a. With the title placeholder selected, click the Text Direction button in the Paragraph group in the Home tab and then click *More Options* at the drop-down list.

b. At the Format Text Effects dialog box with *Text Box* selected in the left panel, click the up-pointing arrow at the right side of the *Left* measurement box until *0.6"* displays in the measurement box.

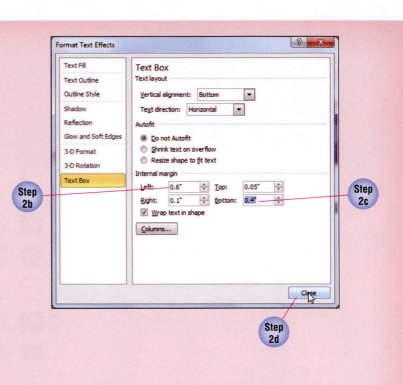

c. Click the up-pointing arrow at the right side of the *Bottom* measurement box until *0.4"* displays in the measurement box.

d. Click the Close button to close the dialog box.

3. Customize the subtitle placeholder by completing the following steps:

a. Click in the subtitle text to select the placeholder.

b. Click the Shape Fill button arrow in the Drawing group, point to *Texture*, and then click *Water droplets* at the drop-down gallery (first option from the left in the second row).

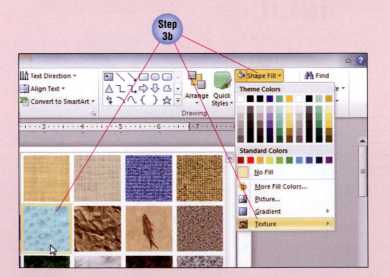

c. Click the Shape Effects button, point to *Bevel*, and then click *Cool Slant* at the side menu (last option in the top row in the *Bevel* section).

4. Change the internal margins for the text in the subtitle placeholder by completing the following steps:
   a. With the subtitle placeholder selected, click the Text Direction button in the Paragraph group in the Home tab and then click *More Options* at the drop-down list.
   b. At the Format Text Effects dialog box with *Text Box* selected in the left panel, click the up-pointing arrow at the right side of the *Left* measurement box until *0.3"* displays in the measurement box.
   c. Click the up-pointing arrow at the right side of the *Top* measurement box until *0.6"* displays in the measurement box.
   d. Click the Close button to close the dialog box.
5. Make Slide 3 active and then change the spacing after paragraphs by completing the following steps:
   a. Select the bulleted text.
   b. Click the Paragraph group dialog box launcher.
   c. At the Paragraph dialog box, click the up-pointing arrow at the right side of the *After* option in the *Spacing* section to display *6 pt* in the option box.
   d. Click OK to close the dialog box.
6. Customize the placeholder by completing the following steps:

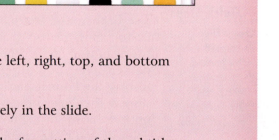

   a. With the bulleted text placeholder selected, click the Quick Styles button in the Drawing group and then click *Subtle Effect - Gold, Accent 6* at the drop-down gallery (last option in the fourth row).
   b. Click the Shape Effects button in the Drawing group, point to *Soft Edges*, and then click *2.5 Point* at the side menu.
   c. Click the Text Direction button in the Paragraph group and then click *More Options* at the drop-down list.
   d. At the Format Text Effects dialog box, change the left, right, top, and bottom measurements to *0.4"*.
   e. Click the Close button to close the dialog box.
   f. Move the placeholder so it is positioned attractively in the slide.
7. Run the presentation.
8. You decide that you do not like the appearance of the formatting of the subtitle placeholder in Slide 1 so you decide to remove the formatting by completing the following steps:
   a. Make Slide 1 active.
   b. Click on any character in the subtitle placeholder text.
   c. Make sure the Home tab is selected.
   d. Click the Quick Styles button in the Drawing group and then click the *Colored Outline - White, Accent 3* option (fourth option from the left in the top row).
9. Print the presentation as a handout with six slides horizontally per page.
10. Save and then close **P-C3-P2-ColorPres.pptx**.

Project 3 — Modify the Theme and Slide Background of a Job Search Presentation   2 Parts

You will open a job search presentation, apply a design theme, and then change the theme colors and fonts. You will also apply and customize a background style.

Modifying Theme Colors and Fonts

HINT

Themes are shared across Office programs such as PowerPoint, Word, and Excel.

Colors

Fonts

Effects

A design theme is a set of formatting choices that includes a color theme (a set of colors), a font theme (heading and text fonts), and an effects theme (a set of lines and fill effects). Use buttons at the right side of the Themes group in the Design tab to change design theme colors, fonts, and effects.

A theme contains specific color formatting, which you can change with options from the Colors button in the Themes group. Click this button and a drop-down gallery displays with named color schemes. The names of the color schemes correspond to the names of the themes. Each theme applies specific fonts, which you can change with options from the Fonts button in the Themes group. Click this button and a drop-down gallery displays with font choices. Each font group in the drop-down gallery contains two choices. The first choice in the group is the font that is applied to slide titles and the second choice is the font that is applied to slide subtitles and text. If you are formatting a presentation that contains graphic elements such as illustrations, pictures, clip art, or text boxes, you can specify theme effects with options at the Effects drop-down gallery.

Changing Slide Background

▼ Quick Steps

Change Slide Background
1. Click Design tab.
2. Click Background Styles button.
3. Click desired style at drop-down gallery.

Background Styles

The Background group in the Design tab contains a button and an option for customizing the background of slides in a presentation. Click the Background Styles button and a drop-down gallery of background styles displays. Click the desired style at this drop-down gallery or click the *Format Background* option to display the Format Background dialog box shown in Figure 3.8. You can also display the dialog box by clicking the Background group dialog box launcher. Use options in this dialog box to customize background fill, gradient, direction, and color. If you make changes to the slide background, you can reset the background to the default by clicking the Reset Background button in the Format Background dialog box. You can also reset the background to the default by clicking the Background Styles button and then clicking *Reset Slide Background* at the drop-down gallery.

Some of the design themes provided by PowerPoint contain a background graphic. You can remove this graphic from a slide by clicking the *Hide Background Graphics* check box in the Background group. This removes the background from the currently active slide. If you want to remove the background from more than one slide, select the slides. You can also remove background graphics from all slides by inserting a check mark in the *Hide background graphics* check box in the Format Background dialog box and then clicking the Apply to All button.

Figure 3.8 Format Background Dialog Box

Use options in this dialog box to specify gradient, texture, and pattern fill of the slide background.

Project 3a   **Customizing Theme Colors and Fonts**   **Part 1 of 2**

1. Open **JobSearch.pptx** and then save the presentation with Save As and name it **P-C3-P3-JobSearch**.
2. Apply a design theme by completing the following steps:
   a. Click the Design tab.
   b. Click the More button at the right side of the design theme thumbnails and then click *Metro* at the drop-down gallery.
3. Change the theme colors by clicking the Colors button in the Themes group, scrolling down the drop-down gallery, and then clicking *Paper*.
4. Change the theme fonts by clicking the Fonts button in the Themes group, scrolling down the drop-down gallery, and then clicking *Solstice*.

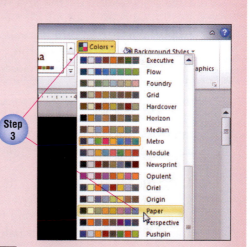

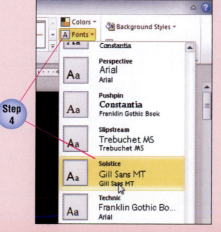

5. Change the background style by clicking the Background Styles button in the Background group and then clicking *Style 10* at the drop-down gallery.

6. With Slide 1 active, run the presentation and notice the formatting applied by the theme, theme colors, theme fonts, and background style.

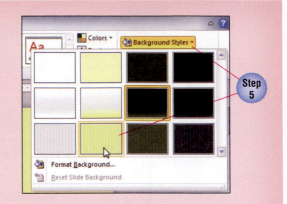

Step 5

7. With the presentation in Normal view, change the background style by clicking the Background Styles button in the Background group in the Design tab and then clicking *Style 7* at the drop-down gallery.

8. Apply and customize a background style by completing the following steps:
   a. Click the Background group dialog box launcher.
   b. At the Format Background dialog box, click the *Picture or texture fill* option.
   c. Click the *Hide background graphics* check box to insert a check mark.
   d. Click the Texture button and then click the *Brown marble* option (first option from the left in the third row).
   e. Click the Apply to All button.
   f. Click the Close button to close the dialog box.

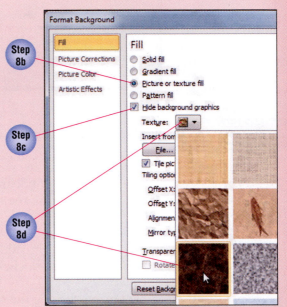

Step 8b

Step 8c

Step 8d

9. Run the presentation and notice the background formatting.

10. Change the background to a pattern rather than texture fill by completing the following steps:
   a. Click the Background group dialog box launcher.
   b. Click the *Pattern fill* option.
   c. Click the *50%* option (second from the left in the top row) in the pattern palette. (See image at right.)
   d. Click the Apply to All button and then click the Close button to close the dialog box.

11. Look at the slides in the Slides/Outline pane and notice the background pattern applied to the slides.

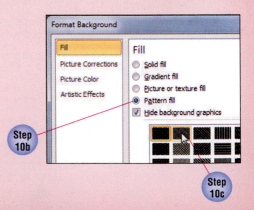

Step 10b

Step 10c

12. Change the background to a gradient fill by completing the following steps:
   a. Click the Background group dialog box launcher.
   b. Click the *Gradient fill* option.
   c. Click the down-pointing arrow to the right of the *Type* option box and then click *Path* at the drop-down list.
   d. Drag the first button on the *Gradient stops* slider bar until *80%* displays in the Position text box.
   e. Click the Color button and then click the *Black, Background 1, Lighter 35%* color (located in the first column).
   f. Drag the button on the *Transparency* slider bar until *15%* displays in the percentage box at the right. (You can also click the up-pointing arrow at the right side of the percentage box until *15%* displays.)
   g. Click the Apply to All button and then click the Close button to close the dialog box.
13. Run the presentation and notice the background formatting.
14. Save **P-C3-P3-JobSearch.pptx**.

Changing Page Setup ■■■■■■■■■■■■■■■■■■■■

You can control page setup and the orientation of slides with buttons in the Page Setup group in the Design tab. The default slide orientation is *Landscape*. You can change this to *Portrait* with the Slide Orientation button. Click the Page Setup button and the Page Setup dialog box displays as shown in Figure 3.9. With options at this dialog box, you can specify how you want the slides sized. By

Slide Orientation

Page Setup

Figure 3.9 Page Setup Dialog Box

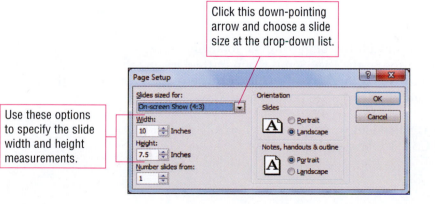

default, slides are sized for an on-screen show with a 4:3 ratio. Click the down-pointing arrow at the right side of the *Slides sized for* option and a drop-down list displays with options for changing the slide size ratio and choosing other paper sizes. With other options in the dialog box, you can specify slide width and height and change the starting slide number. You can also change the orientation of slides and the orientation of notes, handouts, and outline pages.

Project 3b **Changing Orientation and Page Setup** **Part 2 of 2**

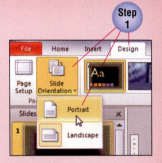

1. With **P-C3-P3-JobSearch.pptx** open, change slide orientation by clicking the Design tab, clicking the Slide Orientation button in the Page Setup group, and then clicking *Portrait* at the drop-down list.
2. Run the presentation and notice how the slides appear in portrait orientation.
3. After running the presentation, click the Slide Orientation button and then click *Landscape* at the drop-down list.
4. Suppose you are going to run the presentation on a wide screen monitor. To do this, you decide to change the slide size ratio by completing the following steps:

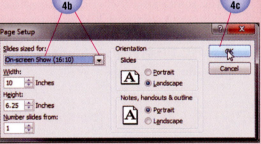

   a. Click the Page Setup button in the Page Setup group in the Design tab.
   b. At the Page Setup dialog box, click the down-pointing arrow at the right side of the *Slides sized for* option and then click *On-screen Show (16:10)*. (Notice that the slide height changed from *7.5* to *6.25*.)
   c. Click OK.
5. Run the presentation.
6. Specify slide width and height by completing the following steps:

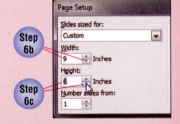

   a. Click the Page Setup button in the Page Setup group in the Design tab.
   b. At the Page Setup dialog box, click the down-pointing arrow at the right side of the *Width* measurement box until *9* displays in the box.
   c. Click the down-pointing arrow at the right side of the *Height* measurement box until *6* displays in the box.
   d. Click OK.
7. Run the presentation.
8. Return the slide size to the default by completing the following steps:
   a. Click the Page Setup button in the Page Setup group in the Design tab.
   b. At the Page Setup dialog box, click the down-pointing arrow at the right side of the *Slides sized for* option and then click *On-screen Show (4:3)*.
   c. Click OK.
9. Print the presentation as a handout with nine slides horizontally per page.
10. Save and then close **P-C3-P3-JobSearch.pptx**.

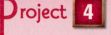

Create and Apply Custom Themes to Presentations

Project 4

4 Parts

You will create custom theme colors and custom theme fonts and then save the changes as a custom theme. You will then apply the custom theme to a job search presentation and a resume writing presentation.

Creating Custom Themes ■■■■■■■■■■■■■■■■■■■■

If the default themes, theme colors, and theme fonts do not provide the formatting you desire for your presentation, you can create your own custom theme colors, custom theme fonts, and a custom theme. A theme you create will display in the Themes drop-down gallery under the *Custom* section. To create a custom theme, change the theme colors, theme fonts, and/or theme effects.

The buttons at the right side of the Themes group in the Design tab display a visual representation of the current theme. If you change the theme colors, the colors are reflected in the small color squares on the Colors button. If you change the theme fonts, the *A* on the Fonts button reflects the change.

Creating Custom Theme Colors

To create custom theme colors, click the Design tab, click the Colors button in the Themes group, and then click *Create New Theme Colors* at the drop-down gallery. This displays the Create New Theme Colors dialog box similar to the one shown in Figure 3.10. Theme colors contain four text and background colors, six accent colors, and two hyperlink colors as shown in the *Themes color* section of the

▼ **Quick Steps**

Create Custom Theme Colors
1. Click Design tab.
2. Click Colors button in Themes group.
3. Click *Create New Theme Colors*.
4. Change to desired background, accent, and hyperlink colors.
5. Type name for custom theme colors.
6. Click Save button.

Figure 3.10 Create New Theme Colors Dialog Box

Click the Reset button to reset color back to the default.

Change a theme color by clicking the color button and then clicking the desired color at the drop-down palette.

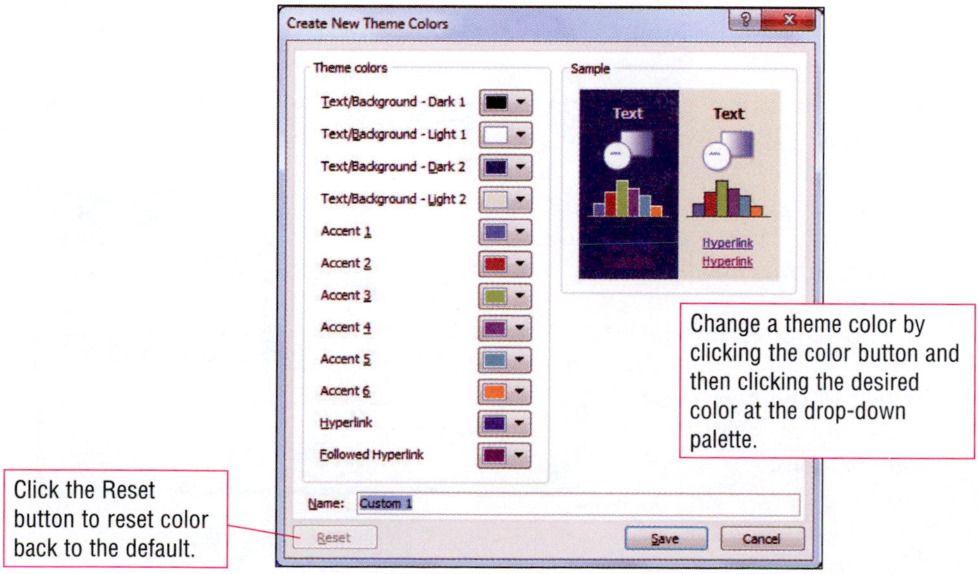

dialog box. Change a color in the list box by clicking the color button at the right side of the color option and then clicking the desired color at the color palette.

After you have made all desired changes to colors, click in the *Name* text box, type a name for the custom theme colors, and then click the Save button. This saves the custom theme colors and applies the color changes to the currently open presentation. Display the custom theme colors by clicking the Colors button in the Themes group in the Design tab. Your custom theme colors will display toward the top of the drop-down gallery in the *Custom* section. If you make changes to colors at the Create New Theme Colors dialog box and then decide you do not like the color changes, click the Reset button located in the lower left corner of the dialog box.

When you create custom theme colors, you can apply the theme to a presentation by clicking the Colors button in the Themes group in the Design tab and then clicking the custom theme colors that display toward the top of the drop-down gallery in the *Custom* section.

Project 4a   Creating Custom Theme Colors   Part 1 of 4

Note: If you are running PowerPoint 2010 on a computer connected to a network in a public environment such as a school, you may need to complete all four parts of Project 4 during the same session. Network system software may delete your custom themes when you exit PowerPoint. Check with your instructor.

1. At a blank presentation, click the Design tab, click the More button at the right side of the theme thumbnails in the Themes group, and then click *Technic* at the drop-down gallery.

2. Create custom theme colors by completing the following steps:
   a. Click the Colors button in the Themes group and then click the *Create New Theme Colors* option at the drop-down gallery.
   b. At the Create New Theme Colors dialog box, click the color button that displays at the right side of the *Text/Background - Dark 1* option and then click the *Olive Green, Accent 4, Lighter 60%* option.
   c. Click the color button that displays at the right side of the *Text/Background - Light 1* option and then click the *Gold, Accent 2, Lighter 80%* option.
   d. Click the color button that displays at the right side of the *Text/Background - Dark 2* option and then click the *Lavender, Accent 3, Darker 25%* option.

3. Save the custom colors by completing the following steps:
   a. Select the current text in the *Name* text box.
   b. Type your first and last names.
   c. Click the Save button.

4. Save the presentation and name it **P-C3-P4-CustomTheme**.

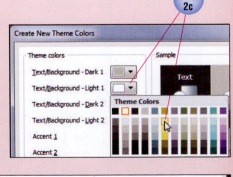

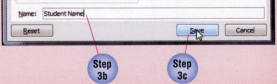

Creating Custom Theme Fonts

To create custom theme fonts, click the Design tab, click the Fonts button, and then click *Create New Theme Fonts* at the drop-down gallery. This displays the Create New Theme Fonts dialog box similar to the one shown in Figure 3.11. At this dialog box, choose a heading font and a font for body text. Type a name for the custom theme fonts in the *Name* box and then click the Save button.

Quick Steps

Create Custom Fonts
1. Click Design tab.
2. Click Theme Fonts button.
3. Click *Create New Theme Fonts*.
4. Choose desired fonts.
5. Type name for custom theme fonts.
6. Click Save button.

Figure 3.11 Create New Theme Fonts Dialog Box

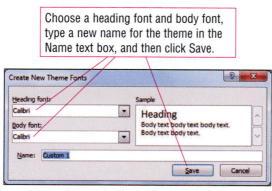

Choose a heading font and body font, type a new name for the theme in the Name text box, and then click Save.

Project 4b **Creating Custom Theme Fonts** **Part 2 of 4**

1. With **P-C3-P4-CustomTheme.pptx** open, create custom theme fonts by completing the following steps:
   a. If necessary, click the Design tab.
   b. Click the Fonts button in the Themes group and then click the *Create New Theme Fonts* option at the drop-down gallery.
   c. At the Create New Theme Fonts dialog box, click the down-pointing arrow at the right side of the *Heading font* option box, scroll up the drop-down list, and then click *Candara*.
   d. Click the down-pointing arrow at the right side of the *Body font* option box, scroll down the drop-down list, and then click *Constantia*.

2. Save the custom theme fonts by completing the following steps:
   a. Select the current text in the *Name* text box.
   b. Type your first and last names.
   c. Click the Save button.
3. Save **P-C3-P4-CustomTheme.pptx**.

Save a Custom Theme
1. Click Design tab.
2. Click More button in Themes group.
3. Click *Save Current Theme.*
4. Type name for custom theme.
5. Click Save button.

Saving a Custom Theme

When you have customized theme colors and fonts, you can save these as a custom theme. To do this, click the More button at the right side of the Themes group in the Design tab and then click *Save Current Theme*. This displays the Save Current Theme dialog box with many of the same options as the Save As dialog box. Type a name for your custom theme in the *File name* text box and then click the Save button. To apply a custom theme, click the More button and then click the desired theme in the *Custom* section of the drop-down gallery.

Project 4c   **Saving and Applying a Custom Theme**   **Part 3 of 4**

1. With **P-C3-P4-CustomTheme.pptx** open, save the custom theme colors and fonts as a custom theme by completing the following steps:
   a. If necessary, click the Design tab.
   b. Click the More button at the right side of the theme thumbnails in the Themes group.
   c. Click the *Save Current Theme* option that displays at the bottom of the drop-down gallery.
   d. At the Save Current Theme dialog box, type **C3** and then type your last name in the *File name* text box.
   e. Click the Save button.

Step 1d

File name:	C3LastName	
Save as type:	Office Theme (*.thmx)	
Authors:	Student Name	Tags: Add a tag

Hide Folders   Tools ▼   Save   Cancel

Step 1e

2. Close **P-C3-P4-CustomTheme.pptx**.
3. Open **JobSearch.pptx** and then save the presentation with Save As and name it **P-C3-P4-JobSearch**.
4. Apply your custom theme by completing the following steps:
   a. Click the Design tab.
   b. Click the More button that displays at the right side of the theme thumbnails.
   c. Click the custom theme that begins with *C3* followed by your last name. (The theme will display in the *Custom* section of the drop-down gallery.)
5. Run the presentation and notice how the slides display with the custom theme applied.
6. Print Slide 1 of the presentation.

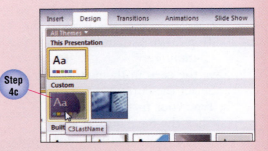

Step 4c

7. Save and then close **P-C3-P4-JobSearch.pptx**.
8. Open **ResumePres.pptx** and then save the presentation with Save As and name it **P-C3-P4-ResumePres**.
9. Apply your custom theme (the theme that displays beginning with *C3* followed by your last name).
10. Make Slide 2 active and then adjust the placeholder containing the bulleted text so it is positioned attractively on the slide.
11. Make Slide 1 active and then run the presentation.
12. Print Slide 1 of the presentation.
13. Save and then close **P-C3-P4-ResumePres.pptx**.

Editing Custom Themes

You can edit the custom theme colors and custom theme fonts. To edit the custom theme colors, click the Colors button in the Themes group in the Design tab. At the drop-down gallery of custom and built-in themes, right-click your custom theme and then click *Edit* at the shortcut menu. This displays the Edit Theme Colors dialog box that contains the same options as the Create New Theme Colors dialog box shown in Figure 3.10 on page 105. Make the desired changes to theme colors and then click the Save button.

To edit custom theme fonts, click the Fonts button in the Themes group in the Design tab, right-click your custom theme fonts, and then click *Edit* at the shortcut menu. This displays the Edit Theme Fonts dialog box that contains the same options as the Create New Theme Fonts dialog box shown in Figure 3.11 on page 107. Make the desired changes and then click the Save button.

Deleting Custom Themes

You can delete custom theme colors from the Colors button drop-down gallery, delete custom theme fonts from the Fonts drop-down gallery, and delete custom themes from the Save Current Theme dialog box. To delete custom theme colors, click the Colors button, right-click the theme you want to delete, and then click *Delete* at the shortcut menu. At the message asking if you want to delete the theme colors, click Yes. Complete similar steps to delete custom theme fonts.

Delete a custom theme at the Save Current Theme dialog box. To display this dialog box, click the More button at the right side of the Themes group in the Design tab and then click *Save Current Theme* at the drop-down gallery. At the dialog box, click the custom theme file name, click the Organize button on the toolbar, and then click *Delete* at the drop-down list. At the message asking if you are sure you want to send the theme to the Recycle Bin, click Yes.

▼ **Quick Steps**

Edit Custom Theme Colors
1. Click Design tab.
2. Click Colors button in Themes group.
3. Right-click desired custom theme.
4. Click *Edit*.
5. Make desired changes.
6. Click Save button.

Edit Custom Theme Fonts
1. Click Design tab.
2. Click Fonts button in Themes group.
3. Right-click desired custom theme.
4. Click *Edit*.
5. Make desired changes.
6. Click Save button.

Delete Custom Theme Colors
1. Click Design tab.
2. Click Colors button in Themes group.
3. Right-click desired custom theme.
4. Click *Delete*.
5. Click Yes.

Delete Custom Theme Fonts
1. Click Design tab.
2. Click Fonts button in Themes group.
3. Right-click desired custom theme.
4. Click *Delete*.
5. Click Yes.

Delete Custom Theme
1. Click Design tab.
2. Click More button in Themes group.
3. Click *Save Current Theme*.
4. Click custom theme.
5. Click Organize button, *Delete*.
6. Click Yes.

Project 4d **Deleting Custom Themes**

1. At a blank presentation, delete the custom theme colors by completing the following steps:
   a. Click the Design tab.
   b. Click the Colors button in the Themes group.
   c. Right-click the custom theme colors named with your first and last names.
   d. Click *Delete* at the shortcut menu.
   e. At the message asking if you want to delete the theme colors, click Yes.
2. Complete steps similar to those in Step 1 to delete the custom theme fonts you created named with your first and last names.
3. Delete the custom theme by completing the following steps:
   a. Click the More button that displays at the right side of the theme thumbnails.
   b. Click *Save Current Theme* located toward the bottom of the drop-down gallery.
   c. At the Save Current Theme dialog box, click the custom theme that begins with *C3* followed by your last name.
   d. Click the Organize button on the toolbar and then click *Delete* at the drop-down list.
   e. At the message asking if you are sure you want to send the theme to the Recycle Bin, click Yes.
   f. Click the Cancel button to close the dialog box.
4. Close the presentation without saving it.

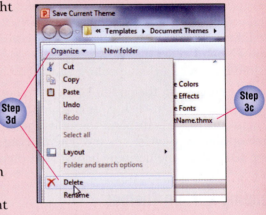

Chapter Summary

- The Font group in the Home tab contains buttons for applying character formatting to text in slides.

- Design themes apply a font to text in slides. You can change this default font with the Font and Font Size buttons in the Font group.

- Some buttons, such as the Font and Font Size buttons, contain the live preview feature, which allows you to see how the formatting affects your text without having to return to the presentation.

- You can also apply character formatting with options at the Font dialog box. Display this dialog box by clicking the Font group dialog box launcher.

- Select text in a slide and the Mini toolbar displays above the selected text in dimmed fashion. Move the mouse pointer to the toolbar and it becomes active.

- Use the Format Painter feature to apply formatting to more than one location in a slide or slides.

- The Paragraph group in the Home tab contains a number of buttons for applying paragraph formatting to text in slides.

- Customize paragraph formatting with options at the Paragraph dialog box with the Indents and Spacing tab selected. Display this dialog box by clicking the Paragraph group dialog box launcher or by clicking the Line Spacing button in the Paragraph group and then clicking *Line Spacing Options* at the drop-down list.

- Use the Columns button in the Paragraph group or options at the Columns dialog box to format selected text into columns. Display the Columns dialog box by clicking the Columns button and then clicking *More Columns* at the drop-down list.

- Use the Text Direction button or options at the Format Text Effects dialog box to rotate or stack text in a slide. Display the Format Text Effects dialog box by clicking the Text Direction button and then clicking *More Options* at the drop-down list.

- Use the Align Text button or options at the Format Text Effects dialog box to vertically align text in a slide.

- Customize bullets with options at the Bullets and Numbering dialog box with the Bulleted tab selected. Display this dialog box by clicking the Bullets button arrow and then clicking *Bullets and Numbering* at the drop-down list.

- Customize numbering with options at the Bullets and Numbering dialog box with the Numbered tab selected. Display this dialog box by clicking the Numbering button arrow and then clicking *Bullets and Numbering* at the drop-down list.

- Click the Quick Styles button in the Drawing group in the Home tab to apply formatting to a placeholder. The Drawing group also contains the Shape Fill, Shape Outline, and Shape Effects buttons you can use to customize a placeholder.

- Use the Colors button in the Themes group in the Design tab to change the theme colors and use the Fonts button to change the theme fonts.

- Use the Background Styles button in the Background group in the Design tab to customize the background of slides and insert a check mark in the *Hide Background Graphics* check box to remove the slide background graphic.

- Click the Page Setup button in the Design tab and the Page Setup dialog box displays containing options for changing the slide size and ratio, starting slide number, and the orientation of slides and notes, handouts, and outline pages.

- Create custom theme colors with options at the Create New Theme Colors dialog box. Display this dialog box by clicking the Colors button in the Themes group in the Design tab and then clicking *Create New Theme Colors* at the drop-down gallery.

- Create custom theme fonts with options at the Create New Theme Fonts dialog box. Display this dialog box by clicking the Fonts button in the Themes group in the Design tab and then clicking *Create New Theme Fonts* at the drop-down gallery.

- Save a custom theme at the Save Current Theme dialog box. Display this dialog box by clicking the Themes button in the Themes group in the Design tab and then clicking *Save Current Theme* at the drop-down gallery.
- Edit custom theme colors with options at the Edit Theme Colors dialog box and edit custom theme fonts with options at the Edit Theme Fonts dialog box.
- Delete custom theme colors by clicking the Theme Colors button, right-clicking the custom theme, and then clicking the *Delete* option.
- Delete custom theme fonts by clicking the Theme Fonts button, right-clicking the custom theme, and then clicking the *Delete* option.
- Delete a custom theme at the Save Current Theme dialog box. Display this dialog box by clicking the Themes button and then clicking *Save Current Theme* at the drop-down gallery.

Commands Review

FEATURE	RIBBON TAB, GROUP	BUTTON, OPTION	KEYBOARD SHORTCUT
Font dialog box	Home, Font		Ctrl + Shift + F
Format Painter	Home, Clipboard		
Paragraph dialog box	Home, Paragraph		
Columns dialog box	Home, Paragraph	, More Columns	
Format Text Effects dialog box	Home, Paragraph	, More Options	
Bullets and Numbering dialog box with Bulleted tab selected	Home, Paragraph	, Bullets and Numbering	
Bullets and Numbering dialog box with Numbered tab selected	Home, Paragraph	, Bullets and Numbering	
Format Background dialog box	Design, Background		
Page Setup dialog box	Design, Page Setup		
Create New Theme Colors dialog box	Design, Themes	, Create New Theme Colors	
Create New Theme Fonts dialog box	Design, Themes	, Create New Theme Fonts	
Save Current Theme dialog box	Design, Themes	, Save Current Theme	

Concepts Check Test Your Knowledge

Completion: In the space provided at the right, indicate the correct term, symbol, or command.

1. The Font button drop-down gallery is an example of this feature, which allows you to see how the font formatting affects your text without having to return to the presentation.   _____

2. Click this button to clear character formatting from selected text.   _____

3. Click this to display the Font dialog box.   _____

4. Select text in a slide and this displays in a dimmed fashion above the selected text.   _____

5. The Format Painter button is located in this group in the Home tab.   _____

6. Press this key to move text to the next tab stop (level).   _____

7. Use options at this dialog box to change text alignment, indentation, and spacing.   _____

8. Click this button in the Paragraph group and a drop-down list displays with options for rotating and stacking text.   _____

9. Use the Align Text button or options at this dialog box to vertically align text in a slide.   _____

10. Customize numbering with options at the Bullets and Numbering dialog box with this tab selected.   _____

11. The Quick Styles button is located in this group in the Home tab.   _____

12. Click this button to apply fill to a placeholder.   _____

13. Create custom theme colors with options at this dialog box.   _____

14. Save a custom theme at this dialog box.   _____

Skills Check Assess Your Performance

Assessment

1 CREATE, FORMAT, AND MODIFY A BENEFITS PRESENTATION

1. At a blank presentation, create the slides shown in Figure 3.12.
2. Apply the Oriel design theme.
3. Make Slide 1 active and then make the following changes:
   a. Select the title *BENEFITS PROGRAM*, change the font to Candara, the font size to 48, the font color to Ice Blue, Accent 5, Darker 50%, and apply italic formatting.
   b. Select the subtitle *Changes to Plans*, change the font to Candara, the font size to 32, the font color to Orange, Accent 1, Darker 50%, and apply shadow formatting.
   c. Click the title placeholder and then drag the placeholder up until the title is vertically centered on the slide.
   d. Click the subtitle placeholder and then drag the placeholder up so the subtitle is positioned just below the title.
4. Make Slide 2 active and then make the following changes:
   a. Select the title *INTRODUCTION*, change the font to Candara, the font size to 48 points, and apply shadow formatting.
   b. Using Format Painter, apply the title formatting to the titles in the remaining slides.
5. Center-align the titles in Slides 2 through 5.
6. Make Slide 2 active, select the bulleted text, and then change the line spacing to *2.0*.
7. Make Slide 3 active, select the bulleted text, and then change the line spacing to *2.0*.
8. Make Slide 4 active, select the bulleted text, and then change the line spacing to *1.5*.
9. Make Slide 5 active, select the bulleted text, and then change the spacing after paragraphs to *18 pt*. **Hint: Do this at the Paragraph dialog box.**
10. Make Slide 2 active and then select the bulleted text. Display the Bullets and Numbering dialog box with the Numbered tab selected, choose the *1. 2. 3.* option, change the size to *85%*, and then close the dialog box.
11. Make Slide 3 active and then select the bulleted text. Display the Bullets and Numbering dialog box with the Numbered tab selected, choose the *1. 2. 3.* option, change the size to *85%*, change the starting number to *5*, and then close the dialog box.
12. Make Slide 4 active, select the bulleted text, and then change the bullets to *Hollow Square Bullets*.
13. Make Slide 5 active, select the bulleted text, and then change the bullets to *Hollow Square Bullets*.
14. Apply the *Style 5* background style to slides.
15. Save the presentation and name it **P-C3-A1-Benefits**.
16. Print the presentation as a handout with six slides horizontally per page.
17. Change the theme colors to *Solstice*.
18. Apply the *Style 2* background style to slides.
19. Apply a transition and sound of your choosing to each slide.

20. Run the presentation.
21. Print the presentation as a handout with six slides horizontally per page.
22. Save and then close **P-C3-A1-Benefits.pptx**.

Figure 3.12 Assessment 1

Slide 1 Title   = BENEFITS PROGRAM
         Subtitle = Changes to Plans

Slide 2 Title   = INTRODUCTION
         Content = • Changes made for 2013
                     • Description of eligibility
                     • Instructions for enrolling new members
                     • Overview of medical and dental coverage

Slide 3 Title   = INTRODUCTION
         Content = • Expanded enrollment forms
                     • Glossary defining terms
                     • Telephone directory
                     • Pamphlet with commonly asked questions

Slide 4 Title   = WHAT'S NEW
         Content = • New medical plans
                       ○ Plan 2013
                       ○ Premier Plan
                     • Changes in monthly contributions
                     • Paying with pretax dollars
                     • Contributions toward spouse's coverage

Slide 5 Title   = COST SHARING
         Content = • Increased deductible
                     • New coinsurance amount
                     • Higher coinsurance amount for retail prescription drugs
                     • Co-payment for mail-order medicines
                     • New stop loss limit

Assessment

2   FORMAT AND MODIFY A PERENNIALS PRESENTATION

1. Open **PerennialsPres.pptx** and then save the presentation with Save As and name it **P-C3-A2-PerennialsPres**.
2. Change the theme fonts to *Opulent*. (Make sure you change the theme fonts and **not** the theme.)
3. Make Slide 3 active, select the bulleted text, and then create and apply a custom bullet using a flower symbol in a complementary color. (You can find a flower symbol in the *Wingdings* font in the Symbol dialog box.)
4. With Slide 3 active, format the bulleted text into two columns and change the line spacing to *2*. Make sure each column contains four bulleted items. If not, make any spacing or other corrections to make the columns even.

5. Make Slide 4 active and then arrange the bulleted text more attractively on the slide. (You determine the formatting and position.)
6. Make Slide 5 active and then format the bulleted text into two columns with three bulleted items in each column. Make any spacing or formatting changes to improve the visual appeal of the slide.
7. Make Slide 6 active and then format the bulleted text into two columns with three bulleted items in each column. Make any spacing or formatting change to improve the visual appeal of the slide.
8. Make any other changes to slides to improve the visual appeal of each slide.
9. Print the presentation with four slides horizontally per page.
10. Add a transition and sound of your choosing to all slides in the presentation.
11. Run the presentation.
12. Save and then close **P-C3-A2-PerennialsPres.pptx**.

Assessment

3   CREATE AND APPLY A CUSTOM THEME TO A TRAVEL PRESENTATION

1. At a blank presentation, apply the *Opulent* design theme.
2. Create custom theme colors named with your first and last names that changes the following colors:
   a. At the Create New Theme Colors dialog box, change the *Text/Background - Light 1* option to *Gold, Accent 4, Lighter 80%*.
   b. Change the *Text/Background - Dark 2* option to *Green* (sixth color from the left in the **Standard Colors** row).
3. Create custom theme fonts named with your first and last names that applies the following fonts:
   a. At the Create New Theme Fonts dialog box, change the *Heading font* to *Copperplate Gothic Bold*.
   b. Change the *Body font* to *Rockwell*.
4. Save the current theme as a custom theme named with your first and last names. ***Hint: Do this at the Save Current Theme dialog box.***
5. Close the presentation without saving it.
6. Open **TravelEngland.pptx** and then save the presentation with Save As and name it **P-C3-A3-TravelEngland**.
7. Apply the custom theme named with your first and last names.
8. Improve the visual display of the bulleted text in Slides 2 and 3 by increasing the spacing between items and positioning the bulleted item placeholders attractively in the slides.
9. Make Slide 4 active, increase the spacing between bulleted items and then format the text into two columns. Make sure that each column contains three bulleted items. Consider decreasing the size of the placeholder.
10. Format the bulleted text in Slides 5 and 6 into two columns with four bulleted items in each column. Consider decreasing the size of the placeholder.
11. Print the presentation as a handout with six slides horizontally per page.
12. Add a transition and sound of your choosing to all slides in the presentation.
13. Run the presentation.
14. Save and then close **P-C3-A3-TravelEngland.pptx**.
15. Display a blank presentation and then delete the custom theme colors, custom theme fonts, and custom theme you created for this assessment.
16. Close the presentation without saving it.

4 PREPARE A PRESENTATION ON ONLINE SHOPPING

1. Open Microsoft Word and then open the document **OnlineShopping.docx** that is located in the PowerPoint2010C3 folder on your storage medium.
2. Print the document by clicking the File tab, clicking the Print tab, and then clicking the Print button at the Print tab Backstage view.
3. Close **OnlineShopping.docx** and then exit Word.
4. At a blank PowerPoint presentation, use the information you printed to create a presentation on online shopping with the following specifications:
   a. Create a slide with the title of your presentation. Type your name as the subtitle.
   b. Create slides (you determine the number of slides) that summarize the information you printed. (Make sure the slides are not crowded with too much information.)
   c. Apply a design theme of your choosing.
   d. Change the design theme colors.
   e. Change the design theme fonts.
   f. Apply a transition and sound of your choosing to all slides.
5. Save the presentation and name it **P-C3-A4-OnlineShopping**.
6. Run the presentation.
7. Print the presentation as a handout with six slides horizontally per page.
8. Close **P-C3-A4-OnlineShopping.pptx**.

Visual Benchmark Demonstrate Your Proficiency

FORMAT A PRESENTATION ON HOME SAFETY

1. Open **HomeSafety.pptx** and then save the presentation with Save As and name it **P-C3-VB-HomeSafety**.
2. Format the presentation so the slides appear as shown in Figure 3.13 with the following specifications.
   a. Apply the *Civic* theme, the *Origin* theme colors, and the *Module* theme fonts.
   b. Apply the *Style 1* background style.
   c. Change the font size of the title in Slide 1 to *48* and apply bold formatting.
   d. Change the font size of the subtitle in Slide 1 to *24* and apply italics.
   e. Change the font of the titles in Slides 2 through 6 to 44-point bold in *Blue-Gray, Accent 1* color.
   f. Change the line spacing, apply column formatting, and then apply other formatting so your slides display similarly to the slides shown in Figure 3.13.
3. Print the presentation as a handout with six slides horizontally per page.
4. Save and then close the presentation.

Figure 3.13 Visual Benchmark

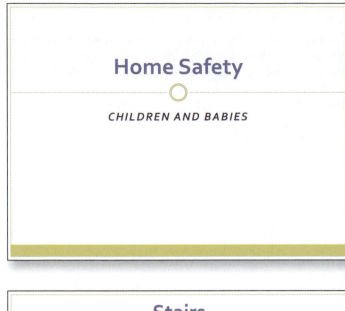

Home Safety

CHILDREN AND BABIES

Stairs

- Fit stair gates at the bottom or top of stairs.
  - ○ Bars of gates should be no more than 2.5 inches apart.
  - ○ Never climb over gate because child may copy you.
- Regularly check that your banister is secured.
- Replace loose or damaged carpet or steps.

Kitchen

- Put safety locks on cabinets and drawers, especially those containing dangerous objects.
- Keep garbage containers in a cabinet with a child-restraint lock.
- Always be aware of what your child can reach and keep dangerous objects out of child's reach on work areas.
- Keep child away from oven doors as some get very hot while the oven is in use.

Figure 3.13 Visual Benchmark

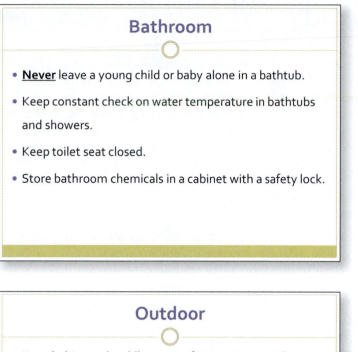

Case Study Apply Your Skills

Part 1

You are the assistant to Gina Coletti, manager of La Dolce Vita, an Italian restaurant. She has been working on a new lunch menu and wants to present the new menu at the upcoming staff meeting. She has asked you to prepare a presentation she can use at the meeting. Open the Word document named **LunchMenu.docx** and then print the document. Close the document and then exit Word. Using the information you printed, create a presentation and apply the Civic design theme to the presentation. Make any formatting changes to improve the visual appeal of the presentation. Save the presentation and name it **P-C3-CS-LunchMenu**.

Part 2

Ms. Coletti has looked over the presentation and has asked you to apply color and font formatting consistent with other restaurant publications. With **P-C3-CS-LunchMenu.pptx** open, create custom theme colors that change the *Text/Background - Light 2* color to *Dark Yellow, Accent 2, Lighter 80%* and the *Accent 3* color to *Green, Accent 5, Darker 25%*. Create custom theme fonts that apply Monotype Corsiva as the heading font and Garamond as the body font. Save the custom theme and name it *LaDolceVita* followed by your initials. Add a transition and sound to all slides in the presentation. Print the presentation as a handout with six slides horizontally per page. Save and then close **P-C3-CS-LunchMenu.pptx**.

Part 3

Ms. Coletti needs further information for the meeting. She wants you to use the Internet to search for two companies that print restaurant menus, two companies that design restaurant menus, and the names of two restaurant menu design software programs. Prepare a presentation with the information you find on the Internet and then apply your custom theme to the presentation. Make any formatting changes to improve the visual appeal of each slide. Add a transition and sound to each slide in the presentation. Save the presentation and name it **P-C3-CS-RestMenus.pptx**. Print the presentation as a handout with six slides horizontally per page. Close **P-C3-CS-RestMenus.pptx**.

Part 4

When running **P-C3-CS-RestMenus.pptx**, Ms. Coletti would like to link to a couple of the sites you list in the presentation. Use PowerPoint's Help feature to learn how to insert a hyperlink in a slide to a web page or website. Create at least two hyperlinks between sites you list in the presentation and the web page or website. Print the slide(s) containing the hyperlinks. Save and then close **P-C3-CS-RestMenus.pptx**.

Inserting Elements in Slides

PERFORMANCE OBJECTIVES

Upon successful completion of Chapter 4, you will be able to:

- Insert, format, select, and align a text box
- Set tabs in a text box
- Insert, format, and copy shapes
- Display rulers, gridlines, and guides
- Group and ungroup objects
- Insert, crop, size, move, and format a picture
- Insert a picture as a slide background
- Insert, size, scale, rotate, and position a clip art image
- Create and insert a screenshot
- Create and format WordArt text
- Insert objects such as a header, footer, date, slide number, and symbol

Tutorials

A presentation consisting only of text slides may have important information in it that will be overlooked by the audience because a slide contains too much text. Adding visual elements, where appropriate, can help deliver the message to your audience by adding interest and impact to the information. In this chapter, you will learn how to create visual elements on slides such as text boxes, shapes, pictures, clip art images, a screenshot, and WordArt text. These elements will make the delivery of your presentation a dynamic experience for your audience. The model answer for this chapter's project appears on the following page.

PowerPoint2010C4

Note: Before beginning the project, copy to your storage medium the PowerPoint2010C4 subfolder from the PowerPoint2010 folder on the CD that accompanies this textbook and then make PowerPoint2010C4 the active folder.

Project 1 Create a Company Presentation Containing Text Boxes, Shapes, and Images
P-C4-P1-AddisonInd.pptx

P-C4-P1-AddisonInd.pptx   8/24/2012

Executive Officers

Shipping Contracts

European Division 2013

Draft Invitation
Grand Opening
Addison Industries
European Division

Technology
Equipment
Software
Personnel

Production Percentages

Addison Industries 2013

Student Name   1
Student Name   2

<table>
<tr><td>ROJECT</td><td>1</td><td>Create a Company Presentation Containing Text Boxes, Shapes, and Images</td><td>14 Parts</td></tr>
</table>

You will create a company presentation that includes slides with text boxes, a slide with tabbed text in a text box, slides with shapes and text, slides with pictures, and slides with clip art images. You will also insert elements in slides such as slide numbers, headers, footers, date, and symbols.

Inserting and Formatting Text Boxes

Many of the slide layouts contain placeholders for entering text and other elements in a document. Along with placeholders, you can insert and format a text box. To insert a text box in a slide, click the Insert tab, click the Text Box button in the Text group, and the mouse pointer displays as a thin, down-pointing arrow. Using the mouse, drag in the slide to create the text box. You can also click in the desired location and a small text box is inserted in the slide.

Formatting a Text Box

When you insert a text box in the document, the Home tab displays. Use options in the Drawing group to format the text box by applying a Quick Style or adding a shape fill, outline, or effect. Format a text box in a manner similar to formatting

Model Answers

a placeholder. In addition to the options in the Drawing group, you can also apply formatting to a text box with options in the Drawing Tools Format tab. Click this tab and the ribbon displays as shown in Figure 4.1. The Shape Styles group contains the same options as the Drawing group in the Home tab. With other options in the tab, you can apply WordArt formatting to text and arrange and size the text box.

Move a text box in the same manner as you move a placeholder. Click the text box to select it, position the mouse pointer on the text box border until the pointer displays with a four-headed arrow attached, and then drag the text box to the desired position. Change the size of a selected text box using the sizing handles that display around the box. You can also use the *Shape Height* and *Shape Width* measurement boxes in the Size group in the Drawing Tools Format tab to specify the text box height and width.

PowerPoint provides dialog boxes with options for formatting and customizing a text box. Click the Shape Styles group dialog box launcher and the Format Shape dialog box displays. Click an option in the left panel to specify what you want to format and then choose options that display at the right side of the dialog box. Click the WordArt Styles group dialog box launcher and the Format Text Effects dialog box displays with options for formatting the text in a text box. Click an option in the left panel to specify what you want to format and then choose options that display at the right side of the dialog box.

You can apply the same formatting to text in a text box that you apply to text in a placeholder. For example, you can use the buttons in the Paragraph group in the Home tab to align text horizontally and vertically in a text box, change text direction, set text in columns, and set internal margins for the text in the text box.

Selecting Multiple Objects

You can select multiple text boxes and other objects in a slide and then apply formatting or align and arrange the objects in the slide. To select all objects in a slide, click the Select button in the Editing group in the Home tab and then click *Select All* at the drop-down list. You can also select all objects in a slide with the keyboard shortcut, Ctrl + A. To select specific text boxes or objects in a slide, click the first object, hold down the Shift key, and then click each of the other desired objects.

Aligning Text Boxes

With the Align button in the Arrange group in the Drawing Tools Format tab, you can align the edge of multiple objects in a slide. Click the Align button and a drop-down list of alignment options displays including options for aligning objects vertically and horizontally and distributing objects.

Figure 4.1 Drawing Tools Format Tab

HINT

Use a text box to place text anywhere in a slide. Text in inserted text boxes does not appear in the Outline view.

▼ **Quick Steps**

Select All Text Boxes
1. Click Select button.
2. Click *Select All.*
OR
Press Ctrl + A.

HINT

To select an object that is behind another object, select the top object and then press the Tab key to cycle through and select the other objects.

Select

Align

1. At a blank presentation, apply a design and change colors by completing the following steps:
   a. Click the Design tab.
   b. Click the More button that displays at the right side of the theme thumbnails and then click *Technic* at the drop-down gallery.
   c. Click the Colors button in the Themes group and then click *Trek* at the drop-down gallery.
2. Click in the title placeholder, type **Addison**, press the Enter key, and then type **Industries**.
3. Click in the subtitle placeholder and then type **Annual Report**.
4. Insert a text box in the slide by completing the following steps:
   a. Click the Insert tab.
   b. Click the Text Box button in the Text group.
   c. Click in the lower right corner of the slide. (This inserts a small, selected text box in the slide.)
   d. Type **January 2013**.
   e. Click outside the text box to deselect it.

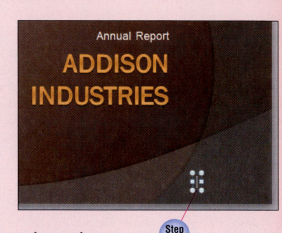

Step 4c

5. After looking at the slide, you decide to delete the text box by completing the following steps:
   a. Click in the text box to select it.
   b. Position the mouse pointer on the text box border until the mouse pointer displays with a four-headed arrow attached and then click the left mouse button. (This changes the text box border from a dashed border line to a solid border line.)
   c. Press the Delete key.
6. Insert a new slide with the *Blank* layout by completing the following steps:
   a. Click the Home tab.
   b. Click the New Slide button arrow.
   c. Click the *Blank* layout at the drop-down list.
7. Insert and format the *Safety* text box shown in Figure 4.2 (on page 127) by completing the following steps:
   a. Click the Insert tab.
   b. Click the Text Box button in the Text group.
   c. Click anywhere in the slide. (This inserts a small, selected text box in the slide.)
   d. Type **Safety**.
   e. Select the text and then change the font to Copperplate Gothic Bold, the font size to 36, and the font color to Orange (third color option from the left in the *Standard Colors* row).
   f. Click the Text Direction button in the Paragraph group in the Home tab and then click *Stacked* at the drop-down list.
   g. Click the Drawing Tools Format tab.
   h. Click the down-pointing arrow at the right side of the *Shape Height* measurement box in the Size group until *4″* displays in the box. (Make sure the measurement in the *Shape Width* box is *0.86″*.)

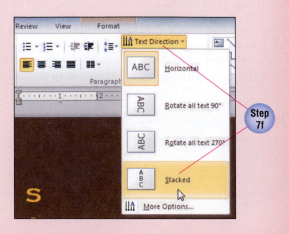

Step 7f

i. Click the More button that displays at the right side of the styles thumbnails in the Shape Styles group and then click the *Moderate Effect - Orange, Accent 6* option (last option in the fifth row).

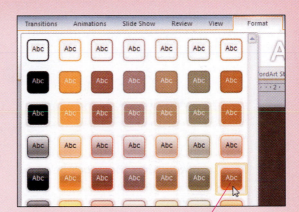

Step 7i

j. Drag the text box so it is positioned as shown in Figure 4.2.

8. Insert and size the other text box shown in Figure 4.2 by completing the following steps:
   a. Click the Insert tab.
   b. Click the Text Box button in the Text group.
   c. Drag in the slide to create a text box. (Drag to the approximate width of the text box in Figure 4.2.)
   d. Type the text shown in the text box in Figure 4.2 in a single column. Type the text in the first column and then type the text in the second column. (Your text will display as shown at the right in one column, in a smaller font, and in a different line spacing than you see in the figure.)

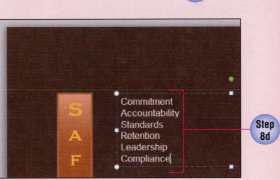

Step 8d

   e. Select the text and then change the font size to 32.
   f. Click the Line Spacing button in the Paragraph group and then click *2.0* at the drop-down list. (The text may flow off the slide.)
   g. Click the Columns button in the Paragraph group and then click *Two Columns* at the drop-down list.
   h. Click the Drawing Tools Format tab.
   i. Click the down-pointing arrow at the right side of the *Shape Height* measurement box until *4″* displays in the box.
   j. Click the up- or down-pointing arrow at the right side of the *Shape Width* measurement box until *7″* displays in the box.

9. Apply a picture fill by completing the following steps:
   a. Click the Shape Styles group dialog box launcher.
   b. With the Fill option selected in the left panel of the Format Shape dialog box, click the *Picture or texture fill* option.
   c. Click the File button in the dialog box.
   d. At the Insert Picture dialog box, navigate to the PowerPoint2010C4 folder on your storage medium and then double-click **Ship.jpg**.
   e. Click the Close button to close the dialog box.

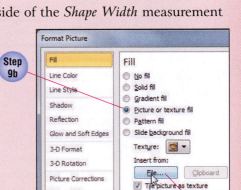

Step 9b

Step 9c

10. Insert a pattern in the text box instead of a picture by completing the following steps:
    a. Click the Shape Styles group dialog box launcher.

b. Click the *Fill* option in the left panel in the Format Shape dialog box and then click the *Pattern fill* option.

c. Click the *80%* option in the pattern palette (second option from the left in the fifth row).

d. Click the Foreground Color button and then click the *Orange, Accent 6, Darker 50%* option (bottom option in the last column in the *Theme Colors* section).

e. Click the Close button to close the dialog box.

11. Change the text box outline weight by clicking the Shape Outline button arrow in the Shape Styles group, pointing to *Weight*, and then clicking the *3 pt* option at the side menu.

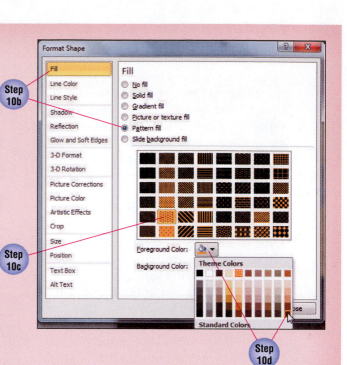

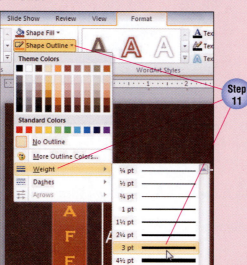

12. Apply a fill color instead of a pattern and change the outline color and effect by completing the following steps:

a. Click the Shape Fill button arrow in the Shape Styles group and then click *Orange, Accent 6, Lighter 40%* at the drop-down gallery.

b. Click the Shape Fill button arrow in the Shape Styles group, point to *Gradient*, and then click *Linear Up* in the *Dark Variations* section at the side menu.

c. Click the Shape Outline button arrow in the Shape Styles group and then click *Dark Red* at the drop-down gallery (first color from the left in the *Standard Colors* row).

d. Click the Shape Outline button arrow in the Shape Styles group, point to *Weight*, and then click ¾ *pt* at the side menu.

e. Click the Shape Effects button in the Shape Styles group, point to *Shadow*, and then click *Inside Diagonal Top Right* at the side menu (last option in the top row of the *Inner* section).

13. Change the internal margins by completing the following steps:
   a. Click the Home tab.
   b. Click the Text Direction button and then click *More Options* at the drop-down list.
   c. In the *Internal margin* section of the Format Text Effects dialog box, change the *Left* measurement to *0.6″* and the *Top* and *Bottom* measurements to *0.4″*.
   d. Click the Close button to close the dialog box.

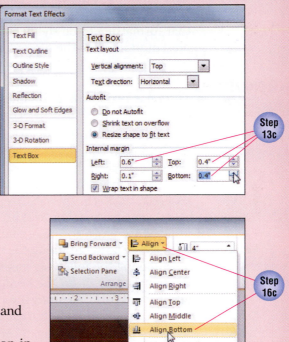

14. With the text box selected, click the Drawing Tools Format tab and then change the shape height measurement to *4″*.

15. Click in the slide outside the text box.

16. Arrange the text boxes by completing the following steps:
   a. Press Ctrl + A to select both text boxes.
   b. Click the Drawing Tools Format tab.
   c. Click the Align button in the Arrange group and then click *Align Bottom* at the drop-down list.
   d. Drag both boxes to the approximate location in the slide as shown in Figure 4.2.

17. Save the presentation and name it **P-C4-P1-AddisonInd**.

Figure 4.2 Project 1a, Slide 2

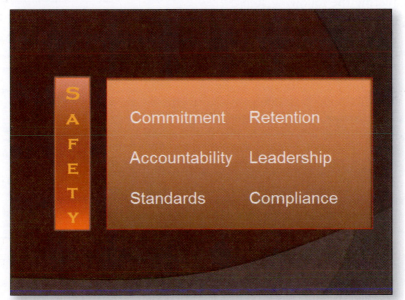

You can format and customize text boxes with options at a shortcut menu. To format a text box with a shortcut menu, position the mouse pointer on the border of the text box until the pointer displays with a four-headed arrow attached and then click the right mouse button. At the shortcut menu, click the *Size and Position* option to display the Format Shape dialog box with the Size option selected or click the *Format Shape* option to display the Format Shape dialog box with the *Fill* option selected. If you apply formatting to a text box and then want that formatting to be the default for other text boxes you create in the current presentation, click the *Set as Default Text Box* option at the shortcut menu.

Project 1b   Format a Text Box and Set the Default Text Box   Part 2 of 15

1. With **P-C4-P1-AddisonInd.pptx** open, make sure Slide 2 is the active slide and then complete the following steps:
    a. Click the Insert tab, click the Text Box button, and then click in the lower right corner of the slide.
    b. Type **Default text box**. (In the next step you will change the default text box. You will use the text box you just inserted to return to the original text box.)
2. Set as default the text box containing the word *SAFETY* by completing the following steps:
    a. Position the mouse pointer on the border of the text box containing the word *SAFETY* until the pointer displays with a four-headed arrow attached and then click the right mouse button.
    b. Click the *Set as Default Text Box* option at the shortcut menu.
3. Make Slide 1 active.
4. Insert a text box by clicking the Insert tab, clicking the Text Box button, and then clicking between the company name and the left side of the slide.
5. Type the text **2012** in the text box.
6. Change the *Autofit* option and wrap text in the text box by completing the following steps:
    a. Position the mouse pointer on the border of the text box until the pointer displays with a four-headed arrow attached and then click the right mouse button.
    b. Click the *Size and Position* option at the shortcut menu.
    c. At the Format Shape dialog box, click the *Text Box* option in the left panel of the dialog box.
    d. Click the *Wrap text in shape* option to insert a check mark.
    e. Click the *Shrink text on overflow* option in the *Autofit* section of the dialog box.
    f. Click the Close button to close the dialog box.
7. Insert text in the text box by clicking immediately above the first *2* (in 2012) in the text box, typing **Report**, and then pressing the spacebar.
8. Press Ctrl + E to center-align the text in the text box.

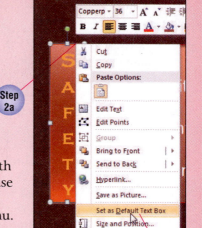

Step 2a

Step 2b

Step 6e

Step 6d

Step 6c

9. With the text box selected, change the shape of the text box by completing the following steps:
   a. Click the Drawing Tools Format tab to make the tab active.
   b. Click the Edit Shape button in the Insert Shapes group, point to *Change Shape*, and then click the *Bevel* option (last option in the second row in the *Basic Shapes* section).

Step 9b

10. Precisely position the text box by completing the following steps:
    a. Right-click the border of the text box and then click *Size and Position* at the shortcut menu.
    b. At the Format Shape dialog box, click the *Position* option in the left panel of the dialog box.
    c. Change the *Horizontal* measurement in the *Position on slide* section to *2.8″*.
    d. Change the *Vertical* measurement in the *Position on slide* section to *2.4″*.
    e. Click the Close button to close the dialog box.
11. Return to the original text box by completing the following steps:
    a. Make Slide 2 active.
    b. Click in the text box containing the words *Default text box*.
    c. Position the mouse pointer on the border of the text box until the pointer displays with a four-headed arrow attached and then click the right mouse button.
    d. Click the *Set as Default Text Box* option at the shortcut menu.
    e. Press the Delete key to delete the text box.
12. Save **P-C4-P1-AddisonInd.pptx**.

Setting Tabs in a Text Box

Inside a text box, you may want to align text in columns using tabs. A text box, by default, contains left alignment tabs that display as light gray marks along the bottom of the horizontal ruler. (If the ruler is not visible, display the horizontal ruler as well as the vertical ruler by clicking the View tab and then clicking the *Ruler* check box in the Show group.) You can change these default left alignment tabs to center, right, or decimal. To change to a different tab alignment, click the Alignment button located at the left side of the horizontal ruler. Display the desired tab alignment symbol and then click at the desired position on the horizontal ruler. When you set a tab on the horizontal ruler, any default tabs to the left of the new tab are deleted. You can move tabs on the horizontal ruler by using the mouse to drag the tab to the desired position. To delete a tab, use the mouse to drag the tab off of the ruler.

You can also set tabs with options at the Tabs dialog box. To display this dialog box, click the Paragraph group dialog box launcher. At the Paragraph dialog box, click the Tabs button that displays in the lower left corner. At the Tabs dialog box, type a tab position in the *Tab stop position* text box, choose a tab alignment with options in the *Alignment* section, and then click the Set button. Clear a specific tab by typing the tab stop position in the *Tab stop position* text box and then clicking the Clear button. Clear all tabs from the horizontal ruler by clicking the Clear All button. When all desired changes are made, click OK to close the Tabs dialog box and then click OK to close the Paragraph dialog box.

HINT
Tab stops help you align your text in a slide.

Left Tab

Center Tab

Right Tab

1. With **P-C4-P1-AddisonInd.pptx** open, make Slide 1 active and then click the Home tab.
2. Click the New Slide button arrow and then click the *Title Only* layout.
3. Click in the placeholder text *Click to add title* and then type **Executive Officers**.
4. Draw a text box by completing the following steps:
   a. Click the Insert tab.
   b. Click the Text Box button in the Text group.
   c. Draw a text box in the slide that is approximately 8 inches wide and 0.5 inch tall.
5. Change tabs in the text box by completing the following steps:
   a. With the insertion point inside the text box, make sure the horizontal ruler displays. (If not, click the View tab and then click the *Ruler* check box in the Show group.)

   b. Check the alignment button at the left side of the horizontal ruler and make sure the left tab symbol displays.

   c. Position the tip of the mouse pointer on the horizontal ruler below the 0.5-inch mark and then click the left mouse button.

   d. Click once on the Alignment button to display the Center alignment symbol.

   e. Click on the horizontal ruler immediately below the 4-inch mark on the horizontal ruler.

   f. Click once on the Alignment button to display the Right alignment symbol.

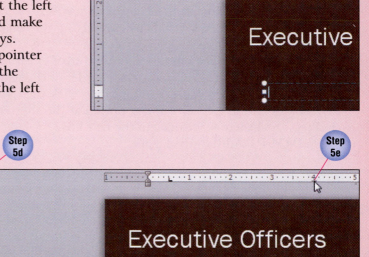

   g. Click on the horizontal ruler immediately below the 7.5-inch mark. (You may need to expand the size of the text box to set the tab at the 7.5-inch mark.)
6. Type the text in the text box as shown in the slide in Figure 4.3. Make sure you press the Tab key before typing text in the first column. (This moves the insertion point to the first tab, which is a left alignment tab.) Bold the three column headings—*Name*, *Title*, and *Number*.
7. When you are finished typing the text in the text box, press Ctrl + A to select all of the text in the text box and then change the line spacing to 1.5.
8. With the text still selected, drag the left alignment marker on the horizontal ruler from the 0.5-inch mark to the 0.25-inch mark and then drag the right alignment marker on the horizontal ruler from the 7.5-inch mark on the ruler to the 7-inch mark.
9. Position the text box as shown in Figure 4.3.
10. Save **P-C4-P1-AddisonInd.pptx**.

Figure 4.3 Project 1c, Slide 2

Executive Officers

Name	Title	Number
Taylor Hallowell	Chief Executive Officer	555-4321
Gina Rodgers	Chief Financial Officer	555-4203
Samuel Weinberg	President	555-4421
Leslie Pena	Vice President	555-3122
Leticia Reynolds	Vice President	555-3004
Gerald Yuan	Vice President	555-2310
Michael Anderson	Vice President	555-3877

Inserting, Formatting, and Copying Shapes

You can draw shapes in a slide using the Shapes button in the Drawing group or with the Shapes button in the Illustrations group in the Insert tab. With the Shapes button drop-down list, you can choose to draw shapes including lines, basic shapes, block arrows, flow chart symbols, callouts, stars, and banners. Click a shape and the mouse pointer displays as crosshairs (plus sign). Click in the slide to insert the shape or position the crosshairs in the slide and then drag to create the shape. Apply formatting to a shape in a manner similar to formatting a text box. Format a shape with buttons in the Drawing group in the Home tab, with buttons in the Drawing Tools Format tab, or with options at the shortcut menu. Display the shortcut menu by right-clicking a shape.

If you choose a shape in the *Lines* section of the drop-down list, the shape you draw is considered a **line drawing**. If you choose an option in the other sections of the drop-down list, the shape you draw is considered an **enclosed object**. When drawing an enclosed object, you can maintain the proportions of the shape by holding down the Shift key while dragging with the mouse to create the shape.

Quick Steps

Insert a Shape
1. Click Insert tab.
2. Click Shapes button.
3. Click desired shape at drop-down list.
4. Drag in slide to create shape.

HINT

Many shapes have an adjustment handle you can use to change the most prominent feature of the shape.

Shapes

Project 1d **Drawing and Formatting Lines and Shapes** **Part 4 of 15**

1. With **P-C4-P1-AddisonInd.pptx** open, make Slide 3 active.
2. Click the New Slide button arrow and then click the *Blank* layout at the drop-down list.
3. Insert and format the square shown in the lower left corner of the slide in Figure 4.4 (on page 134) by completing the following steps:
   a. Make sure the Home tab is selected.
   b. Click the More button located to the right of the shape thumbnails in the Drawing group.

c. Click the *Rectangle* shape in the *Rectangles* section of the drop-down list.

d. Hold down the Shift key and then draw a square the approximate size of the square shown in Figure 4.4.

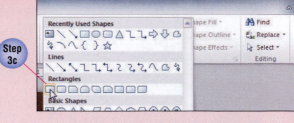

Step 3c

e. With the square selected, click the Quick Styles button in the Drawing group and then click *Moderate Effect - Orange, Accent 1* (second option from the left in the fifth row).

f. Click the Drawing Tools Format tab.

g. Change the *Shape Height* and *Shape Width* to *1.6"*.

h. If necessary, drag the square so it is positioned as shown in Figure 4.4.

Step 3e

4. Insert the word *Safety* in the square by completing the following steps:
   a. With the shape selected, type **Safety**.
   b. Select *Safety* and then change the font to Copperplate Gothic Bold, change the font size to 24, and change the font color to Brown, Accent 2, Darker 50%.

5. Draw and format the line shown in Figure 4.4 by completing the following steps:
   a. Click the Insert tab.
   b. Click the Shapes button in the Illustrations group and then click *Arrow* in the *Lines* section.

Step 5a

Step 5b

   c. Position the mouse pointer (cross hairs) in the upper right corner of the square and then drag up to the approximate location shown in Figure 4.4.
   d. With the arrow line selected, click the Drawing Tools Format tab.
   e. Click the Shape Outline button arrow in the Shape Styles group, point to *Weight*, and then click *4½ pt* at the side menu.
   f. Click the Shape Effects button in the Shape Styles group, point to *Bevel*, and then click *Circle* at the side menu (first option from the left in the top row in the *Bevel* section).

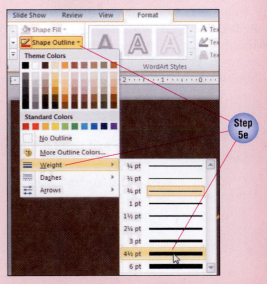

Step 5e

6. Draw a text box and type the text shown in the upper left corner of the slide in Figure 4.4 by completing the following steps:
   a. Click the Text Box button in the Insert Shapes group in the Drawing Tools Format tab.
   b. Click in the upper left side of the slide.

c. With the Home tab active, change the font size to 28 and then click the Bold button in the Font group.

d. Click the Align Text Right button in the Paragraph group.

e. Type **2012**, press the Enter key, and then type **Safety Training**.

f. If necessary, drag the text box so it is positioned as shown in Figure 4.4.

7. Draw and format the text box near the arrow line shown in Figure 4.4 by completing the following steps:

a. Click the Insert tab.

b. Click the Text Box button in the Text group.

c. Click in the slide (you determine the position).

d. Change the font size to 24, click the Bold button in the Font group in the Home tab, and then change the font color to Orange.

e. Type **1,000 ASA-trained employees**.

f. Position the mouse pointer on the green rotation handle, hold down the left mouse button, and then rotate the text box so it is angled as shown in Figure 4.4.

g. Drag the text box so it is positioned next to the arrow line.

8. Insert a shape by completing the following steps (you will use this shape to return to the original default shape):

a. Click the Insert tab, click the Shapes button in the Illustrations group, and then click the *Rectangle* shape in the *Rectangles* section of the drop-down list.

b. Click in the lower right corner of the slide.

9. Set the formatting of the square shape containing the word *SAFETY* as the default for future shapes in the current presentation by completing the following steps:

a. Position the mouse pointer on the shape border until the pointer displays with a four-headed arrow attached.

b. Click the right mouse button and then click the *Set as Default Shape* at the shortcut menu.

10. Make Slide 1 active and then insert a shape by completing the following steps:

a. Click the Insert tab, click the Shapes button, and then click the *Rectangle* shape (first shape in the *Rectangles* section).

b. Click in the lower right corner of the slide.

c. Type **AI**.

11. Size and position the shape by completing the following steps:

a. Right-click the shape border and then click the *Size and Position* option at the shortcut menu.

b. At the Format Shape dialog box with the *Size* option selected in the left panel, change the *Height* measurement and the *Width* measurement to *0.6″*.

c. Click the *Position* option in the left panel.

d. Change the *Horizontal* measurement to *9″* and the *Vertical* measurement to *6.5″*.

e. Click the Close button to close the dialog box.

12. Return to the original default shape by completing the following steps:

a. Make Slide 3 active.

b. Right-click the border of the shape in the lower right corner of the slide and then click *Set as Default Shape* at the shortcut menu.

c. Press the Delete key to delete the shape.

13. Save **P-C4-P1-AddisonInd.pptx**.

Figure 4.4 Project 1d, Slide 4

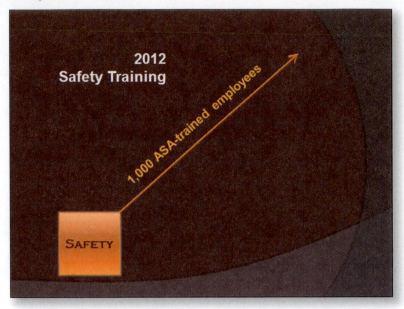

▼ Quick Steps

Copy a Shape
1. Select desired shape.
2. Click Copy button.
3. Position insertion point at desired location.
4. Click Paste button.
OR
1. Select desired shape.
2. Hold down Ctrl key.
3. Drag shape to desired location.

To copy a shape, select the shape and then click the Copy button in the Clipboard group in the Home tab. Position the insertion point at the location where you want the copied image and then click the Paste button. You can also copy a selected shape by holding down the Ctrl key while dragging the shape to the desired location.

Displaying Rulers, Gridlines, and Guides ■■■■■■■■

To help position objects such as placeholders, text boxes, and shapes, consider displaying horizontal and vertical rulers, gridlines, and/or drawing guides as shown in Figure 4.5. You can turn the horizontal and vertical ruler on and off with the *Ruler* check box in the Show group in the View tab. The Show group also contains a *Gridlines* check box. Insert a check mark in this check box and gridlines display in the active slide. Gridlines are intersecting lines that create a grid on the slide and are useful for aligning objects. You can also turn the display of gridlines on and off with the keyboard shortcut, Shift + F9.

Turn on drawing guides to help position objects on a slide. Drawing guides are horizontal and vertical dashed lines that display on the slide in the Slide pane as shown in Figure 4.5. To turn on the drawing guides, display the Grid and Guides dialog box shown in Figure 4.6. Display this dialog box by clicking the Show group dialog box launcher in the View tab. You can also display the Grid and Guides dialog box by selecting an object in the slide, clicking the Drawing Tools Format tab, clicking the Align button in the Arrange group, and then clicking *Grid Settings* at the drop-down list. At the dialog box, insert a check mark in the *Display drawing guides on screen* check box. By default, the horizontal and vertical drawing guides intersect in the middle of the slide. You can move these guides by dragging the guide with the mouse. As you drag the guide, a measurement displays next to the mouse pointer. Drawing guides and gridlines display on the slide but do not print.

Figure 4.5 Rulers, Gridlines, and Drawing Guides

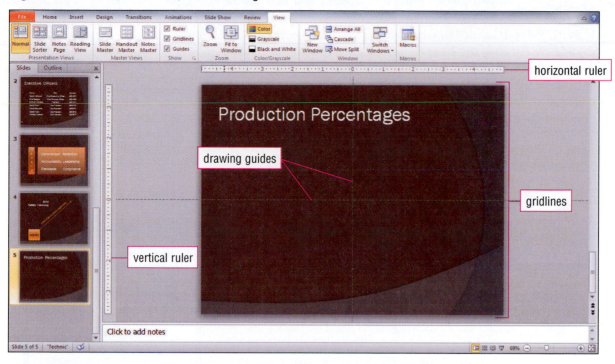

You can turn on gridlines with the *Gridlines* check box in the View tab and you can also turn them on by inserting a check mark in the *Display grid on screen* check box at the Grid and Guides dialog box. The horizontal and vertical spacing between the gridlines is 0.083 inch by default. You can change this measurement with the *Spacing* option at the Grid and Guides dialog box.

As you drag or draw an object on the slide, it is pulled into alignment with the nearest intersection of gridlines. This is because the *Snap objects to grid* option at the Grid and Guides dialog box is active by default. If you want to position an object precisely, you can remove the check mark from the *Snap objects to grid* to turn the feature off or you can hold down the Alt key while dragging an object. If you want an object to be pulled into alignment with another object, insert a check mark in the *Snap objects to other objects* check box.

Figure 4.6 Grid and Guides Dialog Box

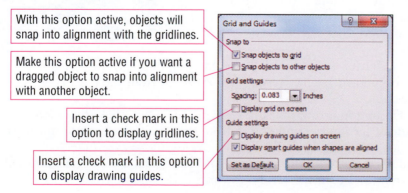

1. With **P-C4-P1-AddisonInd.pptx** open, make sure Slide 4 is active and then insert a new slide by clicking the New Slide button arrow in the Slides group in the Home tab and then clicking *Title Only* at the drop-down list.

2. Turn on the display of gridlines by clicking the View tab and then clicking *Gridlines* to insert a check mark in the check box.

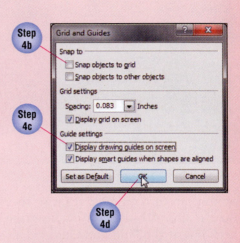

3. Click in the title placeholder and then type **Production Percentages**.

4. Turn on drawing guides and turn off the snap-to-grid feature by completing the following steps:
   a. Make sure the View tab is active and then click the Show group dialog box launcher.
   b. At the Grid and Guides dialog box, click the *Snap objects to grid* check box to remove the check mark.
   c. Click the *Display drawing guides on screen* check box to insert a check mark.
   d. Click OK.

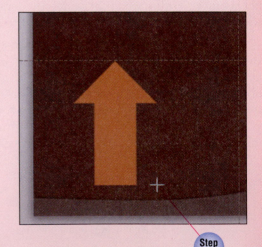

5. Draw the arrow at the left in the slide in Figure 4.7 (on page 138) by completing the following steps:
   a. Click outside the title placeholder to deselect it.
   b. Click the Insert tab.
   c. Click the Shapes button in the Illustrations group and then click the *Up Arrow* shape (third shape from the left in the top row of the *Block Arrows* section).
   d. Position the crosshairs on the intersection of the horizontal drawing guide and the first vertical gridline from the left.
   e. Hold down the left mouse button, drag down and to the right until the crosshairs are positioned on the intersection of the third vertical line from the left and the first horizontal line from the bottom, and then release the mouse button. (Your arrow should be the approximate size shown in Figure 4.7.)
   f. With the arrow selected, click the Drawing Tools Format tab.
   g. Click the Shape Fill button arrow in the Shape Styles group and then click *Light Blue* at the drop-down gallery (seventh color option from the left in the *Standard Colors* section).
   h. Click the Shape Fill button arrow, point to *Gradient*, and then click the *Linear Up* option in the *Dark Variations* section (second option from the left in the bottom row of the *Dark Variations* section).
   i. Click the Shape Effects button, point to *Bevel*, and then click the *Soft round* option (second option from the left in the second row in the *Bevel* section).

6. Insert a text box in the arrow by completing the following steps:
   a. Click the Insert tab.
   b. Click the Text Box button in the Text group.
   c. Drag to create a text box toward the top of the arrow the approximate size shown at the right.
   d. With the Home tab selected, change the font size to 20, turn on Bold, and then change the font color to Dark Blue.
   e. Click the Center button in the Paragraph group.
   f. Type **Plant 3**, press the Enter key, and then type **48%**.
   g. Move and/or size the text box so the text is positioned in the arrow as shown in Figure 4.7.

Step 6c

7. Copy the arrow and text box by completing the following steps:
   a. With the text box selected, hold down the Shift key and then click the arrow. (This selects the arrow and the text box.)
   b. Position the mouse pointer on the border of the selected arrow or text box until the mouse pointer displays with a four-headed arrow attached.
   c. Hold down the Ctrl key and drag the arrow and text box to the right so the tip of the arrow is positioned at the intersection of the horizontal and vertical drawing guides.

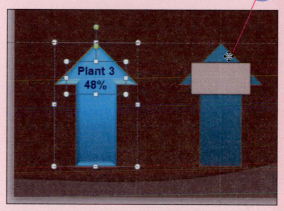

Step 7c

8. Move the vertical drawing guide and then copy the arrow and text box by completing the following steps:
   a. Click outside the arrow to deselect the arrow and the text box.
   b. Position the mouse pointer on the vertical drawing guide, hold down the left mouse button, drag right until the mouse pointer displays with *3.00* and a right-pointing arrow in a box, and then release the mouse button.

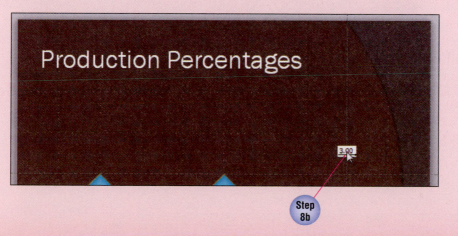

Step 8b

c. Click the arrow at the right, hold down the Shift key, and then click the text box inside the arrow.

d. Hold down the Ctrl key and drag the arrow and text box to the right so the tip of the arrow is positioned at the intersection of the horizontal and vertical drawing guides.

9. Increase the height of the middle arrow by completing the following steps:

a. Click the middle arrow to select it.

b. Using the mouse, drag the top middle sizing handle up to the next horizontal gridline.

c. Click the text box in the middle arrow and then drag the text box up to the position shown in Figure 4.7.

d. Complete similar steps to increase the height of the arrow at the right to the second horizontal gridline. Drag the text box to the position shown in Figure 4.7.

e. Change the text in the text box in the middle arrow to *Plant 1 72%* and change the text in the text box in the arrow at the right to *Plant 2 91%* (see Figure 4.7).

10. Turn off gridlines, drawing guides, and turn on the snap-to-grid feature by completing the following steps:

a. Click the text in the title placeholder.

b. Click the Drawing Tools Format tab.

c. Click the Align button in the Arrange group.

d. Click the *Grid Settings* option at the drop-down list.

e. At the Grid and Guides dialog box, click the *Snap objects to grid* check box to insert a check mark.

f. Click the *Display grid on screen* option to remove the check mark.

g. Click the *Display drawing guides on screen* check box to remove the check mark.

h. Click OK.

11. Save **P-C4-P1-AddisonInd.pptx**.

Figure 4.7 Project 1e, Slide 5

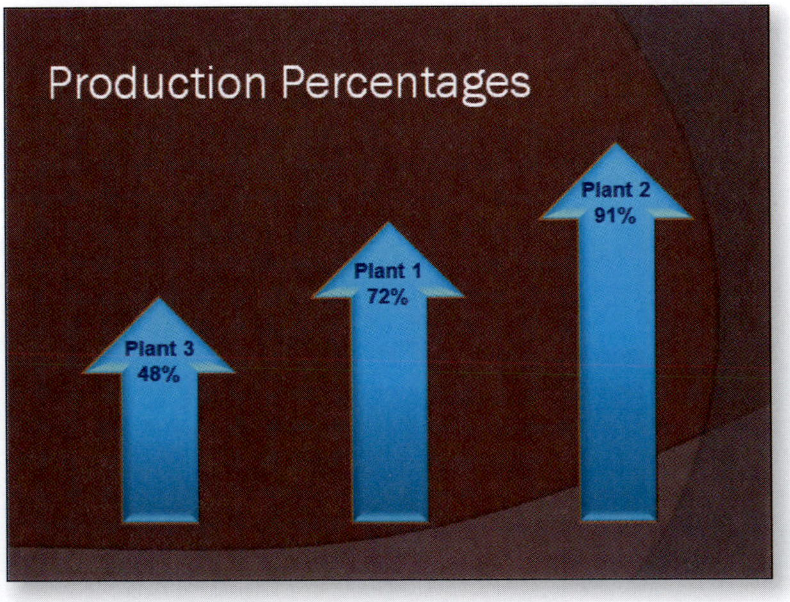

Grouping/Ungrouping Objects

If you want to apply the same formatting or make the same adjustments to the size or rotation of objects, group the objects. If you group objects and then apply a formatting such as a shape fill, effect, or shape style, the formatting is applied to each object within the group. With objects grouped, you can apply formatting more quickly to objects in the slide. To group objects, select the objects you want included in the group. You can do this by clicking each object while holding down the Shift key or you can draw a border around the objects you want included. With the objects selected, click the Drawing Tools Format tab, click the Group button in the Arrange group, and then click *Group* at the drop-down list.

You can format an individual object within a group. To do this, click any object in the group and the group border displays around the objects. Click the individual object and then apply the desired formatting. If you no longer want objects grouped, click the group to select it, click the Drawing Tools Format tab, click the Group button in the Arrange group, and then click *Ungroup* at the drop-down list.

▼ **Quick Steps**

Group Objects
1. Select desired objects.
2. Click Drawing Tools Format tab.
3. Click Group button.
4. Click *Group* at drop-down list.

H I N T

Group objects so you can move, size, flip, or rotate objects at one time.

Group

Project 1f **Grouping and Formatting Objects** **Part 6 of 15**

1. With **P-C4-P1-AddisonInd.pptx** open, make Slide 3 active.
2. Group the objects and apply formatting by completing the following steps:
   a. Using the mouse, draw a border around the two text boxes in the slide. (This selects the text boxes.)
   b. Click the Drawing Tools Format tab.
   c. Click the Group button in the Arrange group and then click *Group* at the drop-down list.

Step 2c

   d. Click the More button at the right side of the shape style thumbnails in the Shape Styles group and then click *Moderate Effect - Orange, Accent 6* at the drop-down gallery (last option in the fifth row).
   e. Click the Shape Outline button arrow and then click *Brown, Accent 3, Darker 50%*.
   f. Click the Shape Outline button arrow, point to *Weight*, and then click *4½ pt*.
3. Make Slide 4 active and then group and format objects by completing the following steps:
   a. Using the mouse, draw a border around all objects in the slide.
   b. Click the Drawing Tools Format tab.
   c. Click the Group button in the Arrange group and then click *Group* at the drop-down list.
   d. Click the Home tab.
   e. Click the Font Color button arrow in the Font group and then click the *Orange, Accent 1, Lighter 60%* option.
4. Make Slide 1 active and then run the presentation.
5. After running the presentation you decide that you want to change the color of the square shape and the arrow in Slide 4. Do this by completing the following steps:
   a. Make Slide 4 active.
   b. Click any object in the slide. (This selects the border around all of the objects.)
   c. Click the gold square located in the lower left corner of the slide.
   d. Click the Drawing Tools Format tab.
   e. Click the More button at the right side of the shape style thumbnails in the Shape Styles group and then click *Moderate Effect - Orange, Accent 6* at the drop-down gallery (last option in the fifth row).

6. Ungroup the objects by completing the following steps:
   a. With the group and square selected, click the Group button in the Arrange group and then click *Ungroup* at the drop-down list.
   b. Click outside any object to deselect the objects.
   c. Click the arrow line.
   d. Click the Drawing Tools Format tab.
   e. Click the More button at the right side of the shape style thumbnails and then click the *Intense Line - Accent 1* option (second option in the bottom row).
7. You also decide that you do not like the light yellow border (outline) around the three arrows in Slide 5. Remove the outlines by completing the following steps:
   a. Make Slide 5 active.
   b. Using the mouse, draw a border around the three arrows in the slide.
   c. Click the Drawing Tools Format tab.
   d. Click the Group button in the Arrange group and then click *Group* at the drop-down list.
   e. Click the Shape Outline button in the Shape Styles group and then click *No Outline* at the drop-down gallery.
8. Save **P-C4-P1-AddisonInd.pptx**.

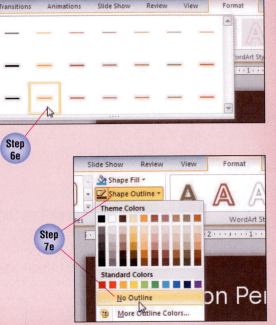

Inserting an Image ■■■■■■■■■■■■■■■■■■

You can insert an image such as a picture or clip art in a slide with buttons in the Images group in the Insert tab. Click the Picture button to display the Insert Picture dialog box where you can specify the desired picture file or click the Clip Art button and then choose from a variety of images available at the Clip Art task pane.

Customizing and Formatting an Image

When you insert an image in a slide, the image is selected and the Picture Tools Format tab is active as shown in Figure 4.8. Use buttons in this tab to apply formatting to the image. With options in the Adjust group in the Picture Tools Format tab you can remove unwanted portions of the image, correct the brightness and contrast, change the image color, apply artistic effects, compress the size of the image file, change to a different image, and reset the image back to the original formatting.

Figure 4.8 Picture Tools Format Tab

Use buttons in the Picture Styles group to apply a predesigned style to the image, change the image border, or apply other effects to the image. With options in the Arrange group, you can position the image on the page, specify how text will wrap around it, align the image with other elements in the document, and rotate the image. Use the Crop button in the Size group to remove any unnecessary parts of the image and specify the image size with the *Shape Height* and *Shape Width* measurement boxes.

Sizing, Cropping, and Moving an Image

You can change the size of an image with the *Shape Height* and *Shape Width* measurement boxes in the Size group in the Picture Tools Format tab or with the sizing handles that display around the selected image. To change size with a sizing handle, position the mouse pointer on a sizing handle until the pointer turns into a double-headed arrow and then hold down the left mouse button. Drag the sizing handle in or out to decrease or increase the size of the image and then release the mouse button. Use the middle sizing handles at the left or right side of the image to make the image wider or thinner. Use the middle sizing handles at the top or bottom of the image to make the image taller or shorter. Use the sizing handles at the corners of the image to change both the width and height at the same time.

The Size group in the Picture Tools Format tab contains a Crop button. Use this button to remove portions of an image. Click the Crop button and the mouse pointer displays with the crop tool attached, which is a black square with overlapping lines, and the image displays with cropping handles around the border. Drag a cropping handle to remove a portion of the image.

Move a selected image by dragging it to the desired location. Move the image by positioning the mouse pointer on the image border until the arrow pointer turns into a four-headed arrow. Hold down the left mouse button, drag the image to the desired position, and then release the mouse button. You can use the arrow keys on the keyboard to move the image in the desired direction. If you want to move the image in small increments (called *nudging*), hold down the Ctrl key while pressing an arrow key.

Use the rotation handle to rotate an image by positioning the mouse pointer on the green, round rotation handle until the pointer displays as a circular arrow. Hold down the left mouse button, drag in the desired direction, and then release the mouse button.

Arranging Objects

With the Bring Forward and Send Backward buttons in the Arrange group in the Drawing Tools Format tab or the Picture Tools Format tab, you can layer one object on top of another. Click the Bring Forward button and the selected object is moved forward one layer. For example, if you have three objects layered on top of each other, selecting the object at the bottom of the layers and then clicking the Bring Forward button will move the object in front of the second object (but not the first object). If you want to move an object to the top layer, select the object, click the Bring Forward button arrow, and then click the *Bring to Front* option at the drop-down list. To move the selected object back one layer, click the Send Backward button. If you want to move the selected object behind all other objects, click the Send Backward button arrow and then click the *Send to Back* option at the drop-down list.

▼ **Quick Steps**

Insert Picture
1. Click Insert tab.
2. Click Picture button.
3. Navigate to desired folder.
4. Double-click desired picture.

H I N T

Insert a picture from your camera by downloading the picture to your computer and then copying the picture into PowerPoint.

Crop

Bring Forward

Send Backward

Inserting a Picture

Picture

To insert a picture in a document, click the Insert tab and then click the Picture button in the Images group. At the Insert Picture dialog box, navigate to the folder containing the desired picture and then double-click the picture. Use buttons in the Picture Tools Format tab to format and customize the picture.

Project 1g   **Inserting and Formatting a Picture**   **Part 7 of 15**

1. With **P-C4-P1-AddisonInd.pptx** open, make Slide 5 active and make sure the Home tab is active.
2. Insert a new slide by clicking the New Slide button arrow in the Slides group and then clicking *Blank* at the drop-down list.
3. Insert a text box by completing the following steps:
   a. Click the Insert tab.
   b. Click the Text Box button in the Text group.
   c. Click in the middle of the slide.
   d. Change the font to Arial Black and the font size to 36.
   e. Click the Center button in the Paragraph group.
   f. Type **Alternative**, press the Enter key, and then type **Energy Resources**.
   g. With the text box selected, click the Drawing Tools Format tab.
   h. Click the Align button in the Arrange group and then click *Distribute Horizontally* at the drop-down list.
   i. Click the Align button and then click *Distribute Vertically* at the drop-down list.

4. Insert a picture by completing the following steps:
   a. Click the Insert tab.
   b. Click the Picture button in the Images group.
   c. At the Insert Picture dialog box, navigate to the PowerPoint2010C4 folder on your storage medium and then double-click **Mountain.jpg**.
5. You decide to insert a picture of the ocean rather than a mountain. Change the picture by completing the following steps:
   a. With the image of the mountain selected, click the Change Picture button in the Adjust group.
   b. Make sure the PowerPoint2010C4 folder on your storage medium is selected and then double-click **Ocean.jpg**.
6. Crop the picture by completing the following steps:
   a. With the picture selected, click the Crop button in the Size group in the Picture Tools Format tab.
   b. Position the mouse pointer (displays with the crop tool attached) on the cropping handle in the middle of the right side of the picture.
   c. Hold down the left mouse button and then drag to the left approximately 0.25 inch. (Use the guideline that displays on the horizontal ruler to crop the picture 0.25 inch.)

d. Complete steps similar to those in Steps 6b and 6c to crop approximately 0.25 inch from the top of the picture. (Use the guideline that displays on the vertical ruler to crop the picture 0.25 inch.)

e. Click the Crop button to turn off cropping.

7. Click in the *Shape Height* measurement box in the Size group, type 5, and then press Enter.

8. Click the Send Backward button arrow in the Arrange group and then click the *Send to Back* option at the drop-down list. (This moves the picture behind the text in the text box.)

9. Align the picture by completing the following steps:

a. With the picture selected, click the Home tab.

b. Click the Arrange button in the Drawing group, point to *Align* at the drop-down list, and then click *Distribute Horizontally*.

c. Click the Arrange button, point to *Align*, and then click *Distribute Vertically*.

10. Format the picture by completing the following steps:

a. With the picture selected, click the Picture Tools Format tab.

b. Click the Artistic Effects button in the Adjust group and then click the *Cutout* option (first option from the left in the bottom row).

c. Click the Corrections button in the Adjust group and then click *Soften: 25%* (second option from the left in the *Sharpen and Soften* section).

d. Click the Picture Border button in the Picture Styles group and then click the orange color in the *Standard Colors* section.

11. After viewing the effects applied to the picture, reset the picture to the original effects by clicking the Reset Picture button arrow in the Adjust group and then clicking *Reset Picture* at the drop-down list.

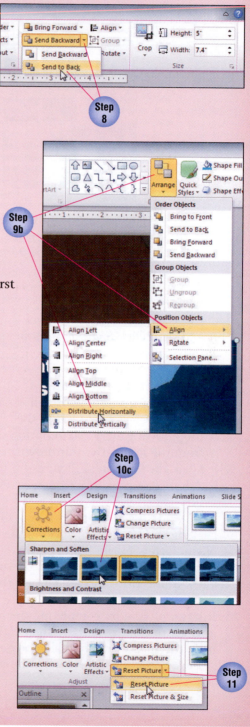

12. Format the picture by completing the following steps:
    a. With the picture selected, click the Picture Tools Format tab, click the Color button in the Adjust group, and then click the *Orange, Accent color 6 Dark* option (last option in the second row in the *Recolor* section).

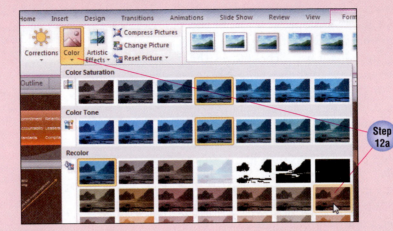

b. Click the Corrections button in the Adjust group and then click *Brightness: +20% Contrast: +20%* (fourth option in the fourth row in the *Brightness and Contrast* section).

c. Click the Corrections button and then click *Sharpen: 25%* in the *Sharpen and Soften* section.

d. Click the More button that displays at the right side of the picture style thumbnails and then click *Soft Edge Oval* at the drop-down gallery (sixth option from the left in the third row).

e. Click the Compress Pictures button in the Adjust group. At the Compress Pictures dialog box, click OK.

13. With Slide 6 active, insert a new slide by clicking the Home tab, clicking the New Slide button arrow in the Slides group, and then clicking *Title Only* at the drop-down list.

14. Click in the title placeholder and then type **Shipping Contracts**.

15. Insert a picture by completing the following steps:
    a. Click the Insert tab and then click the Picture button.
    b. At the Insert Picture dialog box, make sure the PowerPoint2010C4 folder on your storage medium is active and then double-click **Ship.jpg**.

16. With the ship picture selected, remove some of the
background by completing the following steps:
   a. Click the Remove Background button in the Adjust group
      in the Picture Tools Format tab.
   b. Using the left middle sizing handle, drag the border to the
      left to include the back of the ship (see image at the right).
   c. Click the Mark Areas to Remove button in the Refine
      group in the Background Removal tab.
   d. Click anywhere in the water that displays below the
      ship. (This removes the water from the picture. If all of
      the water is not removed, you will need to click in the
      remaining water.)
   e. Using the right middle sizing handle, drag the border to
      the left so the border is near the front of the ship.
   f. If part of the structure above the front of the ship has been
      removed, include it in the picture. To begin, click the Mark
      Areas to Keep button in the Refine group in the Background
      Removal tab. (The mouse pointer displays as a pencil.)
   g. Using the mouse, position the pencil at the top of the
      structure (as shown at the right), drag down to the top of the
      containers on the ship, and then release the mouse button.
   h. Click the Keep Changes button in the Close group in the
      Background Removal tab.
17. Click the Corrections button in the Adjust group in the Picture Tools Format tab and then
    click the *Brightness: +40% Contrast: +40%* option at the drop-down gallery (last option in
    the bottom row in the *Brightness and Contrast* section).
18. Click the Corrections button in the Adjust group and then click the *Sharpen: 50%* option
    at the drop-down gallery (last option in the *Sharpen and Soften* section).
19. Drag the picture down to the middle of the slide.
20. Click outside the picture to deselect it.
21. Save **P-C4-P1-AddisonInd.pptx**.

Inserting a Picture as a Slide Background

You can insert a picture as the background in an entire slide. To do this, click the
Design tab, click the Background Styles button in the Background group, and
then click *Format Background* at the drop-down list. At the Format Background
dialog box, click the *Picture or texture fill* option in the *Fill* section and then click
the File button. At the Insert Picture dialog box, navigate to the desired folder,
and then double-click the picture. Click the Close button to close the Format
Background dialog box. If you want the picture background to display on all
slides, click the Apply to All button at the Format Background dialog box.

▼ **Quick Steps**

**Insert Picture as
Slide Background**
1. Click Design tab.
2. Click Background
   Styles button, *Format
   Background.*
3. Click *Picture or texture
   fill* option.
4. Click File button.
5. Navigate to desired
   folder.
6. Double-click desired
   picture.
7. Click Close button.

1. With **P-C4-P1-AddisonInd.pptx** open, make sure Slide 7 is active and the Home tab is active.
2. Click the New Slide button arrow in the Slides group and then click the *Blank* layout at the drop-down list.
3. Insert a picture background on Slide 8 by completing the following steps:
   a. Click the Design tab.
   b. Click the Background Styles button in the Background group and then click *Format Background* at the drop-down gallery.
   c. At the Format Background dialog box, click the *Picture or texture fill* option in the *Fill* section.
   d. Click the File button that displays near the middle of the dialog box.
   e. At the Insert Picture dialog box, navigate to the PowerPoint2010C4 folder on your storage medium and then double-click *EiffelTower.jpg*.
   f. Click the Close button to close the Format Background dialog box.
   g. Remove the background graphic by clicking the *Hide Background Graphics* check box in the Background group in the Design tab to insert a check mark.

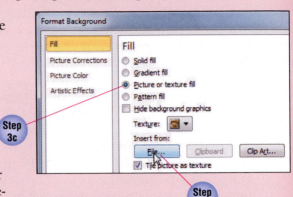

4. Insert a text box by completing the following steps:
   a. Click the Insert tab.
   b. Click the Text Box button in the Text group.
   c. Click in the upper left corner of the slide.
   d. Change the font size to 40.
   e. Type European and then press Enter.
   f. Type Division 2013.
   g. Drag the text box so it is positioned attractively on the slide in the upper left corner.
5. Change the theme colors by completing the following steps:
   a. Click the Design tab.
   b. Click the Colors button in the Themes group and then click *Office* at the drop-down gallery.
6. Save and then close **P-C4-P1-AddisonInd.pptx**.
7. Open **P-C4-P1-AddisonInd.pptx**. (Closing and then opening the presentation will cause the title on Slide 1 to change from orange to blue.)
8. Change the formatting of slide objects by completing the following steps:
   a. Make Slide 3 active and then click in the lower right corner of the text box containing the text in columns (this selects the group).
   b. Click the Drawing Tools Format tab.
   c. Click the More button at the right side of the shape style thumbnails and then click the *Moderate Effect - Blue, Accent 1* option (second option from the left in the fifth row).

d. Make Slide 4 active.

e. Using the mouse, draw a border around all of the objects in the slide, make sure the Home tab is active, and then change the font color to Orange.

f. Make Slide 6 active and then click the picture to select it.

g. Click the Picture Tools Format tab.

h. Click the Color button in the Adjust group and then click the *No Recolor* option in the *Recolor* section.

9. Save **P-C4-P1-AddisonInd.pptx**.

Step 8h

Inserting a Clip Art Image

Microsoft Office includes a gallery of media images you can insert in a slide such as clip art, photographs, and movie images, as well as sound clips. To insert a clip art image in a slide, click the Insert tab and then click the Clip Art button in the Images group. This displays the Clip Art task pane at the right side of the screen as shown in Figure 4.9. You can also choose a slide layout that contains a content placeholder with a Clip Art button.

To view all picture, sound, and motion files, make sure the *Search for* text box in the Clip Art task pane does not contain any text and then click the Go button. When the desired image is visible, click the image to insert it in the document. Use buttons in the Picture Tools Format tab shown in Figure 4.8 to format and customize the clip art image.

If you are searching for specific images, click in the *Search for* text box, type the desired topic, and then click the Go button. For example, if you want to find images related to business, click in the *Search for* text box, type *business*, and then click the Go button. Clip art images related to *business* display in the viewing area of the task pane. If you are connected to the Internet, Word will search for images at the Office.com website matching the topic.

Unless the Clip Art task pane default setting has been customized, the task pane displays all illustrations, photographs, videos, and audio files. The *Results should be* option has a default setting of *All media file types*. Click the down-pointing arrow at the right of this option to display media types. To search for a specific media type, remove the check mark before all options at the drop-down list except for the desired type. For example, if you are searching only for photograph images, remove the check mark before *Illustrations*, *Videos*, and *Audio*.

▼ **Quick Steps**

Insert Clip Art Image
1. Click Insert tab.
2. Click Clip Art button.
3. Type search word or topic.
4. Press Enter.
5. Click desired image.

For additional clip art images, consider buying a commercial package of images.

Preview a clip art image and display properties by positioning the pointer over the image, clicking the arrow that displays, and then clicking *Preview/Properties*.

Clip Art

Figure 4.9 Clip Art Task Pane

Search for specific images by typing the desired category in this text box and then clicking the Go button.

Project 1i **Inserting and Formatting a Clip Art Image**

1. With **P-C4-P1-AddisonInd.pptx** open, make Slide 1 active and then delete the text box (contains the text *Report 2012*) and the shape (contains the text *AI*).
2. Insert a clip art image by completing the following steps:
   a. Click the Insert tab.
   b. Click the Clip Art button in the Images group.
   c. At the Clip Art task pane, click the down-pointing arrow at the right side of the *Results should be* option box and then click in the *Photographs*, *Videos*, and *Audio* check boxes to remove the check marks. (The *Illustrations* check box should be the only option with a check mark.)
   d. Select any text that displays in the *Search for* text box, type **industry**, and then press Enter.
   e. Click the clip art image in the list box as shown at the right.
   f. Close the Clip Art task pane by clicking the Close button (contains an X) located in the upper right corner of the task pane.

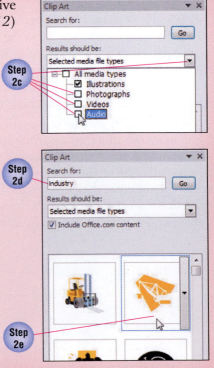

Step 2c

Step 2d

Step 2e

3. Arrange, size, and position the clip art image by completing the following steps:

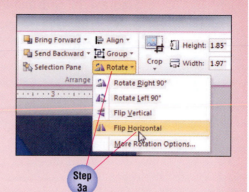

a. With the clip art image selected, click the Rotate button in the Arrange group and then click *Flip Horizontal*.

b. Click in the *Shape Height* measurement box, type 4.5, and then press Enter.

c. Click the Color button in the Adjust group and then click the *Aqua, Accent color 5 Light* option at the drop-down gallery (second option from the right in the third row).

d. Click the Corrections button and then click *Brightness: 0% (Normal) Contrast: +20%* at the drop-down gallery (third option from the left in the fourth row).

e. Click the Send Backward button arrow in the Arrange group and then click *Send to Back* at the drop-down list.

f. Drag the clip art image so it is positioned as shown in Figure 4.10.

4. Save **P-C4-P1-AddisonInd.pptx**.

Figure 4.10 Project 1i, Slide 1

Sizing, Rotating, and Positioning Objects

As you learned in this chapter, you can use the sizing handles that display around an object to increase and decrease the size, and use the *Shape Height* and *Shape Width* measurement boxes. You also learned to position objects by dragging the object with the mouse. You can also size objects with options at the Format Picture dialog box with *Size* selected in the left panel, as shown in Figure 4.11, and position objects with options at the Format Picture dialog box with *Position* selected in the left panel. Display the Format Picture dialog box with *Size* selected in the left panel by clicking the Size group dialog box launcher. Use options at the dialog box to specify the object size, rotation, and scale. Click *Position* in the left panel of the dialog box and use the options to specify the horizontal and vertical position of the object on the slide.

Shape Height

Shape Width

Figure 4.11 Size and Position in the Format Picture Dialog Box

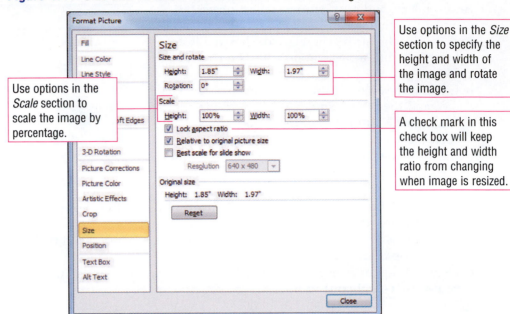

Use options in the *Scale* section to scale the image by percentage.

Use options in the *Size* section to specify the height and width of the image and rotate the image.

A check mark in this check box will keep the height and width ratio from changing when image is resized.

Project 1j **Inserting and Formatting a Clip Art Image** **Part 10 of 15**

1. With **P-C4-P1-AddisonInd.pptx** open, make Slide 8 active.
2. Click the New Slide button arrow in the Slides group in the Home tab and then click the *Two Content* layout at the drop-down list.
3. Click the placeholder text *Click to add title* and then type **Technology**.
4. Click the placeholder text *Click to add text* located in the right side of the slide.
5. Click the Bullets button in the Paragraph group to turn off bullets.
6. Change the font size to 36, turn on bold, and change the font color to Orange.
7. Press the Enter key.
8. Type **Equipment** and then press the Enter key twice.
9. Type **Software** and then press the Enter key twice.
10. Type **Personnel**.
11. Insert a clip art image by completing the following steps:
    a. Click the Clip Art button that displays in the middle of the placeholder at the left side of the slide.

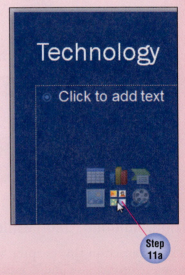

Step 11a

b. At the Clip Art task pane, select any text that displays in the *Search for* text box, type **technology**, and then press Enter.

c. Click the clip art image in the list box as shown at the right.

d. Close the Clip Art task pane by clicking the Close button (contains an X) located in the upper right corner of the task pane.

12. Scale, rotate, and position the clip art image by completing the following steps:

a. With the clip art image selected, click the Size group dialog box launcher.

b. Click the down-pointing arrow at the right of the *Rotation* option until −20° displays in the option box.

c. Select the current percentage in the *Height* option box in the *Scale* section and then type **225**.

d. Click the *Position* option in the left panel.

e. Click the down-pointing arrow at the right side of the *Horizontal* option until *0.7"* displays in the option box.

f. Click the down-pointing arrow at the right side of the *Vertical* option until *1.9"* displays in the option box.

Step 11b

Step 11c

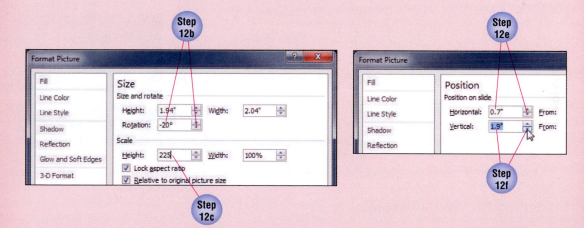

Step 12b

Step 12c

Step 12e

Step 12f

g. Click the Close button to close the dialog box.

13. Bring the text in front of the clip art image by completing the following steps:

a. Click in the text to select the text placeholder.

b. Click the Drawing Tools Format tab.

c. Click the Bring Forward button in the Arrange group.

14. Save **P-C4-P1-AddisonInd.pptx**.

Copying Objects within and between Presentations

Earlier in this chapter you learned how to copy shapes within a slide. You can also copy shapes as well as other objects to other slides within the same presentation or to slides in another presentation. To copy an object, select the object and then click the Copy button in the Clipboard group in the Home tab. Make the desired slide active or open another presentation and display the desired slide and then click the Paste button in the Clipboard group. You can also copy an object by right-clicking the object and then clicking *Copy* at the shortcut menu. To paste the object, make the desired slide active, click the right mouse button, and then click *Paste* at the shortcut menu.

Project 1k   Copying an Object within and between Presentations   Part 11 of 15

1. With **P-C4-P1-AddisonInd.pptx** open, make Slide 1 active.
2. Click the clip art image to select it and then press the Delete key.
3. Open **Addison.pptx**.
4. Click the clip art image located in Slide 1 and then click the Copy button in the Clipboard group.
5. Click the PowerPoint button on the Taskbar and then click the thumbnail representing **P-C4-P1-AddisonInd.pptx**.
6. Click the Paste button. (This inserts the clip art image in Slide 1.)
7. Make the **Addison.pptx** presentation active and then close the presentation.
8. With **P-C4-P1-AddisonInd.pptx** open and the clip art image selected, make Slide 2 active and then click the Paste button.
9. Decrease the size and position the clip art by completing the following steps:
   a. Click the Picture Tools Format tab.
   b. Click in the *Shape Height* measurement text box, type **0.8**, and then press Enter.
   c. Drag the clip art image so it is positioned in the upper right corner of the slide.

10. Copy the clip art image to other slides by completing the following steps:
    a. With the clip art image selected in Slide 2, click the Copy button in the Clipboard group in the Home tab.
    b. Make Slide 3 active and then click the Paste button in the Clipboard group.
    c. Make each of the following slides active and then paste the clip art image: Slide 4, 5, 6, 7, and 9.
11. Save **P-C4-P1-AddisonInd.pptx**.

Creating Screenshots ▪■▪■▪■▪■▪■▪■▪■▪■▪■▪■▪■

Screenshot

The Images group in the Insert tab contains a Screenshot button you can use to capture the contents of a screen as an image or capture a portion of a screen. This is useful for capturing information from a web page or from a file in another program. If you want to capture the entire screen, display the desired web page or open the desired file from a program, make PowerPoint active, and then open a presentation. Click the Insert tab, click the Screenshot button, and then click the desired screen thumbnail at the drop-down list. The currently active presentation does not display as a thumbnail at the drop-down list, only any other file or program you have open. If you do not have another file or program open, the Windows desktop displays. When you click the desired thumbnail, the screenshot is inserted as an image in the active slide in the open presentation, the image is selected, and the Picture Tools Format tab is active. Use buttons in this tab to customize the screenshot image.

In addition to making a screenshot of an entire screen, you can make a screenshot of a specific portion of the screen by clicking the *Screen Clipping* option at the Screenshot button drop-down list. When you click this option, the open web page, file, or Windows desktop displays in a dimmed manner and the mouse pointer displays as crosshairs. Using the mouse, draw a border around the specific area of the screen you want to capture. The specific area you identify is inserted in the active slide in the presentation as an image, the image is selected, and the Picture Tools Format tab is active.

▼ **Quick Steps**

Insert Screenshot
1. Open presentation.
2. Open another file.
3. Display desired information.
4. Make presentation active.
5. Click Insert tab.
6. Click Screenshot button.
7. Click desired window at drop-down list.
OR
6. Click Screenshot button, *Screen Clipping.*
7. Drag to specify capture area.

Project 1l **Inserting and Formatting a Screenshot** **Part 12 of 15**

1. With **P-C4-P1-AddisonInd.pptx** open, make sure that no other programs are open.
2. Make Slide 8 active and then insert a new slide by clicking the New Slide button arrow in the Slides group and then clicking the *Title Only* layout.
3. Click in the title placeholder and then type **Draft Invitation**.
4. Open Word and then open the document named **AddIndInvite.docx** from the PowerPoint2010C4 folder on your storage medium.
5. Click the PowerPoint button on the Taskbar.
6. Insert a screenshot of the draft invitation in the Word document by completing the following steps:
   a. Click the Insert tab.
   b. Click the Screenshot button in the Images group and then click *Screen Clipping* at the drop-down list.

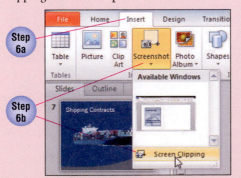

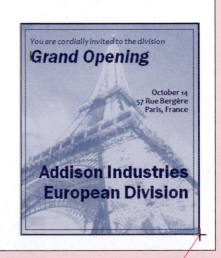

   c. When the **AddIndInvite.docx** document displays in a dimmed manner, position the mouse crosshairs in the upper left corner of the invitation, hold down the left mouse button, drag down to the lower right corner of the invitation, and then release the mouse button. (See image above.)

7. With the screenshot image inserted in the slide in the presentation, make the following changes:
   a. Click in the *Width* measurement box in the Size group in the Picture Tools Format tab, type 4.75, and then press Enter.
   b. Click the Corrections button in the Adjust group and then click the *Sharpen 25%* option (fourth option from the left in the *Sharpen and Soften* section).
   c. Using the mouse, drag the screenshot image so it is centered on the slide.
8. Click outside the screenshot image to deselect it.
9. Save **P-C4-P1-AddisonInd.pptx**.
10. Click the Word button, close **AddIndInvite.docx**, and then exit Word.

Creating WordArt Text

 Quick Steps

Create WordArt Text
1. Click Insert tab.
2. Click WordArt button.
3. Click desired WordArt style.
4. Type WordArt text.

HINT

Use WordArt to create interesting text effects in slides.

HINT

Edit WordArt by double-clicking the WordArt text.

Use the WordArt feature to insert preformatted, decorative text in a slide. You can also use WordArt to modify text to conform to a variety of shapes. Consider using WordArt to create a company logo, letterhead, flier title, or heading. Insert WordArt in a slide by clicking the Insert tab and then clicking the WordArt button in the Text group. This displays the WordArt drop-down list as shown in Figure 4.12. Click the desired WordArt style at this drop-down list and a text box is inserted in the slide containing the text *Your Text Here*. Type the desired WordArt text and then use the options in the Drawing Tools Format tab to customize the WordArt text.

Formatting WordArt Text

When you insert WordArt text in a document, the Drawing Tools Format tab is active. Use options and buttons in this tab to format the WordArt text. Use the WordArt styles to apply predesigned formatting to the WordArt text. Customize the text with the Text Fill, Text Outline, and Text Effects buttons in the WordArt Styles group. Use the Text Fill button to change the fill color, the Text Outline button to change the text outline color, and use the Text Effects button to apply a variety of text effects and shapes.

Figure 4.12 WordArt Drop-down List

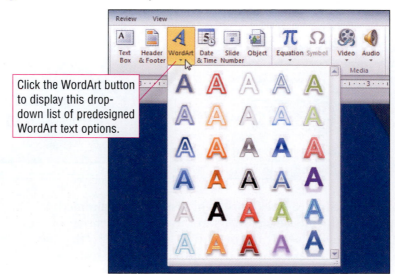

Click the WordArt button to display this drop-down list of predesigned WordArt text options.

Click the Text Effects button and then point to *Transform* and a side menu displays with shaping and warping options as shown in Figure 4.13. Use these options to conform the WordArt text to a specific shape.

WordArt

Figure 4.13 Text Effects Transform Side Menu

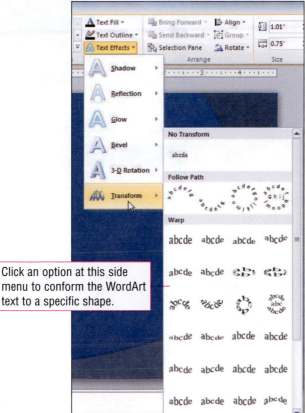

Click an option at this side menu to conform the WordArt text to a specific shape.

Text Fill

Text Outline

Text Effects

 Project 1m   **Inserting and Formatting WordArt**   **Part 13 of 15**

1. With **P-C4-P1-AddisonInd.pptx** open, make Slide 10 active and make sure the Home tab is active.
2. Click the New Slide button arrow in the Slides group and then click the *Blank* layout.
3. Click the Insert tab.
4. Click the WordArt button in the Text group and then click the *Gradient Fill - Orange, Accent 6, Inner Shadow* option (second option from the left in the fourth row).
5. Type **Addison Industries**, press the Enter key, and then type **2013**.
6. Click the WordArt text border to change the border from a dashed line to a solid line. (This selects the text box.)

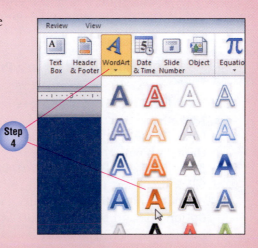

7. Click the Text Outline button arrow in the WordArt Styles group and then click the *Dark Blue* color in the *Standard Colors* section.

8. Click the Text Effects button, point to *Glow*, and then click *Blue, 11 pt glow, Accent color 1* at the side menu (first option from the left in the third row in the *Glow Variations* section).

9. Click the Text Effects button, point to *Transform*, and then click the *Triangle Up* option (third option from the left in the top row of the *Warp* section).

10. Click in the *Shape Height* measurement box, type **3**, and then press Enter.

11. Click in the *Shape Width* measurement box, type **8**, and then press Enter.

12. Click the Align button in the Arrange group and then click *Distribute Horizontally*.

13. Click the Align button and then click *Distribute Vertically*.

14. Make Slide 6 active.

15. Apply WordArt formatting to the text in the text box by completing the following steps:
    a. Click in the text to select the text box.
    b. Click the text box border to change the border line from a dashed line to a solid line.
    c. Click the Drawing Tools Format tab. Click the More button at the right side of the WordArt style thumbnails, and then click *Fill - Orange, Accent 6, Warm Matte Bevel* option (second option from the left in the bottom row).

16. Save **P-C4-P1-AddisonInd.pptx**.

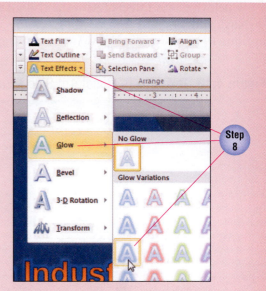

Inserting Symbols ■■■■■■■■■■■■■■■■■■■■■■

Symbol

You can insert symbols in a slide in a presentation with options at the Symbol dialog box. Display this dialog box by clicking the Symbol button in the Symbols group in the Insert tab. At the Symbol dialog box, choose a symbol font with the *Font* option in the dialog box, click the desired symbol in the list box, click the Insert button, and then click the Close button. The symbol is inserted in the slide at the location of the insertion point.

Project 1n   **Inserting Symbols in a Presentation**   **Part 14 of 15**

1. With **P-C4-P1-AddisonInd.pptx** open, insert a symbol by completing the following steps:
   a. Make Slide 2 active.
   b. Click in the text box containing the names, titles, and telephone numbers. (This selects the text box.)
   c. Delete the *n* in *Pena* (the fourth last name).
   d. Click the Insert tab and then click the Symbol button in the Symbols group.
   e. At the Symbol dialog box, click the down-pointing arrow at the right side of the *Font* option box and then click *(normal text)* at the drop-down list (first option in the list).
   f. Scroll down the symbol list box and then click the ñ symbol (located in approximately the eleventh or twelfth row).

g. Click the Insert button and then click the Close button.

2. Insert a text box and a symbol by completing the following steps:

a. With Slide 2 active, click the Text Box button in the Text group in the Insert tab.

b. Click in the lower right corner of the slide below the telephone number column.

c. Change the font size to 24 and the font color to Black.

d. Click the Insert tab.

e. Click the Symbol button.

f. At the Symbol dialog box, click the down-pointing arrow at the right side of the *Font* option, scroll to the end of the list box, and then click *Wingdings*.

g. Click the telephone symbol (☎) located in the top row.

h. Click the Insert button and then click the Close button.

i. If necessary, position the telephone symbol centered below the telephone column.

3. Save **P-C4-P1-AddisonInd.pptx**.

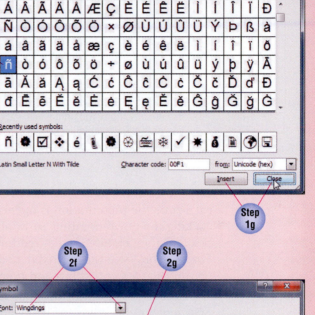

Inserting Headers and Footers ■■■■■■■■■■■■■■■■

As you learned in Chapter 1, if you print a presentation as a handout or an outline, PowerPoint will automatically print the current date in the upper right corner of the page and the page number in the lower right corner. If you print the presentation as notes pages, PowerPoint will automatically print the page number when you print the individual slides. The date and page numbers are considered header and footer elements. You can modify existing header and footer elements or insert additional elements with options in the Header and Footer dialog box. Display the Header and Footer dialog box shown in Figure 4.14 by clicking the Header & Footer button in the Text group in the Insert tab, clicking the Date & Time button in the Text group, or clicking the Slide Number button in the Text group. You can also display the Header and Footer dialog box by displaying the Print tab Backstage view and then clicking the Edit Header & Footer hyperlink that displays below the galleries in the Settings category.

Header & Footer

Slide Number

The Header and Footer dialog box has two tabs, the Slide tab and the Notes and Handouts tab, and the options in the dialog box are similar with either tab selected. With options at the dialog box, you can insert the date and time, a header, a footer, and page numbers. If you insert the date and time in a presentation, you

Figure 4.14 Header and Footer Dialog Box with the Notes and Handouts Tab Selected

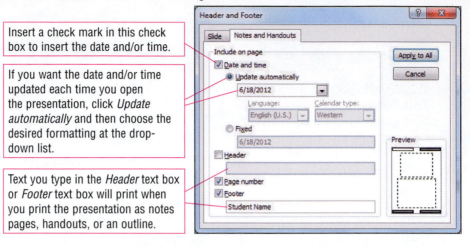

Insert a check mark in this check box to insert the date and/or time.

If you want the date and/or time updated each time you open the presentation, click *Update automatically* and then choose the desired formatting at the drop-down list.

Text you type in the *Header* text box or *Footer* text box will print when you print the presentation as notes pages, handouts, or an outline.

can choose the *Update automatically* option if you want the date and time updated each time the presentation is opened. Choose the date and time formatting by clicking the down-pointing arrow at the right side of the *Update automatically* option box and then choose the desired formatting at the drop-down list. If you choose the *Fixed* option, type the desired date and/or time in the *Fixed* text box. Type header text in the *Header* text box and type footer text in the *Footer* text box.

If you want to print the slide number on slides, insert a check mark in the *Slide number* check box in the Header and Footer dialog box with the Slide tab selected. If you want to include page numbers on handouts, notes pages, or outline pages, insert a check mark in the *Page number* check box in the Header and Footer dialog box with the Notes and Handouts tab selected. If you want all changes you make to the Header and Footer dialog box to apply to all slides or all handouts, notes pages, and outline pages, click the Apply to All button located in the upper right corner of the dialog box.

Project 10 Inserting Headers and Footers   Part 15 of 15

1. With **P-C4-P1-AddisonInd.pptx** open, insert slide numbers on each slide in the presentation by completing the following steps:
   a. Make Slide 1 active.
   b. Click the Insert tab.
   c. Click the Slide Number button in the Text group.
   d. At the Header and Footer dialog box with the Slide tab selected, click the *Slide number* check box to insert a check mark.
   e. Click the Apply to All button.
   f. Scroll through the slides and notice the slide number that displays in the lower right corner of each slide.

2. Insert your name as a footer that displays on each slide in the presentation by completing the following steps:
   a. Click the Header & Footer button in the Text group.
   b. Click the *Footer* check box to insert a check mark and then type your first and last names.
   c. Click the Apply to All button.
   d. Run the presentation and notice that your name displays at the bottom center of each slide.

3. You decide that you also want your name to print as a footer on handout pages. To do this, complete the following steps:
   a. Click the Header & Footer button in the Text group.
   b. At the Header and Footer dialog box, click the Notes and Handouts tab.
   c. Click the *Footer* check box to insert a check mark and then type your first and last names.
   d. Click the Apply to All button.

4. Insert the current date as a header that prints on handout pages by completing the following steps:
   a. Click the Date & Time button in the Text group.
   b. At the Header and Footer dialog box, click the Notes and Handouts tab.
   c. Click the *Date and time* check box to insert a check mark.
   d. Click the Apply to All button.

5. Insert the presentation name as a header that prints on handout pages by completing the following steps:
   a. Click the File tab and then click the Print tab.
   b. At the Print tab Backstage view, click the Edit Header & Footer hyperlink that displays below the galleries in the Settings category.
   c. At the Header and Footer dialog box, select the Notes and Handouts tab.

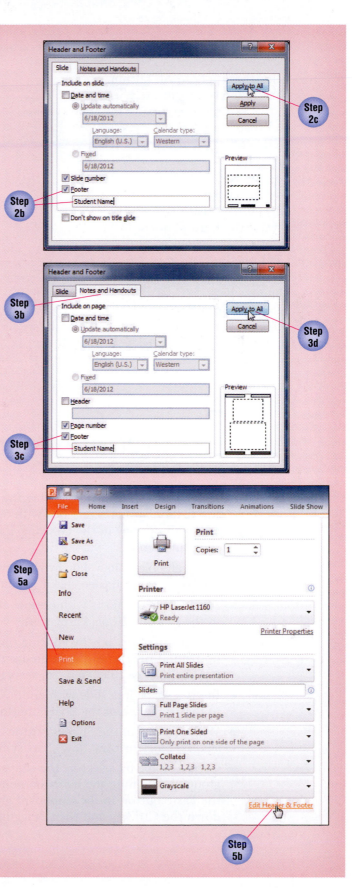

d. Click the *Header* check box to insert a check mark and then type P-C4-P1-AddisonInd.pptx.
e. Click the Apply to All button.
f. Click the second gallery in the Settings category and then click *6 Slides Horizontal* at the drop-down list.

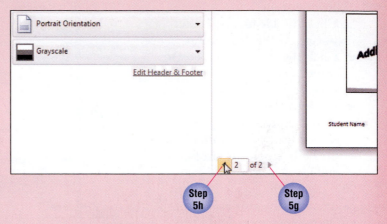

g. Display the next handout page by clicking the Next Page button that displays toward the bottom of the Print tab Backstage view.
h. Click the Previous page button to display the first handout page.
i. Click the Print button to print the presentation as a handout with six slides horizontally per page.

6. Save and then close **P-C4-P1-AddisonInd.pptx**.

Chapter Summary

- Insert a text box in a slide using the Text Box button in the Text group in the Insert tab. Format a text box with options in the Drawing group in the Home tab, with options in the Drawing Tools Format tab, or with options at the shortcut menu.

- Select all objects in a slide by clicking the Select button in the Editing group in the Home tab and then clicking *Select All* or with the keyboard shortcut, Ctrl + A.

- Align selected objects with options from the Align button in the Arrange group in the Drawing Tools Format tab.

- Set tabs in a text box by clicking the Alignment button at the left side of the horizontal ruler until the desired symbol displays and then clicking on a specific location on the ruler. You can set a left, center, right, or decimal tab.

- Insert a shape in a slide with options at the Shapes button in the Drawing group in the Home tab or the Shapes button in the Illustrations group in the Insert tab.

- With options in the Shapes button drop-down list, you can draw a line, basic shapes, block arrows, flow chart symbols, callouts, stars, and banners.

- Copy a shape by selecting the shape, clicking the Copy button in the Clipboard group, positioning the insertion point in the desired position, and then clicking the Paste button in the Clipboard group. You can also copy a shape by holding down the Ctrl key and then dragging the shape to the desired location.

- Turn the horizontal and vertical rulers on and off with the *Ruler* check box in the Show group in the View tab and turn gridlines on and off with the *Gridlines* check box. You can also turn gridlines as well as drawing guides and the snap-to-grid feature on and off with options at the Grid and Guides dialog box.

- You can group objects and then apply the same formatting to objects in the group. To group objects, select the objects, click the Group button in the Arrange group in the Drawing Tools Format tab, and then click *Group* at the drop-down list.

- Size images with the *Shape Height* and *Shape Width* measurement boxes in the Picture Tools Format tab or with the sizing handles that display around a selected image.

- Use the Crop button in the Size group in the Picture Tools Format tab to remove portions of an image.

- Move an image by dragging it to the new location. Move an image in small increments, called nudging, by holding down the Ctrl key while pressing an arrow key.

- Specify how you want to layer objects with the Bring Forward and Send Backward buttons in the Adjust group in the Drawing Tools Format tab or the Picture Tools Format tab.

- Insert a picture in a slide with the Picture button in the Images group in the Insert tab.

- Insert a picture as a slide background with options at the Format Background dialog box. Display this dialog box by clicking the Background Styles button in the Background group in the Design tab and then clicking *Format Background*.

- Insert a clip art image with options in the Clip Art task pane. Display this task pane by clicking the Clip Art button in the Images group in the Insert tab or clicking the Clip Art button in a layout content placeholder.

- You can size objects with options at the Format Picture dialog box with *Size* selected in the left panel. Position an object with options at the Format Picture dialog box with *Position* selected in the left panel.

- Use the Screenshot button in the Images group in the Insert tab to capture the contents of a screen or capture a portion of a screen.

- Use the WordArt feature to distort or modify text to conform to a variety of shapes. Insert WordArt with the WordArt button in the Text group in the Insert tab. Format WordArt with options in the Drawing Tools Format tab.

- Insert symbols in a slide with options at the Symbol dialog box. Display this dialog box by clicking the Symbol button in the Symbols group in the Insert tab.

- Click the Header & Footer button, the Date & Time button, or the Slide Number button to display the Header and Footer dialog box. You can also display the dialog box by clicking the Edit Header & Footer hyperlink at the Print tab Backstage view.

Commands Review

FEATURE	RIBBON TAB, GROUP	BUTTON, OPTION	KEYBOARD SHORTCUT
Text box	Insert, Text		
Shape	Insert, Illustrations OR Home, Drawing		
Gridlines	View, Show	Gridlines	Shift + F9
Rulers	View, Show	Ruler	
Grid and Guides dialog box	View, Show		
Picture	Insert, Images		
Format Background dialog box	Design, Background	, Format Background	
Clip Art task pane	Insert, Images		
Format Picture dialog box	Picture Tools Format, Picture Styles		
Screenshot	Insert, Images		
WordArt	Insert, Text		
Header and Footer	Insert, Text		
Date and Time	Insert, Text		
Slide number	Insert, Text		
Symbol dialog box	Insert, Symbols		

Concepts Check Test Your Knowledge

Completion: In the space provided at the right, indicate the correct term, symbol, or command.

1. The Text Box button is located in the Text group in this tab. _____

2. Use the sizing handles or these measurement boxes to change the size of a text box. _____

3. This is the keyboard shortcut to select all objects in a slide. _____

4. A text box, by default, contains tabs with this alignment.   _____

5. The Drawing group in the Home tab and the Illustrations group in this tab each contain a Shapes button.   _____

6. When dragging a shape to change the size, hold down this key to maintain the proportions of the shape.   _____

7. Copy a shape by holding down this key while dragging the shape to the desired location.   _____

8. Turn drawing guides on and off with options in this dialog box.   _____

9. The Group button is located in this group in the Drawing Tools Format tab.   _____

10. Click the Clip Art button and this displays at the right side of the screen.   _____

11. Use this button in the Size group in the Picture Tools Format tab to remove any unnecessary parts of an image.   _____

12. With the Bring Forward button and this button in the Arrange group in the Drawing Tools Format tab or the Picture Tools Format tab, you can layer one object on top of another.   _____

13. To capture a portion of a screen, click the Screenshot button in the Images group in the Insert tab and then click this option at the drop-down list.   _____

14. Use this feature to distort or modify text to conform to a variety of shapes.   _____

15. The Symbol button is located in the Symbols group in this tab.   _____

16. Click this hyperlink at the Print tab Backstage view to display the Header and Footer dialog box.   _____

Skills Check Assess Your Performance

Assessment

1 FORMAT AND ADD ENHANCEMENTS TO A TRAVEL PRESENTATION

1. Open **TravelEngland.pptx** and then save the presentation with Save As and name it **P-C4-A1-TravelEngland**.
2. Apply the Solstice design theme.
3. Insert the slide shown in Figure 4.15 with the following specifications:
   a. Make Slide 6 active and then insert a new slide with the *Title Only* layout.
   b. Type the title *Travel England* as shown in the slide.
   c. Draw a text box in the slide and then type the text shown in Figure 4.15. Select and then change the text font size to 40 and change the font color to *Brown, Accent 5, Darker 50%*.
   d. Apply *Gold, Accent 2, Lighter 80%* shape fill to the text box.
   e. Apply the *Aqua, 18 pt glow, Accent color 1* shape effect (from the *Glow* side menu).
   f. Size and position the text box so it displays as shown in Figure 4.15.
4. Insert the slide shown in Figure 4.16 with the following specifications:
   a. Make Slide 1 active and then insert a new slide with the *Title Only* layout.
   b. Type the title *Upcoming Tours* as shown in the slide.
   c. Draw a text box in the slide and then set a left tab at the 0.5-inch mark on the horizontal ruler, a center tab at the 4-inch mark, and a right tab at the 6.75-inch mark.
   d. Type the text in columns as shown in Figure 4.16. Bold the heading text *Dates*, *Duration*, and *Price*.
   e. After typing the text, select the text, change the font size to 20, the font color to *Brown, Accent 5, Darker 50%*, and change the line spacing to 1.5.
   f. Size and position the text box so it displays as shown in Figure 4.16.
5. Insert a picture in Slide 6 as shown in Figure 4.17 with the following specifications:
   a. Insert the picture named **WhiteHorse.jpg**.
   b. Size and move the picture so it displays as shown in Figure 4.17.
6. Insert a picture in Slide 4 as shown in Figure 4.18 with the following specifications:
   a. Insert the picture named **Stonehenge.jpg**.
   b. Crop the picture so it displays as shown in Figure 4.18.
   c. Send the picture behind the text.
   d. Size and move the picture so it displays as shown in Figure 4.18.
   e. Size and move the bulleted text placeholder so it displays as shown in Figure 4.18.
7. Insert a clip art image in Slide 7 as shown in Figure 4.19 with the following specification:
   a. In the Clip Art task pane, search only for clip art images related to *umbrella*.
   b. At the Clip Art task pane, click the image shown in Figure 4.19. (The original umbrella colors are green and gray. If this image is not available, choose a different umbrella clip art image and then color and size the image as shown in Figure 4.19.)
   c. Flip the umbrella horizontally. ***Hint: Do this with the Rotate button in the Arrange group in the Picture Tools Format tab.***

d. Change the color of the umbrella to *Aqua, Accent color 1 Light*.

e. Size and position the clip art image as shown in Figure 4.19.

8. Insert a picture as background in Slide 1 as shown in Figure 4.20 with the following specifications:

a. Click the Design tab, click the Background Styles button, and then click *Format Background* at the drop-down list.

b. At the Format Background dialog box, insert a check mark in the *Hide background graphics*.

c. Click the File button, navigate to the PowerPoint2010C4 folder on your storage medium, and then double-click **BigBen.jpg**.

d. At the Format Background dialog box, click the down-pointing arrow at the right side of the *Bottom* option box in the *Stretch Options* section until *-100%* displays in the box.

e. Close the dialog box.

f. Size and move the title placeholder so the title displays as shown in Figure 4.20.

g. Size and move the subtitle placeholder so the subtitle displays as shown in Figure 4.20.

9. Insert the slide shown in Figure 4.21 with the following specifications:

a. Make Slide 8 active and then insert a new slide with the *Title Only* layout.

b. Type the title *Travel Discounts!* as shown in Figure 4.21.

c. Draw the shape shown in the slide in Figure 4.21 using the *Up Ribbon* shape.

d. Apply the *Subtle Effect - Aqua Accent 1* shape style to the shape.

e. Apply the *Gold, 8 pt glow, Accent color 2* shape effect (from the *Glow* side menu).

f. Type the text in the shape as shown in Figure 4.21. Change the font size for the text to 28 and change the font color to *Brown, Accent 5, Darker 50%*.

g. Size and position the shape so it displays as shown in Figure 4.21.

10. Insert a new slide at the beginning of the presentation with the *Blank* layout. **Hint: Click above the Slide 1 miniature in the Slides/Outline pane and then click the New Slide button arrow.** Insert a logo from another presentation by completing the following steps:

a. Open **FCTCruise.pptx** and then copy the First Choice Travel logo from Slide 1 to Slide 1 in the **P-C4-A1-TravelEngland.pptx** presentation.

b. Close **FCTCruise.pptx**.

c. With Slide 1 of **P-C4-A1-TravelEngland.pptx** active and the logo selected, change the logo (picture) color to *Aqua Accent color 1 Light*.

d. Position the logo attractively on the slide.

11. Apply a transition and sound of your choosing to each slide.

12. Insert slide numbers on each slide.

13. Insert a footer for notes and handouts pages that prints your first and last names.

14. Run the presentation.

15. Print the presentation as a handout with six slides horizontally per page.

16. Save and then close **P-C4-A1-TravelEngland.pptx**.

Figure 4.15 Assessment 1 Step 3

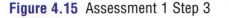

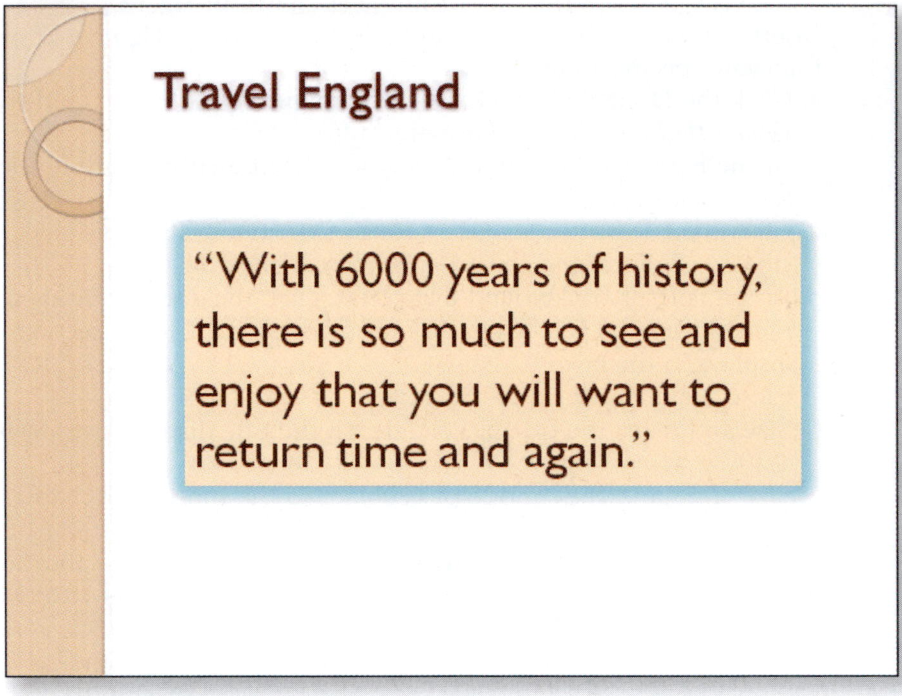

Figure 4.16 Assessment 1 Step 4

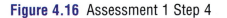

Figure 4.17 Assessment 1 Step 5

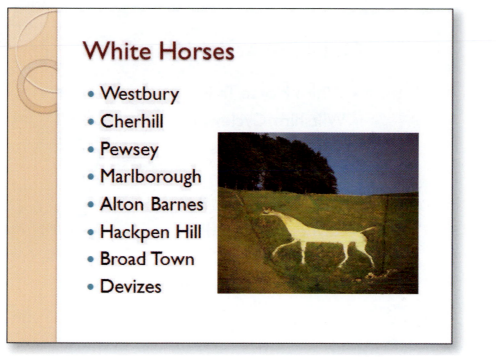

Figure 4.18 Assessment 1 Step 6

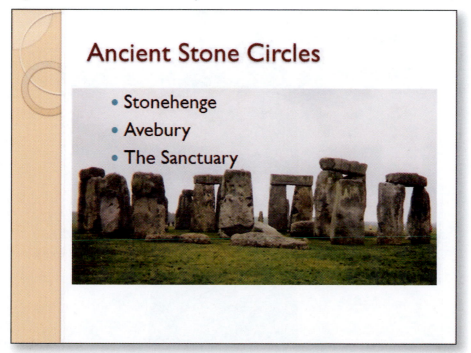

Figure 4.19 Assessment 1 Step 7

Figure 4.20 Assessment 1 Step 8

Figure 4.21 Assessment 1 Step 9

Assessment

2 FORMAT AND ADD ENHANCEMENTS TO A GARDENING PRESENTATION

1. Open **PerennialsPres.pptx** and then save the presentation with Save As and name it **P-C4-A2-PerennialsPres**.
2. Insert the slide shown in Figure 4.22 with the following specifications:
   a. Make Slide 2 active and then insert a new slide with the *Blank* layout.
   b. Hide the background graphics.
   c. Insert the WordArt text using *Gradient Fill - Dark Green, Accent 6, Inner Shadow* (second option from the left in the fourth row).
   d. Change the shape of the WordArt to *Wave 1*. (The *Wave 1* option is the first option in the fifth row in *Warp* section of the Text Effects button Transform side menu.)
   e. Change the height of the WordArt to *3″* and the width to *9″*.
   f. Display the Format Background dialog box (for help, see Assessment 1, Step 8), click the *Gradient fill* option in the *Fill* section, change the *Preset colors* option to *Daybreak*, and then close the dialog box.
   g. Position the WordArt text as shown in Figure 4.22.
3. Insert the slide shown in Figure 4.23 with the following specifications:
   a. Make Slide 8 active and then insert a new slide with the *Title Only* layout.
   b. Insert the title *English/French Translations* as shown in Figure 4.23.
   c. Insert a text box, change the font size to 28, change the font color to *Light Blue, Accent 5, Darker 25%*, set left tabs at the 0.5-inch and the 4-inch marks on the horizontal ruler, and then type the text shown in Figure 4.23 in columns. Bold the headings *English Name* and *French Name* and use the Symbol dialog box to insert the special symbols in the French names.
   d. If necessary, move the text box so it is positioned as shown in Figure 4.23.

4. Make Slide 4 active and then make the following changes:
   a. Select the bulleted text and then change the line spacing to 2.0.
   b. With the bulleted text selected, set the bulleted text in two columns.
      Hint: Refer to Project 1d in Chapter 3.
   c. Make sure four bulleted items display in each column.
5. Make Slide 5 active and then insert a clip art image related to *garden* or *gardening*. Size and position the clip art attractively in the slide.
6. Make Slide 8 active and then insert a clip art image of a flower. Size and position the clip art attractively in the slide.
7. Select and then delete Slide 10.
8. Insert the slide shown in Figure 4.24 with the following specifications:
   a. Make Slide 9 active and then insert a new slide with the *Title Only* layout.
   b. Insert the title *Gardening Magazines*.
   c. Create the top shape using the *Bevel* shape.
   d. Change the font size to 32, turn on bold, turn on italic, change the alignment to Center, and then type the text in the top shape. ***Hint: To vertically center the text in the shape, click the Align Text button in the Paragraph group in the Home tab and then click* Middle *at the drop-down list.***
   e. Select and then copy the shape two times.
   f. Change the text in the second and third shapes to match what you see in Figure 4.24.
   g. Size and position the shapes and text boxes as shown in Figure 4.24.
9. Make Slide 7 active and then insert a clip art image of your choosing.
10. Make Slide 10 active and then insert a new slide with the *Title Only* layout. Type **Gift Certificates Available!** as the title and then insert a screenshot with the following specifications:
    a. Open Word and then open the document named **GAGiftCert.docx** from the PowerPoint2010C4 folder on your storage medium.
    b. Click the PowerPoint button on the Taskbar and then use the *Screen Clipping* option from the Screenshot button drop-down list to capture only the gift certificate in the Word document.
    c. With the gift certificate screenshot inserted in the slide, size and position the gift certificate attractively on the slide.
    d. Make Word active and then exit Word.
11. Run the presentation.
12. Print the presentation as a handout with six slides horizontally per page.
13. Save **P-C4-A2-PerennialsPres.pptx**.

Figure 4.22 Assessment 2 Step 2

Figure 4.23 Assessment 2 Step 3

Figure 4.24 Assessment 2 Step 7

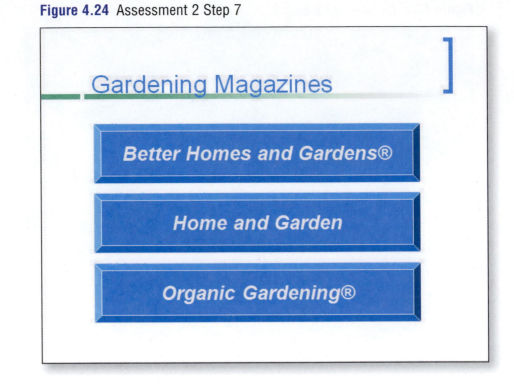

Assessment

3 COPY A PICTURE FROM A WEBSITE TO A PRESENTATION

1. With **P-C4-A2-PerennialsPres.pptx** open, make Slide 6 active.
2. Use the Help feature to find information on copying a picture from a web page. (Begin by entering "insert a picture or clip art" in the PowerPoint Help window and then press Enter. Click the Insert a picture or clip art hyperlink and then click the Insert a picture from a Web page hyperlink.)
3. Using the information you learned about inserting a picture from a web page, open your web browser and then use a search engine of your choosing to search for a picture of at least one flower mentioned in the slide.
4. Save the picture to the PowerPoint2010C4 folder on your storage medium and then insert the image in the slide. Size and move the picture so it is positioned attractively in the slide. (Consider inserting at least one more picture of one of the flowers mentioned.)
5. Print only Slide 6.
6. Run the presentation.
7. Save and then close **P-C4-A2-PerennialsPres.pptx**.

CREATING A STUDY ABROAD PRESENTATION

1. At a blank presentation, create the presentation shown in Figure 4.25 with the following specifications:

   a. Apply the *Slipstream* design theme.

   b. In Slide 1, increase the font size for the subtitle to 32 and then position the subtitle as shown in Figure 4.25.

   c. In Slide 2, insert the WordArt using the *Fill – Turquoise, Accent 2, Matte Bevel* option (located in the *Applies to All Text in the Shape* section) and apply the *Deflate* transform text effect. Size and position the WordArt on the slide as shown in Figure 4.25.

   d. Change the line spacing to *2* for the bulleted text in Slides 3, 4, and 5.

   e. Use the word *apartment* to search for the clip art image in Slide 4. The original color of the clip art image is dark pink. Change the color to *Turquoise, Accent color 2 Light*. (If this clip art image is not available, choose a similar image.)

   f. Insert the picture **Colosseum.jpg** in Slide 5. (This image is located in the PowerPoint2010C4 folder on your storage medium.) Size and position the image as shown in Figure 4.25.

   g. In Slide 6, use the Bevel shape in the *Basic Shapes* section of the Shapes button drop-down list to create the shape and change the fill color to *Turquoise, Accent 2, Darker 50%*.

   h. Make any other changes to placeholders and other objects so your slides display similar to what you see in Figure 4.25.

2. Apply a transition and sound of your choosing to all slides in the presentation.

3. Save the presentation and name it **P-C4-VB-RomeStudy**.

4. Print the presentation as a handout with six slides horizontally per page.

5. Close **P-C4-VB-RomeStudy.pptx**.

Figure 4.25 Visual Benchmark

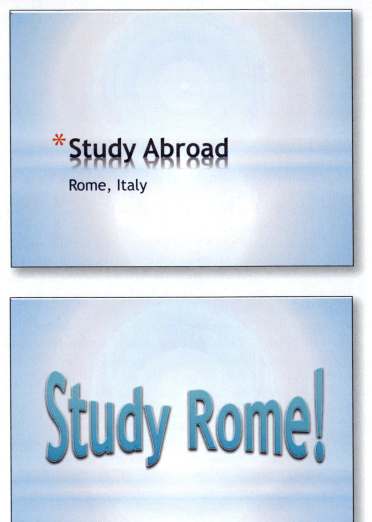

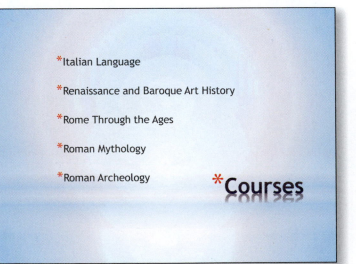

Figure 4.25 Visual Benchmark—*continued*

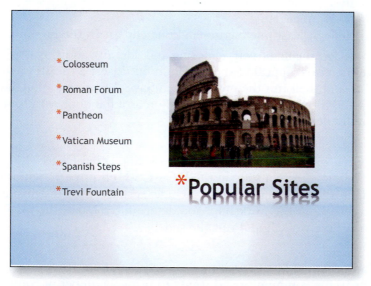

Case Study   Apply Your Skills

Part 1

You work for Honoré Financial Services and the Office Manager, Jason Monroe, has asked you to prepare a presentation for a community workshop he will be conducting next week. Open the Word document named **HFS.docx** and then use the information in the document to create a presentation with the following specifications:

- Slide 1: Include the company name Honoré Financial Services (use the Symbol feature to create the é in Honoré) and the subtitle *Managing Your Money*.
- Slide 2: Insert the word *Budgeting* as WordArt.
- Slides 3, 4, and 5: Use the bulleted and numbered information to create these slides.
- Slide 6: Create a text box, set tabs, and then type the information in the *Managing Records* section that is set in columns.
- Slide 7: Create a shape and then insert the following slogan *"Retirement Planning Made Easy"*.
- Include at least one picture and one clip art in the presentation.

Apply a design theme of your choosing and add any additional features to improve the visual appeal of the presentation. Insert a transition and sound to each slide and then run the presentation. Save the presentation and name it **P-C4-CS-HFS.pptx**. Print the presentation as a handout with four slides horizontally per page.

Part 2

Mr. Monroe will be conducting a free workshop titled *Financial Planning for the College Student*. Create a slide in the **P-C4-CS-HFS.pptx** presentation (make it the last slide in the presentation) that includes a shape with text inside that includes information about the workshop. You determine the day, the time, and the location for the workshop. Print the slide.

Part 3

Mr. Monroe would like to post the information about the workshop in various locations in the community and wants to print a number of copies. You decide to copy the shape and then insert it in a blank Word document. In Word, change the orientation of the page to landscape, increase the size of the shape, and then drag the shape to the middle of the page. Save the Word document and name it **P-C4-CS-HFSWorkshop**. Print and then close **P-C4-CS-HFSWorkshop.docx**.

Part 4

Mr. Monroe has asked you to locate online finance and/or budgeting resources such as newsletters and magazines. He would like you to locate resources and then create a slide with hyperlinks to the resources. Locate at least two online resources and then insert this information with the hyperlinks in a new slide at the end of the **P-C4-CS-HFS.pptx** presentation. Print the slide and then save and close the presentation.

PowerPoint2010U1

Note: Before beginning unit assessments, copy to your storage medium the PowerPoint2010U1 folder from the PowerPoint2010 folder on the CD that accompanies this textbook and then make PowerPoint2010U1 the active folder.

Assessing Proficiency

In this unit, you have learned to create, print, save, close, open, view, run, edit, and format a PowerPoint presentation. You also learned how to add transitions and sound to presentations; rearrange slides; customize presentations by changing the design theme; and add visual appeal to slides by inserting text boxes, shapes, pictures, clip art, screenshots, and symbols.

Assessment 1 Prepare, Format, and Enhance a Conference Presentation

1. Create a presentation with the text shown in Figure U1.1 using the Module design theme. Use the appropriate slide layout for each slide. After creating the slides, complete a spelling check on the text in slides.
2. Add a transition and sound of your choosing to all slides.
3. Save the presentation and name it **P-U1-A1-CSConf**.
4. Run the presentation.
5. Make Slide 1 active and then find all occurrences of *Area* and replace with *Market*.
6. Make the following changes to Slide 2:
   a. Type **Net income per common share** over *Net income*.
   b. Delete *Return on average equity*.
7. Make the following changes to Slide 4:
   a. Delete *Shopping*.
   b. Type **Business finance** between *Personal finance* and *Email*.
8. Rearrange the slides in the presentation so they are in the following order (only the slide titles are shown below):
   - Slide 1 = CORNERSTONE SYSTEMS
   - Slide 2 = Corporate Vision
   - Slide 3 = Future Goals
   - Slide 4 = Industrial Market
   - Slide 5 = Consumer Market
   - Slide 6 = Financial Review
9. Increase spacing to 1.5 for the bulleted text in Slides 2, 3, 5, and 6.
10. Make Slide 4 active, increase the spacing to 2.0 for the bulleted text, and then format the bulleted text into two columns with three entries in each column. (You may need to decrease the size of the placeholder.)

11. Save and then run the presentation.

12. Print the presentation as a handout with six slides horizontally per page.

13. Display the Reuse Slides task pane, browse to the PowerPoint2010U1 folder on your storage medium, and then double-click *CSMktRpt.pptx*.

14. Insert the *Department Reports* slide below Slide 4.

15. Insert the *Services* slide below Slide 2.

16. Close the Reuse Slides task pane.

17. Make Slide 8 active, select the bulleted text, and then create and apply a custom bullet using a dollar sign in a complementary color. (You can find a dollar sign in the normal font in the Symbol dialog box.)

18. With Slide 8 active, insert a clip art image related to *money* or *finances*. Size and position the clip art attractively in the slide.

19. Move Slide 4 (*Future Goals*) to the end of the presentation.

20. Insert a new slide with the *Title and Content* layout at the end of the presentation with the following specifications:
    a. Insert *Future Goals* as the title.
    b. Type International market as the first bulleted item and then press Enter.
    c. Copy *Acquisitions*, *Production*, *Technology*, and *Marketing* from Slide 8 and paste them in the content area of the new slide below the first bulleted text. (When copied, the items should be preceded by a bullet. If a bullet displays on a blank line below the last text item, press the Backspace key twice.)
    d. Select the bulleted text and then change the line spacing to 1.5.

21. Make Slide 8 active, select the bulleted items, and then apply numbering.

22. Make Slide 9 active, select the bulleted items, and then apply numbering and change the beginning number to *6*.

23. With Slide 9 active, create a new slide with the *Blank* layout with the following specifications:
    a. Insert the picture named **Nightscape.jpg** as a background picture and hide the background graphics. *Hint: Do this with the Background Styles button in the Design tab.*
    b. Create a text box toward the top of the slide, change the font color to white, increase the font size to 36, and then change the alignment to center.
    c. Type National Sales Meeting, press Enter, type New York City, press Enter, and then type March 6 - 8, 2013.
    d. Move and/or size the text box so the text is positioned centered above the buildings in the picture.

24. With Slide 10 active, insert a new slide with the *Title Only* layout. Type Doubletree Guest Suites as the title and then insert a screenshot with the following specifications:
    a. Open Word and then open the document named **HotelMap.docx** from the PowerPoint2010U1 folder on your storage medium.
    b. Click the PowerPoint button on the Taskbar and then use the *Screen Clipping* option from the Screenshot button drop-down list to capture only the map in the Word document.
    c. With the map screenshot inserted in the slide, apply the *Sharpen: 25%* correction. Size and position the map attractively on the slide.

25. Insert slide numbers on each slide.

26. Insert a footer for notes and handouts pages that prints your first and last names.

27. Save and then run the presentation.

28. Print the presentation as a handout with six slides horizontally per page.

29. Close **P-U1-A1-CSConf.pptx**.

Slide 1	Title	=	CORNERSTONE SYSTEMS
	Subtitle	=	Executive Conference

Slide 2	Title	=	Financial Review
	Bullets	=	• Net revenues
			• Operating income
			• Net income
			• Return on average equity
			• Return on average asset

Slide 3	Title	=	Corporate Vision
	Bullets	=	• Expansion
			• Increased productivity
			• Consumer satisfaction
			• Employee satisfaction
			• Area visibility

Slide 4	Title	=	Consumer Area
	Bullets	=	• Travel
			• Shopping
			• Entertainment
			• Personal finance
			• Email

Slide 5	Title	=	Industrial Area
	Bullets	=	• Finance
			• Education
			• Government
			• Production
			• Manufacturing
			• Utilities

Slide 6	Title	=	Future Goals
	Bullets	=	• Domestic market
			• Acquisitions
			• Production
			• Technology
			• Marketing

Assessment 2 Format and Enhance a Kraft Artworks Presentation

1. Open **KAPres.pptx** and then save the presentation with Save As and name it **P-U1-A2-KAPres**.
2. With Slide 1 active, insert the text *Kraft Artworks* as WordArt and apply at least the following formatting:
   a. Change the shape of the WordArt.
   b. Change the size so the WordArt better fills the slide.
   c. Change the fill to a purple color.
   d. Apply any other formatting to improve the visual appeal of the WordArt.
3. Duplicate Slides 2 and 3.
4. Change the goal number in Slide 4 from *1* to *3* and change the goal text to *Conduct six art workshops at the Community Center.*
5. Change the goal number in Slide 5 from *2* to *4* and change the goal text to *Provide recycled material to public schools for art classes.*
6. With Slide 5 active, insert a new slide with the *Title Only* layout with the following specifications:
   a. Insert the title *Clients* and then format, size, and position the title in the same manner as the title in Slide 5.
   b. Insert a text box, change the font to Comic Sans MS, the font size to 20, the font color to purple, and then type the following text in columns (you determine the tab settings):

School	Contact	Number
Logan Elementary School	Maya Jones	555-0882
Cedar Elementary School	George Ferraro	555-3211
Sunrise Elementary School	Avery Burns	555-3444
Hillside Middle School	Joanna Myers	555-2211
Douglas Middle School	Ray Murphy	555-8100

   c. Select all of the text in the text box and then change the line spacing to 1.5.
7. With Slide 6 active, insert a new slide with the *Blank* layout, hide the background graphic, and then create the slide shown in Figure U1.2 with the following specifications:
   a. Use the *Explosion 1* shape (in the *Stars and Banners* section) to create the first shape.
   b. Change the fill color of the shape to *Gold, Accent 2, Lighter 40%* and apply the *Lavender, 18 pt glow, Accent color 3* glow effect.
   c. With the shape selected, change the font to 40-point Comic Sans MS bold in purple color, change the alignment to center, change the vertical alignment to middle, and then type the text shown in Figure U1.2.
   d. Copy the shape twice and position the shapes as shown in Figure U1.2.
   e. Type the appropriate text in each text box as shown in Figure U1.2.
8. With Slide 7 active, insert a new slide with the *Blank* layout, hide the background graphic, and then create the slide shown in Figure U1.3 with the following specifications:
   a. Set the text in the two text boxes at the left and right sides of the slide in 54-point Comic Sans MS bold and in purple color. Rotate, size, and position the two text boxes as shown in Figure U1.3.
   b. Use the *Explosion 1* shape to create the shape in the middle of the slide.
   c. Change the fill color of the shape to *Gold, Accent 2, Lighter 40%,* apply the *Perspective Diagonal Upper Left* shadow effect, and change the shape outline color to purple and the weight to *2¼ pt.*

    d. Insert the text in the shape and then change the font to 28-point Comic Sans MS bold in purple color, change the alignment to center, and change the vertical alignment to middle.

9. Create a footer that prints your first and last names and the current date on handout pages.

10. Print the presentation as a handout with four slides horizontally per page.

11. Save and then close **P-U1-A2-KAPres.pptx**.

Figure U1.2 Assessment 2, Slide 7

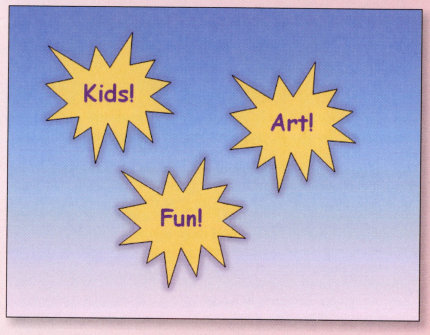

Figure U1.3 Assessment 2, Slide 8

Assessment 3 Create and Apply a Custom Theme to a Job Search Presentation

1. At a blank presentation, apply the *Civic* design theme.
2. Create custom theme colors named with your first and last names that change the following colors:
   a. Change the Text/Background, Dark 1 color, to *Dark Yellow, Followed Hyperlink, Lighter 80%*.
   b. Change the Text/Background, Dark 2 color, to *White, Text 1*.
   c. Change the Text/Background, Light 2 color, to *Turquoise, Hyperlink, Darker 25%*.
   d. Change the Accent 1 color to *Dark Red*.
   e. Change the Accent 2 and the Accent 3 color to *Red, Accent 1, Darker 50%*.
3. Create custom theme fonts named with your first and last names that changes the *Heading font* to Constantia and the *Body font* to Cambria.
4. Save the current theme as a custom theme named with your first and last names. **Hint: Do this at the Save Current Theme dialog box.**
5. Close the presentation without saving it.
6. Open **JobSearch.pptx** and then save the presentation with Save As and name it **P-U1-A3-JobSearch**.
7. Apply the custom theme named with your first and last names.
8. Insert a clip art image in Slide 5 related to *telephone*, *people*, or *Internet*. You determine the size and position of the image.
9. Insert a clip art image in Slide 6 related to *clock* or *time*. You determine the size and position of the image.
10. Improve the visual display of text in Slides 2, 3, 7, 8, and 9 by increasing the spacing between items and positioning the text placeholders attractively in the slides.
11. Insert the current date and slide number on all slides in the presentation. (The slide numbers will appear in the round circle that is part of the design theme.)
12. Create the header *Job Search Seminar*, the footer *Employment Strategies*, and insert the date and page number for notes and handouts.
13. Add the speaker note *Distribute list of Internet employment sites.* to Slide 5.
14. Apply a transition and sound of your choosing to all slides in the presentation.
15. Save and then run the presentation.
16. Print the presentation as a handout with six slides horizontally per page.
17. Print Slide 5 as notes pages.
18. Save and then close **P-U1-A3-JobSearch.pptx**.
19. Display a blank presentation and then delete the custom theme colors, custom theme fonts, and custom theme you created for this assessment.
20. Close the presentation without saving it.

Assessment 4 Format and Enhance a Medical Plans Presentation

1. Open **MedicalPlans.pptx** and then save the presentation with Save As and name it **P-U1-A4-MedicalPlans**.
2. Apply a design theme of your choosing.
3. Create a new slide with a Blank layout between Slides 1 and 2 that contains a shape with the text *Medical Plans 2013 - 2014* inside the shape. You determine the format, position, and size of the shape and the formatting of the text.

4. Change the bullets to custom bullets (you determine the picture or symbol) for the bullets in Slides 3, 4, and 5.
5. Insert a clip art image related to *medicine* in Slide 4. You determine the color, size, and position of the image.
6. Make Slide 5 active, and then apply the following formatting:
   a. Move the insertion point to the beginning of *Eugene* and then press the Enter key.
   b. Select all of the bulleted text and then change the line spacing to 2.0.
   c. With the bulleted text selected, format the text into two columns. (Make sure each column contains four entries.)
   d. Size and/or move the placeholder so the bulleted text displays attractively in the slide.
7. Apply any additional formatting or elements to improve the visual appeal of the slides.
8. Add a transition and sound of your choosing to the presentation.
9. Run the presentation.
10. Print the presentation as a handout with four slides horizontally per page.
11. Save and then close **P-U1-A4-MedicalPlans.pptx**.

Writing Activities ▪▪▪▪▪▪▪▪▪▪▪▪▪▪▪

The following activities provide you with the opportunity to practice your writing skills along with demonstrating an understanding of some of the important PowerPoint features you have mastered in this unit. Use correct spelling, grammar, and appropriate word choices.

Activity 1 Prepare and Format a Health Plan Presentation

Open Word and then open, print, and close **KLHPlan.docx**. Looking at the printing of this document, create a presentation in PowerPoint that presents the main points of the plan. (Use bullets in the presentation.) Add a transition and sound to the slides. Apply formatting and/or insert images to enhance the visual appeal of the presentation. Save the presentation and name it **P-U1-Act1-KLHPlan**. Run the presentation. Print the presentation as a handout with six slides horizontally per page. Save and then close **P-U1-Act1-KLHPlan.pptx**.

Activity 2 Prepare and Format a Presentation on Clip Art

At a blank presentation, use the Help feature to find information on inserting a picture or clip art image. *Hint: Display the PowerPoint Help window, type* insert picture or clip art, *press Enter, and then click the* Insert a picture or clip art *hyperlink that displays in the window.* Print and then read the information and then use the information to create a presentation that includes at least four slides. Format and add visual appeal to the presentation. With the presentation still open, display the Clip Art task pane and then click the Find more at Office.com hyperlink that displays at the bottom of the task pane. (Your computer needs to be connected to the Internet to complete this activity.) At the website, search for information on how to display image categories and then how to specify media types and sizes and how to download images. With the information, create at least three additional slides that contain information about displaying and downloading images from Office.com.

Download and insert at least one image into a slide. Save the completed presentation and name it **P-U1-Act2-ClipArtPres**. Add a transition and sound of your choosing to each slide and then run the presentation. Print the presentation as a handout with four slides horizontally per page. Close **P-U1-Act2-ClipArtPres.pptx**.

Internet Research ∎∎∎∎∎∎∎∎∎∎∎∎∎∎∎∎∎∎

Analyze a Magazine Website

Make sure you are connected to the Internet and then explore the *Time*® magazine website at www.time.com. Discover the following information for the site:

- Magazine sections
- The type of information presented in each section
- Information on how to subscribe

Use the information you discovered about the *Time* magazine website and create a PowerPoint presentation that presents the information in a clear, concise, and logical manner. Add formatting and enhancements to the presentation to make it more interesting. When the presentation is completed, save it and name it **P-U1-TimeMag**. Run, print, and then close the presentation.

Unit 2 ■ Customizing and Enhancing PowerPoint Presentations

Chapter 5 ■ Creating Tables, Charts, and SmartArt Graphics

Chapter 6 ■ Using Slide Masters and Action Buttons

Chapter 7 ■ Applying Custom Animation and Setting Up Shows

Chapter 8 ■ Integrating, Sharing, and Protecting Presentations

185

PERFORMANCE OBJECTIVES

Upon successful completion of Chapter 5, you will be able to:

- Create and format a table
- Modify the design and layout of a table
- Insert an image in a table
- Create SmartArt diagrams
- Modify the design and layout of SmartArt
- Create a SmartArt graphic with bulleted text
- Create and format charts
- Modify the design and layout of charts
- Select and format chart elements
- Create, edit, and format a photo album

Tutorials

5.1 Creating a Table in a Slide
5.2 Inserting and Formatting SmartArt
5.3 Creating and Formatting Charts
5.4 Inserting and Formatting an Excel Spreadsheet
5.5 Creating a Photo Album
5.6 Converting Text and WordArt to a SmartArt Diagram; Converting a SmartArt Diagram to Text and Shapes

---

If you want to present numbers and lists in a slide, consider inserting the information in a table. Use the Tables feature to create data in columns and rows in a manner similar to a spreadsheet. Display data in a slide in a more visual way by creating a SmartArt diagram. The SmartArt feature provides a number of predesigned diagrams and organizational charts. You can create a SmartArt diagram and then modify the design and layout of the diagram.

While a table does an adequate job of representing data, you can create a chart from data to provide a more visual representation of the data. A chart is sometimes referred to as a *graph* and is a picture of numeric data. If you have Microsoft Excel installed on your computer, you can create a chart in a PowerPoint slide. If you do not have Excel installed on your computer, PowerPoint uses the Microsoft Graph feature to create your chart. Projects and assessments in this chapter assume that you have Excel installed on your computer.

You can create a photo album presentation to attractively display personal or business photographs. With the Photo Album feature you can insert pictures and then format the appearance of the pictures in the presentation. Model answers for this chapter's projects appear on the following page.

PowerPoint2010C5

Note: Before beginning the projects, copy to your storage medium the PowerPoint2010C5 folder from the PowerPoint2010 folder on the CD that accompanies this textbook and then make PowerPoint2010C5 the active folder.

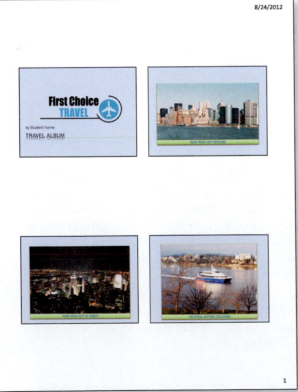

Project 1 Create a Company Sales Conference Presentation

P-C5-P1-Conference.pptx

Project 2 Create and Format a Travel Photo Album

P-C5-P2-Album.pptx

Project 1 — Create a Company Sales Conference Presentation — 14 Parts

You will create a sales conference presentation for Nature's Way that includes a table, a column chart, a pie chart, and four SmartArt graphics.

Creating a Table

Use the Tables feature to create boxes of information called *cells*. A cell is the intersection between a row and a column. A cell can contain text, characters, numbers, data, graphics, or formulas. If you want to arrange the content of a slide in columns and rows, insert a new slide with the slide layout that includes a content placeholder. Click the Insert Table button in the content placeholder and the Insert Table dialog box displays. At the Insert Table dialog box, type the number of columns, press the Tab key, type the number of rows, and then press Enter. You can also insert a table using the Table button in the Tables group in the Insert tab. Click the Table button, drag the mouse down and to the right to select the desired number of columns and rows, and then click the left mouse button.

When you create a table, the insertion point is located in the cell in the upper left corner of the table. Cells in a table contain a cell designation. Columns in a table are lettered from left to right, beginning with *A*. Rows in a table are numbered from top to bottom beginning with *1*. The cell in the upper left corner of the table is cell A1. The cell to the right of A1 is B1, the cell to the right of B1 is C1, and so on.

Entering Text in Cells

With the insertion point positioned in a cell, type or edit text. Move the insertion point to other cells with the mouse by clicking in the desired cell. If you are using the keyboard, press the Tab key to move the insertion point to the next cell or press Shift + Tab to move the insertion point to the previous cell.

If the text you type does not fit on one line, it wraps to the next line within the same cell. Or, if you press Enter within a cell, the insertion point is moved to the next line within the same cell. The cell vertically lengthens to accommodate the text, and all cells in that row also lengthen. Pressing the Tab key in a table causes the insertion point to move to the next cell in the table. If you want to move the insertion point to a tab stop within a cell, press Ctrl + Tab. If the insertion point is located in the last cell of the table and you press the Tab key, PowerPoint adds another row to the table.

Selecting Cells

You can apply formatting to an entire table or to specific cells, rows, or columns in a table. To identify cells for formatting, select the specific cells using the mouse or the keyboard. Press the Tab key to select the next cell or press Shift + Tab to select the previous cell. Refer to Table 5.1 for additional methods for selecting in a table.

▼ Quick Steps

Insert a Table
1. Click Insert Table button in content placeholder.
2. Type number of columns.
3. Press Tab.
4. Type number of rows.
5. Click OK.
OR
1. Click Insert tab.
2. Click Table button.
3. Drag in grid to desired number of columns and rows.

Table

HINT

Add a row to the bottom of a table by positioning the insertion point in the last cell and then pressing the Tab key.

HINT

You can move text to a different cell by selecting the text and then dragging the selected text to a different cell.

Table 5.1 Selecting in a Table

To select this	Do this
A cell	Position the mouse pointer at left side of cell until pointer turns into a small, black, diagonally pointing arrow and then click the left mouse button.
A row	Position the mouse pointer outside the table at the left edge of the row until the pointer turns into a small, black arrow pointing right and then click the left mouse button. Drag to select multiple rows.
A column	Position the mouse pointer outside the table at the top of the column until the pointer turns into a small, black arrow pointing down and then click the left mouse button. Drag to select multiple columns.
All cells in a table	Drag to select all cells or press Ctrl + A.
Text within a cell	Position the mouse pointer at the beginning of the text and then hold down the left mouse button as you drag the mouse across the text. (When a cell is selected, the cell background color changes to blue. When text within cells is selected, only those lines containing text are selected.)

Project 1a Creating a Table   Part 1 of 14

1. Open **Conference.pptx** and then save the presentation with Save As and name it **P-C5-P1-Conference**.
2. Make Slide 4 active.
3. Insert a table in the slide and enter text into the cells by completing the following steps:
   a. Click the Insert Table button located in the middle of the slide in the content placeholder.
   b. At the Insert Table dialog box, type **2** in the *Number of columns* text box.
   c. Press the Tab key.
   d. Type **5** in the *Number of rows* text box.
   e. Click OK or press Enter.
   f. Type the text as displayed in the table below. Press the Tab key to move the insertion point to the next cell or press Shift + Tab to move the insertion point to the previous cell. Do not press Tab after typing the last cell entry.

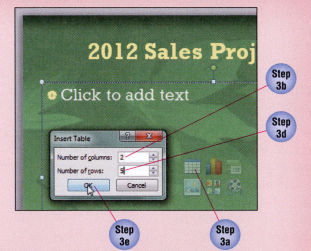

Step 3b
Step 3d
Step 3e
Step 3a
Step 3f

2012 Sales Projections

Region	Sales
North	$1,683,000
South	$1,552,000
East	$1,778,000
West	$1,299,000

4. Apply formatting to text in specific cells by completing the following steps:
   a. With the insertion point positioned in the table, press Ctrl + A to select all of the text in the table.
   b. Click the Home tab and then change the font size to 32.
   c. Looking at the text set in 32 point size, you decide that you want the text below the headings set in a smaller point size. To do this, position the mouse pointer at the left edge of the second row (to the left of the cell containing *North*) until the pointer turns into a small, black, right-pointing arrow. Hold down the left mouse button, drag down so the remaining rows are selected, and then change the font size to 28.
   d. Click outside the table to deselect it.
5. Save **P-C5-P1-Conference.pptx**.

Changing Table Design

When you create a table, the Table Tools Design tab is selected that contains a number of options for enhancing the appearance of the table as shown in Figure 5.1. With options in the Table Styles group, apply a predesigned style that applies color and border lines to a table. Maintain further control over the predesigned style formatting applied to columns and rows with options in the Table Style Options group. For example, if you want your first column to be formatted differently than the other columns in the table, insert a check mark in the *First Column* check box. Apply additional design formatting to cells in a table with the Shading, Borders, and Effects buttons in the Table Styles group. Draw a table or draw additional rows and/or columns in a table by clicking the Draw Table button in the Draw Borders group. Click this button and the mouse pointer turns into a pencil. Drag in the table to create the desired columns and rows. Click the Eraser button and the mouse pointer turns into an eraser. Drag through the column and/or row lines you want to erase in the table.

HINT

Draw a freeform table by clicking the Insert tab, clicking the Table button, and then clicking the *Draw Table* option. Drag in the document to create the table.

Shading   Borders

Effects   Draw Table

Eraser

Figure 5.1 Table Tools Design Tab

Project 1b   **Modifying the Table Design**   **Part 2 of 14**

1. With **P-C5-P1-Conference.pptx** open, make sure Slide 4 is active, the insertion point is positioned in the table, and then click the Table Tools Design tab.
2. Click the *First Column* check box in the Table Style Options group to insert a check mark. (This applies bold formatting to the text in the first column and applies darker shading to the cell.)

3. Click the More button that displays at the right side of the Table Styles thumbnails and then click the *Themed Style 1 - Accent 6* option (last option in the top row).

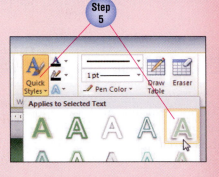

4. Select the first row of the table.
5. Click the Quick Styles button in the WordArt Styles group and then click *Fill - Light Green Accent 3, Outline - Text 2* option (last option in the top row).
6. Click the Text Fill button arrow in the WordArt Styles group and then click *Light Yellow, Text 2, Darker 10%*.

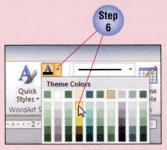

7. Click the Text Outline button arrow in the WordArt Styles group and then click *Green, Accent 6, Lighter 40%*.
8. Click the Pen Weight button arrow in the Draw Borders group and then click *2¼ pt*. (This activates the Draw Table button.)
9. Click the Pen Color button in the Draw Borders group and then click *Green, Accent 6, Darker 25%*.
10. Draw along the border that separates the two columns from the top of the first row to the bottom of the last row.
11. Draw along the border that separates the first row from the second row.
12. Click the Draw Table button to deactivate it.
13. Save **P-C5-P1-Conference.pptx**.

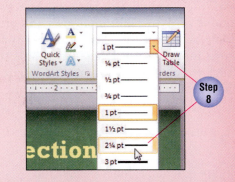

Changing Table Layout

To further customize a table consider changing the table layout by inserting or deleting columns and rows and specifying cell alignments. Change table layout with options at the Table Tools Layout tab shown in Figure 5.2. Use options and buttons in the tab to select specific cells, delete and insert rows and columns, merge and split cells, specify cell and table height and width and text alignment in cells, and arrange elements in a slide.

HINT

If you make a mistake while formatting a table, immediately click the Undo button on the Quick Access toolbar.

Figure 5.2 Table Tools Layout Tab

Project 1c   Modifying Table Layout   **Part 3 of 14**

1. With **P-C5-P1-Conference.pptx** open, make sure Slide 4 is active.
2. Click in any cell in the table and then click the Table Tools Layout tab.
3. Click in the cell containing the word *East*.
4. Click the Insert Above button in the Rows & Columns group.
5. Type **Central** in the new cell at the left, press the Tab key, and then type **$1,024,000** in the new cell at the right.
6. Click in the cell containing the word *Region*.
7. Click the Insert Left button in the Rows & Columns group.
8. Click the Merge Cells button in the Merge group.
9. Type **Sales Projections** in the new cell.
10. Click the Text Direction button in the Alignment group and then click *Rotate all text 270°* at the drop-down list.
11. Click the Center button in the Alignment group and then click the Center Vertically button in the Alignment group.
12. Click in the Width measurement box in the Cell Size group, type **1.2**, and then press Enter.

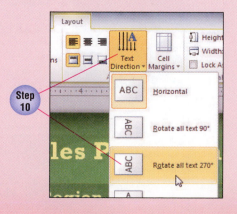

13. Click the Table Tools Design tab.
14. Click the Borders button arrow in the Table Styles group (the name of the button changes depending on the last action performed) and then click *Bottom Border* at the drop-down list.
15. Click in the cell containing the text *Sales* and then click the Table Tools Layout tab.
16. Click in the Height measurement box in the Cell Size group and type **0.7**.
17. Click in the Width measurement box in the Cell Size group, type **2.5**, and then press Enter.
18. Click in the cell containing the text *Region*.
19. Click in the Width measurement box in the Cell Size group, type **4**, and then press Enter.
20. Click in the Height measurement box in the Table Size group, type **4.2**, and then press Enter.
21. Click the Select button in the Table group and then click *Select Table* at the drop-down list.
22. Click the Center button and then click the Center Vertically button in the Alignment group.
23. After looking at the text in cells, you decide that you want the text in the second column left-aligned. To do this, complete the following steps:
    a. Click in the cell containing the text *Region*.
    b. Click the Select button in the Table group and then click *Select Column* at the drop-down list.
    c. Click the Align Text Left button in the Alignment group.
    d. Click in any cell in the table.
24. Align the table by completing the following steps:
    a. Click the Home tab.
    b. Click the Arrange button in the Drawing group, point to *Align*, and then click *Distribute Horizontally*.
    c. Click the Arrange button, point to *Align*, and then click *Distribute Vertically*.
    d. Looking at the table, you decide that it should be moved down in the slide. To do this, position the mouse pointer on the table border until the pointer displays with a four-headed arrow attached. Hold down the left mouse button, drag down approximately one-half inch, and then release the mouse button.
25. Insert a clip art image in the table by completing the following steps:
    a. Click the Insert tab.
    b. Click the Clip Art button in the Illustrations group.

Step 13

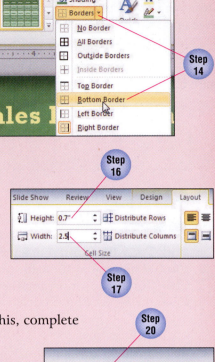

Step 14

Step 16

Step 17

Step 20

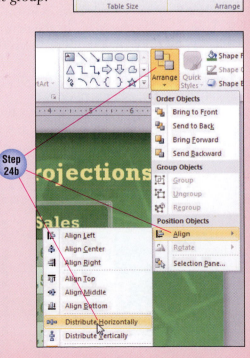

Step 24b

c. Select any text that displays in the *Search for* text box in the Clip Art task pane, type **sales**, and then press Enter.

d. Scroll down the list of clip art images and then click the image shown in Figure 5.3. (If this image is not available, choose a similar clip art image related to sales.)

e. Close the Clip Art task pane.

f. With the image selected, click in the Shape Height measurement box in the Size group in the Picture Tools Format tab, type **2.8**, and then press Enter.

g. Drag the clip art image so it is positioned in the table as shown in Figure 5.3.

h. Click outside the clip art image to deselect it.

26. Save **P-C5-P1-Conference.pptx**.

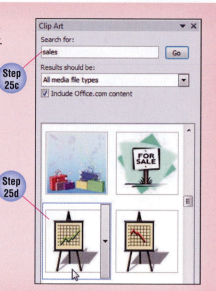

Step 25c

Step 25d

Figure 5.3 Project 1c, Slide 4

2012 Sales Projections

Region	Sales
North	$1,683,000
South	$1,552,000
Central	$1,024,000
East	$1,778,000
West	$1,299,000

Sales Projections

Inserting an Excel Spreadsheet

In addition to inserting a table in a slide, you can insert an Excel spreadsheet, which provides you with some Excel functions. To insert an Excel spreadsheet, click the Insert tab, click the Table button in the Tables group, and then click the *Excel Spreadsheet* option at the drop-down list. This inserts a small worksheet in the slide with two columns and two rows visible. You can increase the number of visible cells by dragging the sizing handles that display around the worksheet. Click outside the worksheet and the cells display as an object that you can format with options in the Drawing Tools Format tab. To format the worksheet with Excel options, double-click the worksheet and the ribbon displays with Excel tabs.

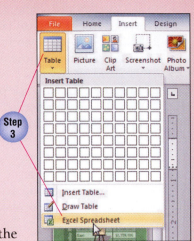

1. With **P-C5-P1-Conference.pptx** open, make Slide 4 active and then insert a new slide with the *Title Only* layout.
2. Click the text *Click to add title* and then type Projected Increase.
3. Insert an Excel spreadsheet by clicking the Insert tab, clicking the Table button in the Tables group, and then clicking *Excel Spreadsheet* at the drop-down list.
4. Increase the size of the worksheet by completing the following steps:
   a. Position the mouse pointer on the sizing handle (small black square) located in the lower right corner of the worksheet until the pointer displays as a black, diagonal, two-headed arrow.
   b. Hold down the left mouse button and drag down and to the right and then release the mouse button. Continue dragging the sizing handles until columns A, B, and C and rows 1 through 6 are visible.
5. Copy a Word table into the Excel worksheet by completing the following steps:
   a. Open Word and then open the **NWSalesInc.docx** document in the PowerPoint2010C5 folder on your storage medium.
   b. Hover your mouse pointer over the table and then click the table move handle (small square containing a four-headed arrow) that displays in the upper left corner of the table. (This selects all cells in the table.)
   c. Click the Copy button in the Clipboard group in the Home tab.
   d. Click the PowerPoint button on the Taskbar.
   e. With Slide 5 active and the first cell in the worksheet active, click the Paste button in the Clipboard group in the Home tab.
6. Size and position the worksheet object by completing the following steps:
   a. Click outside the worksheet to remove the Excel ribbon tabs.
   b. With the worksheet object selected (gray border surrounds the object), click the Drawing Tools Format tab.
   c. Click in the *Shape Width* measurement box, type 7, and then press Enter.
   d. Using the mouse, drag the worksheet object so it is centered on the slide.
7. Format the worksheet and insert a formula by completing the following steps:
   a. Double-click in the worksheet. (This displays the Excel ribbon tabs.)
   b. Increase the width of the second column by positioning the mouse pointer on the column boundary between column B and C and then double-clicking the left mouse button.

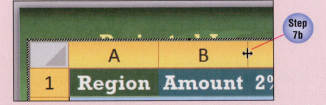

   c. Click in cell C2, type the formula =B2*102, and then press Enter.
8. Copy the formula in C2 to cells C3 through C6 by completing the following steps:
   a. Position the mouse pointer (white plus symbol) in cell C2, hold down the left mouse button, drag down to cell C6, and then release the mouse button.

b. Click the Fill button in the Editing group in the Home tab and then click *Down* at the drop-down list.

9. Click outside the worksheet to remove the Excel ribbon tabs.

10. With the worksheet object selected, drag the object so it is centered on the slide below the title.

11. Click the Word button on the Taskbar and exit Word without saving changes to the document.

12. Save **P-C5-P1-Conference.pptx**.

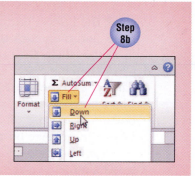

Drawing a Table

You can draw a table in a slide using the *Draw Table* option at the Table button drop-down list. When you click the Table button and then click the *Draw Table* option, the mouse pointer displays as a pen. Drag in the slide to create the table. Use buttons in the Table Tools Design tab and Table Tools Format tab to format the table.

Project 1e **Drawing a Table**   **Part 5 of 14**

1. With **P-C5-P1-Conference.pptx** open, make sure Slide 5 is active.

2. Draw a table and then split the table into two columns and two rows by completing the following steps:

   a. Click the Insert tab, click the Table button in the Tables group, and then click the *Draw Table* option at the drop-down list.

   b. Position the mouse pointer (displays as a pen) below the worksheet and then drag to create a table that is approximately 4 inches wide and 1 inch tall.

   c. Click the Table Tools Layout tab and then click the Split Cells button in the Merge group.

   d. At the Split Cells dialog box, press the Tab key, type **2** and then press the Enter key. (This splits the table into two columns and two rows.)

   e. Select the current measurement in the *Height* measurement box in the Table Size group and then type **1**.

   f. Select the current measurement in the *Width* measurement box in the Table Size group, type **7.5**, and then press Enter.

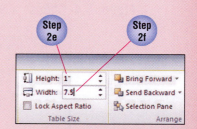

3. With the table selected, make the following formatting changes:

   a. Click the Table Tools Design tab.

   b. Click the Shading button arrow in the Table Styles group and then click *Green, Background 1, Darker 25%* at the drop-down palette (located in the first column).

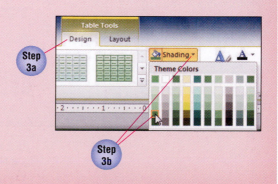

c. Click the Effects button in the Table Styles group, point to *Cell Bevel*, and then click the *Relaxed Inset* option (second option from the left in the top row in the *Bevel* section).

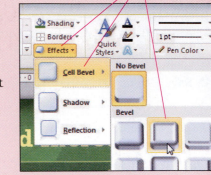

d. Click the Home tab.

e. Click the Center button in the Paragraph group.

f. Make sure the table is positioned evenly between the bottom of the top table and the bottom of the slide.

g. Click the Arrange button in the Drawing group, point to *Align*, and then click *Distribute Horizontally* at the side menu.

4. Type **Maximum** in the first cell in the table, press the Tab key, and then type **$171,666,000**.

5. Press the Tab key and then type **Minimum**.

6. Press the Tab key and then type **$104,448,000**.

7. Click outside the table to deselect it.

8. Save **P-C5-P1-Conference.pptx**.

▼ **Quick Steps**

Insert a SmartArt Diagram
1. Click Insert SmartArt Graphic button in content placeholder.
2. Double-click desired diagram.
OR
1. Click Insert tab.
2. Click SmartArt button.
3. Double-click desired diagram.

Creating SmartArt ■■■■■■■■ ■■■■ ■■ ■■

With the SmartArt feature you can insert diagrams and organizational charts in a slide. SmartArt offers a variety of predesigned diagrams and organizational charts that are available at the Choose a SmartArt Graphic dialog box shown in Figure 5.4. Display the Choose a SmartArt Graphic dialog box by clicking the Insert SmartArt Graphic button that displays in a content placeholder or by clicking the Insert tab and then clicking the SmartArt button in the Illustrations group. At the dialog box, *All* is selected in the left panel and all available predesigned diagrams display in the middle panel.

Figure 5.4 Choose a SmartArt Graphic Dialog Box

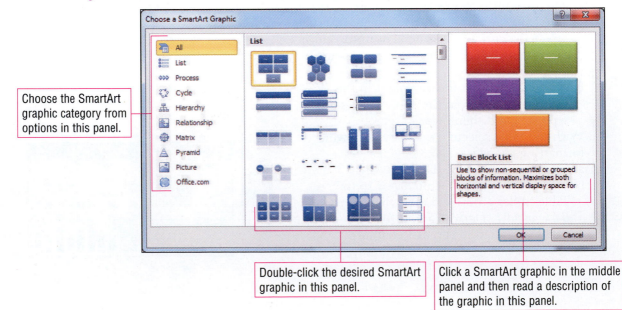

Choose the SmartArt graphic category from options in this panel.

Double-click the desired SmartArt graphic in this panel.

Click a SmartArt graphic in the middle panel and then read a description of the graphic in this panel.

Figure 5.5 SmartArt Tools Design Tab

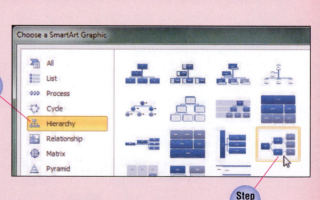

Modifying SmartArt Design

Predesigned diagrams display in the middle panel of the Choose a SmartArt Graphic dialog box. Use the scroll bar at the right side of the middle panel to scroll down the list of diagram choices. Click a diagram in the middle panel and the name of the diagram displays in the right panel along with a description of the diagram type. SmartArt includes diagrams for presenting a list of data; showing data processes, cycles, and relationships; and presenting data in a matrix or pyramid. Double-click a diagram in the middle panel of the dialog box and the diagram is inserted in the slide.

When you double-click a diagram at the dialog box, the diagram is inserted in the slide and a text pane may display at the left side of the diagram. You can type text in the text pane or directly in the diagram. Apply design formatting to a diagram with options at the SmartArt Tools Design tab shown in Figure 5.5. This tab is active when the diagram is inserted in the slide. With options and buttons in this tab you add objects, change the diagram layout, apply a style to the diagram, and reset the diagram back to the original formatting.

HINT
Use SmartArt to communicate your message and ideas in a visual manner.

HINT
Limit the number of shapes and the amount of text to key points in a slide.

SmartArt

Project 1f **Inserting and Modifying a SmartArt Diagram** **Part 6 of 14**

1. With **P-C5-P1-Conference.pptx** open, make sure Slide 5 is active and then insert a new slide with the *Title and Content* layout.
2. Click in the title placeholder and then type **Division Reorganization**.
3. Click the Insert SmartArt Graphic button located in the middle of the slide in the content placeholder.
4. At the Choose a SmartArt Graphic dialog box, click *Hierarchy* in the left panel of the dialog box.
5. Double-click the *Horizontal Hierarchy* option (last option in the third row).
6. If a *Type your text here* window displays at the left side of the organizational chart, close the pane by clicking the Text Pane button in the Create Graphic group.
7. Delete one of the boxes in the organizational chart by clicking the border of the top box at the right side of the slide (the top box of the three stacked boxes) and then pressing the Delete key. (Make sure that the selection border that surrounds the box is a solid line and not a dashed line. If a dashed line displays, click the box border again. This should change it to a solid line.)

8. Click *[Text]* in the first box at the left, type **Andrew Singh**, press the Enter key, and then type **Director**. Click in each of the remaining boxes and type the text as shown below.

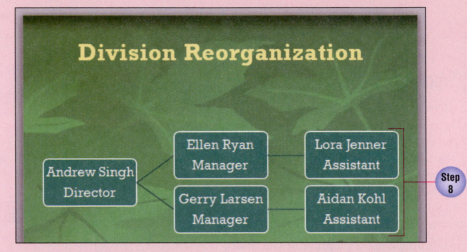

9. Click inside the SmartArt border but outside of any shape.
10. Click the More button located at the right side of the style thumbnails in the SmartArt Styles group and then click the *Polished* style (first option from the left in the top row of the *3-D* section).

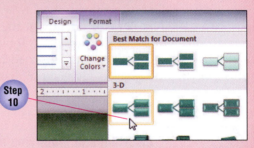

11. Click the Change Colors button in the SmartArt Styles group and then click *Gradient Range - Accent 2* (third option from the left in the *Accent 2* section).
12. Change the layout of the organizational chart by clicking the More button at the right side of the thumbnails in the Layouts group and then click *Table Hierarchy* at the drop-down list. Your slide should now look like the slide shown in Figure 5.6.

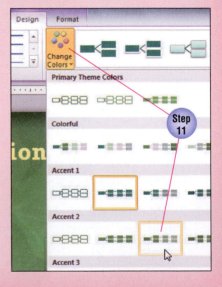

13. Save **P-C5-P1-Conference.pptx**.

Figure 5.6 Project 1f, Slide 6

Division Reorganization

Andrew Singh
Director

Ellen Ryan
Manager

Gerry Larsen
Manager

Lora Jenner
Assistant

Aidan Kohl
Assistant

Formatting SmartArt

Apply formatting to a SmartArt diagram with options at the SmartArt Tools Format tab shown in Figure 5.7. With options and buttons in this tab you can change the size and shape of objects in the diagram; apply shapes styles and WordArt styles; change the shape fill, outline, and effects; and arrange and size the diagram. Move the diagram by positioning the arrow pointer on the diagram border until the pointer turns into a four-headed arrow, holding down the left mouse button, and then dragging the diagram to the desired location.

HINT
Nudge selected shape(s) with the up, down, left, or right arrow keys on the keyboard.

Figure 5.7 SmartArt Tools Format Tab

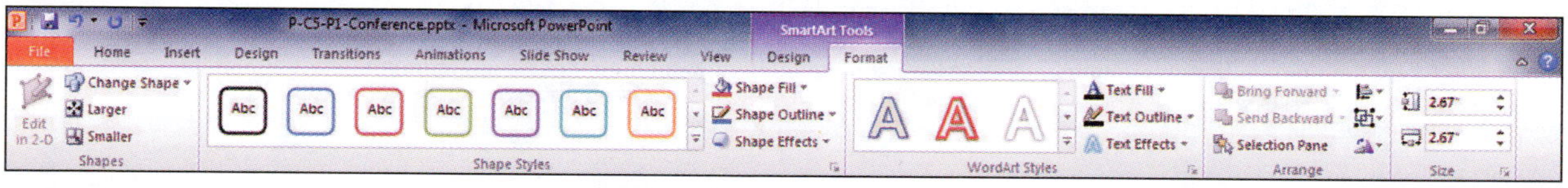

1. With **P-C5-P1-Conference.pptx** open, make Slide 1 active.
2. Click the Insert tab and then click the SmartArt button in the Illustrations group.
3. At the Choose a SmartArt Graphic dialog box, click *Relationship* in the left panel of the dialog box.
4. Double-click the *Basic Venn* option shown at the right.
5. Click in the top shape and type Health.
6. Click in the shape at the left and type Happiness.
7. Click in the shape at the right and type Harmony.
8. Click inside the SmartArt border but outside of any shape.
9. Click the Change Colors button in the SmartArt Styles group and then click *Colored Fill - Accent 2* (second option from the left in the *Accent 2* section).
10. Click the More button at the right side of the thumbnails in the SmartArt Styles group and then click *Polished* at the drop-down gallery (first option from the left in the top row of the *3-D* section).
11. Click the SmartArt Tools Format tab.
12. Click the More button at the right side of the WordArt Styles thumbnails and then click *Fill - Light Green, Accent 3, Powder Bevel* at the drop-down gallery (fourth option from the left in the first row in the *Applies to All Text in the Shape* section).

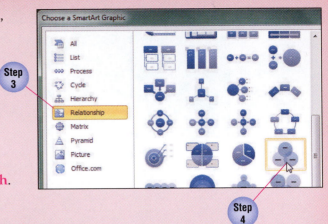

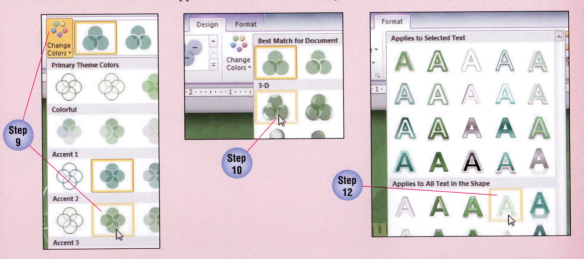

13. Click the Text Outline button arrow in the WordArt Styles group and then click *Light Yellow, Text 2, Darker 25%*.
14. Click in the *Height* measurement box in the Size group and then type 3.6.
15. Click in the *Width* measurement box, type 5.5, and then press Enter.

16. Click the Send Backward button arrow in the Arrange group and then click the *Send to Back* option at the drop-down list.
17. Drag the SmartArt so it is positioned as shown in Figure 5.8.

18. Drag the title and subtitle placeholders so they are positioned as shown in Figure 5.8.
19. You decide to experiment with rotating and changing the orientation of text in a shape. To do this, complete the following steps:
    a. Click the shape containing the word *Happiness*.
    b. Click the Rotate button in the Arrange group in the SmartArt Tools Format tab and then click *Rotate Left 90°* at the drop-down list.
    c. Click the shape containing the word *Harmony*.
    d. Click the Rotate button in the Arrange group and then click *Rotate Left 90°* at the drop-down list.
    e. You decide you do not like the text rotated. Return the text to normal orientation by clicking twice on the Undo button on the Quick Access toolbar.
20. Save **P-C5-P1-Conference.pptx**.

Figure 5.8 Project 1g, Slide 1

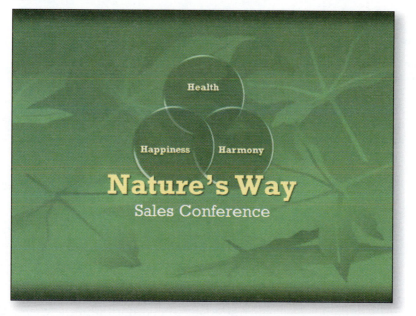

Converting Text and WordArt to a SmartArt Diagram

To improve the visual display of text or WordArt and to create a professionally designed image, consider converting text or WordArt to a SmartArt diagram. To do this, select the placeholder containing the text or WordArt and then click the Convert to SmartArt button in the Paragraph group in the Home tab. Click the desired SmartArt diagram at the drop-down gallery or click the *More SmartArt Graphics* option and then choose a SmartArt diagram at the Choose a SmartArt Graphic dialog box.

Inserting Text in the Text Pane

You can enter text in a SmartArt shape by clicking in the shape and then typing the text. You can also insert text in a SmartArt shape by typing text in the Text pane. Display the Text pane by clicking the Text Pane button in the Create Graphic group in the SmartArt Tools Design tab.

1. With **P-C5-P1-Conference.pptx** open, make Slide 7 active. (This slide contains WordArt text.)
2. Click on any character in the WordArt text.
3. If necessary, click the Home tab.
4. Click the Convert to SmartArt Graphic button in the Paragraph group.
5. At the drop-down gallery that displays, click the *More SmartArt Graphics* option that displays at the bottom of the gallery.
6. At the Choose a SmartArt Graphic dialog box, click *Cycle* in the left panel and then double-click *Diverging Radial* in the middle panel.

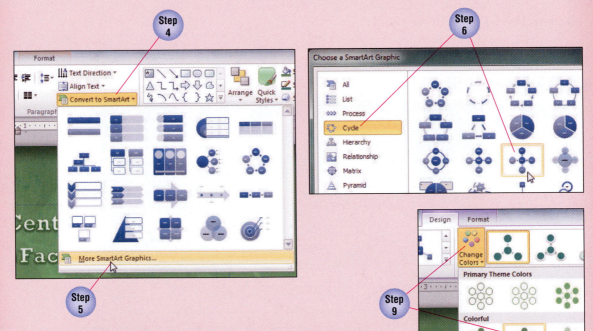

7. Click the Add Shape button in the Create Graphic group in the SmartArt Tools Design tab and then type **Supplies** in the new shape.
8. Change the order of the text in the shapes at the left and right sides of the graphic by clicking the Right to Left button in the Create Graphic group.
9. Click the Change Colors button in the SmartArt Styles group and then click *Colorful Range - Accent Colors 2 to 3* (second option from the left in the *Colorful* section).
10. Click the More button at the right of the SmartArt Styles thumbnails and then click *Inset* (second option from the left in the *3-D* section).
11. Click the SmartArt Tools Format tab.
12. Click the middle circle (contains the text *Central Division*).
13. Click three times on the Larger button in the Shapes group.
14. Click inside the SmartArt border but outside of any shape.
15. Click in the *Height* measurement box in the Size group and then type **6.6**.
16. Click in the *Width* measurement box, type **8.2**, and then press Enter.
17. Click the Home tab.
18. With the SmartArt graphic selected, click the Arrange button in the Drawing group, point to *Align*, and then click *Distribute Horizontally*.

19. Click the Arrange button in the Drawing group, point to *Align*, and then click *Distribute Vertically*.
20. Click the Bold button in the Font group.
21. Make Slide 9 active.
22. Click in any character in the bulleted text and, if necessary, click the Home tab.
23. Click the Convert to SmartArt Graphic button in the Paragraph group and then click the *Vertical Block List* diagram (second diagram from the left in the top row) at the drop-down gallery.
24. Click the shape containing the text *Sales over $2 million* and then click the Demote button in the Create Graphic group in the SmartArt Tools Design tab.
25. Click on any character in the text *One-week all expenses paid trip to Las Vegas* and then click the Promote button in the Create Graphic group.

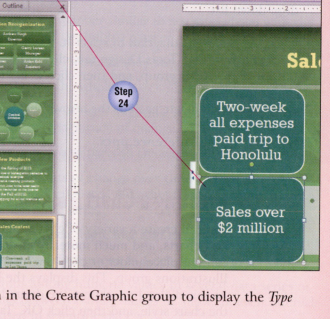

26. If necessary, click the Text Pane button in the Create Graphic group to display the *Type your text here* text pane.
27. Click immediately right of the *s* in *Vegas* in the text pane and then press the Enter key.
28. Press the Tab key and then type **Sales over $1 million**.
29. Close the text pane by clicking the Close button that displays in the upper right corner of the pane.
30. Click the More button that displays at the right side of the SmartArt Styles thumbnails and then click the *Inset* option (second option from the left in the top row of the *3-D* section).
31. Save **P-C5-P1-Conference.pptx**.

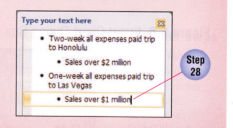

Converting a SmartArt Diagram to Text or Shapes

If you want to remove all formatting from a SmartArt diagram, click the Reset Graphic button in the Reset group in the SmartArt Tools Design tab. With the Convert button, you can convert a SmartArt diagram to text or shapes. Click the Convert button and then click the *Convert to Text* option at the drop-down list to convert the SmartArt to bulleted text. Click the *Convert to Shapes* option at the drop-down list to convert a SmartArt to shapes. With the SmartArt converted to shapes, you can move, resize, or delete a shape independently from the other shapes.

Figure 5.10 Sample Chart

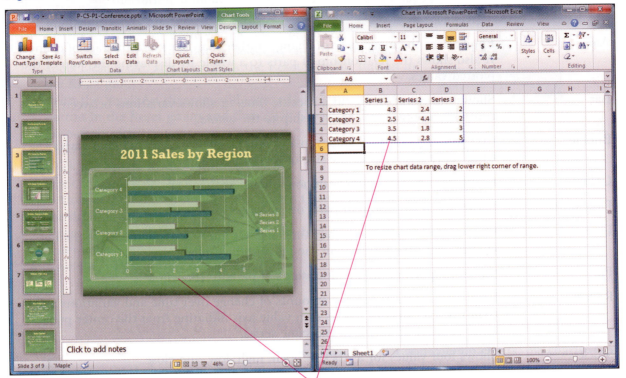

Enter data in cells in the Excel worksheet at right above. The data entered is reflected in the PowerPoint presentation chart at left.

Project 1j   **Creating a Chart**   **Part 10 of 14**

1. With **P-C5-P1-Conference.pptx** open, make Slide 3 active.
2. Click the Insert Chart button in the content placeholder.
3. At the Insert Chart dialog box, click *Bar* in the left panel.
4. Click the *Clustered Bar in 3-D* option that displays in the *Bar* section (fourth option from the left) in the middle panel and then click OK.
5. In the Excel worksheet, position the mouse pointer on the bottom right corner of the blue border until the mouse pointer displays as a double-headed arrow pointing diagonally. Hold down the left mouse button, drag to the left until the border displays at the right side of column C, and then release the mouse button.

Step 3

Step 4

6. Position the mouse pointer on the bottom right corner of the blue border until the pointer displays as a double-headed arrow and then drag down until the border displays at the bottom of row 6.

7. Type the text in cells as shown below by completing the following steps:
   a. Click in cell B1 in the Excel worksheet, type **1st Half**, and then press the Tab key.
   b. With cell C1 active, type **2nd Half** and then press the Tab key.
   c. In cell A2, type **North** and then press the Tab key.
   d. Type **$853,000** and then press the Tab key.
   e. Type **$970,000** and then press the Tab key.
   f. Continue typing the remaining data in cells as indicated below.

8. Click the Close button that displays in the upper right corner of the Excel window.

Step 6

	A	B	C	D	E
1		Series 1	Series 2	Series 3	
2	Category 1	4.3	2.4	2	
3	Category 2	2.5	4.4	2	
4	Category 3	3.5	1.8	3	
5	Category 4	4.5	2.8	5	
6					
7					
8		To resize chart data range, drag lower right co

Step 7

	A	B	C	D	E
1		1st Half	2nd Half	Series 3	
2	North	$853,000	$970,000	2	
3	South	$750,000	$910,000	2	
4	Central	$720,000	$750,000	3	
5	East	$880,000	$950,000	5	
6	West	$830,000	$900,000		
7					
8		To resize chart data range, drag lower rig	

Step 8

9. Save **P-C5-P1-Conference.pptx**.

Changing Chart Design

When the chart is inserted in the slide, the Chart Tools Design tab is active as shown in Figure 5.11. Use options in this tab to change the chart type, edit chart data, change the chart layout, and apply a chart style.

After you create a chart, you can change the chart type by clicking the Change Chart Type button in the Type group in the Chart Tools Design tab. This displays the Change Chart Type dialog box. This dialog box contains the same options as the Insert Chart dialog box shown in Figure 5.9. At the Change Chart Type dialog box, click the desired chart type in the left panel and click the desired chart style in the right panel.

Use options in the Data group in the Chart Tools Design tab to change the grouping of the data in the chart, select specific data, edit data, and refresh the data. When you create a chart, the cells in the Excel worksheet are linked to the chart in the slide. Click the Select Data button in the Data group and Excel opens

▼ **Quick Steps**

Change Chart Type and Style
1. Make the chart active.
2. Click Chart Tools Design tab.
3. Click Change Chart Type button.
4. Click desired chart type.
5. Click desired chart style.
6. Click OK.

Change Chart Type   Select Data

Figure 5.11 Chart Tools Design Tab

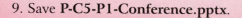

Edit Data

and the Select Data Source dialog box displays. At the Select Data Source dialog box, click the Switch Row/Column button to change the grouping of the selected data. If you need to edit data in the chart, click the Edit Data button and the Excel worksheet opens. Make the desired changes to cells in the Excel worksheet and then click the Close button.

The chart feature provides a number of predesigned chart layouts and styles you can apply to a chart. Click one of the chart layouts that displays in the Chart Layouts group or click the More button and then click the desired layout at the drop-down list. Apply a chart style to a chart by clicking one of the styles in the Chart Styles group or by clicking the More button and then clicking the desired style at the drop-down list.

Project 1k   Changing the Chart Type and Editing Data   Part 11 of 14

1. With **P-C5-P1-Conference.pptx** open, make sure Slide 3 is active.
2. Delete the title placeholder by completing the following steps:
   a. Click on any character in the title *2011 Sales by Region*.
   b. Position the mouse pointer on the placeholder border until the pointer displays with a four-headed arrow attached and then click the left mouse button. (This changes the placeholder border from a dashed line to a solid line.)
   c. Press the Delete key. (This removes the title *2011 Sales by Region* and displays the placeholder text *Click to add title*.)
   d. Position the mouse pointer on the placeholder border until the pointer displays with a four-headed arrow attached and then click the left mouse button. (This changes the placeholder border from a dashed line to a solid line.)
   e. Press the Delete key.
3. Click near the chart (but outside any chart elements) to select the chart. (A light gray border displays around the chart.)
4. Select data and switch rows and columns by completing the following steps:
   a. Click the Chart Tools Design tab.
   b. Click the Select Data button in the Data group. (This opens Excel and displays the Select Data Source dialog box.)
   c. Click the Switch Row/Column button in the Select Data Source dialog box.
   d. Click OK. (This switches the grouping of the data from Region to Half Yearly Sales.)
   e. Click the PowerPoint Title bar to make PowerPoint the active program.
   f. After viewing the chart in the PowerPoint slide, switch the rows and columns back to the original groupings by clicking the Switch Row/Column button in the Data group in the Chart Tools Design tab.
   g. Click the Close button that displays in the upper right corner of the Excel window.
5. Looking at the chart, you decide that the bar chart was not the best choice for the data and decide to change to a column chart. To do this, click the Change Chart Type button in the Type group.

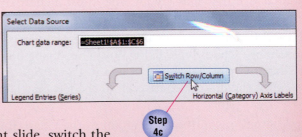

Step 4c

6. At the Change Chart Type dialog box, click the *Column* option in the left panel.
7. Click the *3-D Clustered Column* option (fourth option from the left in the top row in the *Column* section of the dialog box).
8. Click OK to close the dialog box.
9. Click the Edit Data button in the Data group.
10. Click in cell B4 (the cell containing the amount *$720,000*), type **650000**, and then press Enter. (When you press Enter, a dollar sign is automatically inserted in front of the number and a thousand separator comma is inserted.)
11. Click in cell B6 (the cell containing the amount *$830,000*), type **730000**, and then press Enter.
12. Click the Close button that displays in the upper right corner of the Excel window.
13. Click the Layout 3 thumbnail (third layout from the left) in the Chart Layouts group.
14. Click the More button that displays at the right side of the Chart Styles group and then click the *Style 18* option (second option from the left in the third row).
15. Save **P-C5-P1-Conference.pptx**.

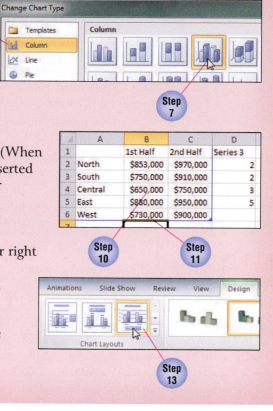

Formatting Chart Layout

Click the Chart Tools Layout tab and options display for changing and customizing chart elements as shown in Figure 5.12. With options in this tab you can specify chart elements, insert objects, add labels to the chart, customize the chart background, and add analysis items to the chart.

To format or modify a specific element in a chart, select the element. Do this by clicking the element or by clicking the Chart Elements button in the Current Selection group in the Chart Tools Layout tab. With the element selected, apply the desired formatting. Click the Format Selection button in the Current Selection group and a dialog box displays with options for formatting the selected element.

Insert objects in a chart with buttons in the Insert group in the Chart Tools Layout tab. Click the Picture button and the Insert Picture dialog box displays. At this dialog box, navigate to the desired folder and then double-click the desired picture. Use the Shapes button to draw a shape in the chart and use the Draw Text Box button to insert a text box in the chart.

▼ **Quick Steps**

Position Labels in Chart
1. Make the chart active.
2. Click Chart Tools Layout tab.
3. Click desired button.
4. Choose desired option at drop-down list.

H I N T

Right-click text in a chart element to display the Mini toolbar.

Figure 5.12 Chart Tools Layout Tab

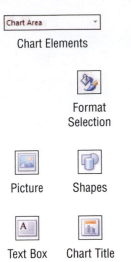

Chart Elements

Format Selection

Picture   Shapes

Text Box   Chart Title

Use options in the Labels group in the Chart Tools Layout tab to insert and position labels. For example, click the Chart Title button and a drop-down list displays with options for removing the chart title, centering the title and overlaying on the chart, and displaying the title above the chart. You can also position a label by dragging it. To do this, select the label, position the mouse pointer over the selected label or over the label border until the pointer displays with a four-headed arrow attached, hold down the left mouse button, and then drag the label to the desired location.

With buttons in the Axes, Background, and Analysis groups, you can further customize a chart. Use buttons in the Axes group to specify if you want major and/or minor horizontal and vertical lines in the chart. With buttons in the Background group, you can format the chart wall and floor and rotate the chart. Depending on the type of chart, some of the buttons in the Background group may not be active. Use buttons in the Analysis group to add analysis elements such as trendlines and up and down bars and error bars.

Project 1l   **Modifying Chart Layout**   **Part 12 of 14**

1. With **P-C5-P1-Conference.pptx** open, make sure Slide 3 is active and the chart is selected.
2. Click the Chart Tools Layout tab.
3. Click the Text Box button in the Insert group.
4. Click in the lower left corner of the chart (outside any chart elements).
5. Change the font size to 16, turn on bold, change the font color to Green, Accent 6, Darker 50%, and then type **Nature's Way**.
6. Click the Drawing Tools Format tab.
7. Click in the *Shape Height* measurement box in the Size group and then type **0.4**.
8. Click in the *Shape Width* measurement box, type **1.7**, and then press Enter.
9. Drag the text box down to the lower left corner of the chart.
10. Click inside the chart border but outside any chart elements and then click the Chart Tools Layout tab.
11. Click the Chart Elements button arrow in the Current Selection group and then click *Chart Title* at the drop-down list.
12. Type **2011 Regional Sales**.
13. Click the Data Table button in the Labels group and then click the *Show Data Table with Legend Keys* option at the drop-down list.
14. After looking at the data table, you decide to remove it by clicking the Data Table button in the Labels group and then clicking *None* at the drop-down list.
15. Click the Gridlines button in the Axes group, point to *Primary Vertical Gridlines*, and then click *Major & Minor Gridlines* at the side menu.
16. Click the Axes button in the Axes group, point to *Primary Horizontal Axis*, and then click the *Show Right to Left Axis* option.

17. Customize the chart wall and floor by completing the following steps:
    a. Click the Chart Wall button in the Background group and then click the *More Walls Options* option at the drop-down list.

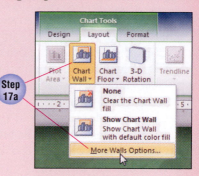

    b. At the Format Walls dialog box with the *Fill* option selected in the left panel, click the *Gradient fill* option and then click the Close button to close the dialog box.
    c. Click the Chart Floor button in the Background group and then click the *More Floor Options* option at the drop-down list.
    d. At the Format Floor dialog box with the *Fill* option selected in the left panel, click the *Gradient fill* option and then click the Close button to close the dialog box.
18. Return the horizontal axis back to the original location by clicking the Axes button in the Axes group, pointing to *Primary Horizontal Axis*, and then clicking the *Show Left to Right Axis* option.
19. Increase the height of the chart by positioning the mouse pointer on the four dots that display in the middle of the top border until the pointer displays as a two-headed arrow pointing up and down. Hold down the left mouse button, drag up approximately one inch, and then release the mouse button.
20. Click on any character in the chart title *2011 Regional Sales*.
21. Click the Home tab, change the font size to 32, and change the font color to Light Yellow, Text 2, Darker 10%.
22. Save **P-C5-P1-Conference.pptx**.

Changing Chart Formatting

Customize the format of the chart and chart elements with options in the Chart Tools Format tab as shown in Figure 5.13. The tab contains the same Current Selection group as the Chart Tools Layout tab. With the other options in the tab you can apply a predesigned style to a shape, a predesigned WordArt style to text, and arrange and size the chart.

The Shape Styles group in the Chart Tools Format tab contains predesigned styles you can apply to shapes in the chart. Click the More button at the right side of the style in the group and a drop-down gallery displays of shape styles. Use the buttons that display at the right side of the Shape Styles group to apply fill, an outline, and an effect to a selected shape. The WordArt Styles group contains predesigned styles you can apply to text in a chart. Use the buttons that display at the right side of the WordArt Styles group to apply fill, an outline, or an effect to text in a chart.

HINT Chart elements can be repositioned for easier viewing.

Figure 5.13 Chart Tools Format Tab

1. With **P-C5-P1-Conference.pptx** open, make sure Slide 3 is the active slide and the chart is selected.
2. Click the Chart Tools Format tab.
3. Click the Chart Elements button arrow in the Current Selection group and then click *Series "2nd Half"* at the drop-down list. (This selects the green bars in the chart representing second half sales.)
4. Click the More button at the right side of the Shape Styles thumbnails and then click the *Colored Fill - Green, Dark 1* option (first option from the left in the second row).

5. With the second half bars still selected, click the Shape Fill button arrow in the Shape Styles group, point to *Gradient*, and then click *Linear Down* in the *Dark Variations* section (second option from the left in the top row).
6. With the second half bars still selected, click the Shape Effects button in the Shape Styles group, point to *Bevel*, and then click the *Circle* option (first option from the left in the *Bevel* section of the side menu).
7. Click one of the teal bars that represent the first half sales amounts. (This selects all teal bars in the chart.)
8. Click the Shape Fill button arrow in the Shape Styles group and then click *Light Yellow, Text 2, Darker 10%*.
9. With the first half bars still selected, click the Shape Effects button in the Shape Styles group, point to *Bevel*, and then click the *Circle* option at the side menu.
10. Format the legend by completing the following steps:
    a. Click the Chart Elements button arrow in the Current Selection group and then click *Legend* at the drop-down list.
    b. Using the mouse, drag to the right approximately one-half inch the square sizing handle that displays in the middle of the right border of the legend.
    c. Click the Home tab.

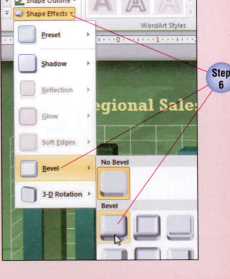

d. Click the Quick Styles button in the Drawing group and then click the *Moderate Effect - Green, Accent 2* option (third option from the left in the fifth row).

e. Click the Chart Tools Format tab.

f. Click the Format Selection button in the Current Selection group. (This displays the Format Legend dialog box.)

g. Click the *Border Color* option in the left panel.

h. Make sure the *Solid line* option is selected.

i. Click the Color button and then click the *Light Yellow, Text 2* option (fourth option from the left in the top row).

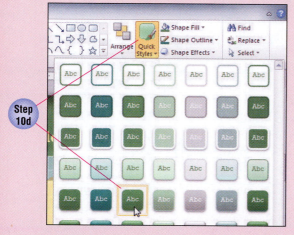

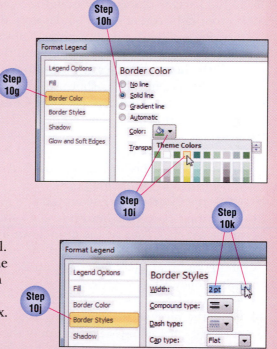

j. Click the *Border Styles* option in the left panel.

k. Click the up-pointing arrow at the right of the *Width* measurement box until *2 pt* displays in the box.

l. Click the Close button to close the dialog box.

11. Precisely position the chart on the slide by completing the following steps:

a. Click inside the chart border but outside any chart elements.

b. With the Chart Format Tools tab selected, click the Size group dialog box launcher. (This displays the Format Chart Area dialog box with the *Size* option selected in the left panel.)

c. Click the *Position* option in the left panel.

d. Change the *Horizontal* measurement to *0.5˝* and change the *Vertical* measurement to *0.9˝*.

e. Click the Close button to close the dialog box.

12. Save **P-C5-P1-Conference.pptx**.

Use buttons in the Arrange group to send the chart behind other objects, move it to the front of other objects, specify the alignment, and rotate the chart. You can size a chart by selecting the chart and then dragging a border. You can also size a chart to specific measurements with the Shape Height and Shape Width measurement boxes in the Size group in the Chart Tools Format tab. Change the height or width by clicking the up- or down-pointing arrows that display at the right side of the measurement box or click the current measurement in the measurement box and then type a specific measurement.

Shape Height   Shape Width

▼ **Quick Steps**

Change Chart Height and/or Width
1. Make the chart active.
2. Click Chart Tools Format tab.
3. Insert desired height and/or width in *Shape Height* and/or *Shape Width* measurement boxes.

1. With **P-C5-P1-Conference.pptx** open, make Slide 6 active and then insert a new slide with the *Title and Content* layout.
2. Click the title placeholder text and then type **Division Budget**.
3. Click the Insert tab and then click the Chart button in the Illustrations group.
4. At the Insert Chart dialog box, click *Pie* in the left panel.
5. Click the *Pie in 3-D* option (second option from the left in the *Pie* section) and then click OK.
6. In the Excel worksheet, position the mouse pointer on the bottom right corner of the border until the mouse pointer displays as a double-headed arrow pointing diagonally. Hold down the left mouse button and then drag down until the border displays at the bottom of row 7.

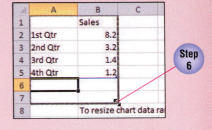

7. Type the text in cells as shown below.
8. When all data is entered, click the Close button that displays in the upper right corner of the Excel window.
9. With the Chart Tools Design tab selected, click the More button at the right side of the Chart Styles group and then click the *Style 26* option (second option from the left in the fourth row).

10. Click the Chart Tools Layout tab.
11. Click the Chart Title button in the Labels group and then click *None* at the drop-down list.
12. Click the Data Labels button in the Labels group and then click *Inside End* at the drop-down list.

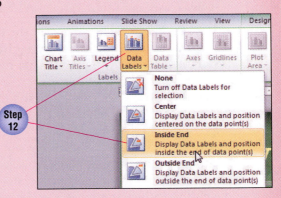

13. Click the Chart Tools Format tab.
14. Click the piece of pie containing *10%* and then click it again. (Make sure only the one piece of pie is selected.)
15. Click the Shape Fill button arrow in the Shape Styles group and then click *Light Yellow, Text 2, Darker 75%*.
16. Click the piece of pie containing *9%*. (Make sure only the one piece of pie is selected.)
17. Click the Shape Fill button arrow in the Shape Styles group and then click *Light Green, Accent 5, Darker 50%*.
18. Click the piece of pie containing *12%*. (Make sure only the one piece of pie is selected.)
19. Click the Shape Fill button arrow in the Shape Styles group and then click *Dark Teal, Accent 1, Lighter 40%*.
20. Click the Chart Elements button in the Current Selection group and then click *Chart Area* at the drop-down list.
21. Click in the *Shape Height* measurement box in the Size group, type **6**, and then press Enter.
22. Click the Align button in the Arrange group and then click *Distribute Vertically*.
23. Drag the chart down approximately one-half inch.
24. Apply a transition and sound of your choosing to all slides in the presentation.
25. Save **P-C5-P1-Conference.pptx**.
26. Run the presentation.
27. Print the presentation as a handout with six slides horizontally per page and then close **P-C5-P1-Conference.pptx**.

Project 2 Create and Format a Travel Photo Album 3 Parts

You will use the photo album feature to create a presentation containing travel photographs. You will also apply formatting and insert elements in the presentation.

Creating a Photo Album ■■■■■■■■■■■■■■■■■■

With PowerPoint's photo album feature, you can create a presentation containing personal or business pictures. You can customize and format the appearance of pictures by applying interesting layouts, frame shapes, and themes and you can also insert elements such as captions and text boxes. To create a photo album, click the Insert tab, click the Photo Album button arrow, and then click *New Photo Album* at the drop-down list. This displays the Photo Album dialog box as shown in Figure 5.14.

To insert pictures in the photo album, click the File/Disk button and the Insert New Pictures dialog box displays. At this dialog box, navigate to the desired folder and then double-click the picture you want inserted in the album. This inserts the picture name in the *Pictures in album* list box in the dialog box and also previews the picture in the *Preview* section. As you insert pictures in the photo album, the picture names display in the *Pictures in album* list box in the order in which they will appear in the presentation. When you have inserted the desired pictures in the photo album, click the Create button. This creates the photo album as a presentation and displays the first slide. The photo album feature creates the first slide with the title *Photo Album* and inserts the user's name.

▼ Quick Steps

Create Photo Album
1. Click Insert tab.
2. Click Photo Album button arrow.
3. Click *New Photo Album*.
4. Click File/Disk button.
5. Double-click desired picture.
6. Repeat Steps 4 and 5 for all desired pictures.
7. Make desired changes at Photo Album dialog box.
8. Click Create button.

Photo Album

Figure 5.14 Photo Album Dialog Box

Insert a picture by clicking this button and then double-clicking the picture at the Insert New Pictures dialog box.

Choose a picture and then preview it in this Preview box.

1. At a blank screen, click the Insert tab, click the Photo Album button arrow, and then click *New Photo Album* at the drop-down list.
2. At the Photo Album dialog box, click the File/Disk button.
3. At the Insert New Pictures dialog box, navigate to the PowerPoint2010C5 folder on your storage medium and then double-click *Cityscape.jpg*.
4. At the Photo Album dialog box, click the File/Disk button, and then double-click *Nightscape.jpg* at the Insert New Pictures dialog box.
5. Insert the following additional pictures: *Stonehenge.jpg*, *BigBen.jpg*, *WhiteHorse.jpg*, and *VictoriaBC.jpg*.
6. Click the Create button. (This opens a presentation with each image in a slide and the first slide containing the default text *Photo Album* followed by your name (or the user name for the computer).
7. Save the presentation and name it **P-C5-P2-Album.pptx**.
8. Run the presentation.

Editing and Formatting a Photo Album

▼ Quick Steps

Edit Photo Album
1. Click Insert tab.
2. Click Photo Album button arrow.
3. Click *Edit Photo Album*.
4. Make desired changes at Edit Photo Album dialog box.
5. Click Update button.

If you want to make changes to a photo album presentation, open the presentation, click the Insert tab, click the Photo Album button arrow, and then click *Edit Photo Album* at the drop-down list. This displays the Edit Photo Album dialog box, which contains the same options as the Photo Album dialog box.

Rearrange the order of slides in the photo album presentation by clicking the desired slide in the *Pictures in album* list box and then clicking the button containing the up-pointing arrow to move the slide up in the order or clicking the button containing the down-pointing arrow to move the slide down in the order. Remove a slide by clicking the desired slide in the list box and then clicking the Remove button. With the buttons below the *Preview* box in the Edit Photo Album dialog box, you can rotate the picture in the slide, increase or decrease the contrast, and increase or decrease the brightness of the picture.

The *Picture layout* option in the Album Layout group has a default setting of *Fit to slide*. At this setting the picture in each slide will fill most of the slide. You can change this setting by clicking the down-pointing arrow at the right side of the option. With options at the drop-down list, you can specify that you want one picture inserted in the slide, two pictures, or four pictures. You can also specify that you want the one, two, or four pictures inserted in slides with titles.

If you change the *Picture layout* option to something other than the default of *Fit to slide*, the *Frame shape* option becomes available. Click the down-pointing arrow at the right side of the option and a drop-down list displays with framing options. You can choose a rounded frame, simple frame, double frame, or a soft or shadow effect frame.

You can apply a theme to the photo album presentation by clicking the Browse button located at the right side of the *Theme* option box and then double-clicking the desired theme in the Choose Theme dialog box. This dialog box contains the predesigned themes provided by PowerPoint.

If you want to include a caption with the pictures, change the *Picture layout* to one, two, or four slides, and then click the *Captions below ALL pictures* check box located in the *Picture Options* section of the dialog box. PowerPoint will insert a caption below each picture that contains the name of the picture. You can edit the caption in the slide in the presentation. If you want to display all of the pictures in your photo album in black and white, click the *ALL pictures black and white* check box in the *Picture Options* section.

Click the New Text Box button in the Edit Photo Album dialog box and a new slide containing a text box is inserted in the presentation. In the presentation, you can edit the information in the text box. When all changes are made to the photo album, click the Update button located toward the bottom right side of the dialog box.

Project 2b **Editing and Formatting a Photo Album** **Part 2 of 3**

1. With **P-C5-P2-Album.pptx** open, click the Insert tab, click the Photo Album button arrow in the Images group, and then click *Edit Photo Album* at the drop-down list.
2. At the Edit Photo Album dialog box, make the following changes:
   a. Click the *ALL pictures black and white* option to insert a check mark.
   b. Click *VictoriaBC* in the *Pictures in album* list box and then click three times on the up-pointing arrow that displays below the list box. (This moves *VictoriaBC* so it is positioned between *Nightscape* and *Stonehenge*).
   c. Click *Cityscape* in the *Pictures in album* list box and then click twice on the Increase Contrast button located below the *Pictures in album* list box (the third button to the right of the Remove button).
   d. Click *VictoriaBC* in the *Pictures in album* list box and then click once on the rotate button located below the *Pictures in album* list box (the first button to the right of the Remove button). Click three more times on the Rotate button to return the image to the original orientation.

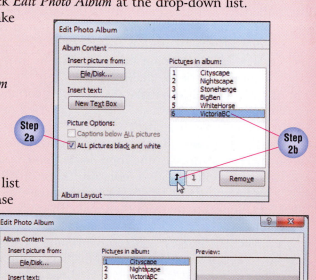

e. Click *Stonehenge* in the *Pictures in album* list box, click twice on the Increase Contrast button (the third button to the right of the Remove button), and then click twice on the Increase Brightness button (fifth button to the right of the Remove button).

f. Click the down-pointing arrow at the right side of the *Picture layout* option and then click *1 picture* at the drop-down list.

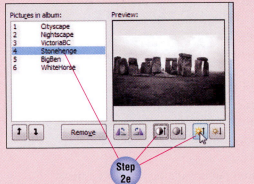

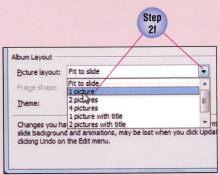

g. Click the down-pointing arrow at the right side of the *Frame shape* option and then click *Center Shadow Rectangle* at the drop-down list.

h. Click the Browse button located at the right side of the *Theme* option box. At the Choose Theme dialog box, scroll down the list box and then double-click *Trek.thmx*.

i. Click the *Captions below ALL pictures* check box to insert a check mark.

j. Click *WhiteHorse* in the *Pictures in album* list box and then click the New Text Box button that displays at the left side of the list box. (This inserts a new slide containing a text box at the end of the presentation.)

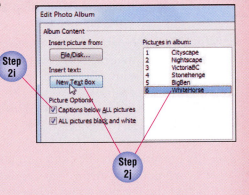

k. Click the Update button located in the lower right corner of the dialog box.

3. At the presentation, make the following formatting changes:
   a. Click the Design tab.
   b. Click the Colors button in the Themes group and then click *Metro* at the drop-down gallery.
   c. Click the Background Styles button in the Background group and then click *Style 2* at the drop-down list.

4. Make Slide 1 active and then make the following changes:
   a. Select the text *PHOTO ALBUM* and then type **travel album**. (The text will display in all caps.)
   b. Select any text that displays after the word *by* and then type your first and last names.
   c. Click the Insert tab and then click the Picture button.
   d. At the Insert Picture dialog box, navigate to the PowerPoint2010C5 folder on your storage medium and then double-click *FCTLogo.jpg*.
   e. Click the Color button in the Adjust group in the Picture Tools Format tab and then click *Set Transparent Color* at the drop-down list.

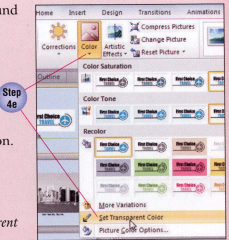

f. Move the mouse pointer (pointer displays with a tool attached) to any white portion of the logo and then click the left mouse button. (This changes the white fill to transparent fill and allows the blue background to show through.)

   g. Change the height of the logo to *3.5"* and then position the logo attractively in the slide.

5. Make Slide 2 active and then edit the caption by completing the following steps:
   a. Click on any character in the caption *Cityscape*.
   b. Select *Cityscape* and then type **New York City Skyline**.

6. Complete steps similar to those in Step 5 to change the following captions:
   a. Slide 3: Change *Nightscape* to *New York City at Night*.
   b. Slide 4: Change *VictoriaBC* to *Victoria, British Columbia*.
   c. Slide 5: Change *Stonehenge* to *Stonehenge, Wiltshire County*.
   d. Slide 6: Change *BigBen* to *Big Ben, London*.
   e. Slide 7: Change *WhiteHorse* to *White Horse, Wiltshire County*.

7. Make Slide 8 active and then make the following changes:
   a. Select the text *Text Box* and then type **Call First Choice Travel at 555-4500 to book your next travel tour.**
   b. Select the text, change the font size to 48, change the font color to Blue, and change the alignment to Center.

8. Apply a transition and sound of your choosing to each slide.
9. Run the presentation.
10. Save **P-C5-P2-Album.pptx**.

Formatting Pictures

If you format slides in the presentation instead of the Edit Photo Album dialog box, you may lose some of those changes if you subsequently display the Edit Photo Album dialog box, make changes, and then click the Update button. Consider making your initial editing and formatting changes at the Edit Photo Album dialog box and then make final editing and formatting changes in the presentation.

Since a picture in a slide in a photo album is an object, you can format it with options at the Drawing Tools Format tab and the Picture Tools Format tab. With options at the Drawing Tools Format tab, you can insert shapes, apply a shape style to the picture and caption (if one is displayed), apply a WordArt style to caption text, and arrange and size the picture. Use options in the Picture Tools Format tab to adjust the color of the picture, apply a picture style, and arrange and size the picture.

| Project 2c | Formatting Pictures in a Presentation | Part 3 of 3 |

1. With **P-C5-P2-Album.pptx** open, make Slide 2 active.
2. Change the pictures back to color by completing the following steps:
   a. Click the Insert tab.
   b. Click the Photo Album button arrow in the Images group and then click *Edit Photo Album* at the drop-down list.
   c. Click the *ALL pictures black and white* check box to remove the check mark.
   d. Click the Update button.

3. Format the picture in Slide 2 by completing the following steps:
   a. Click the picture to select it.
   b. Click the Drawing Tools Format tab.
   c. Click the More button at the right side of the thumbnails in the Shape Styles group and then click *Subtle Effect - Green, Accent 1* (second option from the left in the fourth row).

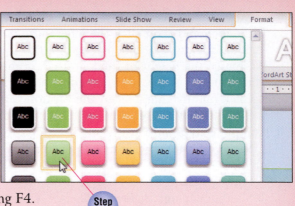

Step 3c

4. Apply the same style to the pictures in Slides 3 through 7 by making each slide active, clicking the picture, and then pressing F4. (Pressing F4 repeats the style formatting.)
5. Make Slide 2 active and then apply a WordArt style to the caption text by completing the following steps:
   a. With Slide 2 active, click the picture to select it.
   b. Click the Drawing Tools Format tab.
   c. Click the More button at the right side of the thumbnails in the WordArt Styles group and then click *Gradient Fill - Turquoise, Accent 4, Reflection* (last option in the fourth row).
6. Apply the same WordStyle style to caption text in Slides 3 through 7 by making each slide active, clicking the picture, and then pressing F4.
7. Run the presentation.
8. Print the presentation as a handout with four slides horizontally per page.
9. Save and then close **P-C5-P2-Album.pptx**.

Chapter Summary

- With the Table button in the Tables group in the Insert tab, you can create a table, insert an Excel spreadsheet, and draw a table in a slide.
- Change the table design with options and buttons in the Table Tools Design tab. Change the table layout with options and buttons in the Table Tools Layout tab.
- Use the SmartArt feature to insert predesigned diagrams and organizational charts in a slide.
- Use options and buttons in the SmartArt Tools Design tab to change the diagram layout, apply a style to the diagram, and reset the diagram back to the original formatting.
- Use options and buttons in the SmartArt Tools Format tab to change the size and shapes of objects in the diagram; apply shape styles; change the shape fill, outline, and effects; and arrange and size the diagram.
- You can insert text directly into a SmartArt diagram shape or at the Text pane. Display this pane by clicking the Text Pane button in the Create Graphic group in the SmartArt Tools Design tab.

- You can convert text or WordArt to a SmartArt diagram and convert a SmartArt diagram to text or shapes.
- A chart is a visual presentation of data and you can create a variety of charts as described in Table 5.2.
- To create a chart, display the Insert Chart dialog box by clicking the Insert Chart button in a content placeholder or clicking the Chart button in the Illustrations group in the Home tab.
- Enter chart data in an Excel worksheet. When entering data, press Tab to make the next cell active, press Shift + Tab to make the previous cell active, and press Enter to make the cell below active.
- Modify a chart design with options and buttons in the Chart Tools Design tab.
- Cells in the Excel worksheet used to create a chart are linked to the chart in the slide. To edit chart data, click the Edit Data button in the Chart Tools Design tab and then make changes to text in the Excel worksheet.
- The Chart Tools Layout tab contains options and buttons for inserting objects in a chart such as a picture, shape, or text box and inserting and removing labels, axes, gridlines, and backgrounds.
- Customize the format of a chart and chart elements with options and buttons in the Chart Tools Format tab. You can select the chart or a specific element, apply a style to a shape, apply a WordArt style to text, and arrange and size the chart.
- Use the Photo Album feature to create a presentation containing pictures and then edit and format the pictures.
- At the Photo Album dialog box (or the Edit Photo Album dialog box), insert pictures and then use options to customize the photo album.
- Use options in the Drawing Tools Format tab and the Picture Tools Format tab to format pictures in a photo album presentation.

Commands Review

FEATURE	RIBBON TAB, GROUP	BUTTON, FILE TAB	PLACEHOLDER BUTTON
Insert Table dialog box	Insert, Tables	, Insert Table	
Choose a SmartArt Graphic dialog box	Insert, Illustrations		
Convert bulleted text to SmartArt	Home, Paragraph		
Text pane	SmartArt Tools Design, Create Graphic		
Insert Chart dialog box	Insert, Illustrations		
Create photo album	Insert, Illustrations	, New Photo Album	
Edit photo album	Insert, Illustrations	, Edit Photo Album	

Concepts Check Test Your Knowledge

Completion: In the space provided at the right, indicate the correct term, symbol, or command.

1. This term refers to the intersection between a row and a column.

   _____

2. Display the Insert Table dialog box by clicking this button in a content placeholder.

   _____

3. Use this keyboard shortcut to move the insertion point to the next cell.

   _____

4. This is the keyboard shortcut to select all cells in a table.

   _____

5. The Table Styles group is located in this tab.

   _____

6. Use options and buttons in this tab to delete and insert rows and columns and merge and split cells.

   _____

7. Click this button in a content placeholder to display the Choose a SmartArt Graphic dialog box.

   _____

8. When you insert a SmartArt diagram in a slide, this tab is active.

   _____

9. Create a SmartArt diagram with bulleted text by clicking in the text placeholder, clicking this button, and then clicking the desired SmartArt graphic at the drop-down gallery.

   _____

10. Click the Chart button in this group in the Insert tab to display the Insert Chart dialog box.

   _____

11. Insert a chart in a slide and this tab is active.

   _____

12. To edit data in a chart, click the Edit Data button in this group in the Chart Tools Design tab.

   _____

13. This group in the Chart Tools Format tab contains predesigned styles you can apply to shapes in a chart.

   _____

14. This group in the Chart Tools Format tab contains predesigned styles you can apply to chart text.

   _____

15. To create a photo album, click the Insert tab, click the Photo Album button arrow, and then click this at the drop-down list.

   _____

16. Click the down-pointing arrow at the right of this option in the Edit Photo Album dialog box to display a list of framing choices. _____

17. To insert captions below pictures in a photo album, insert a check mark in this check box in the Edit Photo Album dialog box. _____

Skills Check Assess Your Performance

Assessment

1 CREATE AND FORMAT TABLES AND SMARTART IN A RESTAURANT PRESENTATION

1. Open **Dockside.pptx** and then save the presentation with Save As and name it **P-C5-A1-Dockside**.
2. Make Slide 6 active and then create the table shown in the slide in Figure 5.15 with the following specifications:
   a. Create a table with three columns and six rows.
   b. Type the text in cells as shown in Figure 5.15.
   c. Apply the *Medium Style 4 - Accent 3* style to the table.
   d. Select all of the text in the table, center the text vertically, change the font size to 20 points, and change the font color to *Turquoise, Accent 2, Darker 50%*.
   e. Change the height of the table to 3.7 inches. (The width should be set at 9 inches.)
   f. Center the text in the first row.
   g. Center the text in the third column.
   h. Make sure the table is positioned as shown in Figure 5.15.
3. Make Slide 4 active and then create the table shown in the slide in Figure 5.16 with the following specifications:
   a. Create a table with four columns and three rows.
   b. Select the entire table, change the vertical alignment to center, and then change the font size to 28.
   c. Merge the cells in the first column, change the text direction to *Rotate all text 270°*, change the alignment to center, change the font size to 40, and then type Lunch.
   d. Merge the cells in the third column, change the text direction to *Rotate all text 270°*, change the alignment to center, change the font size to 40, and then type Dinner.
   e. Type the remaining text in cells as shown in Figure 5.16.
   f. Change the height of the table to 3 inches.
   g. Change the width of the first and third columns to 1.2 inches.
   h. Change the width of the second and fourth columns to 2.5 inches.
   i. Insert a check mark in the *Banded Columns* check box in the Table Style Options group in the Table Tools Design tab and remove the check marks from the other check boxes in the group.
   j. Apply the *Medium Style 4 - Accent 3* style to the table.
   k. Select all of the text in the table and then change the font color to *Turquoise, Accent 2, Darker 50%*.
   l. Change the height of all of the rows to 1 inch.
   m. Position the table on the slide as shown in Figure 5.16.

4. Make Slide 5 active and then create the SmartArt organizational chart shown in the slide in Figure 5.17 with the following specifications:
   a. Choose the *Half Circle Organization Chart* diagram at the Choose a SmartArt Graphic dialog box.
   b. Delete the second box so your chart appears with the same number of boxes and in the same order as the organizational chart in Figure 5.17.
   c. Type the text in the boxes as shown in Figure 5.17.
   d. Change the color to *Colorful Range - Accent Colors 3 to 4*.
   e. Apply the *Cartoon* SmartArt style.
   f. Apply the *Gradient Fill - Blue, Accent 1* WordArt style to text.
   g. Change the height of the organizational chart to 5 inches and change the width to 8.5 inches.
   h. Position the organizational chart in the slide as shown in Figure 5.17.
5. Make Slide 1 active and then format the title and create the SmartArt diagram shown in the slide in Figure 5.18 with the following specifications:
   a. Select the title *The Dockside Café* and then change the font to Lucida Calligraphy.
   b. Create the SmartArt diagram with the *Linear Venn* option located in the *Relationship* group. Type the text in the shapes as shown in Figure 5.18.
   c. Change the colors to *Colorful - Accent Colors*.
   d. Apply the *Intense Effect* SmartArt style.
   e. Apply the *Fill - White, Drop Shadow* WordArt style to text.
   f. Change the height of the diagram to 4.2 inches and the width to 6.8 inches.
   g. Position the SmartArt diagram on the slide as shown in Figure 5.18.
6. Make Slide 2 active, select the bulleted text placeholder, and then convert the bulleted text to a *Basic Matrix* diagram as shown in the slide in Figure 5.19 with the following specifications:
   a. Change the colors to *Colorful - Accent Colors*.
   b. Apply the *Cartoon* SmartArt style.
   c. Apply the *Fill - White, Drop Shadow* WordArt style to text.
   d. Change the height of the diagram to 4.8 inches and the width to 5.5 inches.
   e. Position the SmartArt diagram on the slide as shown in Figure 5.19.
7. Make Slide 3 active and then insert a clip art image related to "menu." Size and position the image attractively on the slide.
8. Apply a transition and sound of your choosing to all slides in the presentation.
9. Run the presentation.
10. Print the presentation as a handout with six slides horizontally per page.
11. Save and then close **P-C5-A1-Dockside.pptx**.

Figure 5.15 Assessment 1, Slide 6

Suppliers

Supplier	Contact Person	Telephone
Seaside Fish Market	Iliana Kovich	253-555-4331
MacDougal's Bakery	Joseph Loeberg	253-555-0099
Oakridge Winery	Michelle Woodring	206-555-3156
Tanner Supplies	Rose Patterson	425-555-1165
Pier 90 Company	Miguel Trujillo	206-555-7761

Figure 5.16 Assessment 1, Slide 4

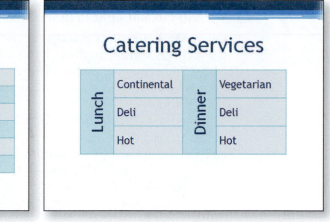

Catering Services

Lunch		Dinner	
	Continental		Vegetarian
	Deli		Deli
	Hot		Hot

Figure 5.17 Assessment 1, Slide 5

Restaurant Team — Tanya Mitchell, Owner; Ryan Holbrook, Catering Manager; Roslyn Jones, Restaurant Manager; Jean Lawson, Personnel Manager

Figure 5.18 Assessment 1, Slide 1

The Dockside Café — Lunch, Dinner, Catering, Banquets

Figure 5.19 Assessment 1, Slide 2

Accommodations — Dining Area, Salon, Banquet Rooms, Wine Cellar

Assessment

2 CREATE AND FORMAT CHARTS IN A MARKETING PRESENTATION

1. Open **MarketingPres.pptx** and save the presentation with Save As and name it **P-C5-A2-MarketingPres**.
2. Make Slide 2 active, insert a new slide with the *Title and Content* layout, and then create the chart shown in the slide in Figure 5.20 with the following specifications:
   a. Type the slide title as shown in Figure 5.20.
   b. Use the pie chart option *Pie in 3-D* to create the chart.
   c. Type the following information in the Excel worksheet:

	Amount
Salaries	47%
Equipment	18%
Supplies	4%
Production	21%
Distribution	10%

   d. Change the chart layout to *Layout 3*.
   e. Insert data labels on the outside end.
   f. Change the shape fill of the piece of pie containing *10%* to *White, Accent 3, Darker 35%*.
3. Print Slide 3.
4. After looking at the slide, you realize that two of the percentages are incorrect. Edit the Excel data and change *47%* to *42%* and change *10%* to *15%*.
5. With Slide 3 active, insert a new slide with the *Title and Content* layout and then create the chart shown in the slide in Figure 5.21 with the following specifications:
   a. Type the slide title as shown in Figure 5.21.
   b. Use the line chart option *Line with Markers* to create the chart.
   c. Type the following information in the Excel worksheet:

	Revenues	Expenses
1st Qtr	$789,560	$670,500
2nd Qtr	$990,450	$765,000
3rd Qtr	$750,340	$780,000
4th Qtr	$980,400	$875,200

   d. Apply the *Style 42* chart style.

Figure 5.20 Assessment 2, Slide 3   **Figure 5.21** Assessment 2, Slide 4

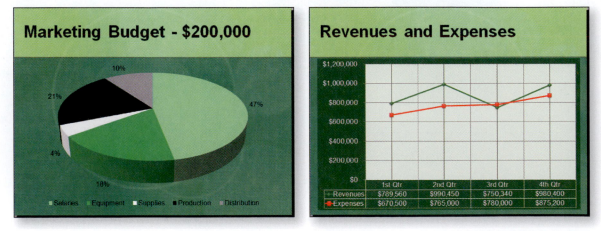

e. Click the Data Table button in the Chart Tools Layout tab and then click the *Show Data Table with Legend Keys* option.

f. Click the Legend button and then click *None* at the drop-down list.

g. Insert major and minor vertical gridlines.

h. Select the plot area and then change the shape fill color to *Light Green, Accent 1, Lighter 80%*. (The Shape Fill button is located in the Chart Tools Format tab.)

i. Select the chart area and then change the shape fill color to *Green, Accent 2, Darker 50%*.

j. Select the expenses line (*Series "Expenses"*) and then change the shape fill to Red and the shape outline to Red.

k. Select the revenues line (*Series "Revenues"*) and then change the shape fill and the shape outline to *Light Green, Accent 1, Darker 50%*.

6. Apply a transition and sound of your choosing to each slide in the presentation.

7. Run the presentation.

8. Print the presentation as a handout with three slides per page.

9. Save and then close **P-C5-A2-MarketingPres.pptx**.

Assessment

3 CREATE A SCENERY PHOTO ALBUM

1. At a blank screen, create a new photo album.

2. At the Photo Album dialog box, insert the following images:
   AlderSprings.jpg
   CrookedRiver.jpg
   Mountain.jpg
   Ocean.jpg
   Olympics.jpg
   River.jpg

3. Change the *Picture layout* option to *1 picture with title*.

4. Change the *Frame shape* option to *Simple Frame, White*.

5. Apply the *Paper* theme.

6. Click the Create button.

7. At the presentation, change the theme colors to *Solstice* and the background style to *Style 8*. **Hint: Do this with buttons in the Design tab.**

8. Insert the following titles in the specified slides:
   Slide 2 = Alder Springs, Oregon
   Slide 3 = Crooked River, Oregon
   Slide 4 = Mt. Rainier, Washington
   Slide 5 = Pacific Ocean, Washington
   Slide 6 = Olympic Mountains, Washington
   Slide 7 = Salmon River, Idaho

9. Make Slide 1 active, select any name that follows *by*, and then type your first and last names.

10. Save the presentation and name it **P-C5-A3-PhotoAlbum**.

11. Print the presentation as a handout with four slides horizontally per page.

12. Close **P-C5-A3-PhotoAlbum.pptx**.

4 CREATE A SALES AREA CHART

1. Open **P-C5-A2-MarketingPres.pptx** and then save the presentation with Save As and name it **P-C5-A4-MarketingPres**.
2. Make Slide 4 active and then insert a new slide with the *Title and Content* layout.
3. Use Excel's Help feature to learn more about chart types and then create an area chart (use the *Area* chart type) with the data shown below. Apply design, layout, and/or formatting to improve the visual appeal of the chart. Type **Sales by Region** as the slide title.

	Region 1	Region 2	Region 3
Sales 2009	$650,300	$478,100	$225,500
Sales 2010	$623,100	$533,600	$210,000
Sales 2011	$725,600	$478,400	$296,500

4. Print Slide 5.
5. Save and then close **P-C5-A4-MarketingPres.pptx**.

Visual Benchmark Demonstrate Your Proficiency

CREATE AND FORMAT A MEDICAL CENTER PRESENTATION

1. Open **RMCPres.pptx** and then save the presentation with Save As and name it **P-C5-VB-RMCPres**.
2. Create the presentation shown in Figure 5.22 with the following specifications:
   a. Apply the *Aspect* design theme and change the theme colors to *Hardcover*.
   b. In Slide 2, create the SmartArt with the *Hierarchy* relationship diagram and apply the *Colorful Range - Accent Colors 2 to 3* colors to the diagram.
   c. In Slide 3, create the SmartArt with the *Basic Venn* relationship diagram and apply the *Colorful Range - Accent Colors 2 to 3* colors to the diagram.
   d. Use the Bevel shape to create the shape in Slide 4.
   e. Insert the table as shown in Slide 5.
   f. Use the information shown in the legend and the data information shown above the bars to create a 3-D bar chart as shown in Slide 6.
   g. Use the information shown in the legend and the data information at the outside end of each pie to create a 3-D pie chart as shown in Slide 7.
3. Apply a transition and sound of your choosing to all slides in the presentation.
4. Print the presentation as a handout with four slides horizontally per page.
5. Save and then close **P-C5-VB-RMCPres.pptx**.

Figure 5.22 Visual Benchmark

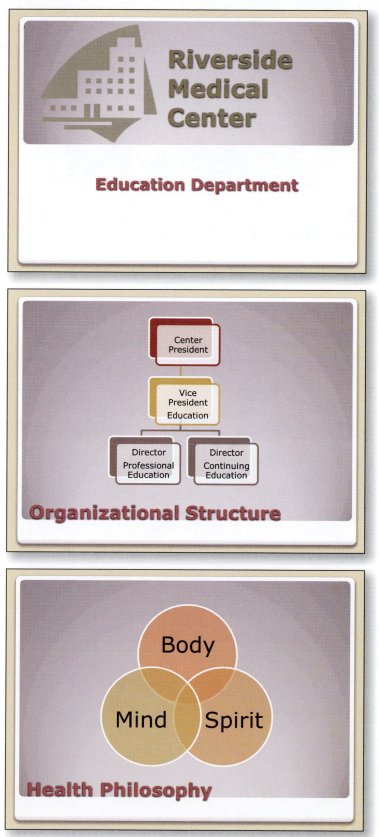

Figure 5.22 Visual Benchmark—*continued*

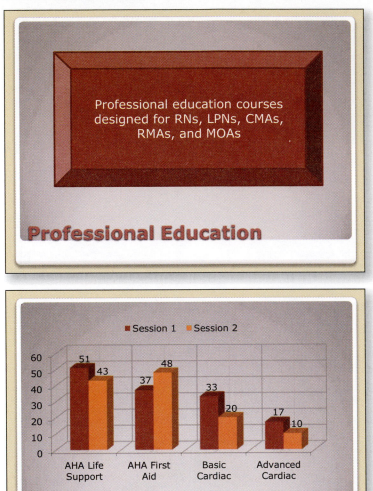

Professional education courses designed for RNs, LPNs, CMAs, RMAs, and MOAs

Professional Education

Current Enrollment

Course	Session 1	Session 2
AHA Basic Life Support	October 1	October 3
AHA First Aid	October 9	October 11
Basic Cardiac Care	October 15	October 17
Advanced Cardiac Life Support	October 30	November 1
Trauma Nursing Care	November 6	November 8
Emergency Pediatric Nursing Care	November 12	November 14

Course Offerings

Figure 5.22 Visual Benchmark—*continued*

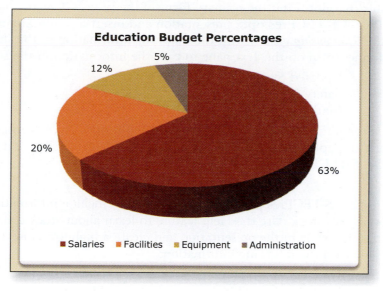

Case Study   Apply Your Skills

You are an administrator for Terra Energy Corporation and you are responsible for preparing a presentation for a quarterly meeting. Open the Word document named **TerraEnergy.docx** and then use the information to prepare a presentation with the following specifications:

- Create the first slide with the company name and the subtitle of *Quarterly Meeting*.
- Create a slide that presents the Executive Team information in a table.
- Create a slide that presents the phases information in a table (the three columns of text in the *Research and Development* section). Insert a column at the left side of the table that includes the text *New Product* rotated.
- Create a slide that presents the development team information in a SmartArt organizational chart.
- Create a slide that presents the revenues information in a chart (you determine the type of chart).
- Create a slide that presents the United States sales information in a chart (you determine the type of chart).

Apply a design theme of your choosing and add any additional features to improve the visual appeal of the presentation. Insert a transition and sound to each slide and then run the presentation. Save the presentation and name it **P-C5-CS-TECPres.pptx**. Print the presentation as a handout with four slides horizontally per page.

Part 2

Last year, a production project was completed and you want to display a graphic that illustrates the primary focus of the project. Create a new slide in the **P-C5-CS-TECPres.pptx** presentation and insert a *Funnel* SmartArt graphic (in the *Relationship* group) with the following information in the shapes inside the funnel (turn on the Text pane to type the information in the shapes):

> Updated Systems
> Safety Programs
> Market Expansion

Insert the information *Higher Profits* below the funnel. Apply formatting to the SmartArt graphic to improve the visual appeal. Print the slide and then save **P-C5-CS-TECPres.pptx**.

Part 3

The **P-C5-CS-TECPres.pptx** presentation should include information on the corporation's stock. Use the Help feature to learn about stock charts and then insert a new slide in the presentation and create a high-low-close stock chart in the slide with the following information:

Date	High	Low	Close
01/01/2012	23	20.25	21.875
02/01/2012	28.625	25.25	26.375
03/01/2012	32.375	28	30.125
04/01/2012	27.125	24.5	26.375
05/01/2012	25.125	22.875	24.25

Apply formatting to the chart to improve the readability and appeal of the chart. Print the slide and then save **P-C5-CS-TECPres.pptx**.

Part 4

You have created an Excel chart containing information on department costs. You decide to improve the visual appeal of the chart and then create a link from the presentation to the chart. Open Excel and then open **DepartmentCosts.xlsx**. Apply additional formatting to the pie chart to make it easy to read and understand the data. Save and then close the workbook and exit Excel. Create a new slide in the **P-C5-CS-TECPres.pptx** presentation that includes a hyperlink to the **DepartmentCosts.xlsx** workbook. Run the presentation and when the slide displays containing the hyperlinked text, click the hyperlink, view the chart in Excel, and then exit Excel. Print the presentation as a handout with four slides horizontally per page. Save and then close **P-C5-CS-TECPres.pptx**.

PowerPoint

Using Slide Masters and Action Buttons

PERFORMANCE OBJECTIVES

Upon successful completion of Chapter 6, you will be able to:
- **Format slides in Slide Master view**
- **Apply themes and backgrounds in Slide Master view**
- **Delete placeholders and slide master layouts**
- **Insert elements in Slide Master view**
- **Create and rename a custom slide layout**
- **Insert a new slide master**
- **Save a presentation as a template**
- **Customize a handout in Handout Master view**
- **Customize notes pages in Notes Master view**
- **Insert action buttons**
- **Create hyperlinks**

Tutorials

6.1 Formatting with a Slide Master
6.2 Working in Slide Master View
6.3 Saving a Presentation as a Template
6.4 Customizing a Handout and Notes Pages
6.5 Inserting Action Buttons and Hyperlinks

If you make design or formatting changes and you want the changes to affect all slides in the presentation, consider making the changes in a slide master in the Slide Master view. Along with the Slide Master view, you can make changes to all pages in a handout with options in the Handout Master view and all notes pages in the Notes Master view. You can insert action buttons in a presentation to connect to slides within the same presentation, connect to another presentation, connect to a website, or connect to another program. You can also connect to a website by inserting a hyperlink to the site. Model answers for this chapter's projects appear on the following pages.

PowerPoint2010C6

Note: Before beginning the projects, copy to your storage medium the PowerPoint2010C6 folder from the PowerPoint2010 folder on the CD that accompanies this textbook and then make PowerPoint2010C6 the active folder.

235

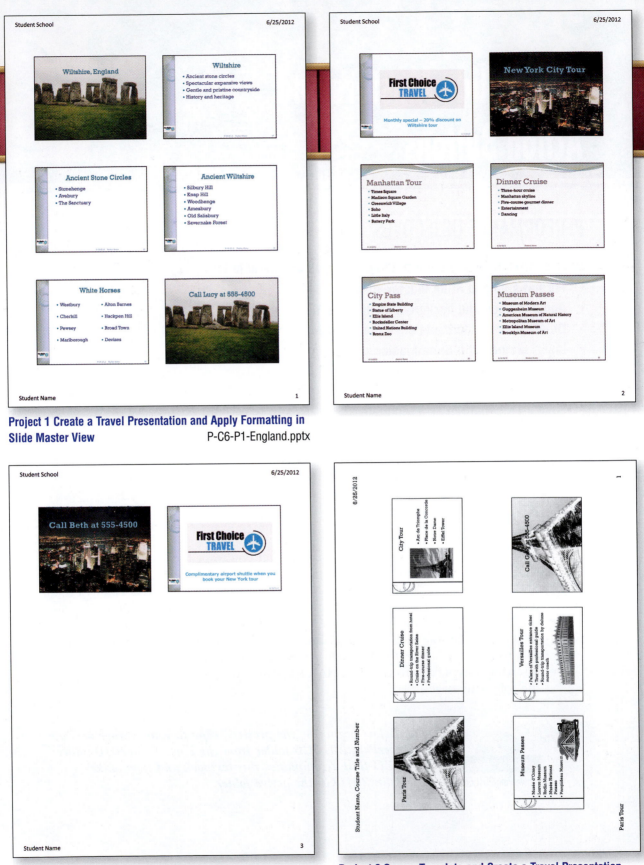

Project 1 Create a Travel Presentation and Apply Formatting in Slide Master View P-C6-P1-England.pptx

Project 2 Save a Template and Create a Travel Presentation with the Template P-C6-P2-ParisTour.pptx

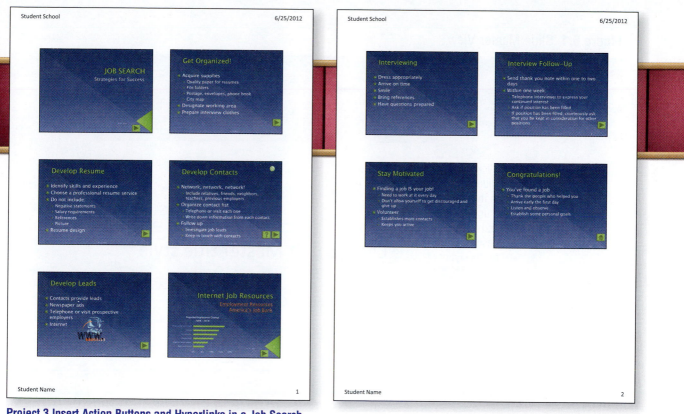

Project 3 Insert Action Buttons and Hyperlinks in a Job Search Presentation
P-C6-P3-JobSearch.pptx

Project **1** **Create a Travel Presentation and Apply Formatting in Slide Master View**   **6 Parts**

You will apply formatting to a blank presentation in Slide Master view, insert slides in the presentation, insert elements in Slide Master view, insert a custom slide layout, and insert a new slide master.

Customizing Slide Masters ■■■■■■■■■■ ■■ ■■ ■■■

When creating a presentation, you can apply a design theme to the presentation to provide colors and formatting. If you make changes to a slide and want the changes to affect all slides in the presentation, make the change in a slide master. You can customize a slide master by changing the theme, theme colors, and/ or theme fonts; changing the location of and inserting placeholders; applying a background style; and changing the page setup and slide orientation. If you know you want to customize slides, consider making the changes in Slide Master view before you create each slide. If you apply a slide master to an existing presentation, some items on slides may not conform to the new formatting.

To display the Slide Master view, click the View tab and then click the Slide Master button in the Master Views group. This displays the Slide Master tab, a blank slide master in the Slide pane, and inserts slide master thumbnails in the slide thumbnail pane. The largest thumbnail in the pane is the slide master and the other thumbnails represent associated layouts. Position the mouse pointer on a

▼ **Quick Steps**

Display Slide Master View
1. Click View tab.
2. Click Slide Master button.

Slide Master

Close Master View

Figure 6.1 Slide Master View

Click the desired slide master in the slide thumbnail pane and then make desired changes to the layout.

Click to edit Master title style

Click to edit Master subtitle style

HINT

Create a consistent look to your slides by customizing slides in Slide Master view.

slide thumbnail and the name of the thumbnail displays in a box by the thumbnail. Figure 6.1 displays a blank presentation in Slide Master view. To specify the slide master or layout you want to customize, click the desired thumbnail in the slide thumbnail pane. With the slide master layout displayed in the Slide pane, make the desired changes and then click the Close Master View button.

Applying Themes to Slide Masters

Themes

You can apply themes, theme colors, theme fonts, and theme effects with buttons in the Edit Theme group in the Slide Master tab. Click the Themes button and a drop-down gallery displays with available predesigned themes and also any custom themes you have created. Click the desired theme and the theme formatting is applied to the slide master. Complete similar steps to apply theme colors, theme fonts, and theme effects.

Project 1a **Formatting a Slide Master**   **Part 1 of 6**

1. Display a blank presentation.
2. Click the View tab and then click the Slide Master button in the Master Views group.

3. Click the top (and largest) slide master thumbnail in the slide thumbnail pane (*Office Theme Slide Master*). (This displays the slide master layout in the Slide pane.)
4. Click the Themes button in the Edit Theme group in the Slide Master tab.
5. Click *Solstice* at the drop-down gallery.
6. Click the Colors button in the Edit Theme group and then click *Metro* at the drop-down gallery.
7. Click the Fonts button in the Edit Theme group and then click the *Foundry* option at the drop-down gallery.

8. Change the font color and alignment for the title style by completing the following steps:
   a. Select the text *Click to edit Master title style* that displays in the slide master in the Slide pane.
   b. Click the Home tab.
   c. Click the Font Color button arrow in the Font group and then click the *Turquoise, Accent 4, Darker 25%* option.
   d. Click the Center button in the Paragraph group.

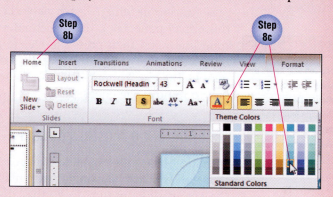

9. Change the font color of the bulleted text in the slide master by completing the following steps:
   a. Select all of the bulleted text in the slide master.
   b. Make sure the Home tab is selected.
   c. Click the Font Color button arrow in the Font group and then click the *Periwinkle, Accent 5, Darker 50%* option.
10. Change the color of the first bullet by completing the following steps:
    a. Select the text following the first bullet.
    b. Click the Bullets button arrow in the Paragraph group in the Home tab and then click *Bullets and Numbering* at the drop-down gallery.
    c. At the Bullets and Numbering dialog box with the Bulleted tab selected, click the Color button and then click the *Turquoise, Accent 4, Darker 25%* color option.
    d. Click OK to close the dialog box.

11. Select the text following the second bullet and then complete steps 10b through 10d to change the bullet color to *Turquoise, Accent 4, Darker 25%*.
12. Click the Slide Master tab.
13. Click the Close Master View button.
14. Save the presentation and name it **P-C6-P1-TravelMaster.pptx**.

▼ Quick Steps

Delete Slide Master Layouts
1. Display presentation in Slide Master view.
2. Click desired slide layout thumbnail.
3. Click Delete button.

Delete

Applying and Formatting Backgrounds

Like the Background group in the Design tab, the Background group in the Slide Master tab contains the Background Styles button and the *Hide Background Graphics* check box. If you want to change the background graphic for all slides, make the change at the slide master. To do this, display the presentation in Slide Master view and then click the desired slide master layout in the slide thumbnail pane. Click the Background Styles button and then click a background at the drop-down gallery. Or, click the *Format Background* option and choose the desired options at the Format Background dialog box. If you want to remove the background graphic for slides, click the *Hide Background Graphics* check box to insert a check mark.

Deleting Placeholders

If you want to remove a placeholder for all slides in a presentation, consider deleting the placeholder in the Slide Master view. To do this, display the presentation in Slide Master view, click the desired slide master layout in the slide thumbnail pane, click the placeholder border (make sure the border displays as a solid line), and then press the Delete key. You can also remove a title placeholder from a slide master by clicking the *Title* check box in the Master Layout group to remove the check mark. Remove footer placeholders by clicking the *Footer* check box to remove the check mark.

Deleting Slide Master Layouts

In Slide Master view, a slide master displays for each available layout. If you know that you will not be using a particular layout in the presentation, you can delete the layout slide master. To do this, display the presentation in Slide Master view, click the desired slide layout thumbnail in the slide thumbnail pane, and then click the Delete button in the Edit Master group.

Project 1b **Applying and Formatting Background Graphics**   **Part 2 of 6**

1. With **P-C6-P1-TravelMaster.pptx** open, click the View tab and then click the Slide Master button in the Master Views group.
2. Click the top slide layout thumbnail (*Solstice Slide Master*) in the slide thumbnail pane.
3. Format the background by completing the following steps:
   a. Click the Background Styles button in the Background group in the Slide Master tab and then click *Format Background* at the drop-down gallery.
   b. At the Format Background dialog box, click the *Gradient fill* option.
   c. Click the Preset colors button and then click the *Fog* option at the drop-down list (last option in the second row).

Step 3b

Step 3c

Format Background

Fill
Picture Corrections
Picture Color
Artistic Effects

Fill
○ Solid fill
● Gradient fill
○ Picture or texture fill
○ Pattern fill
☐ Hide background graphics

Preset colors:
Type:
Direction:
Angle:
Gradient stops

d. Click the down-pointing arrow at the right side of the *Type* option and then click *Path* at the drop-down list.

e. Click the Close button.

4. Apply a picture to the background of the title slide layout (the picture will appear only on this layout) by completing the following steps:

a. Click the second slide layout thumbnail (*Title Slide Layout*) in the slide thumbnail pane.

b. Click the *Hide Background Graphics* check box in the Background group in the Slide Master tab to insert a check mark.

c. Click the Background Styles button in the Background group and then click *Format Background* at the drop-down list.

d. At the Format Background dialog box, click the *Picture or texture fill* option.

e. Click the File button (located in the Insert from group).

f. At the Insert Picture dialog box, navigate to the PowerPoint2010C6 folder on your storage medium and then double-click **Stonehenge.jpg**.

g. Click the Close button to close the Format Background dialog box.

h. Remove the two small green circles that appear in the slide master in the Slide pane by clicking each circle and then pressing the Delete key.

i. Click on any character in the text *Click to edit Master title style* and then press Ctrl + E. (This is the keyboard shortcut for centering.)

j. Drag the placeholder so it is positioned above the stones and centered horizontally. (Make sure the bottom border of the placeholder is positioned above the stones.)

k. Delete the Master subtitle style placeholder by clicking the placeholder border (make sure the border displays as a solid line) and then pressing the Delete key.

l. Remove the footer placeholders from the layout by clicking the *Footers* check box in the Master Layout group to remove the check mark.

Step 4l

5. Delete slide layouts that you will not be using in the presentation by completing the following steps:

a. Click the fourth slide layout thumbnail (*Section Header Layout*) in the slide thumbnail pane.

b. Scroll down the pane until the last slide layout thumbnail is visible.

c. Hold down the Shift key and then click the last slide layout thumbnail.

d. Click the Delete button in the Edit Master group. (The slide thumbnail pane should contain the slide master and two associated layouts.)

Step 5d

6. Click the Close Master View button.

7. Delete the slide that currently displays in the Slide pane. (This displays a gray background with the text *Click to add first slide*. The presentation does not contain any slides, just formatting.)

8. Save **P-C6-P1-TravelMaster.pptx**.

Inserting Slides in a Customized Presentation

If you customize slides in a presentation in Slide Master view, you can use the presentation formatting in other presentations. You can save the formatted presentation as a template or you can save the presentation in the normal manner and then open the presentation, save it with a new name, and then type text in slides. You can also insert slides into the current presentation using the Reuse

Slides task pane. (You learned about this task pane in Chapter 2.) To use this task pane, click the Home tab, click the New Slide button arrow, and then click *Reuse Slides* at the drop-down list. This displays the Reuse Slides task pane at the right side of the screen. Click the Browse button and then click the *Browse File* option at the drop-down list. At the Browse dialog box, navigate to the desired folder and then double-click the desired presentation. Insert slides into the current presentation by clicking the desired slide in the task pane.

Project 1c Inserting Slides in a Presentation   Part 3 of 6

1. With **P-C6-P1-TravelMaster.pptx** open, save the presentation with Save As and name it **P-C6-P1-England**.
2. Make sure the Home tab is active, click the New Slide button arrow, and then click *Title Slide* at the drop-down list.
3. Click the *Click to add title* text in the current slide and then type Wiltshire, England.
4. Insert slides into the current presentation from an existing presentation by completing the following steps:
   a. Click the New Slide button arrow and then click *Reuse Slides* at the drop-down list.
   b. Click the Browse button in the Reuse Slides task pane and then click *Browse File* at the drop-down list.
   c. At the Browse dialog box, navigate to the PowerPoint2010C6 folder on your storage medium and then double-click *TravelEngland.pptx*.
   d. Click the *Wiltshire* slide in the Reuse Slides task pane. (This inserts the slide in the presentation and applies the custom formatting to the slide.)
   e. Click the *Ancient Stone Circles* slide in the Reuse Slides task pane.
   f. Click the *Ancient Wiltshire* slide in the Reuse Slides task pane.
   g. Click the *White Horses* slide in the Reuse Slides task pane.
   h. Click the Close button located in the upper right corner of the Reuse Slides task pane to close the task pane.
5. With Slide 5 active, format the bulleted text into two columns by completing the following steps:
   a. Click in any character in the bulleted text.
   b. Move the insertion point so it is positioned immediately following *Marlborough*.
   c. Press the Enter key (to insert a blank line) and then click the Bullets button in the Paragraph group in the Home tab to remove the bullet.
   d. Press Ctrl + A to select all of the bulleted text.
   e. Click the Line Spacing button in the Paragraph group and then click *2.0* at the drop-down list.
   f. Click the Columns button in the Paragraph group and then click *Two Columns* at the drop-down list.
6. With Slide 5 active, insert a new slide by completing the following steps:
   a. Click the New Slide button arrow and then click the *Title Slide* layout at the drop-down list.
   b. Click in the text *Click to add title* and then type Call Lucy at 555-4500.
7. Save **P-C6-P1-England.pptx**.

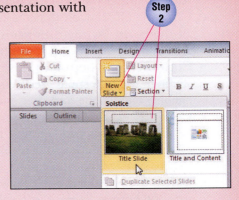

Step 2

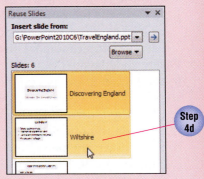

Step 4d

Inserting Elements in a Slide Master

As you learned in Chapter 4, you can insert a header, footer, or the date and time that print on every slide in the presentation. You can also insert these elements in a slide master. For example, to insert a header or footer in slides, display the presentation in Slide Master view, click the Insert tab, and then click the Header & Footer button in the Text group. At the Header and Footer dialog box with the Slide tab selected, make the desired changes, click the Notes and Handouts tab, make the desired changes, and then click the Apply to All button. You can also insert additional elements in the Slide Master view such as a picture, clip art image, shape, SmartArt graphic, or chart. Insert any of these elements in the normal manner in a slide in Slide Master view.

Project 1d   Inserting Elements in Slide Master View   Part 4 of 6

1. With **P-C6-P1-England.pptx** open, insert a header, a footer, and the date and time by completing the following steps:
   a. Click the View tab.
   b. Click the Slide Master button in the Master Views group.
   c. Click the slide master thumbnail (the top slide thumbnail in the slide thumbnail pane).
   d. Click the Insert tab.
   e. Click the Header & Footer button in the Text group.
   f. At the Header and Footer dialog box with the Slide tab selected, click the *Date and time* check box to insert a check mark.
   g. Make sure the *Update automatically* option is selected. (With this option selected, the date and/or time will automatically update each time you open the presentation.)
   h. Click the *Slide number* check box to insert a check mark.
   i. Click the *Footer* check box to insert a check mark and then type your first and last names in the *Footer* text box.
   j. Click the Notes and Handouts tab.
   k. Click the *Date and time* check box to insert a check mark.
   l. Make sure the *Update automatically* option is selected.
   m. Click the *Header* check box and then type the name of your school in the *Header* text box.
   n. Click the *Footer* check box and then type your first and last names in the *Footer* text box.
   o. Click the Apply to All button.

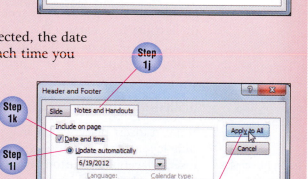

2. Insert the First Choice Travel logo in the lower left corner of the slide master by completing the following steps:
  a. Click the Picture button in the Images group.
  b. At the Insert Picture dialog box, navigate to the PowerPoint2010C6 folder on your storage medium and then double-click *FCTLogo.jpg*.
  c. Click in the *Shape Height* measurement box in the Size group in the Picture Tools Format tab, type 0.55, and then press Enter.
  d. Drag the logo so it is positioned in the lower left corner of the slide as shown at the right.
  e. Click the Send Backward button in the Arrange group.
  f. Click outside the logo to deselect it.
3. With the Slide Master tab selected, click the Close Master View button.
4. Run the presentation and notice the logo and other elements in the slides.
5. Save **P-C6-P1-England.pptx**.

Creating and Renaming a Custom Slide Layout

Insert Layout

Rename

You can create your own custom slide layout in Slide Master view and then customize the layout by inserting or deleting elements and applying formatting to placeholders and text. To create a new slide layout, click the Insert Layout button in the Edit Master group in the Slide Master tab. This inserts in the Slide pane a new slide containing a Master title style placeholder and footer placeholders. Customize the layout by inserting or deleting placeholders and applying formatting to placeholders.

PowerPoint will automatically assign the name *Custom Layout* to a slide layout you create. If you create another slide layout, PowerPoint will name it *1_Custom Layout*, and so on. Consider renaming your custom layout to a name that describes the layout. To rename a layout, make sure the desired slide layout is active, and then click the Rename button in the Edit Master group. At the Rename Layout dialog box, type the desired name, and then click the Rename button.

Inserting Placeholders

Insert Placeholder

Master Layout

You can insert placeholders in a predesigned slide layout or you can insert a custom slide layout and then insert placeholders. Insert a placeholder by clicking the Insert Placeholder button arrow in the Master Layout group and then clicking the desired placeholder option at the drop-down list. If you click the slide master, the Insert Placeholder button is dimmed. If you delete a placeholder from the slide master, you can reinsert the placeholder with options at the Master Layout dialog box. Display this dialog box by clicking the Master Layout button and any placeholder that has been removed from the slide master displays in the dialog box as an active option with an empty check box. Reinsert the placeholder by inserting a check mark in the desired placeholder check box and then clicking OK to close the dialog box.

Creating Custom Prompts

Some placeholders in a custom layout may contain generic text such as *Click to add Master title style* or *Click to edit Master text styles*. In Slide Master view, you can select this generic text and replace it with custom text. You might want to insert text that describes what you want entered into the placeholder.

Project 1e   Inserting a Layout and Placeholder   **Part 5 of 6**

1. With **P-C6-P1-England.pptx** open, click the View tab and then click the Slide Master button in the Master Views group.
2. Click the bottom slide layout thumbnail in the slide thumbnail pane.
3. Click the Insert Layout button in the Edit Master group. (This inserts in the Slide pane a new slide with a Master title style placeholder, the logo, and the footer information.)
4. Format and move the placeholder by completing the following steps:
   a. Select the text *Click to edit Master title style*.
   b. Click the Home tab, click the Text Shadow button (to turn off shadowing), turn on bold, change the font to Tahoma, change the font size to 28 points, and change the font color to Light Blue.
   c. Move the placeholder so it is positioned along the bottom of the slide just above the footer placeholder.

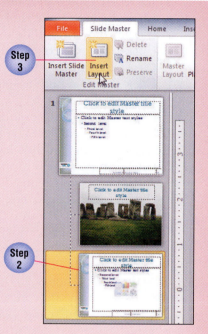

5. Click the Slide Master tab.
6. Insert a Picture placeholder by completing the following steps:
   a. Click the Insert Placeholder button arrow.
   b. Click *Picture* at the drop-down list.
   c. Drag in the slide in the Slide pane to create a placeholder that is approximately 7.5 inches wide and 3.5 inches high.
   d. Click the Drawing Tools Format tab.

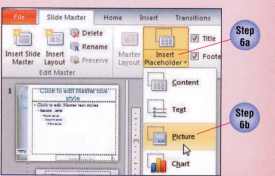

e. Click in the *Shape Height* measurement box and then type 3.5.

f. Click in the *Shape Width* measurement box, type 7.5, and then press Enter.

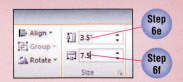

g. Drag the placeholder so it is balanced in the slide.

h. Click anywhere in the word *Picture* in the placeholder. (This removes the word *Picture* and inserts the insertion point in the placeholder.)

i. Type Insert company logo.

7. Remove the footer and slide number placeholders by completing the following steps:

a. Click the footer placeholder. (The placeholder contains your name and is located along the bottom of the slide in the Slide pane.)

b. Click the border of the placeholder to select it (the border turns into a solid line) and then press the Delete key.

c. Click the slide number placeholder, click the placeholder border, and then press the Delete key.

d. Drag the date placeholder so it is positioned at the right side of the slide.

8. If necessary, click the Slide Master tab.

9. Rename the custom slide layout by completing the following steps:

a. Click the Rename button in the Edit Master group.

b. At the Rename Layout dialog box, select the text that displays in the *Layout name* text box and then type Logo.

c. Click the Rename button.

10. Click the Close Master View button.

11. Insert a slide using the new slide layout by completing the following steps:

a. Make Slide 6 active.

b. Click the New Slide button arrow.

c. Click the Logo layout at the drop-down list.

d. Click the Insert Picture from File button in the slide.

e. At the Insert Picture dialog box, navigate to the PowerPoint2010C6 folder on your storage medium and then double-click *FCTLogo.jpg*.

f. Click in the text *Click to add title* and then type Monthly special – 20% discount on Wiltshire tour.

12. Save P-C6-P1-England.pptx.

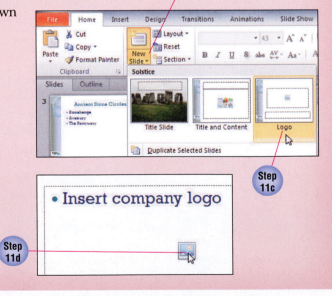

Inserting a New Slide Master

Insert Slide Master

A PowerPoint presentation can contain more than one slide master (and associated layouts). To insert a new slide master, display the presentation in Slide Master view and then click the Insert Slide Master button in the Edit Master group. This inserts the slide master and all associated layouts below the existing slide master and layouts in the slide thumbnail pane. You can also insert a slide master and all associated layouts with a design theme applied. To do this, click below the existing slide master and associated layouts, click the Themes button in the Edit Theme group, and then click the desired theme at the drop-down gallery. A slide master containing the chosen design theme is inserted below the existing thumbnails.

Preserving Slide Masters

If you delete all slide layouts that follow a slide master, PowerPoint will automatically delete the slide master. You can protect a slide master from being deleted by "preserving" the master. To do this, click the desired slide master thumbnail and then click the Preserve button in the Edit Master group. If you insert a slide master using the Insert Slide Master button, the Preserve button is automatically active. When a slide master is preserved, a preservation icon displays below the slide number in the slide thumbnail pane.

Changing Page Setup

The Page Setup group in the Slide Master tab contains two buttons. By default, slides display in the landscape orientation (wider than tall). You can change this to portrait orientation (taller than wide) by clicking the Slide Orientation button in the Page Setup group and then clicking *Portrait* at the drop-down list. Click the Page Setup button and the Page Setup dialog box displays with options for changing slide width and height; slide numbering; and applying slide orientation to slides or notes, handouts, and outline pages.

▼ **Quick Steps**

Preserve Slide Master
1. Display presentation in Slide Master view.
2. Click desired slide master thumbnail.
3. Click Preserve button.

Preserve

Slide Orientation

Page Setup

Project 1f | **Applying a Second Slide Master and Changing Slide Numbering** | **Part 6 of 6**

1. With **P-C6-P1-England.pptx** open, insert a second slide master by completing the following steps:
   a. Click the View tab and then click the Slide Master button in the Master Views group.
   b. Click below the bottom slide layout in the slide thumbnail pane. (You want the slide master and associated layouts to display below the original slide master and not take the place of the original.)
   c. Click the Themes button in the Edit Theme group and then click *Flow* at the drop-down gallery. (Notice the slide master and associated layouts that display in the slide thumbnail pane below the original slide master and associated layouts and notice the preservation icon that displays below the slide master number 2.)
   d. Click the new slide master (Flow Slide Master) in the slide thumbnail pane.
   e. Click the Colors button in the Edit Theme group and then click *Apex* at the drop-down gallery.
   f. Click the Fonts button and then click *Foundry* at the drop-down gallery.

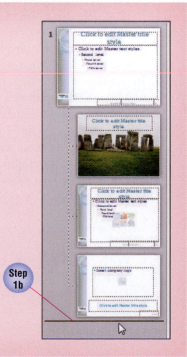

Step 1b

2. Insert a footer, the date and time, and slide numbers in the slide master by completing the following steps:
   a. Click the Insert tab.
   b. Click the Header & Footer button in the Text group.
   c. At the Header and Footer dialog box with the Slide tab selected, click the *Date and time* check box to insert a check mark.
   d. Make sure the *Update automatically* option is selected. (With this option selected, the date and/or time will automatically update each time you open the presentation.)
   e. Click the *Slide number* check box to insert a check mark.
   f. Click the *Footer* check box to insert a check mark and then type your first and last names in the *Footer* text box.
   g. Click the Apply to All button.
3. Click the Slide Master tab.
4. Click the third layout below the new slide master (*Section Header Layout*), scroll down to the bottom of the slide thumbnail pane, hold down the Shift key, click the bottom thumbnail, and then click the Delete button in the Edit Master group. (This deletes all but two of the associated layouts with the new slide master.)
5. Format the slide layout below the new slide master by completing the following steps:
   a. Click the first layout (*Title Slide Layout*) below the new slide master.
   b. Click the Background Styles button in the Background group and then click *Format Background*.
   c. At the Format Background dialog box, click the *Picture or texture fill* option.
   d. Click the File button (located in the Insert from group).
   e. At the Insert Picture dialog box, navigate to the PowerPoint2010C6 folder on your storage medium and then double-click *Nightscape.jpg*.
   f. Click the *Hide background graphics* check box to insert a check mark.
   g. Click the Close button.
   h. Click in the text *Click to edit Master title style* and then press Ctrl + E. (This centers the text.)
   i. Drag the placeholder up so the text displays above the buildings.
   j. Select and then delete the subtitle placeholder.
   k. Click the *Footers* check box in the Master Layout group to remove footer placeholders.
6. Click the Close Master View button.
7. Insert a new slide by completing the following steps:
   a. Make Slide 7 active.
   b. Click the New Slide button arrow and then click the Flow Title Slide (the slide with the image of the New York City night skyline).
   c. Click in the text *Click to add title* and then type New York City Tour.
8. Insert a new slide by completing the following steps:
   a. With Slide 8 active, click the New Slide button. (This inserts the Flow Title and Content layout.)
   b. Click the text *Click to add title* and then type Manhattan Tour.

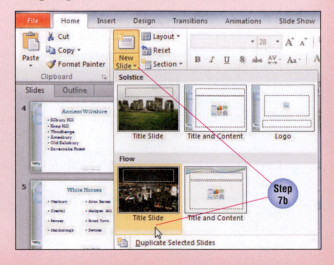

c. Click the text *Click to add text* and then type the following bulleted text:
- Times Square
- Madison Square Garden
- Greenwich Village
- Soho
- Little Italy
- Battery Park

9. Insert the following text in slides using the Flow Title and Content layout:

Slide 10   Dinner Cruise
- Three-hour cruise
- Manhattan skyline
- Five-course gourmet dinner
- Entertainment
- Dancing

Slide 11   City Pass
- Empire State Building
- Statue of Liberty
- Ellis Island
- Rockefeller Center
- United Nations Building
- Bronx Zoo

Slide 12   Museum Passes
- Museum of Modern Art
- Guggenheim Museum
- American Museum of Natural History
- Metropolitan Museum of Art
- Ellis Island Museum
- Brooklyn Museum of Art

10. Insert a new slide by completing the following steps:
    a. With Slide 12 active, click the New Slide button arrow and then click the Flow Title Slide (the slide with the image of the New York City night skyline).
    b. Click in the text *Click to add text* and then type Call Beth at 555-4500.

11. Insert a new slide with the logo layout by completing the following steps:
    a. With Slide 13 active, click the New Slide button arrow and then click the Solstice Logo Layout.
    b. Click the Insert Picture from File button in the slide.
    c. At the Insert Picture dialog box, navigate to the PowerPoint2010C6 folder on your storage medium and then double-click *FCTLogo.jpg*.
    d. Click in the text *Click to add title* and then type Complimentary airport shuttle when you book your New York tour.

12. Assume that the presentation is going to be inserted into a larger presentation and that the starting slide number will be 12 (instead of 1). Change the beginning slide number by completing the following steps:
    a. Click the View tab and then click the Slide Master button.
    b. Click the top slide master in the slide thumbnail pane.
    c. Click the Page Setup button in the Page Setup group.

d. At the Page Setup dialog box, select the current number in the *Number slides from* text box and then type 12.

e. Click OK to close the dialog box.

f. Click the Close Master View button.

13. Make Slide 12 active and then run the presentation.

14. Print the presentation as a handout with six slides horizontally per page.

15. Save and then close **P-C6-P1-England.pptx**.

You will save a travel presentation as a template and then use the template to create and format a travel presentation. You will insert elements in the presentation in Handout Master view and Notes Master view, change the presentation zoom, and view the presentation in grayscale and black and white.

Saving a Presentation as a Template ▪▪▪▪▪▪▪▪▪▪

▼ Quick Steps

Save Presentation as a Template
1. Click File tab, Save As button.
2. Click *Save as type* option.
3. Click *PowerPoint Template (*.potx).
4. Type presentation name.
5. Click Save button.

If you create custom formatting that you will use for future presentations, consider saving the presentation as a template. The advantage to saving your presentation as a template is that you cannot accidentally overwrite the presentation. When you open a template and then click the Save button on the Quick Access toolbar, the Save As dialog box automatically displays.

To save a presentation as a template, click the File tab and then click Save As. At the Save As dialog box, click the *Save as type* option button and then click *PowerPoint Template (*.potx)* at the drop-down list. Type a name for the template in the *File name* text box and then click the Save button. The template is automatically saved in a Templates folder on the hard drive. If you want to save the template to another location, navigate to the desired folder in the Save As dialog box and then save the template.

To create a presentation based on a template, click the File tab and then click the New tab. At the New tab Backstage view, click the *My templates* option in the Available Templates and Themes category. At the New Presentation dialog box, double-click the desired theme in the list box.

If you saved a template in a location other than the default, open a presentation based on the template by displaying the New tab Backstage view and then clicking the *New from existing* option in the Available Templates and Themes category. At the New from Existing Presentation dialog box, navigate to the desired folder and then double-click the desired template.

After opening a presentation template, insert the desired slides and make any other formatting or design changes and then click the Save button on the Quick Access toolbar. At the Save As dialog box, type a name for the presentation and then click the Save button.

If you no longer need a template, delete the template at the New Presentation dialog box. To do this, display the New tab Backstage view and then click the *My templates* option in the Available Templates and Themes category. At the New Presentation dialog box, right-click the template you want to delete and then click *Delete* at the shortcut menu. At the message asking if you want to delete the template, click the Yes button. If you saved a template to a location other than the default, delete the template in the same manner as you delete a presentation. To do this, display the Open dialog box, navigate to the desired folder, click the template you want to delete, click the Organize button, click *Delete* at the drop-down list, and then click Yes at the message that displays.

Project 2a   **Saving a Presentation as a Template**   **Part 1 of 4**

1. Open **P-C6-P1-TravelMaster.pptx**.
2. Click the File tab and then click the Save As button.
3. At the Save As dialog box, click the *Save as type* option button and then click *PowerPoint Template (*.potx)* at the drop-down list.

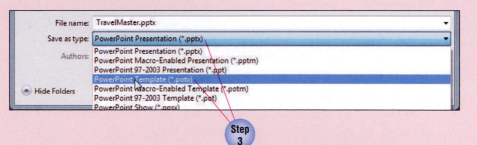

4. Navigate to the PowerPoint2010C6 folder on your storage medium.
5. Select the name that currently displays in the *File name* text box and then type **XXXTravelTemplate**. (Type your initials rather than the *XXX*.)
6. Click the Save button.

7. Close the **XXXTravelTemplate.potx** template.

8. Open the template and save it as a presentation by completing the following steps:
   a. Click the File tab and then click the New tab.
   b. At the New tab Backstage view, click the *New from existing* option in the Available Templates and Themes category.

Step 8a

Step 8b

   c. At the New from Existing Presentation dialog box, navigate to the PowerPoint2010C6 folder on your storage medium and then double-click **XXXTravelTemplate.potx** (where the *XXX* represents your initials).
9. Save the presentation and name it **P-C6-P2-ParisTour**.

Customizing the Handout Master ■■■■■■■■■■■■■■

Handout Master

As you learned in Chapter 1, you can choose to print a presentation as individual slides, handouts, notes pages, or an outline. If you print a presentation as handouts or an outline, PowerPoint will automatically print the current date in the upper right corner of the page and the page number in the lower right corner. You can customize the handout with options in the Print Preview tab and you can also customize a handout in the Handout Master view. Display a presentation in Handout Master view by clicking the View tab and then clicking the Handout Master button in the Presentation Views group. With options in the Handout Master tab, you can move, resize, and format header and footer placeholders, change page orientation, and specify the number of slides you want printed on each page.

With buttons in the Page Setup group, you can display the Page Setup dialog box with options for changing the size and orientation of the handout page, changing the handout and/or slide orientation, and specifying the number of slides you want printed on the handout page. By default, a handout will contain a header, footer, date, and page number placeholder. You can remove any of these placeholders by removing the check mark before the placeholder option in the Placeholders group. For example, to remove the page number placeholder, click the *Page Number* check box in the Placeholders group to remove the check mark.

The Edit Theme group contains buttons for changing the theme color, font, and effects. Click the Themes button and the options in the drop-down gallery are dimmed, indicating that the themes are not available for the handout. If you apply a background style to the handout master, you can change theme colors by clicking the Colors button and then clicking the desired color theme at the drop-down gallery. Apply theme fonts by clicking the Fonts button and then clicking the desired fonts theme at the drop-down gallery.

Apply a background style to the handout page by clicking the Background Styles button in the Background group and then clicking one of the predesigned styles. You can also click the *Format Background* option and then make changes at the Format Background dialog box. Remove any background graphics by clicking the *Hide background graphics* check box to insert a check mark.

Background
Styles

Project 2b   **Customizing the Handout Master**   **Part 2 of 4**

1. With **P-C6-P2-ParisTour.pptx** open, click the New Slide button arrow and then click *Reuse Slides* at the drop-down list.
2. In the Reuse Slides task pane, click the Browse button, and then click the *Browse File* option at the drop-down list.
3. Navigate to the PowerPoint2010C6 folder on your storage medium and then double-click *ParisTour.pptx*.
4. Insert the second, third, fourth, and fifth slides from the Reuse Slides task pane into the current presentation.
5. Close the Reuse Slides task pane.
6. Edit the Title Slide Layout in Slide Master view by completing the following steps:
   a. Click the View tab and then click the Slide Master button.
   b. Click the second thumbnail in the slide thumbnail pane (*Title Slide Layout*).
   c. Click the Background Styles button in the Background group and then click *Format Background* at the drop-down list.
   d. At the Format Background dialog box, click the File button (displays in the *Insert from* section).
   e. At the Insert Picture dialog box, navigate to the PowerPoint2010C6 folder on your storage medium and then double-click *EiffelTower.jpg*.
   f. Click the Close button to close the Format Background dialog box.
   g. Select the text *Click to edit Master title style*, click the Home tab, click the Font Color button arrow, and then click *Turquoise, Accent 4, Lighter 60%* at the drop-down gallery.
   h. Click the Slide Master tab.
   i. Click the Close Master View button.
7. Make Slide 1 active, click in the text *Click to add title*, and then type **Paris Tour**.
8. Size and move the text placeholder so *Paris Tour* displays in a blue area on the slide (not over the tower).
9. Display each slide and then make adjustments to the position of clip art images and/or placeholders.
10. Make Slide 5 active and then create a new slide with the *Title Slide* layout. Type **Call Greg at 555-4500**.
11. Save **P-C6-P2-ParisTour.pptx**.
12. Click the View tab and then click the Handout Master button in the Master Views group.
13. Click the Handout Orientation button in the Page Setup group and then click *Landscape* at the drop-down list.

14. Click in the Header placeholder on the page and then type your first and last names.
15. Click in the Footer placeholder and then type **Paris Tour**.
16. Click the Background Styles button and then click *Style 10* at the drop-down list (second option from the left in the third row).
17. Click the Colors button in the Edit Theme group and then click *Metro* at the drop-down list.
18. Click the Fonts button in the Edit Theme group and then click *Foundry* at the drop-down list.
19. Edit the header text by completing the following steps:
    a. Click in the header placeholder and then click on any character in your name.
    b. Move the insertion point so it is positioned immediately right of the last character in your last name.
    c. Type a comma, press the spacebar, and then type your course number and title.
    d. Click in the handout page outside of any placeholder.
20. Click the Close Master View button.
21. Save **P-C6-P2-ParisTour.pptx**

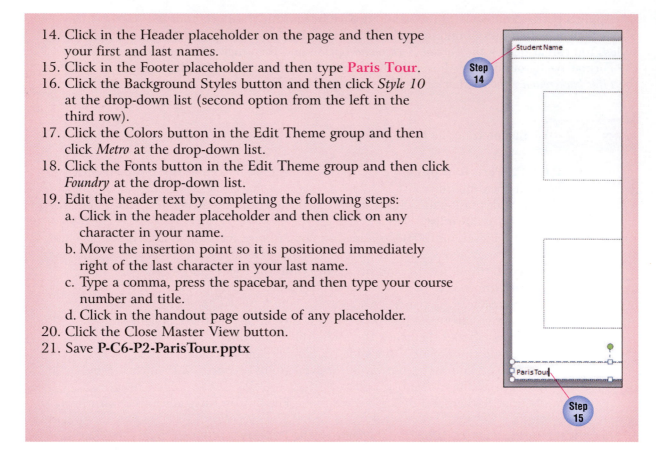

Step 14

Step 15

Customizing the Notes Master ∎■∎■∎■∎▪▪▪▪▪

Notes Master

You can insert notes in a presentation and then print the presentation as notes pages and the notes will print below the slide. If you want to insert or format text or other elements as notes on all slides in a presentation, consider making the changes in the Notes Master view. Display this view by clicking the View tab and then clicking the Notes Master button in the Master Views group. This displays a notes page along with the Notes Master tab. Many of the buttons and options in this tab are the same as the ones in the Handout Master tab.

Project 2c — Customizing the Notes Master — Part 3 of 4

1. With **P-C6-P2-ParisTour.pptx** open, click the View tab and then click the Notes Master button in the Master Views group.
2. Click the *Body* check box in the Placeholders group to remove the check mark.
3. Click the Fonts button in the Edit Theme group and then click *Foundry* at the drop-down list.
4. Click the Insert tab.
5. Click the Text Box button in the Text group.
6. Click in the notes page below the slide.
7. Type **Visit www.first-choice.emcp.net for a listing of all upcoming tours.**

Step 2

254 PowerPoint ∎ Unit 2

8. Size and position the text box below the slide as shown below.

Step 8 (slide master view showing)

Header   6/19/2012

Click to edit Master title
style
- Click to edit Master text styles
  - Second level
    - Third level
      - Fourth level
        - Fifth level

Visit www.first-choice.emcp.net
for a listing of all upcoming tours.

9. Click the Insert tab and then click the Picture button in the Images group.
10. At the Insert Picture dialog box, navigate to the PowerPoint2010C6 folder on your storage medium and then double-click *FCTLogo.jpg*.
11. Change the height of the logo to *0.5"*. (This changes the width to *1"*.)
12. Drag the logo so it is positioned below the text.
13. Click the Notes Master tab and then click the Close Master View button.
14. Print Slides 2 and 4 as notes pages by completing the following steps:
   a. Display the Print tab Backstage view.
   b. Click the second gallery in the Settings category and then click *Notes Pages* in the *Print Layout* section.
   c. Click in the *Slides* text box located below the first gallery in the Settings category and then type 2,4.
   d. Click the Print button.
15. Save **P-C6-P2-ParisTour.pptx**.

Step 12 (slide master view showing)

Click to edit Master title
style
- Click to edit Master text styles
  - Second level
    - Third level
      - Fourth level
        - Fifth level

Visit www.first-choice.emcp.net
for a listing of all upcoming tours.

First Choice
TRAVEL

Step 14d Print   Copies: 1
Step 14c Slides: 2,4
Step 14b Notes Pages — Print slides with notes

File   Home   Insert   Design   Transitions   Animations   Slide Show

Save
Save As
Open
Close
Info
Recent
New
Print
Save & Send
Help
Options
Exit

Print
Copies: 1

Printer
HP LaserJet 1160
Ready
Printer Properties

Settings
Custom Range
Enter specific slides to print
Slides: 2,4
Notes Pages
Print slides with notes
Print One Sided
Only print on one side of the page

Using View Tab Options ■■■■■■■■■■■■■■■■■■■■■■

You have used buttons in the Presentation Views group and Master Views group in the View tab to display your presentation in various views such as Normal, Slide Sorter, Slide Master, Handout Master, and Notes Master. In addition to viewing buttons, the View tab includes options for showing or hiding the ruler and gridlines; zooming in or out in the slide; viewing the slide in color, grayscale, or black and white; and working with windows including opening a new window containing the current presentation and arranging, splitting, and switching windows.

Zoom

You can change the display size of the slide in the Slide pane or slides in the Slides/Outline pane with the Zoom button in the View tab and also with the Zoom slider bar located at the right side of the Status bar. Click the Zoom button in the View tab and the Zoom dialog box displays. Use options in this dialog box to increase or decrease the display size of slides in the Slides/Outline pane or the slide in the Slide pane. To change the zoom with the Zoom slider bar, use the mouse to drag the slider bar button to the left to decrease the display size or to the right to increase the display size. Click the button with the minus symbol that displays at the left side of the Zoom slider bar to decrease the display percentage or click the button with the plus symbol that displays at the right side of the Zoom slider bar to increase the display percentage. Click the percentage number that displays at the left side of the slider bar and the Zoom dialog box displays.

Project 2d   Viewing a Presentation   Part 4 of 4

1. With **P-C6-P2-ParisTour.pptx** open, make Slide 1 active and then click the slide in the Slide pane.
2. Click the View tab.
3. Increase and decrease the zoom by completing the following steps:
   a. Click the Zoom button in the Zoom group. (This displays the Zoom dialog box.)
   b. At the Zoom dialog box, click the *33%* option and then click OK.
   c. Click the Zoom button, click the *100%* option in the Zoom dialog box, and then click OK.
   d. Click the Slide 2 thumbnail in the Slides/Outline pane.
   e. Click the Zoom button, click the *66%* option in the Zoom dialog box, and then click OK. (Because the slide in the Slides/Outline pane was active, the percentage display changed for the thumbnails in the pane.)
   f. Position the mouse pointer on the Zoom slider bar button (located at the right side of the Status bar), drag the button to the right to increase the size of the slide in the Slide pane, and then drag the slider bar to the left to decrease the size of the slide.
   g. Click the percentage number that displays at the left side of the Zoom slider bar (this displays the Zoom dialog box).
   h. Click the *66%* option in the Zoom dialog box and then click OK.
   i. Click the Slide 3 thumbnail in the Slides/Outline pane.
   j. Click the Zoom button in the View tab.
   k. Type 45 in the *Percentage* text box and then click OK. (This changes the zoom display for the slides in the Slides/Outline pane.)

4. View the slides in grayscale by completing the following steps:
   a. Click the slide in the Slides pane to make it active and then click the Grayscale button in the Color/Grayscale group in the View tab.
   b. Click some of the buttons in the Grayscale tab to display the slides in varying grayscale options.
   c. Click the Back To Color View button.

Step 4a

5. View the slides in black and white by completing the following steps:
   a. Click the View tab and then click the Black and White button in the Color/Grayscale group in the View tab.
   b. Click some of the buttons in the Black And White tab to display the slides in varying black and white options.
   c. Click the Back To Color View button.

6. Open a new window and arrange the windows by completing the following steps:
   a. Click the View tab and then click the New Window button in the Window group. (This opens the same presentation in another window. Notice that the name on the title bar displays followed by a colon and the number 2.)

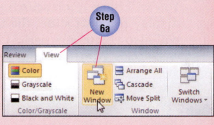

Step 6a

   b. Click the View tab and then click the Arrange All button to arrange the two presentation windows. (This arranges the presentations as tiles with the title bar of each presentation visible as well as a portion of each presentation.)
   c. Click the Window button in either window and then click the Cascade button at the drop-down list. (This arranges the two presentations with the presentations overlapping with the title bar for each presentation visible as well as a portion of the top presentation.)

Step 6c

   d. Click the Switch Windows button and then click the *P-C6-P2-ParisTour.pptx:1* option at the drop-down list. (Notice the presentation name in the title bar now displays followed by a colon and the number 1.)
   e. Click the Close button that displays in the upper right corner of the currently active presentation. (The Close button contains an X.)
   f. Click the Maximize button that displays in the upper right corner of the presentation window. (The Maximize button displays immediately left of the Close button.)

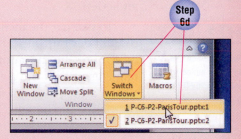

Step 6d

7. With the View tab active, click the Grayscale button in the Color/Grayscale group and then click the Inverse Grayscale button in the Change Selected Object group.
8. Print the presentation by completing the following steps:
   a. Display the Print tab Backstage view.
   b. If any text displays in the *Slides* text box, select and then delete the text.
   c. If you are using a color printer, click the Color gallery that displays at the bottom of the Settings category and then click *Grayscale*. (Skip this step if you are using a black and white printer.)

d. Click the second gallery in the Settings category and then click *6 Slides Horizontal* in the Handout section.

e. Click the Print button.

9. Click the Back To Color View button in the Grayscale tab.

10. Make Slide 1 active and then run the presentation.

11. Save and then close **P-C6-P2-ParisTour.pptx**.

ℙroject 3   Insert Action Buttons and Hyperlinks in a Job Search Presentation   5 Parts

You will open a job search presentation and then insert action buttons that display the next slide, the first slide, a website, and another presentation. You will also create a hyperlink from text, a graphic image, and a chart in a slide to a website, a Word document, and another presentation.

▼ **Quick Steps**

Create Action Button

1. Make desired slide active.
2. Click Insert tab.
3. Click Shapes button.
4. Click desired action button.
5. Drag in slide to create button.
6. Make desired changes at Action Settings dialog box.
7. Click OK.

HINT

Apply formatting to an action button with options in the Drawing Tools Format tab.

Inserting Action Buttons ■■■■■■■■■■■■■■■■■■■■■

Action buttons are drawn objects on a slide that have a routine attached to them which is activated when the viewer or the speaker clicks the button. For example, you could include an action button that displays the next slide in the presentation, a file in another program, or a specific web page. Creating an action button is a two-step process. You draw the button using an Action Button shape in the Shapes button drop-down list and then you define the action that will take place with options in the Action Settings dialog box. You can customize an action button in the same manner as customizing a drawn object. When the viewer or speaker moves the mouse over an action button during a presentation, the pointer changes to a hand with a finger pointing upward to indicate clicking will result in an action.

To display the available action buttons, click the Insert tab and then click the Shapes button in the Illustrations group. Action buttons display at the bottom of the drop-down list. Hover the mouse pointer over a button and the name as well as the action it performs displays in a box above the button. The action attached to an action button occurs when you run the presentation and then click the button.

ℙroject 3a   Inserting Action Buttons   Part 1 of 5

1. Open **JobSearch.pptx** and then save the presentation with the name **P-C6-P3-JobSearch**.

2. Make the following changes to the presentation:

a. Change the design theme to *Verve*.

b. Change the theme colors to *Metro*.

c. Change the theme fonts to *Concourse*.

d. Click the Insert tab and then click the Header & Footer button in the Text group.

e. At the Header and Footer dialog box with the Slide tab selected, click the *Date and time* check box and make sure *Update automatically* is selected.

---

f. Click the *Slide number* check box to insert a check mark.

g. Click the Notes and Handouts tab.

h. Click the *Date and time* check box and make sure *Update automatically* is selected.

i. Click the *Header* check box and then type the name of your school.

j. Click the *Footer* check box and then type your first and last names.

k. Click the Apply to All button.

3. Insert an action button in Slide 1 that will display the next slide by completing the following steps:

a. Make Slide 1 active.

b. Click the Insert tab and then click the Shapes button.

c. At the drop-down list, click *Action Button: Forward or Next* (second option from the left in the Action Buttons group) that displays at the bottom of the drop-down list.

d. Move the crosshair pointer to the lower right corner of the slide and then drag to create a button as shown below.

Step 3d

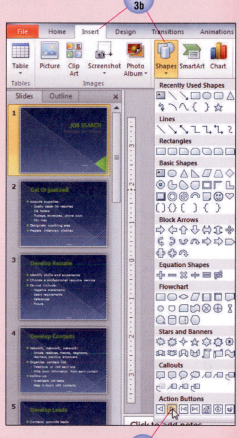

Step 3b

Step 3c

e. At the Action Settings dialog box, click OK. (The default setting is *Hyperlink to Next Slide*.)

4. Insert an action button in Slide Master view that will display the next slide by completing the following steps:

a. Display the presentation in Slide Master view.

b. Click the top slide master thumbnail.

c. Click the Insert tab and then click the Shapes button.

d. At the drop-down list, click *Action Button: Forward or Next* (second option from the left in the Action Buttons group).

e. Move the crosshair pointer to the lower right corner of the slide master and then drag to create a button as shown at the right.

f. At the Action Settings dialog box, click OK. (The default setting is *Hyperlink to Next Slide*.)

g. Click the Slide Master tab and then click the Close Master View button.

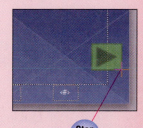

Step 4e

5. Make Slide 1 active and then run the presentation, clicking the action button to advance slides. When you click the action button on the last slide (Slide 9) nothing happens because it is the last slide. Press the Esc key to end the presentation.

6. Change the action button on Slide 9 by completing the following steps:
   a. Make Slide 9 active.
   b. Click the Insert tab and then click the Shapes button.
   c. At the drop-down list, click *Action Button: Home* (fifth button from the left in the Action Buttons group).
   d. Drag to create a button on top of the previous action button. (Make sure it completely covers the previous action button.)
   e. At the Action Settings dialog box with the *Hyperlink to: First Slide* option selected, click OK.
   f. Deselect the button.
7. Display Slide 1 in the Slide pane and then run the presentation. Navigate through the slide show by clicking the action button. When you click the action button on the last slide, the first slide displays. End the slide show by pressing the Esc key.
8. Save **P-C6-P3-JobSearch.pptx**.

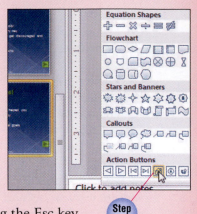

Step 6c

Applying an Action to an Object ■■■■■■■■■■■■■■■

Action

The Links group in the Insert tab contains an Action button you can use to specify an action to a selected object. To use this button, select the desired object in the slide, click the Insert tab, and then click the Action button. This displays the Action Settings dialog box, which is the same dialog box that displays when you draw an action button in a slide.

You can specify that an action button or a selected object link to another PowerPoint presentation or other file as well as a website. To link to another PowerPoint presentation, click the *Hyperlink to* option at the Action Settings dialog box, click the down-pointing arrow at the right side of the *Hyperlink to* option box, and then click *Other PowerPoint Presentation* at the drop-down list. At the Hyperlink to Other PowerPoint Presentation dialog box, navigate to the desired folder, and then double-click the PowerPoint presentation. To link to a website, click the *Hyperlink to* option at the Action Settings dialog box, click the down-pointing arrow at the right side of the *Hyperlink to* option box, and then click *URL* at the drop-down list. At the Hyperlink To URL dialog box, type the web address in the URL text box, and then click OK. Click OK to close the Action Settings dialog box. Other actions you can link to using the *Hyperlink to* drop-down list include: Next Slide, Previous Slide, First Slide, Last Slide, Last Slide Viewed, End Show, Custom Show, Slide, and Other File.

Project 3b | Linking to Another Presentation and a Website

Part 2 of 5

1. With **P-C6-P3-JobSearch.pptx** open, add an action button that will link to another presentation by completing the following steps:
   a. Make Slide 4 active.
   b. Click the Insert tab and then click the Shapes button in the Illustrations group.
   c. At the drop-down list, click *Action Button: Help* (second button from the right in the Action Buttons group).

d. Draw the action button to the left of the existing button located in the lower right corner of the slide.

e. At the Action Settings dialog box, click the *Hyperlink to* option.

f. Click the down-pointing arrow at the right side of the *Hyperlink to* option box and then click *Other PowerPoint Presentation* at the drop-down list. (You will need to scroll down the list to display this option.)

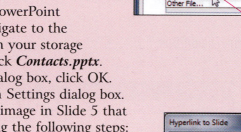

g. At the Hyperlink to Other PowerPoint Presentation dialog box, navigate to the PowerPoint2010C6 folder on your storage medium and then double-click **Contacts.pptx**.

h. At the Hyperlink to Slide dialog box, click OK.

i. Click OK to close the Action Settings dialog box.

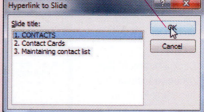

2. Apply an action to the clip art image in Slide 5 that links to a website by completing the following steps:

a. Make Slide 5 active and then click the clip art image to select it.

b. Click the Insert tab and then click the Action button in the Links group.

c. At the Action Settings dialog box, click the *Hyperlink to* option.

d. Click the down-pointing arrow at the right of the *Hyperlink to* option box, and then click *URL* at the drop-down list.

e. At the Hyperlink To URL dialog box, type **www.usajobs.gov** and then click OK.

f. Click OK to close the Action Settings dialog box.

g. Click outside the clip art image to deselect it.

3. Run the presentation by completing the following steps:

a. Make sure you are connected to the Internet.

b. Make Slide 1 active.

c. Click the Slide Show button in the view area on the Status bar.

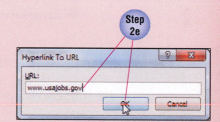

d. Navigate through the slide show to Slide 4.

e. Click the action button in Slide 4 containing the question mark. (This displays Slide 1 of **Contacts.pptx**.)

f. Navigate through the three slides in **Contacts.pptx**. Continue clicking the mouse button until you return to Slide 4 of **P-C6-P3-JobSearch.pptx**.

g. Display Slide 5 and then click the clip art image. (If you are connected to the Internet, the job site of the United States Federal Government displays.)

h. Click a few links at the website.

i. When you are finished viewing the website, close your web browser.

j. Continue viewing the remainder of the presentation by clicking the action button in the lower right corner of each slide.

k. When Slide 1 displays, press the Esc key to end the presentation.

4. Save **P-C6-P3-JobSearch.pptx**.

Inserting Hyperlinks ■■■■■ ■■ ■ ■■ ■■■■ ■ ■■■■

▼ **Quick Steps**

Insert Hyperlink
1. Click Insert tab.
2. Click Hyperlink button.
3. Make desired changes at Insert Hyperlink dialog box.
4. Click OK.

In Project 3b, you created hyperlinks with options at the Action Settings dialog box. You can also create hyperlinks with options at the Insert Hyperlink dialog box shown in Figure 6.2. To display this dialog box, select a key word, phrase, or object in a slide, click the Insert tab, and then click the Hyperlink button in the Links group. You can also display the Insert Hyperlink dialog box with the keyboard shortcut Ctrl + K. You can link to a website, another presentation, a place in the current presentation, a new presentation, or to an email address. To insert a hyperlink to a website or an existing presentation, click the Existing File or Web Page button in the *Link to* group at the Insert Hyperlink dialog box.

Figure 6.2 Insert Hyperlink Dialog Box

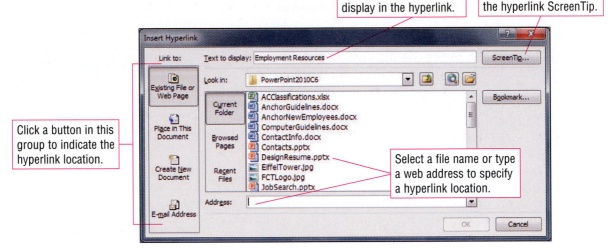

Type the text you want to display in the hyperlink.

Click this button to edit the hyperlink ScreenTip.

Click a button in this group to indicate the hyperlink location.

Select a file name or type a web address to specify a hyperlink location.

Project 3c Inserting Hyperlinks to a Website   Part 3 of 5

1. With **P-C6-P3-JobSearch.pptx** open, insert a new slide by completing the following steps:
   a. Make Slide 5 active.
   b. Click the Home tab.
   c. Click the New Slide button arrow and then click the *Title Slide* layout.
   d. Click the text *Click to add title* and then type **Internet Job Resources**.
   e. Click the text *Click to add subtitle* and then type **Employment Resources**, press Enter, and then type **America's Job Bank**.
2. Add a hyperlink to the Employment Resources site by completing the following steps:
   a. Select *Employment Resources* in Slide 6.
   b. Click the Insert tab and then click the Hyperlink button in the Links group.
   c. At the Insert Hyperlink dialog box, type **www.employment-resources.com** in the *Address* text box. (PowerPoint automatically inserts *http://* at the beginning of the address.)
   d. Click OK to close the Insert Hyperlink dialog box.

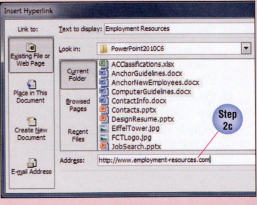

Step 2c

3. Add a hyperlink to the America's Job Bank website by completing the following steps:
    a. Select *America's Job Bank* in Slide 6.
    b. Click the Hyperlink button in the Links group.
    c. At the Insert Hyperlink dialog box, type **www.ajb.dni.us** in the *Address* text box.
    d. Click OK to close the Insert Hyperlink dialog box.
4. Copy the action button in Slide 1 to Slide 6 by completing the following steps:
    a. Make Slide 1 active.
    b. Click the action button to select it.
    c. Press Ctrl + C to copy the button.
    d. Make Slide 6 active.
    e. Press Ctrl + V to paste the button.
5. Save **P-C6-P3-JobSearch.pptx**.

In addition to linking to a website, you can create a hyperlink to another location in the presentation with the Place in This Document button in the *Link to* group in the Insert Hyperlink dialog box. Click the slide you want to link to in the *Select a place in this document* list box. With the Create New Document button in the Insert Hyperlink dialog box, you can create a hyperlink to a new presentation. When you click this button, you will be prompted to type a name for the new presentation and specify if you want to edit the new presentation now or later.

You can use a graphic such as a clip art image, picture, chart, or text box, to hyperlink to a file or website. To hyperlink with a graphic, select the graphic, click the Insert tab, and then click the Hyperlink button. You can also right-click the graphic and then click *Hyperlink* at the shortcut menu. At the Insert Hyperlink dialog box, specify what you want to link to and the text you want to display in the hyperlink.

You can insert a hyperlink to an email address at the Insert Hyperlink dialog box. To do this, click the E-Mail Address button in the *Link to* group, type the desired address in the *E-mail address* text box, and type a subject for the email in the *Subject* text box. Click in the *Text to display* text box and then type the text you want to display in the document. To use this feature, the email address you use must be set up in Outlook 2010.

Navigate to a hyperlink by clicking the hyperlink in the slide. Hover the mouse over the hyperlink and a ScreenTip displays with the hyperlink. If you want specific information to display in the ScreenTip, click the ScreenTip button in the Insert Hyperlink dialog box, type the desired text in the Set Hyperlink ScreenTip dialog box, and then click OK.

HINT
Hyperlinks are active when running the presentation, not when creating it.

Project 3d | **Inserting Hyperlinks to a Website, to Another Presentation, and to a Word Document** | **Part 4 of 5**

1. With **P-C6-P3-JobSearch.pptx** open, make Slide 3 active.
2. Create a link to another presentation by completing the following steps:
    a. Move the insertion point immediately right of the word *Picture*, press the Enter key, press Shift + Tab, and then type **Resume design**.
    b. Select *Resume design*.
    c. Make sure the Insert tab is active and then click the Hyperlink button in the Links group.

d. At the Insert Hyperlink dialog box, make sure the Existing File or Web Page button is selected.

e. Click the down-pointing arrow at the right side of the *Look in* option and then navigate to the PowerPoint2010C6 folder on your storage medium.

f. Double-click *DesignResume.pptx*.

3. Create a hyperlink from a graphic to a Word document by completing the following steps:

   a. Make Slide 4 active.

   b. Right-click the small clip art image that displays in the upper right corner of the slide and then click *Hyperlink* at the shortcut menu.

   c. At the Insert Hyperlink dialog box, make sure the Existing File or Web Page button is selected.

   d. Click the down-pointing arrow at the right side of the *Look in* option and then navigate to the PowerPoint2010C6 folder on your storage medium.

   e. Double-click *ContactInfo.docx*.

4. Make Slide 6 active and then insert a chart by completing the following steps:

   a. Press Ctrl + O to display the Open dialog box.

   b. Navigate to the PowerPoint2010C6 folder on your storage medium and then double-click *USBLSChart.pptx*.

   c. Select the chart.

   d. Click the Copy button.

   e. Click the PowerPoint button on the Status bar and then click the thumbnail representing the **P-C6-P3-JobSearch.pptx** presentation.

   f. Click the Paste button.

   g. With the chart selected, drag the chart to the lower left corner of the slide.

5. Create a hyperlink from the chart to the United States Bureau of Labor Statistics website by completing the following steps:

   a. With the chart selected, click the Hyperlink button in the Links group in the Insert tab.

   b. At the Insert Hyperlink dialog box, make sure the Existing File or Web Page button is selected and then type www.bls.gov in the *Address* text box.

   c. Click OK to close the Insert Hyperlink dialog box.

6. Hover the mouse pointer on the PowerPoint button on the Taskbar, click the thumbnail representing the **USBLSChart.pptx** presentation, and then close the presentation.

7. Run the presentation by completing the following steps:

   a. Make sure you are connected to the Internet.

   b. Make Slide 1 active.

   c. Click the Slide Show button in the view area on the Status bar.

   d. Navigate through the slides to Slide 3 and then click the Resume design hyperlink in the slide.

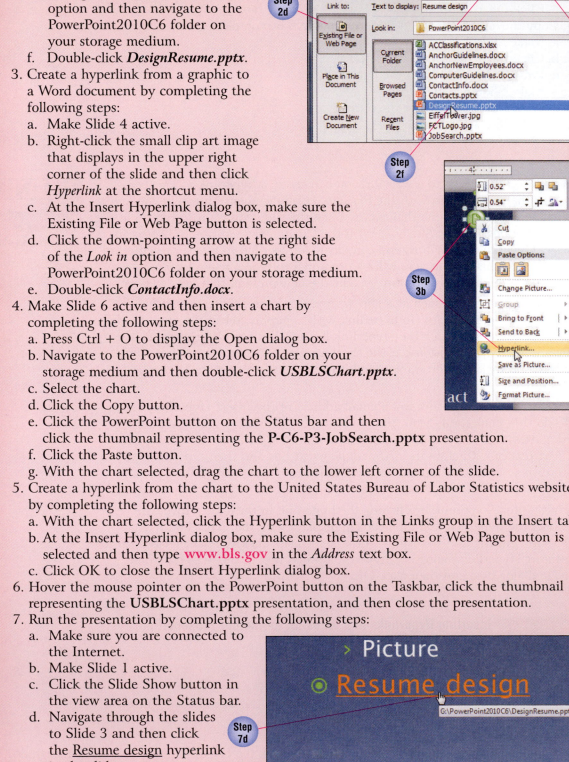

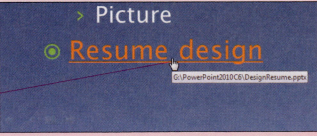

e. Run the **DesignResume.pptx** presentation that displays and then press the Esc key when the presentation has ended.

f. Click the mouse button to display Slide 4.

g. Display the Word document by clicking the small clip art image in the upper right corner of the slide.

h. Look at the information that displays in the Word document and then click the Close button located in the upper right corner of the Word window.

i. Continue running the presentation to Slide 6.

j. At Slide 6, click the <u>Employment Resources</u> hyperlink.

k. Scroll through the employment website and then close the web browser.

l. Click the <u>America's Job Bank</u> hyperlink.

m. Scroll through the America's Job Bank website and then close the web browser.

n. Click the chart.

o. Scroll through the Bureau of Labor Statistics website and then close the web browser.

p. Continue viewing the remainder of the presentation. (When Slide 1 displays, press the Esc key to end the presentation.)

8. Save **P-C6-P3-JobSearch.pptx**.

You can modify or change hyperlink text or the hyperlink destination. To do this, right-click the hyperlink and then click *Edit Hyperlink* at the shortcut menu. At the Edit Hyperlink dialog box, make any desired changes and then close the dialog box. The Edit Hyperlink dialog box contains the same options as the Insert Hyperlink dialog box.

In addition to modifying the hyperlink, you can edit hyperlink text by making the desired editing changes. For example, you can apply a different font or font size, change the text color, and apply a text effect. Remove a hyperlink from a slide by right-clicking on the hyperlinked text and then clicking *Remove Hyperlink* at the shortcut menu.

Project 3e Modifying, Editing, and Removing a Hyperlink   Part 5 of 5

1. With **P-C6-P3-JobSearch.pptx** open, make Slide 4 active and then modify the hyperlink in the clip art image by completing the following steps:

a. Position the mouse pointer on the small clip art image in the upper right corner of the slide, click the right mouse button, and then click *Edit Hyperlink* at the shortcut menu.

b. At the Edit Hyperlink dialog box, click the ScreenTip button located in the upper right corner of the dialog box.

c. At the Set Hyperlink ScreenTip dialog box, type **Click this image to display information on typing contact information.**

d. Click OK to close the Set Hyperlink ScreenTip dialog box.

e. Click OK to close the Edit Hyperlink dialog box.

2. Make Slide 3 active and then remove the <u>Resume design</u> hyperlink by right-clicking the hyperlinked text (the text is dimmed and barely visible) and then clicking *Remove Hyperlink* at the shortcut menu.

3. Run the presentation and click the hyperlinks as they appear in slides.
4. Print the presentation as a handout with six slides horizontally per page.
5. Save and then close **P-C6-P3-JobSearch.pptx**.

Chapter Summary

- Display a presentation in Slide Master view by clicking the View tab and then clicking the Slide Master button in the Master Views group. In Slide Master view, slide master thumbnails display in the slide thumbnail pane.

- Use buttons in the Edit Theme group in the Slide Master tab to apply a design theme, theme colors, and theme fonts.

- Use buttons in the Background group in the Slide Master tab to apply a predesigned background style, display the Format Background dialog box with options for applying background styles, and hide background graphics.

- Delete a placeholder by clicking in the placeholder, clicking the placeholder border, and then pressing the Delete key.

- Delete a slide master in Slide Master view by clicking the desired slide master thumbnail in the slide thumbnail pane and then clicking the Delete button in the Edit Master group.

- In Slide Master view, you can display the Header and Footer dialog box with the Slide tab selected and then insert the date and time, slide number, and/or a footer. At the Header and Footer dialog box with the Notes and Handouts tab selected, you can insert the date and time, a header, page numbers, and/or a footer.

- Create a custom slide layout by clicking the Insert Layout button in the Edit Master group in the Slide Master tab. Rename the custom slide layout with the Rename button in the Edit Master group.

- Insert placeholders in a slide layout or custom slide layout by clicking the Insert Placeholder button arrow in the Master Layout group and then clicking the desired placeholder at the drop-down list.

- In Slide Master view, create custom prompts by selecting generic text in a placeholder and then typing the desired text.

- Click the Insert Slide Master button in Slide Master view to insert a new slide master and associated slide layouts. You can also insert a new slide master by applying a design theme in Slide Master view.

- Save a presentation as a template by changing the *Save as type* option at the Save As dialog box to *PowerPoint Template (*.potx)*.

- Open a presentation based on a template by clicking the My templates button or the New from existing button at the New tab Backstage view.

- You can customize a handout with options in the Handout Master view and customize notes pages with options in the Notes Master view.

- In addition to changing the view, you can use buttons in the View tab to show/hide the ruler and/or gridlines; change the zoom display; view slides in color, grayscale, or black and white; and arrange, split, and switch windows.
- Action buttons are drawn objects in a slide that have a routine attached, such as displaying the next slide, the first slide, a website, or another PowerPoint presentation.
- Create an action button by clicking the Insert tab, clicking the Shapes button, clicking the desired button at the drop-down list, and then dragging in the slide to create the button.
- Apply an action to text or an object in a slide by selecting the text or object, clicking the Insert tab, and then clicking the Action button.
- With options at the Insert Hyperlink dialog box, you can create a hyperlink to a web page, another presentation, a location within a presentation, a new presentation, or to an email. You can also create a hyperlink using a graphic.
- You can modify, edit, and remove hyperlinks.

Commands Review

FEATURE	RIBBON TAB, GROUP	BUTTON, FILE TAB	KEYBOARD SHORTCUT
Slide Master view	View, Master Views		
New tab Backstage view	File	New	
Handout Master view	View, Master Views		
Notes Master view	View, Master Views		
Action buttons	Insert, Illustrations		
Insert Hyperlink dialog box	Insert, Links		Ctrl + K
Action Settings dialog box	Insert, Links		

Concepts Check   Test Your Knowledge

Completion: In the space provided at the right, indicate the correct term, symbol, or command.

1. To display a presentation in Slide Master view, click this tab and then click the Slide Master button.

   _____

2. Click this button to close Slide Master view.

   _____

3. This group in the Slide Master tab contains buttons for applying a theme, theme colors, and theme fonts.

   _____

4. This dialog box with the Slide tab selected contains options for inserting the date and time, a slide number, and a footer.

   _____

5. To create a new slide layout in Slide Master view, click this button in the Edit Master group.

   _____

6. To save a presentation as a template, choose this option at the *Save as type* option drop-down list at the Save As dialog box.

   _____

7. Change to this view to customize handouts.

   _____

8. Change to this view to customize notes pages.

   _____

9. The Zoom slider bar is located at the right side of this bar.

   _____

10. Click this button to display a drop-down list that includes action buttons.

    _____

11. Insert this action button in a slide to display the next slide in the presentation.

    _____

12. Insert this action button in a slide to display the first slide in the presentation.

    _____

13. This is the keyboard shortcut to display the Insert Hyperlink dialog box.

    _____

Skills Check Assess Your Performance

Assessment

1 FORMAT A PRESENTATION IN SLIDE MASTER VIEW AND THEN SAVE THE PRESENTATION AS A TEMPLATE

1. Display a blank presentation, click the View tab, and then click the Slide Master button.
2. Click the top slide master thumbnail in the slide thumbnail pane.
3. Apply the *Urban* theme, change the theme colors to *Paper*, and change the theme fonts to *Flow*.
4. Apply the *Style 2* background style.
5. Select the text *Click to edit Master title style*, click the Home tab, change the font color to *Olive Green, Accent 1, Darker 50%*, and then turn on bold.
6. Select the text *Second level* in the slide master and then change the font color to *Orange, Accent 2, Darker 50%*.
7. Insert the **WELogo.jpg** image in the master slide and then change the background of the logo to transparent by clicking the Color button in the Picture Tools Format tab, clicking the *Set Transparent Color* option, and then clicking on a white portion of the logo. This removes the white background so the yellow slide background displays. Change the height of the logo to 0.5 inch and drag the logo to the lower left corner of the slide master.
8. Select the date placeholder and then move the placeholder to the lower right corner of the slide.
9. Select the footer placeholder and then drag it down to the lower right corner of the slide immediately left of the date placeholder.
10. Click the Slide Master tab.
11. Click the first slide layout below the slide master.
12. Click the *Footers* check box in the Master Layout group to remove the footer and date placeholders.
13. Select and then delete the slide layouts from the third layout below the slide master (the *Section Header Layout*) to the last layout.
14. Preserve the slide masters by clicking the top slide master in the slide thumbnail pane, clicking the Slide Master tab, and then clicking the Preserve button in the Edit Master group.
15. Click the Close Master View button.
16. Save the presentation as a template to the PowerPoint2010C6 folder on your storage medium and name the template **XXXPublicationTemplate** (use your initials in place of the *XXX*).
17. Close **XXXPublicationTemplate.potx**.

2 USE A TEMPLATE TO CREATE A PUBLICATIONS PRESENTATION

1. Open **XXXPublicationTemplate.potx** (where the *XXX* represents your initials). (To do this, display the New tab Backstage view and then click the New from existing button. At the New from Existing Presentation dialog box, navigate to the PowerPoint2010C6 folder on your storage medium, and then double-click *XXXPublicationTemplate.potx*.)

2. Save the presentation and name it **P-C6-A2-WEnterprises**.

3. Click the *Click to add title* text in the current slide and then type Worldwide Enterprises.

4. Click the *Click to add subtitle* text and then type Company Publications.

5. Display the Reuse Slides task pane, browse to PowerPoint2010C6 folder on your storage medium, and then double-click **Publications.pptx**.

6. Insert the second, third, fourth, and fifth slides from the Reuse Slides task pane into the current presentation and then close the task pane.

7. Insert a second slide master with the following specifications:
   a. Display the presentation in Slide Master view.
   b. Click in the slide thumbnail pane below the bottom slide layout.
   c. Change the theme to *Foundry*.
   d. Click the Foundry Slide Master thumbnail in the slide thumbnail pane and then change the colors to *Paper* and the fonts to *Flow*.
   e. Apply the *Style 2* background style.
   f. Select the *Click to edit Master title style* text, click the Home tab, turn off text shadow, turn on bold, and change to left alignment.
   g. Select the text *Second level* and then change the font color to *Orange, Accent 2, Darker 50%*.
   h. Click the Slide Master tab.

8. Select and then delete slide layouts from the third layout (*Section Header Layout*) below the new slide master to the last layout.

9. Insert headers, footers, slide numbers, and dates with the following specifications:
   a. Click the Insert tab, display the Header and Footer dialog box with the Slide tab selected, insert the date to update automatically, and insert slide numbers.
   b. Click the Notes and Handouts tab, insert the date to update automatically, insert a header that prints your first and last names, insert a footer that prints *Worldwide Enterprises*, and then click the Apply to All button.

10. Close Slide Master view.

11. Make Slide 5 active and then insert a new slide using the new Foundry Title Slide layout and then type *Worldwide Enterprises* as the title and *Preparing the Company Newsletter* as the subtitle.

12. Insert the following text in slides using the Foundry Title and Content layout:
    Slide 7   Preparing the Newsletter
    - Maintain consistent elements from issue to issue
    - Consider the following when designing the newsletter
       ◦ Focus
       ◦ Balance
       ◦ White space
       ◦ Directional flow

Slide 8   Preparing the Newsletter
- Choose paper size and weight
- Determine margins
- Specify column layout
- Choose nameplate layout and format
- Specify heading format
- Determine newsletter colors

13. Select the bulleted text in Slide 8 and then change the line spacing to *1.5*.

14. Make Slide 7 active and then insert a clip art image related to newsletters.

15. Insert a transition and sound of your choosing to the presentation.

16. Run the presentation.

17. Print the presentation as a handout with four slides horizontally per page.

18. Save and then close **P-C6-A2-WEnterprises.pptx**.

Assessment

3   INSERT ACTION BUTTONS IN A GARDENING PRESENTATION

1. Open **PerennialsPres.pptx** and then save the presentation with the name **P-C6-A3-PerennialsPres**.

2. Make Slide 1 active and then insert an action button in the lower right corner of the slide that displays the next slide.

3. Display the presentation in Slide Master view, click the top slide master in the slide thumbnail pane, create an action button in the lower right corner of the slide that displays the next slide, and then close Slide Master view.

4. Make Slide 8 active and then create an action button that displays the first slide in the presentation.

5. Make Slide 2 active, click the flowers clip art image, and then create a link to the presentation **MaintenancePres.pptx** (located in the PowerPoint2010C6 folder on your storage medium). ***Hint: Use the Action button in the Links group in the Insert tab.***

6. Display Slide 8 and then make the following changes:
   a. Delete the text *Better Homes and Gardens®* and then type **Organic Gardening®**.
   b. Select *Organic Gardening®* and then create a hyperlink with the text to the website www.organicgardening.com.

7. Make sure you are connected to the Internet and then run the presentation beginning with Slide 1. Navigate through the slide show by clicking the next action button and display the connected presentation by clicking the clip art image in Slide 2. At Slide 8, click the <u>Organic Gardening®</u> hyperlink (if you are connected to the Internet). Scroll through the website and click a couple different hyperlinks that interest you. After viewing a few web pages in the magazine, close your web browser. When you click the action button on the last slide, the first slide displays. End the slide show by pressing the Esc key.

8. Print the presentation as a handout with four slides horizontally per page.

9. Save and then close **P-C6-A3-PerennialsPres.pptx**.

4 **CREATE AN ACTION BUTTONS PRESENTATION**

1. In this chapter, you learned to insert a number of action buttons in a slide. Experiment with the other action buttons (click the Insert tab, click the Shapes button, and then point to Action Buttons) and then prepare a PowerPoint presentation with the following specifications:
    a. The first slide should contain the title of your presentation.
    b. Include one slide for each of the action buttons that includes the specific name as well as an explanation of the button.
    c. Apply a design theme of your choosing to the presentation.
2. Save the presentation and name it **P-C6-A4-ActionButtons**.
3. Print the presentation as a handout with six slides horizontally per page.
4. Close **P-C6-A4-ActionButtons.pptx**.

Visual Benchmark Demonstrate Your Proficiency

CREATE AND FORMAT A COMPANY BRANCH OFFICE PRESENTATION

1. Create the presentation shown in Figure 6.3 with the following specifications:
    a. Apply the *Concourse* design theme, the *Module* theme colors, and the *Aspect* theme fonts.
    b. Insert **WELogo.jpg** in Slide 1 and then size and position the logo as shown in the figure. Insert the Forward or Next action button in the lower right corner of the slide as shown in the figure.
    c. Display the presentation in Slide Master view and then click the top slide master thumbnail. Insert **WELogo.jpg**, change the height of the logo to 0.5 inch, and then position the logo in the lower left corner of the side as shown in Figure 6.3. Click the *Click to edit Master Title style* text, click the Home tab, remove the text shadow effect, and then change the font color to *Gold, Accent 1, Darker 25%*. Insert the Forward or Next action button in the lower right corner of the slide master as shown in the figure and then close the Slide Master view.
    d. In Slide 4, create the clustered column chart with the *Style 26* chart style applied using the following numbers:

	>$25,000	>$50,000	>$100,000
Under 25	184	167	0
25 to 44	1,228	524	660
45 to 64	519	1,689	1,402
Over 64	818	831	476

    e. In Slide 5, insert the Information action button that links to the website www.clearwater-fl.com/gov and size and position the action button as shown in the figure.
    f. In Slide 6, insert the clip art image of the hospital (the original clip art image is black and light purple), change the clip art color to *Gold, Accent color 1 Dark*, and then size and position the clip art as shown in the figure. Insert a Home action button over the Forward or Next action button.
    g. Change the line spacing in slides so your slides display similar to the slides in Figure 6.3.

2. Apply a transition and sound of your choosing to all slides in the presentation.
3. Save the presentation and name it **P-C6-VB-WEClearwater**.
4. Run the presentation.
5. Print the presentation as a handout with six slides horizontally per page.
6. Close **P-C6-VB-WEClearwater.pptx**.

Figure 6.3 Visual Benchmark

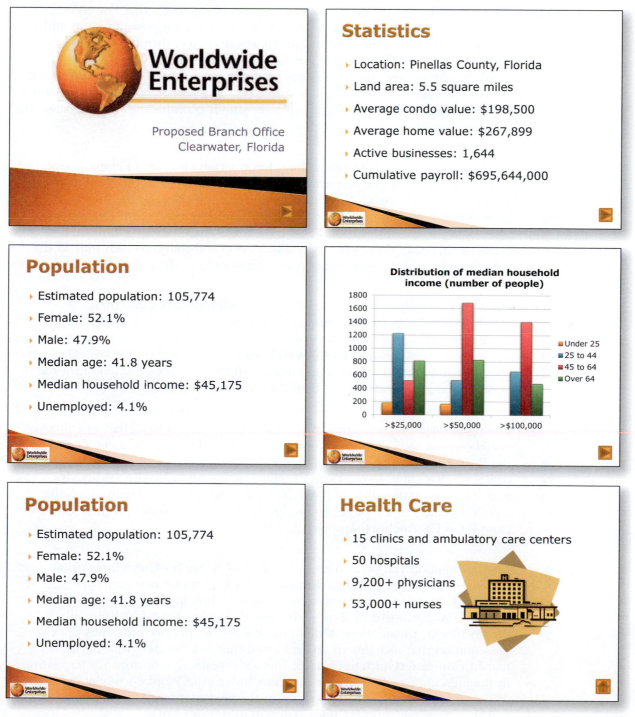

Case Study Apply Your Skills

Part 1

You are the training manager for Anchor Corporation and one of your job responsibilities is conducting new employee orientations. You decide that a PowerPoint presentation will help you deliver information to new employees during the orientation. You know that you will be creating other PowerPoint presentations so you decide to create a template. Create a presentation template with attractive formatting that includes a design theme, theme colors, theme fonts, and include an anchor clip art image in the lower left corner of most of the slides. Apply any other formatting or design elements to increase the appeal of the presentation. Save the presentation as a template on your storage medium with the name **AnchorTemplate** and make sure it contains the file extension *.potx*. Close the template.

Part 2

You have a document with notes about information on types of employment appointments, employee performance, and compensation. Open the Word document named **AnchorNewEmployees.docx** and then use the information to prepare a presentation using the **AnchorTemplate.potx** template. Save the completed presentation with the name **P-C6-CS-AnchorEmp** and make sure it has the file extension *.pptx*. Apply a transition and sound to each slide in the presentation, print the presentation as a handout, and then close the presentation.

Part 3

Open the Word document named **AnchorGuidelines.docx** and then use the information in the document to prepare a presentation using the **AnchorTemplate.potx** template. Save the completed presentation with the name **P-C6-CS-AnchorGuidelines** and make sure it contains the file extension *.pptx*. Apply a transition and sound to each slide in the presentation, print the presentation as a handout, and then close the presentation.

Part 4

During the new employee presentation you want to refer to a chart of employee classifications, so you decide to create a link to an Excel spreadsheet. Open the **P-C6-CS-AnchorEmp.pptx** presentation and then create a new slide that contains a hyperlink to the Excel workbook named **ACClassifications.xlsx**. Run the presentation, link to the Excel chart, and then continue running the remaining slides in the presentation. Print only the new slide and then save and close **P-C6-CS-AnchorEmp.pptx**.

Part 5

The information you used to create the **P-C6-CS-AnchorGuidelines.pptx** presentation was taken from a document that is part of a new employee handbook. You decide that you want to create a link in your presentation to the Word document to show employees the additional information in the document. Create a new slide in the **P-C6-CS-AnchorGuidelines.pptx** presentation that includes an action button that links to the Word document named **ComputerGuidelines.docx**. Include other action buttons for navigating in the presentation. Run the presentation, link to the Word document, and then continue running the remaining slides in the presentation. Print only the new slide and then save and close **P-C6-CS-AnchorGuidelines.pptx**.

Applying Custom Animation and Setting Up Shows

PERFORMANCE OBJECTIVES

Upon successful completion of Chapter 7, you will be able to:

- **Apply animations**
- **Modify and remove animations**
- **Apply a build**
- **Animate shapes, images, SmartArt, and chart elements**
- **Draw motion paths**
- **Set up a slide show**
- **Set rehearse timings for slides**
- **Hide slides**
- **Create, run, edit, and print a custom show**
- **Insert and customize audio and video files**

Tutorials

7.1 Applying Animation to Objects and Text

7.2 Animating Shapes, Images, SmartArt, and Chart Elements

7.3 Setting Up a Slide Show

7.4 Creating and Running a Custom Show

7.5 Adding Audio and Video

7.6 Broadcasting a Presentation; Compressing Audio and Video Files

7.7 Applying Sound to Animations; Recording Narrations

Animation or movement will add visual appeal and interest to your presentation when used appropriately. PowerPoint provides a number of animation effects you can apply to elements in a slide. In this chapter, you will learn how to apply animation effects as well as how to insert audio and video files to create dynamic presentations.

In some situations, you may want to prepare a self-running presentation where the presentation runs on a continuous loop. You can customize a presentation to run continuously and also rehearse the time you want each slide to remain on the screen. You can also create a custom slide show to present only specific slides in a presentation. In this chapter, you will learn how to prepare self-running presentations and how to create and edit custom slide shows. Model answers for this chapter's projects appear on the following pages.

PowerPoint2010C7

Note: Before beginning the projects, copy to your storage medium the PowerPoint2010C7 folder from the PowerPoint2010 folder on the CD that accompanies this textbook and then make PowerPoint2010C7 the active folder.

Model Answers

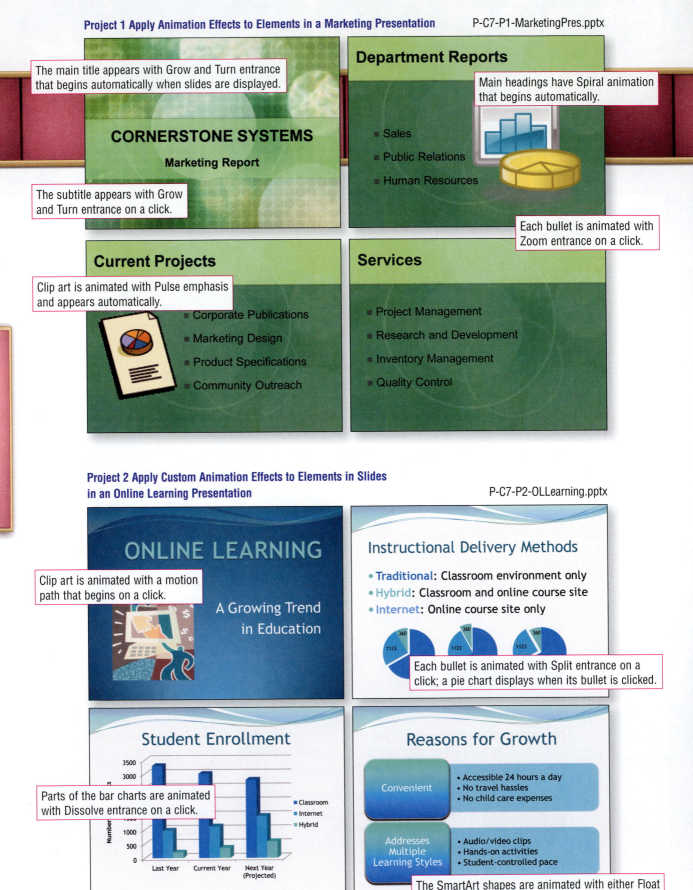

The main title appears with Grow and Turn entrance that begins automatically when slides are displayed.

CORNERSTONE SYSTEMS

Marketing Report

The subtitle appears with Grow and Turn entrance on a click.

Department Reports

Main headings have Spiral animation that begins automatically.

- Sales
- Public Relations
- Human Resources

Each bullet is animated with Zoom entrance on a click.

Current Projects

Clip art is animated with Pulse emphasis and appears automatically.

- Corporate Publications
- Marketing Design
- Product Specifications
- Community Outreach

Services

- Project Management
- Research and Development
- Inventory Management
- Quality Control

Project 2 Apply Custom Animation Effects to Elements in Slides in an Online Learning Presentation   P-C7-P2-OLLearning.pptx

ONLINE LEARNING

Clip art is animated with a motion path that begins on a click.

A Growing Trend in Education

Instructional Delivery Methods

- Traditional: Classroom environment only
- Hybrid: Classroom and online course site
- Internet: Online course site only

Each bullet is animated with Split entrance on a click; a pie chart displays when its bullet is clicked.

Student Enrollment

Parts of the bar charts are animated with Dissolve entrance on a click.

- Classroom
- Internet
- Hybrid

Reasons for Growth

Convenient
- Accessible 24 hours a day
- No travel hassles
- No child care expenses

Addresses Multiple Learning Styles
- Audio/video clips
- Hands-on activities
- Student-controlled pace

The SmartArt shapes are animated with either Float In (Up) or Grow and Turn entrance on a click.

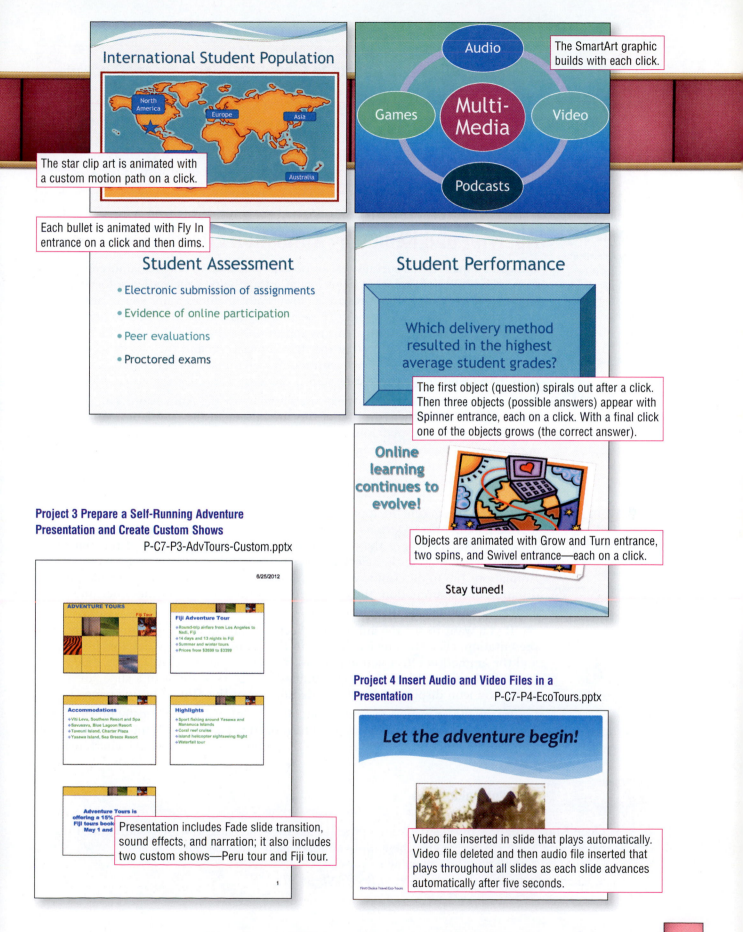

International Student Population

The star clip art is animated with a custom motion path on a click.

The SmartArt graphic builds with each click.

Audio

Games

Multi-Media

Video

Podcasts

Each bullet is animated with Fly In entrance on a click and then dims.

Student Assessment

- Electronic submission of assignments
- Evidence of online participation
- Peer evaluations
- Proctored exams

Student Performance

Which delivery method resulted in the highest average student grades?

The first object (question) spirals out after a click. Then three objects (possible answers) appear with Spinner entrance, each on a click. With a final click one of the objects grows (the correct answer).

Online learning continues to evolve!

Objects are animated with Grow and Turn entrance, two spins, and Swivel entrance—each on a click.

Stay tuned!

Project 3 Prepare a Self-Running Adventure Presentation and Create Custom Shows

P-C7-P3-AdvTours-Custom.pptx

6/25/2012

ADVENTURE TOURS

Fiji Tour

Fiji Adventure Tour
- Round-trip airfare from Los Angeles to Nadi, Fiji
- 14 days and 13 nights in Fiji
- Summer and winter tours
- Prices from $2699 to $3399

Accommodations
- Viti Levu, Southern Resort and Spa
- Savusavu, Blue Lagoon Resort
- Taveuni Island, Charter Plaza
- Yasawa Island, Sea Breeze Resort

Highlights
- Sport fishing around Yasawa and Mamanuca Islands
- Coral reef cruise
- Island helicopter sightseeing flight
- Waterfall tour

Adventure Tours is offering a 15% ... Fiji tours book... May 1 and ...

Presentation includes Fade slide transition, sound effects, and narration; it also includes two custom shows—Peru tour and Fiji tour.

1

Project 4 Insert Audio and Video Files in a Presentation

P-C7-P4-EcoTours.pptx

Let the adventure begin!

Video file inserted in slide that plays automatically. Video file deleted and then audio file inserted that plays throughout all slides as each slide advances automatically after five seconds.

First Choice Travel Eco-Tours

You will open a marketing presentation and then apply animation effects to the title slide and apply animation effects in Slide Master view to the remaining slides. You will remove some of the animation effects and then apply custom animation effects to elements in slides such as entrance and emphasis effects.

Effects Options

Preview

Applying and Removing Animation Effects ■■■■■■■■■

You can animate items such as text or objects in a slide to add visual interest to your presentation. Displaying items one at a time helps your audience focus on a single topic or point as you present it. PowerPoint includes a number of animations you can apply to items in a slide. These animations can be modified to fit your specific needs. You may want items to appear one right after the other or in groups. You can control the direction that the item comes from and the rate of speed. Try not to overwhelm your audience with too much animation. In general, you want them to remember the content of your presentation and not the visual effects.

To animate an item, click the desired item, click the Animations tab, click the More button at the right side of the animations in the Animation group, and then click the desired animation at the drop-down gallery. Once you have applied an animation, you can specify the animation effects with options in the Effect Options button drop-down gallery. Some of the animation effect options may include the direction from which you want the item to appear, and if you want the items such as bulleted text or SmartArt to appear as one object, all at once, or by paragraph. To apply effects to an animation, apply an animation to an item, click the Effect Options button located in the Animation group, and then click the desired effect at the drop-down gallery. (The appearance of this button changes depending on the selected effect.) Use options in the Timing group of the Animations tab to determine when the animation needs to start on a slide, the duration of the animation, the delay between animations, and the order in which animations should appear on the slide.

If you want to see the animation effects in your slide without running the presentation, click the Preview button in the Animations tab. Click this button and the animation effect you applied to the active slide displays on the slide in the Slide pane. When you apply animation effects to items in a slide, an animation icon displays below the slide number in the Slides/Outline pane.

If you add or change an animation, PowerPoint will automatically preview the animation in the slide. If you want to turn off this feature, click the Preview button arrow and then click *AutoPreview* at the drop-down list to remove the check mark.

Project 1a **Applying Animations** **Part 1 of 6**

1. Open **MarketingPres.pptx** and save the presentation with the name **P-C7-P1-MarketingPres**.
2. Make sure Slide 1 is active and then apply animations to the title and subtitle by completing the following steps:
   a. Click anywhere in the title *CORNERSTONE SYSTEMS*.

b. Click the Animations tab.
c. Click the *Fade* animation in the Animation group. (If you hover the mouse pointer over the animation option, the slide in the Slide pane will preview the animation.)

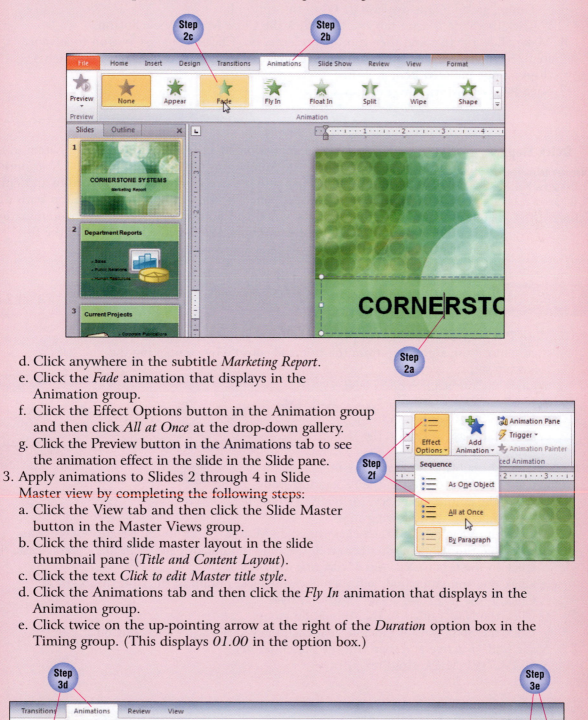

d. Click anywhere in the subtitle *Marketing Report*.
e. Click the *Fade* animation that displays in the Animation group.
f. Click the Effect Options button in the Animation group and then click *All at Once* at the drop-down gallery.
g. Click the Preview button in the Animations tab to see the animation effect in the slide in the Slide pane.

3. Apply animations to Slides 2 through 4 in Slide Master view by completing the following steps:
a. Click the View tab and then click the Slide Master button in the Master Views group.
b. Click the third slide master layout in the slide thumbnail pane (*Title and Content Layout*).
c. Click the text *Click to edit Master title style*.
d. Click the Animations tab and then click the *Fly In* animation that displays in the Animation group.
e. Click twice on the up-pointing arrow at the right of the *Duration* option box in the Timing group. (This displays *01.00* in the option box.)

f. Click the bulleted text *Click to edit Master text styles*.

g. Click the *Fly In* animation that displays in the Animation group.

h. Click twice on the up-pointing arrow at the right of the *Duration* option box in the Timing group. (This displays *01.00* in the option box.)

i. Click the Slide Master tab and then click the Close Master View button.

4. Make Slide 1 active and then run the presentation. Click the mouse button to advance items in slides and advance slides. Notice how the bulleted text in Slides 2 through 4 displays one bulleted item at a time.

5. Save **P-C7-P1-MarketingPres.pptx**.

▼ **Quick Steps**

Remove Animation
1. Click desired item.
2. Click Animations tab.
3. Click *None* option.

If you want to remove an animation effect from an item, click the item in the slide in the Slides pane, click the Animations tab, and then click the *None* option in the Animation group. You can also remove an animation effect from an item by clicking the item in the Slides pane, clicking the assigned animation button, and then pressing the Delete key. You will need to remove an assigned animation first if you want to apply a different animation. If you do not delete the first animation, both animations will be assigned to the item.

Project 1b **Removing Animations** **Part 2 of 6**

1. With **P-C7-P1-MarketingPres.pptx** open, make Slide 1 active and then remove the animation from the title and subtitle by completing the following steps:

    a. Click the title *CORNERSTONE SYSTEMS*.

    b. Click the Animations tab.

    c. Click the *None* option in the Animation group.

    d. Click the subtitle *Marketing Report*.

    e. Click the *None* option in the Animation group.

2. Remove the animation effects for Slides 2 through 4 by completing the following steps:

    a. Click the View tab and then click the Slide Master button in the Master Views group.

    b. Click the third slide master layout in the slide thumbnail pane (*Title and Content Layout*).

    c. Click in the text *Click to edit Master title style*.

    d. Click the Animations tab and then click the *None* option in the Animation group.

    e. Click in the text *Click to edit Master text styles*.

    f. Click the *None* option in the Animation group.

    g. Click the Slide Master tab and then click the Close Master View button.

3. Make Slide 1 active and then run the presentation.

4. Save **P-C7-P1-MarketingPres.pptx**.

Applying Animation Effects ■■■■■■ ■■■■ ■■■■ ■■

The Add Animation button in the Advanced Animation group in the Animations tab provides four types of animation effects you can apply to an item. You can apply an effect as an item enters the slide and also as an item exits the slide. You can apply emphasis to an item and you can apply a motion path to an item that will cause it to move in a specific pattern or even off the slide.

To apply an entrance effect to an item, click the Add Animation button in the Advanced Animation group and then click the desired animation effect in the *Entrance* section of the drop-down gallery. Customize the entrance effect by clicking the Effect Options button in the Animation group and then clicking the desired entrance effect. Additional entrance effects are available at the Add Entrance Effect dialog box. Display this dialog box by clicking the Add Animation button and then clicking *More Entrance Effects* at the drop-down gallery. Complete similar steps to apply an emphasis effect and an exit effect. Display additional emphasis effects by clicking the Add Animation button and then clicking *More Emphasis Effects* and display additional exit effects by clicking the Add Animation button and then clicking *More Exit Effects*.

Applying Animations with Animation Painter

If you apply an animation or animations to items in a slide and want to apply the same animation in more than one location in a slide or slides, use the Animation Painter. To use the Animation Painter, apply the desired animation to an item, position the insertion point anywhere in the animated item, and then double-click the Animation Painter button in the Advanced Animation group in the Animations tab. Using the mouse, select or click on additional items to which you want the animation applied. After applying the animation in the desired locations, click the Animation Painter button to deactivate it. If you need to apply animation in only one other location, click the Animation Painter button once. The first time you click an item, the animation is applied and the Animation Painter is deactivated.

▼ **Quick Steps**

Apply Animation Effect
1. Click desired item.
2. Click Animations tab.
3. Click Add Animation button.
4. Click desired animation effect at drop-down gallery.

Apply Effects with Animation Painter
1. Click item, then apply desired animation effect.
2. Click item with animation effect.
3. Double-click Animation Painter button.
4. Click each item to which you want animation effect applied.
5. Click Animation Painter button to deactivate it.

Add Animation

Animation Painter

Project 1c **Applying Animation Effects**   **Part 3 of 6**

1. With **P-C7-P1-MarktingPres.pptx** open, apply an animation effect to the title and subtitle in Slide 1 by completing the following steps:
   a. Make Slide 1 active.
   b. Click the title *CORNERSTONE SYSTEMS*.
   c. Click the Animations tab.
   d. Click the Add Animation button in the Advanced Animation group and then click the *Wipe* animation in the *Entrance* section of the drop-down gallery.

e. Click the Effect Options button in the Animation group and then click *From Top* at the drop-down gallery.

f. Click the subtitle *Marketing Report*.

g. Click the Add Animation button and then click the *Zoom* animation in the *Entrance* section.

2. Apply an animation effect to the title in Slides 2 through 4 by completing the following steps:

   a. Click the View tab and then click the Slide Master button in the Master Views group.

   b. Click the third slide master layout in the slide thumbnail pane (*Title and Content Layout*).

   c. Click in the text *Click to edit Master title style*.

   d. Click the Animations tab, click the Add Animation button in the Advanced Animation group, and then click the *More Emphasis Effects* option at the drop-down gallery.

   e. At the Add Emphasis Effects dialog box, click the *Grow With Color* option in the *Moderate* section.

   f. Click OK to close the dialog box.

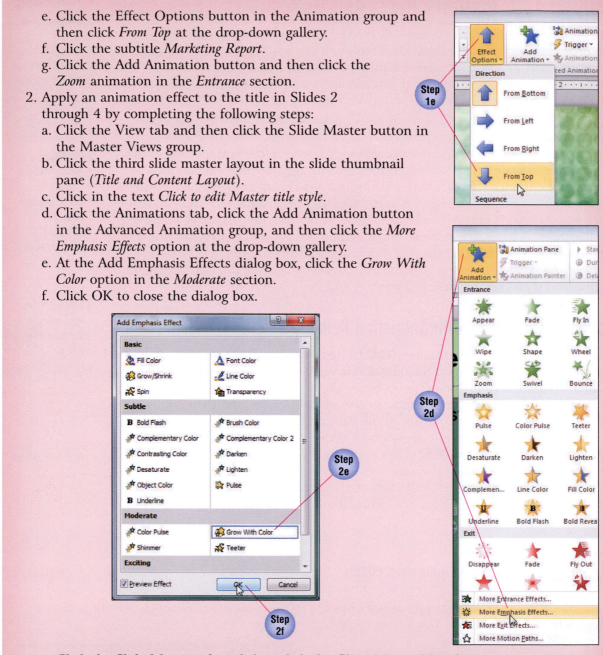

g. Click the Slide Master tab and then click the Close Master View button.

3. Apply an animation effect to the bulleted text in Slides 2 through 4 using the Animation Painter by completing the following steps:

   a. Make Slide 2 active.

   b. Click anywhere in the bulleted text to make the placeholder active.

   c. Click the Animations tab, click the Add Animation button, and then click the *Split* animation in the *Entrance* section.

   d. Click anywhere in the bulleted text.

   e. Double-click the Animation Painter button in the Advanced Animation group.

   f. Click the Next Slide button to display Slide 3.

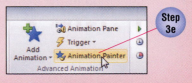

g. Click anywhere in the bulleted text. (The mouse pointer displays as an arrow with a paintbrush attached. The animations are applied to all four bulleted items.)

h. Make Slide 4 active and then click anywhere in the bulleted text.

i. Click the Animation Painter button to deactivate it.

4. Click the Preview button to view the animation effects.

5. Make Slide 1 active and then run the presentation by clicking the Slide Show button located toward the bottom of the task pane. Click the mouse button to begin animation effects and to advance slides.

6. Save **P-C7-P1-MarketingPres.pptx**.

Modifying Animation Effects

When you apply an animation effect to an item, you can use options in the Timing group to modify the animation effect. Use the *Start* option drop-down list to specify when you want the item inserted in the slide. Generally, items display in a slide when you click the mouse button. Click the *Start* option down-pointing arrow and then click *With Previous* or *With Next* at the drop-down list to make the item appear on the slide with the previous item or the next item.

Use the *Duration* option to specify the length of an animation. For example, click the up-pointing arrow to the right of the *Duration* option box to increase the length of time the animation takes to display on the slide and click the down-pointing arrow to decrease the length of time the animation takes to display. You can also select the current time in the *Duration* option box and then type the desired time.

The *Delay* option allows you to specify when to play an animation after a certain number of seconds. Click the up-pointing arrow to increase the amount of time between when an animation displays and the item that displays before it and click the down-pointing arrow to decrease the amount of time between when an animation displays after the previous animation. You can also select the current time in the *Delay* option box and then type the desired time.

Start

Duration

Delay

Move Earlier

Move Later

Reordering Items

When you apply an animation effect to an item, the item displays with an assigned animation number in the Slides pane. This number indicates the order in which items will appear in the slide. When more than one item displays in the slide, you can change the order with options in the *Reorder Animation* section of the Timing group in the Animations tab. Click the Move Earlier button to move an item before other items or click the Move Later button to move an item after other items.

▼ **Quick Steps**

Reorder Animation Item
1. Click item in slide.
2. Click Move Earlier or Move Later button.

Project 1d   **Removing, Modifying, and Reordering Animation Effects**   **Part 4 of 6**

1. With **P-C7-P1-MarketingPres.pptx** open, make Slide 1 active.
2. Modify the start setting for the slide title animation effect by completing the following steps:
   a. Click anywhere in the title to activate the placeholder.

b. Click the down-pointing arrow at the right of the *Start* option in the Timing group.

c. Click *With Previous* at the drop-down list. (At this setting, the title animation effect will begin as soon as the slide displays without you having to click the mouse button. Notice that the number 1 located to the left of the item changed to a zero.)

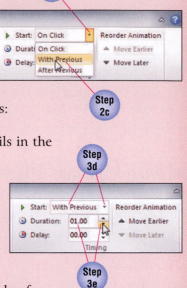

3. Change the animation effect applied to the subtitle and modify the animation effect by completing the following steps:

   a. Click anywhere in the subtitle *Marketing Report* in the slide.

   b. Click the More button located to the right of the thumbnails in the Animation group and then click the *None* option in the drop-down gallery.

   c. Click the Add Animation button in the Advanced Animation group and then click the *Grow/Shrink* animation in the *Emphasis* section.

   d. Click the down-pointing arrow at the right side of the *Start* option and then click *With Previous* at the drop-down list.

   e. Click four times on the down-pointing arrow at the right side of the *Duration* option. (This displays *01.00* in the option box.)

4. Remove animations from slide titles in Slide Master view by completing the following steps:

   a. Click the View tab and then click the Slide Master button in the Master Views group.

   b. Click the third slide master layout in the slide thumbnail pane (*Title and Content Layout*).

   c. Click in the text *Click to edit Master title style*.

   d. Click the Animations tab.

   e. Click the More button located to the right of the thumbnails in the Animation group and then click the *None* option in the Animation group.

   f. Click the Slide Master tab and then click the Close Master View button.

5. Remove animations from bulleted text in Slides 2 through 4 by completing the following steps:

   a. Make Slide 2 active.

   b. Click in the bulleted text.

   c. Click the *None* option in the Animation group in the Animations tab.

   d. Make Slide 3 active, click in the bulleted text, and then click the *None* option in the Animation group.

   e. Make Slide 4 active, click in the bulleted text, and then click the *None* option in the Animation group.

6. Make Slide 2 active and then apply and customize animation effects by completing the following steps:

   a. Click the title *Department Reports*.

   b. Click the Add Animation button in the Advanced Animation group and then click the *More Entrance Effects* option at the drop-down gallery.

   c. At the Add Entrance Effect dialog box, scroll down the list box and then click *Spiral In* in the *Exciting* section.

   d. Click OK to close the dialog box.

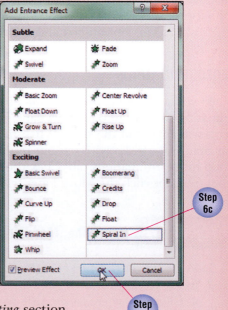

e. Click the bulleted text.

f. Click the Add Animation button and then click the *Zoom* animation in the *Entrance* section.

g. Click the clip art image.

h. Click the Add Animation button and then click the *Zoom* animation in the *Entrance* section.

7. Click the Preview button located at the left side of the Animations tab to view the animation effects.

8. After viewing the animation effects, you decide that you want the clip art to animate before the bulleted text and you want the animation effects to begin with the previous animation (instead of with a mouse click). With Slide 2 active, complete the following steps:

a. Click the clip art image. (The number 5 will display in the assigned animation button located to the left of the clip art placeholder because the clip art is the fifth item to enter the slide.)

b. Click the Move Earlier button located in the *Reorder Animation* section of the Timing group. (This displays the number 2 in the assigned animation button because you moved the clip art animation before the three bulleted items.)

c. Click the down-pointing arrow at the right side of the *Start* option in the Timing group and then click *With Previous* at the drop-down list.

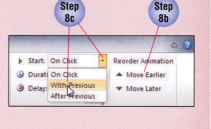

d. Click the title *Department Reports*.

e. Click the down-pointing arrow at the right side of the *Start* option in the Timing group and then click *With Previous* at the drop-down list.

9. Make Slide 3 active and then apply the same animation effects you applied in Slide 2. (Do this by completing steps similar to those in Steps 6a through 6h and Steps 8a through 8e.)

10. Make Slide 4 active and then apply the same animation effects you applied to Slide 2. (Do this by completing steps similar to those in Steps 6a through 6e and Steps 8d through 8e.)

11. Make Slide 1 active and then run the presentation. After running the presentation, make any changes or modifications to animation effects.

12. Save **P-C7-P1-MarketingPres.pptx**.

Customizing Animation Effects at the Animation Pane

You can use the Animation Pane to customize and modify animation effects in a presentation. Display the Animation Pane, shown in Figure 7.1, by clicking the Animation Pane button in the Advanced Animation group in the Animations tab. When you apply an animation to an item, the item name or description displays in the *Animation Pane* list box. Hover the mouse pointer over an item and a description of the animation effect applied to the item displays in a box below the item. If you click the down-pointing arrow at the right side of an item in the list box, a drop-down list displays with options for modifying or customizing the animation effect. For example, you can use options at the drop-down list to specify when you want the item inserted in the slide, the delay and duration of the animation, and specify that you want the animation effect removed.

Animation Pane

Up Re-Order

Down Re-Order

When you apply an effect to an item, the item name and/or description displays in the *Animation Pane* list box preceded by a number. This number indicates the order in which items will appear in the slide. When more than one item displays in the list box, you can change the order of an item by clicking the item in the list box and then clicking the Up Re-Order button or the Down Re-Order button located toward the bottom of the Animation Pane.

Figure 7.1 Animation Pane

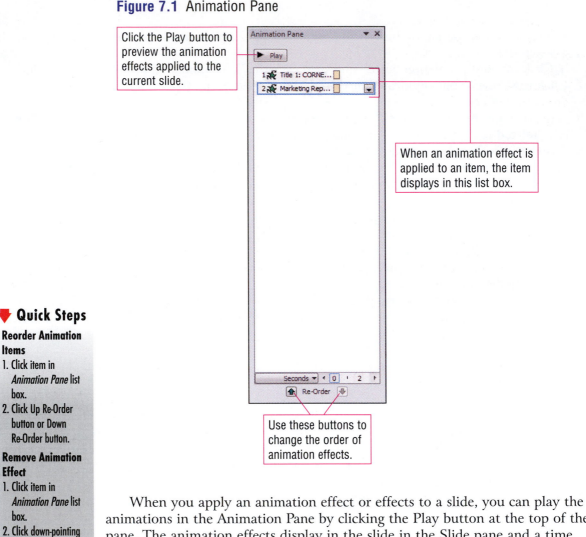

Click the Play button to preview the animation effects applied to the current slide.

When an animation effect is applied to an item, the item displays in this list box.

Use these buttons to change the order of animation effects.

▼ **Quick Steps**

Reorder Animation Items
1. Click item in *Animation Pane* list box.
2. Click Up Re-Order button or Down Re-Order button.

Remove Animation Effect
1. Click item in *Animation Pane* list box.
2. Click down-pointing arrow.
3. Click *Remove.*

When you apply an animation effect or effects to a slide, you can play the animations in the Animation Pane by clicking the Play button at the top of the pane. The animation effects display in the slide in the Slide pane and a time indicator displays along the bottom of the Animation Pane with a vertical line indicating the progression of time (in seconds).

Project 1e   **Removing, Modifying, and Reordering Animation Effects in the Animation Pane**   **Part 5 of 6**

1. With **P-C7-P1-MarketingPres.pptx** open, make Slide 1 active.
2. Click in the title *CORNERSTONE SYSTEMS*, click the Animations tab, and then click the *None* option in the Animation group.
3. With the title placeholder selected, click the Add Animation button in the Advanced Animation group and then click the *Grow & Turn* animation in the *Entrance* section.
4. Click twice on the down-pointing arrow at the right side of the *Duration* option. (This displays *00.50* in the option box.)
5. Click in the subtitle *Marketing Report*, click the More button located to the right of the animation thumbnails in the Animation group, and then click the *None* option.

6. With the subtitle placeholder selected, click the Add Animation button in the Advanced Animation group and then click the *Grow & Turn* animation in the *Entrance* section.

7. Click twice on the down-pointing arrow at the right side of the *Duration* option. (This displays *00.50* in the option box.)

8. Modify the start setting for the slide title animation effect in the Animation Pane by completing the following steps:

    a. Click the Animation Pane button located in the Advanced Animation group in the Animations tab. (This displays the Animation Pane at the right side of the screen.)

    b. Click the Title 1 item that displays in the *Animation Pane* list box.

    c. Click the down-pointing arrow at the right side of the item and then click *Start With Previous* at the drop-down list.

9. Remove animations from slides using the Animation Pane by completing the following steps:

    a. Make Slide 2 active.

    b. Click the Picture 3 item in the *Animation Pane* list box.

    c. Click the down-pointing arrow at the right side of the item and then click *Remove* at the drop-down list.

    d. Click the clip art image in the Slides pane, click the Add Animation button in the Advanced Animation group, and then click the *Pulse* animation in the *Emphasis* section.

10. Make Slide 3 active and then complete steps similar to those in Steps 9b through 9d to remove the animation effect from the clip art image and add the *Pulse* emphasis effect.

11. Click the Play button located toward the top of the Animation Pane to view the animation effects.

12. After viewing the animation effects, you decide that you want the clip art image to animate before the title and bulleted text and you want the animation effect to begin with the previous animation. With Slide 3 active, complete the following steps:

    a. Click the Picture 6 item in the *Animation Pane* list box.

    b. Click twice on the Up Re-Order button located at the bottom of the task pane. (This moves the Picture 6 item above the Title 1 and the content placeholder items.)

    c. Click the down-pointing arrow at the right side of the Picture 3 item and then click *Start With Previous* at the drop-down list.

13. Reorder animation effects in Slide 2 to match the changes made to Slide 3.

14. Make Slide 1 active and then run the presentation. After running the presentation, make any changes or modifications to animation effects.

15. Close the Animation Pane.

16. Save **P-C7-P1-MarketingPres.pptx**.

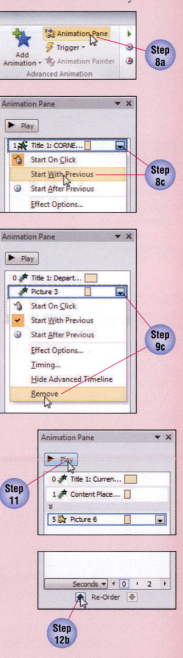

Applying Sound to Animations

You can enhance an animation by applying a sound to the animation. To apply a sound, click the Animation Pane button to display the Animation Pane, click the desired animated item in the Animation Pane list box, click the down-pointing arrow at the right side of the item, and then click *Effect Options* at the drop-down list. At the Effect Options dialog box with the Effect tab selected, click the down-pointing arrow at the right side of the *Sound* option box and then click the desired sound at the drop-down list. You can also apply sound to an animation by clicking the desired animated item in the slide in the Slides pane, clicking the Animation group dialog box launcher, and then choosing the desired sound effect at the dialog box that displays.

Applying a Build

![HINT]

You can group text (in a bulleted text placeholder) at the Effect Options dialog box by first, second, third, fourth, or fifth levels.

In Project 1a, you applied a build to bulleted text in a slide. A *build* displays important points on a slide one point at a time, keeping the audience's attention focused on the current point. You can further customize a build by causing a previous point to dim when the next point displays. To customize a build, click the Animation Pane button to display the Animation Pane, click the desired bulleted item in the Animation Pane list box, click the down-pointing arrow at the right side of the item, and then click *Effect Options* at the drop-down list. At the Effect Options dialog box with the Effect tab selected, choose a color option with the *After animation* option.

Project 1f — Applying Sound and a Build to Animations — Part 6 of 6

1. With **P-C7-P1-MarketingPres.pptx** open, make Slide 2 active and then apply sound and a build to the bulleted text by completing the following steps:
   a. Click in the bulleted text.
   b. Open the Animation Pane by clicking the Animation Pane button in the Advanced Animation group in the Animations tab.
   c. Click the down-pointing arrow at the right side of the Content Placeholder item in the Animation Pane list box and then click *Effect Options* at the drop-down list.
   d. At the Zoom dialog box, make sure the Effect tab is selected, click the down-pointing arrow at the right side of the *Sound* option, scroll down the list box, and then click the *Chime* option.
   e. Click the down-pointing arrow at the right side of the *After animation* option and then click the light green color (fifth color from the left).
   f. Click OK to close the dialog box.

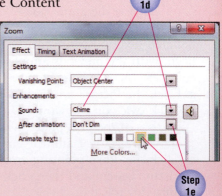

2. Click in the bulleted text in the slide.
3. Double-click the Animation Painter button.
4. Display Slide 3 and click anywhere in the bulleted text.
5. Display Slide 4 and click anywhere in the bulleted text.
6. Click the Animation Painter button to deactivate it.
7. Close the Animation Pane.
8. Make Slide 1 active and then run the presentation. After running the presentation, make any necessary changes or modifications to animation effects.
9. Save and then close **P-C7-P1-MarketingPres.pptx**.

Project 2 — Apply Custom Animation Effects to Elements in Slides in an Online Learning Presentation

6 Parts

You will open an online learning presentation and then apply animation effects to shapes, a clip art image, elements in SmartArt graphics, and elements in a chart. You will also draw a motion path in a slide.

Animating Shapes and Images

You can animate individual shapes or images such as clip art images in a slide in the same manner as animating a title or text content placeholder. You can select more than one shape and then apply the same animation effect to the shapes. To select more than one shape, click the first shape, hold down the Shift key, and then click any additional shapes.

Project 2a — Animating Shapes and a Clip Art Image

Part 1 of 6

1. Open **OLLearning.pptx** and then save the presentation with Save As and name it **P-C7-P2-OLLearning**.
2. Make Slide 8 active (this slide contains one large object with three smaller objects hidden behind it) and then animate objects and apply exit effects by completing the following steps:
   a. Click the Animations tab and then click the Animation Pane button in the Advanced Animation group. (This displays the Animation Pane at the right side of the screen.)
   b. Click the large object in the slide.
   c. Click the Add Animation button in the Advanced Animation group.
   d. Click the *More Exit Effects* option at the drop-down gallery.
   e. At the Add Exit Effect dialog box, click the *Spiral Out* option in the *Exciting* section. (You will need to scroll down the list to display this option.) Watch the animation effect in the slide and then click OK.

   f. Click the large object to select it and then drag it down the slide to display a portion of the three objects behind.
   g. Click the small object at the left, click the Add Animation button, and then click the *More Entrance Effects* option at the drop-down gallery.
   h. At the Add Entrance Effect dialog box, click *Spinner* in the *Moderate* section, and then click OK.
   i. Select the middle object, hold down the Shift key, and then click the object at the right. (This selects both objects.)
   j. Click the Add Animation button and then click the *More Entrance Effects* option at the drop-down gallery.

   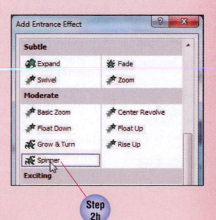

k. At the Add Entrance Effect dialog box, click *Spinner* in the *Moderate* section and then click OK. (Notice that the two objects are numbered *3* in the Animation Pane list box and are set to enter the slide at the same time. You will change this in the next step.)

l. Click the small object at the right, click the down-pointing arrow at the right of the *Start* option in the Timing group, and then click *On Click* at the drop-down list.

m. Apply emphasis to the middle object by clicking the middle object, clicking the Add Animation button, and then clicking the *Grow/Shrink* option in the *Emphasis* section of the drop-down gallery.

n. Click the large object to select it and then reposition it over the three smaller objects.

o. Click the Preview button to play the animation effects in the slide.

3. Make Slide 9 active and apply and modify animation effects and change animation order by completing the following steps:

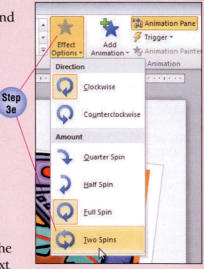

a. Click in the text *Online learning continues to evolve!* (this selects the text box), click the Add Animation button, and then click *Grow & Turn* in the *Entrance* section.

b. Click in the text *Stay tuned!* (this selects the text box), click the Add Animation button, and then click the *Swivel* option in the *Entrance* section.

c. Click the clip art image to select it.

d. Click the Add Animation button and then click the *Spin* animation in the *Emphasis* section.

e. Click the Effect Options button in the Animation group and then click *Two Spins* at the drop-down gallery.

f. Click the down-pointing arrow at the right side of the *Duration* option until *01.00* displays.

g. Click once on the Up Re-Order button (located toward the bottom of the Animation Pane). This moves the clip art image item in the list box above the *Stay tuned!* text box item.

h. Click the Preview button to play the animation effects in the slide.

4. Save **P-C7-P2-OLLearning.pptx**.

Animating a SmartArt Graphic

▼ **Quick Steps**

Animate SmartArt Graphic
1. Click SmartArt graphic.
2. Apply animation effect.
3. Click Effect Options button.
4. Specify the desired sequence.

You can apply animation effects to a SmartArt graphic and specify if you want the entire SmartArt graphic to display at once or if you want the individual elements in the SmartArt graphic to display one at a time. Specify a sequence for displaying elements in a SmartArt graphic with the Effect Options button in the Animation group.

When you apply an animation effect to a SmartArt graphic, you can apply animations to individual elements in the graphic. To do this, click the Effect Options button and then click the *One by One* option at the drop-down list. Display the Animation Pane and then expand the list of SmartArt graphic objects by clicking the small double arrows that display in a gray shaded box below the item in the Animation Pane list box. Click the individual item in the Animation Pane that you want to apply a different animation effect to and then click the desired animation in the Animation group.

1. With **P-C7-P2-OLLearning.pptx** open, make Slide 4 active and then animate objects in the SmartArt graphic by completing the following steps:

   a. Click the shape in the SmartArt graphic containing the word *Convenient*. (Make sure white sizing handles display only around the shape.)

   b. Make sure the Animations tab is selected and then click the *Float In* animation in the Animation group.

   c. Click the Effect Options button in the Animation group and then click *One by One* at the drop-down gallery. (This will allow you to apply different effects to the objects in the SmartArt graphic.)

   d. Make sure the Animation Pane displays.

   e. Expand the list of SmartArt graphic objects in the Animation Pane list box by clicking the small double arrows that display in a gray shaded box below the content placeholder item. (This expands the list to display four items.)

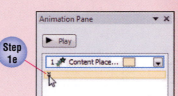

   f. Click the second item in the Animation Pane list box (the item that begins with the number *2*).

   g. Click the More button at the right side of the animations in the Animation group and then click the *Grow & Turn* animation in the *Entrance* section.

   h. Click the fourth item in the Animation Pane list box (the item that begins with the number *4*).

   i. Click the More button at the right side of the animations in the Animation group and then click the *Grow & Turn* animation in the *Entrance* section.

2. Click the Play button located toward the top of the Animation Pane to view the animation effects applied to the SmartArt graphic objects.

3. Make Slide 6 active and then apply animation effects by completing the following steps:

   a. Click the shape in the SmartArt graphic containing the text *Multi-Media*. (Make sure white sizing handles display only around the shape.)

   b. Click the Add Animation button and then click the *More Entrance Effects* option.

   c. At the Add Entrance Effect dialog box, click the *Circle* option in the *Basic* section.

   d. Click OK to close the dialog box.

   e. Click the Effect Options button and then click *Out* in the *Direction* section of the drop-down list.

   f. Click the Effect Options button and then click *One by One* in the *Sequence* section of the drop-down list.

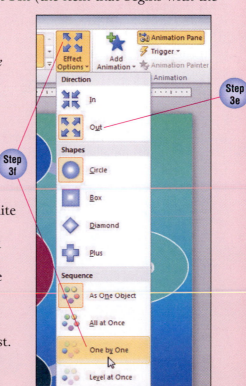

   g. Click the down-pointing arrow at the right of the *Duration* option until *00.50* displays.

4. Click the Play button located toward the top of the Animation Pane to view the animation effects applied to the SmartArt graphic objects.

5. Save **P-C7-P2-OLLearning.pptx**.

Animating a Chart

Like a SmartArt graphic, you can animate a chart or elements in a chart. Displaying data in a chart may have a more dramatic effect if the chart is animated. Bringing in one element at a time also allows you to discuss each piece of the data as it displays. Specify how you want the chart animated in the slide and how you want chart elements grouped. For example, you can group chart elements on one object or by series or category. Apply animation to elements in a chart in a manner similar to animating elements in a SmartArt graphic.

Project 2c   **Animating Elements in a Chart**   **Part 3 of 6**

1. With **P-C7-P2-OLLearning.pptx** open, make Slide 3 active and then animate chart elements by completing the following steps:
   a. Click in the chart placeholder to select the chart. (Make sure you do not have a chart element selected.)
   b. Click the Add Animation button and then click the *More Entrance Effects* option.
   c. At the Add Entrance Effect dialog box, click the *Dissolve In* option in the *Basic* section.
   d. Click OK to close the dialog box.
   e. Make sure the Animation Pane displays and then click the down-pointing arrow at the right side of the Content Placeholder item in the list box.
   f. At the drop-down list that displays, click *Effect Options*.
   g. At the Dissolve In dialog box, click the down-pointing arrow at the right side of the *Sound* option, scroll down the drop-down list, and then click the *Click* option.
   h. Click the Timing tab.
   i. Click the down-pointing arrow at the right side of the *Duration* option and then click *1 seconds (Fast)* at the drop-down list.
   j. Click the Chart Animation tab.
   k. Click the down-pointing arrow at the right side of the *Group chart* option and then click *By Category* at the drop-down list.

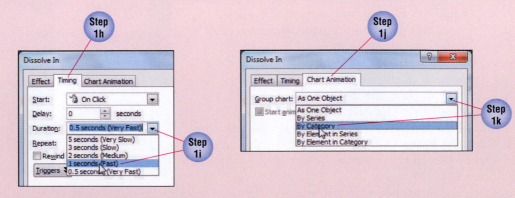

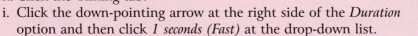

   l. Click OK to close the dialog box.
2. Make Slide 7 active and then apply a build animation effect to the bulleted text by completing the following steps:
   a. Click in the bulleted text.

b. Click the *Fly In* animation in the Animation group in the Animations tab.

c. Click the Effect Options button and then click *From Right* at the drop-down gallery.

d. Make sure the Animation Pane displays, click the down-pointing arrow at the right side of the Content Placeholder item in the list box, and then click *Effect Options* at the drop-down list.

e. At the Fly In dialog box, make sure the Effect tab is selected, click the down-pointing arrow at the right side of the *After animation* option, and then click the yellow color (second from the right).

f. Click OK to close the dialog box.

3. Save **P-C7-P2-OLLearning.pptx**.

Creating a Motion Path

▼ **Quick Steps**

Insert Motion Path
1. Click desired item in slide.
2. Click Animations tab.
3. Click Add Animation button.
4. Click desired path in *Motion Path* section.

Draw Motion Path
1. Click desired item in slide.
2. Click Animations tab.
3. Click Add Animation button.
4. Click *Custom Path* in *Motion Path* section.
5. Drag in slide to create path.
6. Double-click mouse button.

With options in the *Motion Paths* section of the Add Animation button drop-down gallery, you can specify a motion path. A ***motion path*** is a path you create for an object that specifies the movements of the object when you run the presentation. Click the Add Animation button in the Advanced Animation group, and a gallery of options for drawing a motion path in a specific direction can be found in the *Motion Paths* section. For example, if you want an item to move left in a line when running the presentation, click the Add Animation button in the Advanced Animation group and then click the *Lines* option in the *Motion Paths* section of the drop-down gallery. Click the Effect Options button in the Animation group and then click *Left* at the drop-down gallery. You can also apply a motion path by clicking the Add Animation button, clicking *More Motion Paths* at the drop-down gallery, and then clicking the desired motion path at the Add Motion Path dialog box.

To draw your own motion path, select the object in the slide you want to move in the slide, click the Add Animation button, and then click the *Custom Path* option in the *Motion Paths* section of the drop-down gallery. Using the mouse, drag in the slide to create the path. When the path is completed, double-click the mouse button.

Project 2d   Drawing a Motion Path   Part 4 of 6

1. With **P-C7-P2-OLLearning.pptx** open, make Slide 1 active and then apply a motion path to the clip art image by completing the following steps:
   a. Click the clip art image.
   b. Click the Add Animation button and then click the *More Motion Paths* option at the drop-down gallery.

c. At the Add Motion Path dialog box, scroll down the list box and then click the *Spiral Right* option in the *Lines & Curves* section.

d. Click OK to close the dialog box.

e. Notice that a spiral line object displays in the slide and the object is selected. Using the mouse, drag the spiral line object so it is positioned in the middle of the clip art image.

f. Click the down-pointing arrow at the right side of the *Start* option box in the Timing group and then click *With Previous* at the drop-down list.

g. Click the up-pointing arrow at the right side of the *Duration* option box in the Timing group until *03.00* displays in the option box.

h. Click the up-pointing arrow at the right side of the *Delay* option box in the Timing group until *01.00* displays in the option box.

2. Make Slide 5 active and then animate the star on the map by completing the following steps:

a. Click the star object in the slide (located below the heading *North America*).

b. Click the Add Animation button, scroll down the drop-down gallery, and then click the *Custom Path* option in the *Motion Paths* section.

c. Position the mouse pointer (displays as crosshairs) on the star, hold down the left mouse button, drag a path through each of the five locations on the map ending back in the original location, and then double-click the left mouse button.

3. Run the presentation and click the mouse to advance slides and elements on slides as needed.

4. Save **P-C7-P2-OLLearning.pptx**.

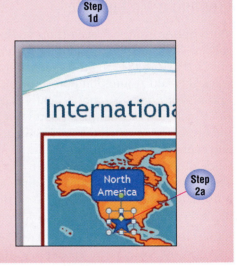

Applying a Trigger

▼ Quick Steps

Apply a Trigger
1. Click desired object in slide.
2. Click Animations tab.
3. Click Trigger button, point to *On Click of,* and then click trigger object.

With the Trigger button in the Advanced Animation group, you can make an animation effect occur during a slide show by clicking an item on the slide. For example, you can apply a trigger to a specific bulleted item in a presentation. A *trigger* creates a link between two items and triggers another item such as a picture or chart that provides additional information about the bulleted item. When running the presentation, you hover the mouse over the item containing the trigger until the mouse pointer displays as a hand and then you click the mouse button. This displays the trigger item.

The advantage to applying a trigger to an item is that you control whether or not the item displays when running the presentation. For example, suppose you created a presentation with product sales information and you wanted to provide additional specific sales data to one group you will be presenting to but not another group. When presenting to the group that you want to share the additional sales data, click the item to trigger the display of the data. When presenting to the other group, you would not click the item and the sales data would remain hidden.

Trigger

To insert a trigger, apply an animation effect to both items, display the Animation Pane, and then click in the list box the item to which you want to apply the trigger. Click the Trigger button in the Advanced Animation group, point to *On Click of*, and then click the item you want triggered at the side menu.

Part 5 of 6

Project 2e — Inserting Triggers

1. With **P-C7-P2-OLLearning.pptx** open, make Slide 2 active.
2. Apply animation effects to the text and charts by completing the following steps:
   a. Click anywhere in the bulleted text.
   b. Click the Animations tab.
   c. Click the *Split* animation in the Animation group.
   d. Select the pie chart at the left. (To do this, click outside the chart at the left side. Make sure the chart is selected and not an individual chart element.)
   e. Click the *Split* animation in the Animation group.
   f. Select the middle pie chart and then click the *Split* animation. (Make sure you select the chart and not a chart element.)
   g. Select the pie chart at the right and then click the *Split* animation. (Make sure you select the chart and not a chart element.)
3. Make sure the Animation Pane displays.
4. Apply a trigger to the first bulleted item that, when clicked, will display the chart at the left by completing the following steps:
   a. Click the *Chart 3* item in the list box in the Animation Pane.
   b. Click the Trigger button in the Advanced Animation group, point to *On Click of*, and then click *Content Placeholder 2* at the side menu.
   c. Click the *Chart 4* item in the list box in the Animation Pane, click the Trigger button, point to *On Click of*, and then click *Content Placeholder 2* at the side menu.
   d. Click the *Chart 5* item in the list box in the Animation Pane, click the Trigger button, point to *On Click of*, and then click *Content Placeholder 2* at the side menu.
5. Close the Animation Pane.
6. Run the presentation by completing the following steps:
   a. Run the presentation from the beginning and when you get to Slide 2, click the mouse button until the first bulleted item displays (the item that begins with *Traditional*).

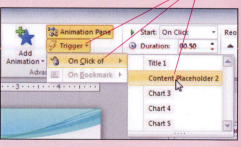

Step 4b

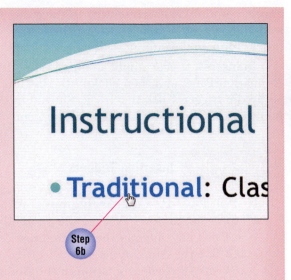

b. Hover your mouse over the bulleted text until the pointer turns into a hand and then click the left mouse button. (This displays the first chart.)

c. Position the mouse pointer anywhere in the white background of the slide and then click the left mouse button to display the second bulleted item (the item that begins with *Hybrid*).

d. Hover your mouse over the text in the second bulleted item until the pointer turns into a hand and then click the left mouse button. (This displays the middle chart.)

e. Position the mouse pointer anywhere in the white background of the slide and then click the left mouse button to display the third bulleted item (the item that begins with *Internet*).

f. Hover your mouse over the text in the third bulleted item until the pointer turns into a hand and then click the left mouse button. (This displays the third chart.)

g. Continue running the remaining slides in the presentation.

7. Save **P-C7-P2-OLLearning.pptx**.

8. Print the presentation as a handout with all nine slides printed horizontally on the page.

Setting Up a Slide Show ■■■■■ ■ ■ ■ ■ ■ ■ ■ ■ ■ ■ ■

Set Up
Slide Show

You can control how the presentation displays with options at the Set Up Show dialog box shown in Figure 7.2. With options at this dialog box, you can set slide presentation options, specify how you want slides to advance, and set screen resolution. Display the Set Up Show dialog box by clicking the Slide Show tab and then clicking the Set Up Slide Show button in the Set Up group.

Figure 7.2 Set Up Show Dialog Box

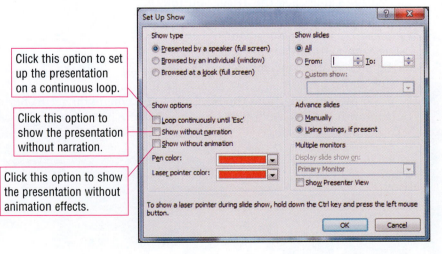

Click this option to set up the presentation on a continuous loop.

Click this option to show the presentation without narration.

Click this option to show the presentation without animation effects.

Running a Presentation without Animation

If a presentation contains numerous animation effects, you can choose to run the presentation without the animations. To do this, display the Set Up Show dialog box, click the *Show without animation* check box to insert a check mark, and then click OK. Changes you make to the Set Up Show dialog box are saved with the presentation.

Quick Steps

Run Presentation without Animation
1. Click Slide Show tab.
2. Click Set Up Slide Show button.
3. Click *Show without animation.*
4. Click OK.

Project 2f | **Running a Presentation without Animation** | **Part 6 of 6**

1. With **P-C7-P2-OLLearning.pptx** open, specify that you want to run the presentation without animation by completing the following steps:
   a. Click the Slide Show tab.
   b. Click the Set Up Slide Show button in the Set Up group.
   c. At the Set Up Show dialog box, click the *Show without animation* check box to insert a check mark.
   d. Click OK to close the dialog box.
2. Run the presentation and notice that the animation effects do not play.
3. Specify that you want the presentation to run with animations by completing the following steps:
   a. Click the Set Up Slide Show button in the Slide Show tab.
   b. At the Set Up Show dialog box, click the *Show without animation* check box to remove the check mark and then click OK.
4. Save and then close **P-C7-P2-OLLearning.pptx**.

Step 1c

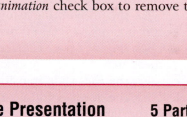

Project 3 **Prepare a Self-Running Adventure Presentation and Create Custom Shows** **5 Parts**

You will open a travel tour presentation and then customize it to be a self-running presentation set on a continuous loop. You will also hide slides and create and edit custom shows.

Setting Up a Presentation to Loop Continuously

In Chapter 1, you learned how to set automatic times for advancing slides. To advance a slide automatically, insert a check mark in the *After* check box in the Advance Slide section of the Timing group in the Transitions tab and then insert the desired number of seconds in the time box. If you want to have the ability to advance a slide more quickly than the time applied, leave the check mark in the *On Mouse Click* option. With this option active, you can let the slide advance the specified number of seconds or you can click the left mouse button to advance the slide sooner. Remove the check mark from the *On Mouse Click* button if you do not want to advance slides with the mouse.

Quick Steps

Loop Presentation Continuously
1. Click Slide Show tab.
2. Click Set Up Slide Show button.
3. Click *Loop continuously until 'Esc'.*
4. Click OK.

HINT
Use a self-running presentation to communicate information without a presenter.

In some situations, such as at a trade show or convention, you may want to prepare a self-running presentation. A self-running presentation is set up on a continuous loop and does not require someone to run the presentation. To design a self-running presentation, display the Set Up Show dialog box and then insert a check mark in the *Loop continuously until 'Esc'* option. With this option active, the presentation will continue running until you press the Esc key.

Project 3a Preparing a Self-Running Presentation   Part 1 of 5

1. Open **AdvTours.pptx** and then save the presentation with the name **P-C7-P3-AdvTours**.
2. Insert slides by completing the following steps:
   a. Click below the last slide thumbnail in the Slides/Outline pane.
   b. Make sure the Home tab is selected, click the New Slide button arrow, and then click *Reuse Slides* at the drop-down list.
   c. At the Reuse Slides task pane, click the Browse button and then click *Browse File*.
   d. At the Browse dialog box, navigate to the PowerPoint2010C7 folder on your storage medium and then double-click *PeruTour.pptx*.
   e. Click each slide in the Reuse Slides task pane in the order in which they display beginning with the top slide.
   f. Close the Reuse Slides task pane.
3. Add transition and sound effects and specify a time for automatically advancing slides by completing the following steps:
   a. Click the Transitions tab.
   b. Click in the *After* check box in the Timing group to insert a check mark.
   c. Click the up-pointing arrow at the right side of the *after* box until *00:05.00* displays.
   d. Click the *On Mouse Click* check box to remove the check mark.
   e. Click the *Fade* slide transition in the Transition to This Slide group.
   f. Click the down-pointing arrow at the right side of the *Sound* option in the Timing group and then click *Breeze* at the drop-down list.
   g. Click the Apply To All button.

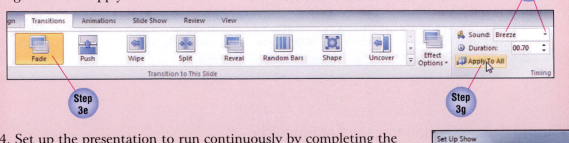

4. Set up the presentation to run continuously by completing the following steps:
   a. Click the Slide Show tab.
   b. Click the Set Up Slide Show button in the Set Up group.
   c. At the Set Up Show dialog box, click in the *Loop continuously until 'Esc'* check box to insert a check mark. (Make sure *All* is selected in the *Show slides* section and *Using timings, if present* is selected in the *Advance slides* section.)
   d. Click OK to close the dialog box.

5. Click Slide 1 to select it and then run the presentation. (The slides will advance automatically after five seconds.)
6. After viewing the presentation, press the Esc key on the keyboard.
7. Save **P-C7-P3-AdvTours.pptx**.

Setting Automatic Times for Slides

Applying the same time to all slides is not very practical unless the same amount of text occurs on every slide. In most cases, some slides should be left on the screen longer than others. Apply specific times to a slide with buttons on the Recording toolbar. Display this toolbar by clicking the Slide Show tab and then clicking the Rehearse Timings button in the Set Up group. This displays the first slide in the presentation in Slide Show view with the Recording toolbar located in the upper left corner of the slide. The buttons on the Recording toolbar are identified in Figure 7.3.

When the slide displays on the screen, the timer on the Recording toolbar begins. Click the Next button on the Recording toolbar when the slide has displayed for the appropriate amount of time. If you want to stop the timer, click the Pause button. Click the Resume Recording button to resume the timer. Use the Repeat button on the Recording toolbar if you get off track and want to reset the time for the current slide. Continue through the presentation until the slide show is complete. After the last slide, a message displays showing the total time for the presentation and asks if you want to record the new slide timings. At this message, click Yes to set the times for each slide recorded during the rehearsal. If you do not want to use the rehearsed timings when running a presentation, click the Slide Show tab and then click in the Use Timings check box to remove the check mark.

The time you apply to each slide will display below slides in the Slide Sorter view. The time that displays below the slide will generally be one second more than the time you applied to the slide. So, if you applied 5 seconds to Slide 1, *00.06* will display below the slide in Slide Sorter view.

▼ **Quick Steps**

Set Automatic Times for Slides
1. Click Slide Show tab.
2. Click Rehearse Timings button.
3. Using Recording toolbar, specify time for each slide.
4. Click Yes.

HINT

You can enter a specific recording time by selecting the time in the Slide Time text box, typing the desired time, and then pressing Enter.

Rehearse Timings

Figure 7.3 Recording Toolbar

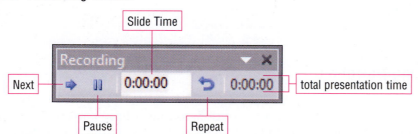

1. With **P-C7-P3-AdvTours.pptx** open, remove the automatic times for slides by completing the following steps:
   a. Click the Slide Show tab.
   b. Click the Set Up Slide Show button.
   c. At the Set Up Show dialog box, click the *Loop continuously until 'Esc'* check box to remove the check mark.
   d. Click OK to close the dialog box.
2. Set times for the slides to display during a slide show by completing the following steps:
   a. Make Slide 1 active.
   b. With the Slide Show tab active, click the Rehearse Timings button in the Set Up group.
   c. The first slide displays in Slide Show view and the Recording toolbar displays. Wait until the time displayed for the current slide reaches four seconds and then click Next. (If you miss the time, click the Repeat button to reset the clock back to zero for the current slide.)

   d. Set the times for remaining slides as follows:
      Slide 2 = 5 seconds
      Slide 3 = 6 seconds
      Slide 4 = 5 seconds
      Slide 5 = 6 seconds
      Slide 6 = 3 seconds
      Slide 7 = 6 seconds
      Slide 8 = 7 seconds
      Slide 9 = 7 seconds
   e. After the last slide displays, click Yes at the message asking if you want to record the new slide timings. (The slide times may display each with one additional second.)
   f. Click the Normal button in the view area on the Status bar.
3. Click the Set Up Slide Show button to display the Set Up Show dialog box, click the *Loop continuously until 'Esc'* check box to insert a check mark, and then click OK to close the dialog box.
4. Run the presentation. (The slide show will start and run continuously.) Watch the presentation until it has started for the second time and then end the show by pressing the Esc key.
5. Save **P-C7-P3-AdvTours.pptx**.

Recording Narration

You can record narration with your presentation that will play when the presentation is running. To record narration you must have a microphone connected to your computer. To begin the narration, click the Record Slide Show button in the Set Up group in the Slide Show tab. At the Record Slide Show dialog box, click the Start Recording button. Your presentation begins and the first slide fills the screen. Begin your narration, clicking the mouse to advance each slide. When you have narrated all of the slides in the presentation, your presentation displays in Slide Sorter view.

If you click the Record Slide Show button arrow, a drop-down list displays with three options. Click the *Start Recording from Beginning* option to begin recording your narration with the first slide in the presentation or click the *Start Recording from Current Slide* if you want to begin recording your narration with the currently active slide. Position your mouse on the third option, *Clear*, and a side menu displays with options for clearing the timing on the current slide or all slides and clearing the narration from the current slide or all slides.

When you click the Record Slide Show button in the Slide Show tab, the Record Slide Show dialog box displays. This dialog box contains two options: *Slide and animation timings* and *Narrations and laser pointer*. You can choose to record just the slide timings, just the narration, or both at the same time. With the *Slide and animation timings* option active (contains a check mark), PowerPoint will keep track of the timing for each slide. When you run the presentation, the slides will remain on the screen the number of seconds recorded. If you want to narrate a presentation but do not want slides timed, remove the check mark from the *Slide and animation timings* check box. With the *Narrations and laser pointer* option active (contains a check mark), you can record your narration and record laser pointer gestures you can make with the mouse. To make laser pointer gestures, hold down the Ctrl key, hold down the left mouse button, and then drag in the slide.

The narration in a presentation plays by default when you run the presentation. You can run the presentation without the narration by displaying the Set Up Show dialog box and then inserting a check mark in the *Show without narration* check box in the *Show options* section.

▼ **Quick Steps**

Record Narration
1. Click Slide Show tab.
2. Click Record Slide Show button.
3. Click Start Recording button.
4. Narrate slides.

Project 3c **Recording Narration**   **Part 3 of 5**

This is an optional project. Before beginning the project, check with your instructor to determine if you have a microphone available for recording.

1. With **P-C7-P3-AdvTours.pptx** open, save the presentation and name it **P-C7-P3-AdvTours-NarrateSlide**.
2. Make Slide 9 active and then narrate the slide by completing the following steps:
   a. Click the Slide Show tab.
   b. Click the Record Slide Show button arrow in the Set Up group and then click *Start Recording from Current Slide* at the drop-down list.
   c. At the Record Slide Show dialog box, make sure both options contain a check mark and then click the Start Recording button.
   d. Speak into the microphone the following text: Call Adventure Tours today to receive an additional ten percent savings when you book a Fiji or Peru tour.
   e. Press the Esc key to end the narration.

3. Make Slide 1 active and then run the presentation. If your computer has speakers, you will hear your narration when Slide 9 displays. After viewing the presentation at least once, press the Esc key to end it.
4. Save and then close **P-C7-P3-AdvTours-NarrateSlide.pptx**.
5. Open **P-C7-P3-AdvTours.pptx** and then save the presentation and name it **P-C7-P3-AdvTours-Narration**.

6. Remove the timings and the continuous loop option by completing the following steps:
   a. Click the Slide Show tab.
   b. Click the Record Slide Show button arrow, point to *Clear* at the drop-down list, and then click *Clear Timings on All Slides* at the side menu.
   c. Click the Set Up Slide Show button.
   d. At the Set Up Show dialog box, click the *Loop continuously until 'Esc'* check box to remove the check mark.
   e. Click OK to close the dialog box.

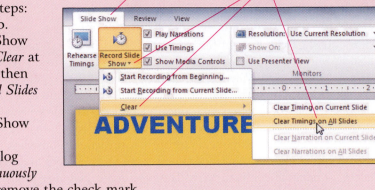

7. Make Slide 1 active and then record narration by completing the following steps:
   a. Click the Record Slide Show button in the Set Up group in the Slide Show tab.
   b. At the Record Slide Show dialog box, make sure both options contain a check mark and then click the Start Recording button.
   c. When the first slide displays, either read the information or provide your own narrative of the slide and then click the left mouse button. (You can also click the Next button on the Recording toolbar that displays in the upper left corner of the slide.)
   d. Continue narrating each slide (either using some of the information in the slides or creating your own narration). Try recording laser pointer gestures by holding down the Ctrl key, holding down the left mouse button, and then dragging in the slide.
   e. After narrating the last slide (the slide about accommodations for the Peru tour), the presentation will display in Slide Sorter view.

8. Make Slide 1 active and then run the presentation. If your computer has speakers, you will hear your narration as the presentation runs.

9. Run the presentation without narration by completing the following steps:
   a. Click the Set Up Slide Show button in the Set Up group in the Slide Show tab.
   b. At the Set Up Show dialog box, click in the *Show without narration* check box to insert a check mark.
   c. Click OK.
   d. Run the presentation beginning with Slide 1. (The presentation will run automatically with the timing established when you were recording your narration but without the narration.)

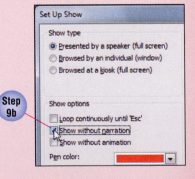

10. Save and then close **P-C7-P3-AdvTours-Narration.pptx**.

Hiding Slides

Hide Slide

A presentation you create may be presented to a number of different groups or departments. In some situations, you may want to hide specific slides in a presentation depending on the audience. To hide a slide in a presentation, make the desired slide active, click the Slide Show tab, and then click the Hide Slide button in the Set Up group. When a slide is hidden, a square with a slash through it displays behind the slide number in the Slides/Outline pane. The slide is visible in the Slides/Outline pane in Normal view and also in the Slide Sorter view. To remove the hidden icon and redisplay the slide when running a presentation, click the slide miniature in the Slides/Outline pane, click the Slide Show tab, and then click the Hide Slide button.

▼ **Quick Steps**

Hide Slide
1. Make slide active.
2. Click Slide Show tab.
3. Click Hide Slide button.

Setting Up Monitors

With options in the Monitors group in the Slide Show tab, you can specify screen resolution and show the presentation on two different monitors. The Resolution option in the Slide Show tab displays the default setting of *Use Current Resolution*. If you hover your mouse over the option, an expanded ScreenTip displays with information telling you that you can choose a screen resolution and that a smaller resolution generally displays faster while a larger resolution generally displays the presentation slower but with more visual detail.

If you have two monitors connected to your computer or are running PowerPoint on a laptop with dual-display capabilities, you can choose the *Use Presenter View* option in the Monitors group. With this option active, you display your presentation in full-screen view on one monitor and display your presentation in a special speaker view on the other.

Project 3d   **Changing Monitor Resolution**   **Part 4 of 5**

Check with your instructor before completing this project to determine if you can change monitor resolution.

1. Open **P-C7-P3-AdvTours.pptx**.
2. Remove the continuous loop option and remove timings by completing the following:
   a. Click the Slide Show tab.
   b. Click the Set Up Slide Show button.
   c. At the Set Up Show dialog box, click the *Loop continuously until 'Esc'* check box to remove the check mark.
   d. Click OK to close the dialog box.
   e. Click the Transitions tab.
   f. Click the down-pointing arrow at the right side of the *After* option box until *00:00* displays.
   g. Click the *After* check box to remove the check mark.
   h. Click the *On Mouse Click* option to insert a check mark.
   i. Click the Apply To All button.
3. Hide Slide 2 by completing the following steps:
   a. Click the Slide 2 thumbnail in the Slides/Outline pane.
   b. Click the Slide Show tab and then click the Hide Slide button in the Set Up group.

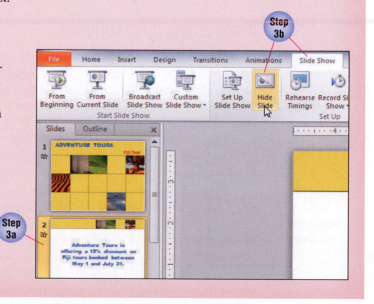

4. Change the monitor resolution by clicking the down-pointing arrow at the right side of the *Resolution* option in the Monitors group and then clicking *800×600* at the drop-down list.

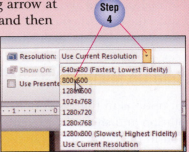

5. Run the presentation and notice the resolution and that Slide 2 does not display (since it is hidden).

6. Unhide Slide 2 by clicking the Slide 2 thumbnail in the Slides/Outline pane and then clicking the Hide Slide button in the Set Up group in the Slide Show tab.

7. Return the monitor resolution to the original setting by clicking the down-pointing arrow at the right side of the *Resolution* option in the Monitors group in the Slide Show tab and then clicking *Use Current Resolution* at the drop-down list.

If you have two monitors connected to your computer, you can run the presentation in Presenter View. Complete these optional steps only if you have two monitors available with your computer.

8. Make sure the Slide Show tab is active and then click the *Use Presenter View* check box in the Monitors group to insert a check mark.

9. At the Display Settings dialog box (from the Windows Control Panel) that displays, click the Monitor tab.

10. Click the monitor icon that you want to use to view your speaker notes and then click the *This is my main monitor* check box to insert a check mark.

11. Click the monitor icon for the second monitor that will show the presentation to the audience and then click the *Extend my Windows Desktop onto this monitor* check box to insert a check mark.

12. Click OK to close the dialog box.

13. Run the presentation.

14. Make sure the Slide Show tab is active and then click the *Show Presenter View* check box to remove the check mark.

15. Save **P-C7-P3-AdvTours.pptx**.

Broadcasting a Presentation

With the Broadcast Slide Show feature, you can share a slide show with others over the Internet by sending a link to the people you want to view the presentation and then everyone watches the slide show in their browser. To use this feature, you need a network service to host the slide show. You can use the PowerPoint Broadcast Service, which is available to anyone with a Windows Live ID, or you can use a broadcast service provided by an organization with a SharePoint server with Microsoft Office Web Apps installed. You can view a broadcast presentation in Internet Explorer, Firefox, and Safari.

Broadcast
Slide Show

To broadcast a presentation, click the Broadcast Slide Show button in the Start Slide Show group in the Slide Show tab. At the Broadcast Slide Show dialog box that displays, make sure the service you want to use displays in the *Broadcast Service* section (if not, click the Change Broadcast Service button and then specify the desired service), and then click the Start Broadcast button. PowerPoint creates a unique link for your presentation and you can send that link in an email or copy the link information. When everyone you want to view the presentation has received the link, click the Start Slide Show button. When the slide show has ended, press the Esc key and then click the End Broadcast button.

To complete this project, you will need either a Windows Live ID account or access to an organization's SharePoint service with Microsoft Office Web Apps installed. Depending on your system configuration and what services are available, these steps will vary.

1. With **P-C7-P3-AdvTours.pttx** open, click the Slide Show tab and then click the Broadcast Slide Show button in the Start Slide Show group.
2. At the Broadcast Slide Show dialog box that displays, make sure the service you want to use displays in the *Broadcast Service* section. If not, click the Change Broadcast Service button and then specify the desired service.
3. Click the Start Broadcast button.
4. Click the Copy Link hyperlink and then send the link to colleagues in any method you prefer. Or, if you are using Microsoft Outlook, click the Send in Email hyperlink and Microsoft Outlook 2010 opens in Compose mail mode with the link inserted in the message. In Outlook, send the link to people you want to view the presentation.
5. When everyone has received the link, click the Start Slide Show button.
6. When the slide show has ended, press the Esc key and then click the End Broadcast button.
7. At the message that displays telling you that all remote viewers will be disconnected if you continue, click the End Broadcast button.

Creating a Custom Show

You can create a *custom slide show*, which is a presentation within a presentation. This might be useful in situations where you want to show only a select number of slides to a particular audience. To create a custom show, click the Slide Show tab, click the Custom Slide Show button in the Start Slide Show group, and then click *Custom Shows* at the drop-down list. At the Custom Shows dialog box, click the New button and the Define Custom Show dialog box displays similar to what you see in Figure 7.4.

HINT

Create custom shows to customize a presentation for a variety of audiences.

Custom
Slide Show

Figure 7.4 Define Custom Show Dialog Box

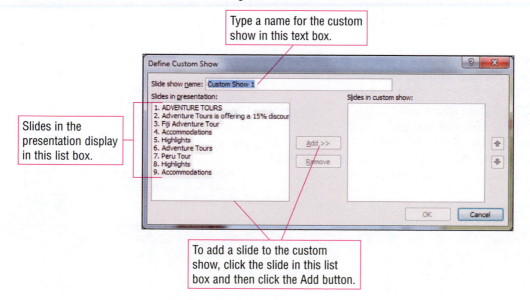

Type a name for the custom show in this text box.

Slides in the presentation display in this list box.

To add a slide to the custom show, click the slide in this list box and then click the Add button.

Create Custom Show
1. Click Slide Show tab.
2. Click Custom Slide Show button.
3. Click *Custom Shows*.
4. Click New button.
5. Make desired changes at Define Custom Show dialog box.
6. Click OK.

Run Custom Show
1. Click Slide Show tab.
2. Click Custom Slide Show button.
3. Click desired custom show.

Edit Custom Show
1. Click Slide Show tab.
2. Click Custom Slide Show button.
3. Click *Custom Shows*.
4. Click desired custom show.
5. Click Edit button.
6. Make desired changes at Define Custom Show dialog box.
7. Click OK.

Print Custom Show
1. Display Print tab Backstage view.
2. Click first gallery in Settings category.
3. Click desired custom show at drop-down list.
4. Click Print button.

At the Define Custom Show dialog box, type a name for the custom presentation in the *Slide show name* text box. To insert a slide in the custom show, click the slide in the *Slides in presentation* list box and then click the Add button. This inserts the slide in the *Slides in custom show* list box. Continue in this manner until all desired slides are added to the custom show. If you want to change the order of the slides in the *Slides in custom show* list box, click one of the arrow keys to move the selected slide up or down in the list box. When the desired slides are inserted in the *Slides in custom show* list box and in the desired order, click OK. You can create more than one custom show in a presentation.

Running a Custom Show

To run a custom show within a presentation, click the Custom Slide Show button in the Slide Show tab and then click the desired custom show at the drop-down list. You can also choose a custom show by displaying the Set Up Show dialog box and then clicking the *Custom show* option. If the presentation contains more than one custom show, click the down-pointing arrow at the right of the *Custom show* option and then click the show name at the drop-down list.

Editing a Custom Show

A custom show is saved with the presentation and can be edited. To edit a custom show, open the presentation, click the Custom Slide Show button in the Slide Show tab, and then click *Custom Shows* at the drop-down list. At the Custom Shows dialog box, click the custom show name you want to edit and then click the Edit button. At the Define Custom Show dialog box, make the desired changes to the custom show such as adding or removing slides or changing the order of slides. When all changes have been made, click the OK button.

Printing a Custom Show

You can print a custom show with options in the Settings category of the Print tab Backstage view. To do this, click the File tab and then click the Print tab to display the Print tab Backstage view. Click the first gallery in the Settings category and then click the desired custom show in the *Custom Shows* section.

Project 3e **Creating, Editing, and Running Custom Shows** **Part 5 of 5**

1. With **P-C7-P3-AdvTours.pptx** open, save the presentation and name it **P-C7-P3-AdvTours-Custom**.
2. Create two custom shows by completing the following steps:
   a. Click the Slide Show tab, click the Custom Slide Show button, and then click *Custom Shows* at the drop-down list.
   b. At the Custom Shows dialog box, click the New button.

Step 2b

c. At the Define Custom Show dialog box, type **PeruTourCustom** in the *Slide show name* text box.

d. Click Slide 6 in the *Slides in presentation* list box and then click the Add button. (This adds the slide to the *Slides in custom show* list box.)

e. Click each of the following slides in the list box (Slides 7, 8, and 9) and click the Add button.

f. Click OK to close the Define Custom Show dialog box.

g. At the Custom Shows dialog box, click the New button.

h. At the Define Custom Show dialog box, type **FijiTourCustom** in the *Slide show name* text box.

i. Add Slides 1 through 5 to the *Slides in custom show* list box.

j. Click OK to close the dialog box.

k. Click the Close button to close the Custom Shows dialog box.

3. Run the *PeruTourCustom* custom show by completing the following steps:

a. Click the Custom Slide Show button in the Slide Show tab and then click *PeruTourCustom* at the drop-down list.

b. Click the left mouse button to advance slides.

c. Click the Custom Slide Show button, click *FijiTourCustom* at the drop-down list, and then view the presentation. (Click the left mouse button to advance slides.)

4. Edit the FijiTourCustom custom slide show by completing the following steps:

a. Click the Custom Slide Show button in the Slide Show tab and then click *Custom Shows* at the drop-down list.

b. At the Custom Shows dialog box, click *FijiTourCustom* in the *Custom shows* list box and then click the Edit button.

c. At the Define Custom Show dialog box, click Slide 2 in the *Slides in custom show* list box and then click three times on the down-pointing arrow at the right side of the list box. (This moves the slide to the bottom of the list.)

d. Click OK to close the dialog box.

e. Click the Close button to close the Custom Shows dialog box.

5. Run the FijiTourCustom custom show.

6. Print the FijiTourCustom custom show by completing the following steps:

a. Click the File tab and then click the Print tab.

b. At the Print tab Backstage view, click the first gallery in the Settings category and then click *FijiTourCustom* in the *Custom Shows* section.

c. Click the second gallery in the Settings category and then click *6 Slides Horizontal* at the drop-down list.

d. Click the Print button.

7. Save and then close **P-C7-P3-AdvTours-Custom.pptx**.

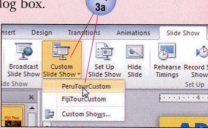

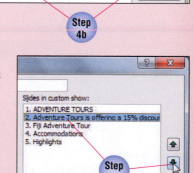

You will open a presentation and then insert an audio file, video file, and clip art image with motion. You will also customize the audio and video files to play automatically when running the presentation.

Inserting Audio and Video Files ■■■■■■■■■■■■■

Adding audio and/or video files to a presentation will turn a slide show into a true multimedia experience for your audience. Including a variety of elements in a presentation will stimulate interest in your presentation and keep the audience motivated.

Inserting an Audio File

▼ **Quick Steps**

Insert Audio File
1. Click Insert tab.
2. Click Audio button.
3. Double-click desired audio file.

Audio

To add an audio file to your presentation, click the Insert tab and then click the Audio button in the Media group. At the Insert Audio dialog box, navigate to the desired folder and then double-click the audio file. You can also insert audio by clicking the Audio button arrow and then clicking an option at the drop-down list. With the list options you can choose to insert audio from a file, insert a clip art audio, or record audio.

When you insert an audio file in a presentation, the Audio Tools Format tab and the Audio Tools Playback tab display. Click the Audio Tools Format tab and options display that are similar to options in the Picture Tools Format tab. Click the Audio Tools Playback tab and the Audio Tools Playback tab displays as shown in Figure 7.5. With options in the tab, you can preview the audio clip, insert a bookmark at a specific time in the audio file, trim the audio file, specify a fade in and fade out time, and specify how you want the audio file to play.

Figure 7.5 Audio Tools Playback Tab

Project 4a Inserting an Audio File   **Part 1 of 4**

1. Open **EcoTours.pptx** and then save the presentation with Save As and name it **P-C7-P4-EcoTours**.
2. Insert an audio file that plays music at the end of the presentation by completing the following steps:
   a. Make Slide 8 active.
   b. Click the Insert tab and then click the Audio button in the Media group.
   c. At the Insert Audio dialog box, navigate to the PowerPoint2010C7 folder on your storage medium and then double-click *AudioFile-01.mid*.

d. Click the Audio Tools Playback tab.

e. Click the down-pointing arrow at the right side of the *Start* option in the Audio Options group and then click *Automatically* at the drop-down list.

f. Click the *Hide During Show* check box in the Audio Options group to insert a check mark.

g. Click the *Loop until Stopped* check box to insert a check mark.

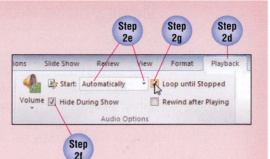

3. Make Slide 1 active and then run the presentation. When the last slide displays, listen to the audio clip and then press the Esc key to return to the Normal view.

4. Save **P-C7-P4-EcoTours.pptx**.

Inserting a Video File

Inserting a video file in a presentation is a similar process to inserting an audio file. Click the Video button in the Media group in the Insert tab to display the Insert Video dialog box. At this dialog box, navigate to the folder containing the video file and then double-click the file. You can also click the Video button arrow and then click *Video from File* to display the Insert Video dialog box.

You can insert a link in a slide to a video file at a website. To do this, click the Video button arrow in the Media group in the Insert tab and then click *Video from Web Site* at the drop-down list. This displays the Insert Video From Web Site dialog box. Information in this dialog box tells you that you can insert a link to a video file you have uploaded to a website by copying the embedded code from the website and pasting it into the dialog box text box. Click the *Clip Art Video* option at the Media button drop-down list and the Clip Art task pane displays with clip art images containing animation effects.

When you insert a video file in a presentation, the Video Tools Format tab and the Video Tools Playback tab display. Click the Video Tools Format tab and options display for adjusting the video file color and frame, applying video styles, and arranging and sizing the video file. Click the Video Tools Playback tab and options display that are similar to the options in the Audio Tools Playback tab shown in Figure 7.5.

▼ **Quick Steps**

Insert Video File
1. Click Insert tab.
2. Click Video button.
3. Double-click desired video file.

Video

Compressing Audio and Video Files

If you insert an audio and/or video file in a presentation, consider compressing the file(s) to improve playback performance and save disk space. If a presentation contains audio and/or video files, the Info tab Backstage view contains the Compress Media button. Click this button and a drop-down list displays with options for specifying the compressed quality of the video. Click the *Presentation Quality* option to save space and maintain the quality of the audio and/or video files. Click the *Internet Quality* option and the compressed video or audio files will be comparable to audio or video files streamed over the Internet. Choose the last option, *Low Quality*, to compress the audio or video files when space is limited such as when sending the presentation as an email attachment.

Showing/Hiding Media Controls

When a slide with an audio or video file displays when running a slide show, media controls display along the bottom of the audio icon or video window. You can use these media controls to play the audio or video file, move to a specific location in the file, or change the audio level. The media controls display when you move the mouse pointer over the audio icon or video window. You can turn off the display of media controls by displaying the Slide Show tab and then clicking the *Show Media Controls* check box in the Set Up group to remove the check mark.

Project 4b **Inserting a Video File in a Presentation** **Part 2 of 4**

1. With **P-C7-P4-EcoTours.pptx** open, make Slide 8 active.
2. You will insert a video file in the slide that contains audio so delete the audio file you inserted in Project 4a by clicking the audio file icon that displays in the middle of Slide 8 and then pressing the Delete key.
3. Insert a video file by completing the following steps:
   a. Click the Insert tab and then click the Video button in the Media group.
   b. At the Insert Video dialog box, navigate to the PowerPoint2010C7 folder on your storage medium and then double-click the file named *EcoTours.wmv*. (The **EcoTours.wmv** file is a low-resolution video. If you have access to sample videos in Windows 7, use the **Wildlife.wmv** video located in the Videos folder in the Libraries section of the hard drive. Double-click the Sample Videos folder and then double-click *Wildlife.wmv*. This video is high resolution.)
   c. Click the Play button in the Preview group (left side of the Video Tools Format tab) to preview the video clip. (The video plays for approximately 37 seconds.)
4. Format the video by completing the following steps:
   a. Make sure the video image is selected on the slide and the Video Tools Format tab is selected.
   b. Click the Beveled Frame, Gradient thumbnail in the Video Styles group.
   c. Click the Corrections button in the Adjust group and then click *Brightness: 0% (Normal) Contrast: +20%* at the drop-down gallery (third option from the right in the fourth row).

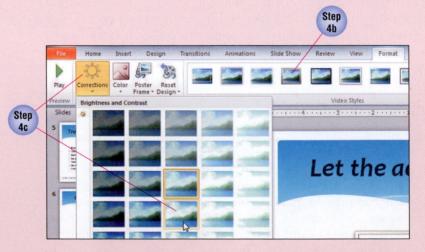

   d. Click the Rotate button in the Arrange group and then click *Flip Horizontal* at the drop-down list.
   e. Click the Video Tools Playback tab.

f. Click the up-pointing arrow at the right side of the *Fade In* text box until *01.00* displays and then click the up-pointing arrow at the right side of the *Fade Out* text box until *01.00* displays.

g. Click the Volume button in the Video Options group and then click *Low* at the drop-down list.

h. Click the *Loop until Stopped* check box in the Video Options group to insert a check mark.

5. Make Slide 1 active and then run the presentation. When the slide containing the video clip displays, move the mouse over the video clip window and then click the Play button located at the bottom left side of the window.

6. After viewing the video a couple of times, press the Esc key twice.

7. Specify that you want the video window to fill the slide, the video to automatically start when the slide displays, the video to play only once, and the display of media controls turned off by completing the following steps:

a. Make sure Slide 8 is active, click the video clip window, and then click the Video Tools Playback tab.

b. Click the *Play Full Screen* check box in the Video Options group to insert a check mark and click the *Loop until Stopped* check box to remove the check mark.

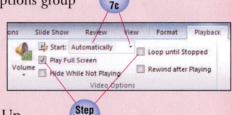

c. Click the down-pointing arrow at the right side of the *Start* option in the Video Options group and then click *Automatically* at the drop-down list.

d. Click the Slide Show tab.

e. Click the *Show Media Controls* check box in the Set Up group to remove the check mark.

8. Make Slide 1 active and then run the presentation. When the slide displays containing the video, the video will automatically begin. When the video is finished playing, press the Esc key to return to Normal view.

9. Print Slide 8.

10. Compress the video file by completing the following steps:

a. Make Slide 8 active and then click the video clip window.

b. Click the File tab.

c. At the Info tab Backstage view, click the Compress Media button and then click *Internet Quality* at the drop-down list.

d. At the Compress Media dialog box, wait until the compression is complete (notice the progress bar along the bottom of the dialog box) and then notice the initial size of the video file and the number of megabytes saved by the compression.

e. Click the Close button to close the dialog box and then click the File tab to return to the presentation.

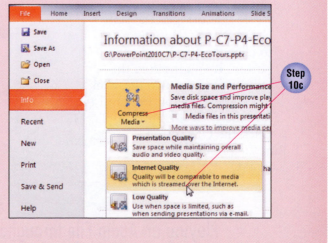

11. Save **P-C7-P4-EcoTours.pptx**.

Trimming a Video File

Quick Steps

Trim Video
1. Insert video file.
2. Click Video Tools Playback tab.
3. Click Trim Video button.
4. Specify start time and/or end time.
5. Click OK.

Trim Video

With the Trim Video button in the Video Tools Playback tab, you can trim the beginning and end of your video. This might be helpful in a situation where you want to remove a portion of the video that is not pertinent to the message in your presentation. You are limited in trimming the video to trimming a portion of the beginning of the video or the end.

To trim a video, insert the video file in the slide, click the Video Tools Playback tab, and then click the Trim Video button in the Editing group. At the Trim Video dialog box, specify the time you want the video to start and/or the time you want the video to end. To trim the start of the video, you can insert a specific time in the *Start Time* text box or drag the green start point marker that displays on the slider bar below the video. You can zero in on a very specific starting point by clicking the Next Frame button or the Previous Frame button to move the display of the video a frame at a time. Complete similar steps to trim the ending of the video except use the red end point marker on the slider bar or insert the specific ending time in the *End Time* text box.

Project 4c   **Trimming a Video**   **Part 3 of 4**

1. With **P-C7-P4-EcoTour.pptx** open, make Slide 8 active.
2. Trim out the first part of the video that shows the wolf howling by completing the following steps:
   a. Click the video to select it.
   b. Click the Video Tools Playback tab.
   c. Click the Trim Video button in the Editing group.
   d. At the Trim Video dialog box, position the mouse pointer on the green start point marker on the slider bar until the pointer displays as a double-headed arrow pointing left and right. Hold down the left mouse button, drag the start point marker to approximately the *00:04.5* time and then release the mouse button. (If you inserted the high-resolution **Wildlife.wmv** file from Windows 7, trim the horses running from the first part of the video by dragging the start point marker to approximately the *00:04.0* time.)
   e. Click the Next Frame button until the first image of the sunset displays. (Depending on where you dragged the start point marker, you may need to click the Previous Frame button. If you inserted the **Wildlife.wmv** video file, click the Next Frame button until the first image of the birds displays.)

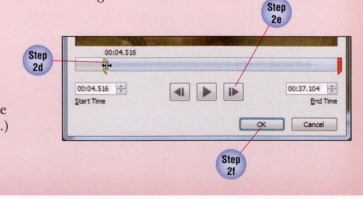

   f. Click the OK button.
3. Run the presentation.
4. Save **P-C7-P4-EcoTours.pptx**.

Playing an Audio File throughout a Presentation

In Project 4a, you inserted an audio file that played when a specific slide displayed. You can also insert an audio file in a presentation and have the audio play continually through all slides in the presentation. Generally you would add an audio file for the entire presentation when setting up a self-running presentation. To specify that you want the audio file to play throughout the presentation, click the down-pointing arrow at the right side of the *Start* option in the Audio Options group in the Audio Tools Playback tab and then click *Play across slides* at the drop-down list. To make the presentation self-running, display the Set Up Show dialog box and then insert a check mark in the *Loop continuously until 'Esc'* check box.

Project 4d   **Playing an Audio File throughout a Presentation**   **Part 4 of 4**

1. With **P-C7-P4-EcoTours.pptx** open, make Slide 8 active and then make the following changes:
   a. Select and then delete the video file.
   b. Select and then delete the bulleted text placeholder.
   c. Select the title placeholder and then drag the title down to the middle of the slide.
2. Make Slide 1 active and then insert an audio file that plays throughout all files by completing the following steps:
   a. Click the Insert tab and then click the Audio button in the Media group.
   b. At the Insert Audio dialog box, navigate to the PowerPoint2010C7 folder on your storage medium and then double-click **AudioFile-02.mid**.
   c. Click the Audio Tools Playback tab.
   d. Click the down-pointing arrow at the right side of the *Start* option in the Audio Options group and then click *Play across slides* at the drop-down list.
   e. Click the *Hide During Show* check box in the Audio Options group to insert a check mark.
   f. Click the *Loop until Stopped* check box to insert a check mark.
   g. Click the Volume button in the Audio Options group and then click *Medium* at the drop-down list.
3. Specify that you want slides to automatically advance after five seconds by completing the following steps:
   a. Click the Transitions tab.
   b. Click the up-pointing arrow at the right side of the *After* option in the Timing group until *00:05.00* displays.
   c. Click in the *On Mouse Click* check box to remove the check mark.
   d. Click the Apply To All button.

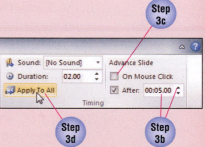

4. Set up the presentation to run continuously by completing the following steps:
   a. Click the Slide Show tab.
   b. Click the Set Up Slide Show button.
   c. At the Set Up Show dialog box, click in the *Loop continuously until 'Esc'* check box to insert a check mark.
   d. Click OK to close the dialog box.
5. Make Slide 1 active and then run the presentation. When the presentation begins for the second time, press the Esc key to return to Normal view.
6. Save and then close **P-C7-P4-EcoTours.pptx**.

Chapter Summary

- Apply animation to an item in a slide with options in the Animation group in the Animations tab. Specify animation effects with options from the Effect Options button drop-down gallery.

- Click the Preview button in the Animations tab to view the animation effects without running the presentation.

- Remove an animation effect from an item in a slide by clicking the *None* option in the Animation group in the Animations tab.

- The Add Animation button in the Advanced Animation group in the Animations tab provides four types of animation effects—entrance, exit, emphasis, and motion paths.

- Use the Animation Painter, located in the Advanced Animation group in the Animations tab, to apply the same animation to items in more than one location in a slide or slides.

- Use options in the Timing group in the Animations tab to determine when an animation starts on a slide, the duration of the animation, the delay between animations, and the order in which animations appear on the slide.

- Use the Animation Pane to customize and modify animation effects. Display the pane by clicking the Animation Pane button in the Advanced Animation group in the Animations tab.

- Apply a sound to an animation with the *Sound* option at the Effect Options dialog box with the Effect tab selected.

- A build displays important points on a slide one point at a time. You can apply a build that dims the previous bulleted point with the *After animation* option at the effect options dialog box with the Effect tab selected.

- Specify a path you want an item to follow when it displays on the slide with options in the *Motion Paths* section of the Add Animation button drop-down gallery. To draw a motion path, choose the *Custom path* option at the drop-down gallery.

- Use the Trigger button in the Advanced Animation group to specify that you want to make an animation effect occur during a slide show by clicking an item on the slide.

- Customize a slide show with options in the Set Up Show dialog box.

- To prepare a self-running presentation, insert a check mark in the *Loop continuously until 'Esc'* check box at the Set Up Show dialog box.

- To apply specific times to slides, click the Rehearse Timings button in the Set Up group in the Slide Show tab. Use buttons on the Recording toolbar to set, pause, or repeat times.

- To record a narration for a presentation, click the Record Slide Show button in the Set Up group in the Slide Show tab and then click the Start Recording button at the Record Slide Show dialog box.

- Hide or unhide a slide in a presentation by clicking the Hide Slide button in the Set Up group in the Slide Show tab.

- Specify screen resolutions with the *Resolution* option in the Monitors group in the Slide Show tab.

- Use the Broadcast Slide Show feature to share a slide show with others over the Internet. Send a link to the people you want to view the presentation and then everyone watches the slide show in their browser.

- Create a custom slide show, which is a presentation within a presentation, with options in the Define Custom Show dialog box.

- To run a custom slide show, click the Custom Slide Show button in the Start Slide Show group in the Slide Show tab and then click the desired custom show at the drop-down list.

- Print a custom show at the Print tab Backstage view by clicking the first gallery in the Settings category and then clicking the desired custom show in the *Custom Shows* section.

- Insert an audio file in a slide with the Audio button in the Media group in the Insert tab. Use options in the Audio Tools Format tab and the Audio Tools Playback tab to format and customize the audio file.

- Insert a video file in a slide with the Video button in the Media group in the Insert tab. Use options in the Video Tools Format tab and the Video Tools Playback tab to format and customize the video file.

- When running a slide show, media controls display along the bottom of an audio icon or video window in a slide when you move the mouse over the icon or window. You can turn on or off the display of these media controls with the *Show Media Controls* check box in the Set Up group in the Slide Show tab.

- Compress audio and video files to improve playback performance and save disk space. Compress audio and video files by clicking the File tab to display the Info tab Backstage view, clicking the Compress Media button, and then clicking the desired compression.

- With the Trim Video button in the Video Tools Playback tab, you can trim the beginning and end of your video.

Commands Review

FEATURE	RIBBON TAB, GROUP	BUTTON, OPTION
Animations	Animations, Animation	
Add Animations	Animations, Advanced Animation	
Animation Painter	Animations, Advanced Animation	
Animation Pane	Animations, Advanced Animation	
Set Up Show dialog box	Slide Show, Set Up	
Recording toolbar	Slide Show, Set Up	
Hide/unhide slide	Slide Show, Set Up	

FEATURE	RIBBON TAB, GROUP	BUTTON, OPTION
Define Custom Show dialog box	Slide Show, Set Up	, Custom Shows, New
Insert audio file	Insert, Media	
Insert video file	Insert, Media	
Trim Video dialog box	Video Tools Playback, Editing	
Compress audio and video files	File	
Broadcast slide show	Slide Show, Start Slide Show	

Concepts Check   Test Your Knowledge

Completion: In the space provided at the right, indicate the correct term, symbol, or command.

1. Once you have applied an animation, specify the animation effects with options in this button drop-down gallery. _____

2. Remove an animation effect from an item in a slide by clicking this option in the Animation group in the Animations tab. _____

3. The Add Animation button in the Advanced Animation group in the Animations tab provides four types of animation effects you can apply to an item—entrance, exit, motion paths, and this. _____

4. Use this feature if you apply an animation or animations to items in a slide and want to apply the same animation in more than one location in a slide or slides. _____

5. The *Duration* option is located in this group in the Animations tab. _____

6. Display the Animation Pane by clicking the Animation Pane button in this group in the Animations tab. _____

7. This term refers to displaying important points one at a time in a slide when running a presentation. _____

8. To draw your own motion path in a slide, click the Add Animation button in the Animations tab and then click this option in the *Motion Paths* section of the drop-down gallery. _____

9. The Hide Slide button is located in this tab. _____

10. Specify the slides you want included in a custom show with options at this dialog box. _____

11. The Audio and Video buttons are located in this group in the Insert tab.

_____

12. The Volume button for an audio file is located in the Audio Options group in this tab.

_____

13. The Trim Video button is located in this tab.

_____

Skills Check Assess Your Performance

Assessment

1 APPLY ANIMATION EFFECTS TO A TRAVEL PRESENTATION

1. Open **FCTCruise.pptx** and then save the presentation with Save As and name it **P-C7-A1-FCTCruise**.
2. With Slide 1 active, click the company logo and then apply the *Fade* animation. ***Hint: Click the Animations tab.***
3. Click the subtitle *Vacation Cruise* and then apply the *Fly In* animation.
4. Display the presentation in Slide Master view, click the top slide master layout (Japanese Waves Slide Master) in the slide thumbnail pane, apply the *Fade* animation to the title style, and then close the Slide Master view.
5. Make Slide 2 active and then complete the following steps:
   a. Click in the bulleted text.
   b. Apply the *Wipe* animation.
   c. Click in the bulleted text.
   d. Double-click the Animation Painter button.
   e. Make Slide 3 active and then click in the bulleted text.
   f. Make Slide 4 active and then click in the bulleted text.
   g. Make Slide 5 active and then click in the bulleted text.
   h. Click the Animation Painter button to deactivate it.
6. Make Slide 3 active and then insert a trigger by completing the following steps:
   a. Click the banner that displays toward the bottom of the slide and then apply the *Wipe* animation and change the direction to *From Left*. ***Hint: Change the direction with the Effect Options button.***
   b. Display the Animation Pane.
   c. Click the *Horizontal Scroll* item in the list box.
   d. Click the Trigger button, point to *On Click of*, and then click *Content Placeholder 2* at the side menu.
   e. Close the Animation Pane.
7. Run the presentation and, when the third bulleted item displays in Slide 3, click the bulleted item to trigger the display of the banner.
8. Save and then close **P-C7-A1-FCTCruise.pptx**.

Assessment

2 APPLY ANIMATION EFFECTS TO AN EMPLOYEE ORIENTATION PRESENTATION

1. Open **GEOrientation.pptx** and then save the presentation with Save As and name it **P-C7-A2-GEOrientation**.
2. Make Slide 2 active and then apply the following animations to the SmartArt graphic:
   a. Apply the *Blinds* entrance animation effect. ***Hint: You will need to click the More button at the right of the animations in the Animation group and then click* More Entrance Effects.**
   b. Change the SmartArt animation so the sequence is *One by One* and change the direction to *Vertical*. ***Hint: Do this with the Effect Options button.***
3. Make Slide 3 active and then apply the following animations to the organizational chart.
   a. Apply the *Blinds* entrance animation effect.
   b. Change the SmartArt animation so the sequence is *Level at Once*.
4. Make Slide 4 active and then apply the following animations to the bulleted text (click on any character in the bulleted text):
   a. Apply the *Zoom* entrance animation effect.
   b. Display the Animation Pane and then set the text to dim after animation to a light blue color. ***Hint: Click the down-pointing arrow at the right side of the content placeholder in the Animation Pane list box and then click* Effect Options.**
5. Apply the following animations to the clip art image in Slide 4:
   a. Apply the *Spin* emphasis animation effect.
   b. Set the amount of spin for the clip art image to *Two Spins* and change the duration to *01.00*.
   c. Change the *Start* option to *With Previous*.
   d. Reorder the items in the Animation Pane list box so the clip art displays first when running the presentation.
6. Make Slide 5 active, select the SmartArt graphic, and then apply an animation effect so the elements in the SmartArt graphic fade in one by one.
7. Make Slide 6 active and then apply the following animation effects to the images with the following specifications:
   a. Apply the *Fly Out* exit animation effect to the *Free Education* gift package, change the direction to *To Right*, and change the duration to *00.25*.
   b. Apply the *Shape* entrance animation effect to the diploma/books clip art image and change the duration to *01.00*.
   c. Move the *Free Education* gift package so the bulleted text underneath displays, apply the *Grow & Turn* entrance animation effect to the bulleted text, and then move the gift package back to the original location.
   d. Apply the *Fly Out* exit animation effect to the *Free Toys and Fitness* gift package, change the direction to *To Left*, and change the duration to *00.25*.
   e. Apply the *Shape* entrance animation effect to the notebook computer clip art image and change the duration to *01.00*.
   f. Move the *Free Toys and Fitness* gift package so the bulleted text underneath displays, apply the *Grow & Turn* entrance animation effect to the bulleted text, and then move the gift package back to the original location.
8. Make Slide 1 active and then run the presentation.
9. Save **P-C7-A2-GEOrientation.pptx**.

10. Display the presentation in Slide Master view, click the top slide master layout in the slide thumbnail pane, apply an entrance animation effect of your choosing to the title, and then close Slide Master view.
11. Make Slide 1 active and then apply the following animation effects:
    a. Click the globe clip art image and then draw a motion path (using the *Custom Path* option) so the image will circle around the slide and return back to the original location.
    b. Apply the *Spiral In* entrance animation effect to the *New Employee Orientation* placeholder.
12. Run the presentation.
13. Print the presentation as a handout with nine slides horizontally per page.
14. Save and then close **P-C7-A2-GEOrientation.pptx**.

Assessment

3   APPLY ANIMATION EFFECTS, VIDEO, AND AUDIO TO A JOB SEARCH PRESENTATION

1. Open **JobSearch.pptx** and then save the presentation with Save As and name it **P-C7-A3-JobSearch**.
2. Apply the *Clarity* design theme to the presentation.
3. Add appropriate clip art images to at least two slides.
4. Make Slide 10 active and then insert the video file named **Flight.wmv** from the PowerPoint2010C7 folder on your storage medium. Make the following changes to the video:
    a. Click the Video Tools Format tab and then change the height to 5.3 inches.
    b. Click the Video Tools Playback tab and then specify that you want the video to play automatically (do this with the *Start* option), that you want the video to play full screen, and that you want the video to hide when not playing.
    c. Click the Trim Video button and then trim approximately the first nine seconds from the start of the video. Click OK to close the dialog box.
5. With Slide 10 active, insert the **AudioFile-03.mid** audio file in the slide (located in the PowerPoint2010C7 folder on your storage medium) so it plays automatically, loops until stopped, and is hidden when running the presentation.
6. Compress the video file.
7. Run the presentation. After listening to the music for a period of time, end the presentation.
8. Print only Slide 10.
9. Create a custom show named *Interview* that contains Slides 1, 3, 6, 7, and 9.
10. Run the Interview custom show.
11. Print the Interview custom show as a handout with all slides printed horizontally on one page.
12. Edit the Interview custom show by removing Slide 2.
13. Print the Interview custom show again as a handout with all slides printed horizontally on one page.
14. Save and then close **P-C7-A3-JobSearch.pptx**.

4 **INSERT AN AUDIO CLIP FROM THE CLIP ART TASK PANE**

1. Open **JamaicaTour.pptx** and then save the presentation with Save As and name it **P-C7-A4-JamaicaTour**.
2. Click the Insert tab, click the Audio button arrow, and then click *Clip Art Audio*. (This displays the Clip Art task pane with audio files.)
3. Scroll down the list of audio files and then click *Jamaica Bounce (1 or 2)*. (If this audio file is not available, choose another audio file such as *Rainforest music*, *African song*, or a different audio file of your choosing.)
4. Set the audio file to play across all slides and hide when running the presentation.
5. Display the Transitions tab and specify that each slide should advance automatically after five seconds.
6. Set up the presentation to run on an endless loop. (Do this at the Set Up Show dialog box.)
7. Run the presentation.
8. Print the presentation as a handout with six slides horizontally per page.
9. Save and then close **P-C7-A4-JamaicaTour.pptx**.

Visual Benchmark Demonstrate Your Proficiency

CREATE AND FORMAT A MEDICAL CENTER PRESENTATION

1. Open **RMCPres.pptx** and then save the presentation with Save As and name it **P-C7-VB-RMCPres**.
2. Create the presentation shown in Figure 7.6 with the following specifications:
   a. Apply the *Aspect* design theme and change the theme colors to *Hardcover*.
   b. Find the clip art image for Slide 2 by using the search word *medicine*. Change the color of the clip art to *Gold, Accent color 3 Light*.
   c. Create the SmartArt in Slide 3 using the *Staggered Process* diagram (located in the *Process* section) and apply the *Colorful - Accent Colors* option to the diagram.
   d. Use the information shown in the legend and the data information shown above the bars to create a *3-D Clustered Column* chart as shown in Slide 4.
   e. Use the *Heart* shape (located in the *Basic Shapes* section) to create the hearts in Slide 5.
   f. Use the *Frame* shape (located in the *Basic Shapes* section) to create the shape in Slide 6.
3. Apply the following animation effects to items in slides:
   a. Display the presentation in Slide Master view, click the top slide master layout in the slide thumbnail pane (Aspect Slide Master), apply the *Float In* animation to the title style, and then close the Slide Master view.
   b. Make Slide 1 active and then apply an animation effect of your choosing to the subtitle.
   c. Make Slide 2 active and then apply an animation effect of your choosing to the clip art image and then apply an animation effect to the bulleted text.

Figure 7.6 Visual Benchmark

d. Make Slide 3 active and then apply an animation effect of your choosing to the SmartArt and specify a sequence of *One by One*.

e. Make Slide 4 active and then apply an animation effect of your choosing to the chart and specify a sequence of *By Category*.

f. Make Slide 5 active and then apply the *Shape* entrance animation effect to the heart at the left side of the slide. Using the Add Animation button, apply the *Pulse* emphasis animation effect. Click the same heart and then use the Animation Painter button to apply the entrance and emphasis animation effect to the middle heart and the heart at the right side of the slide.

g. Make Slide 6 active and then insert the **AudioFile-04.mid** audio file to play automatically, loop until stopped, and be hidden when running the presentation.

4. Run the presentation.

5. Print the presentation as a handout with six slides horizontally per page.

6. Save and then close **P-C7-VB-RMCPres.pptx**.

Case Study   Apply Your Skills

Part 1

You are a trainer in the Training Department at Riverside Services. You are responsible for coordinating and conducting software training in the company. Your company hires contract employees and some of those employees work at home and need to have a computer available. You will be conducting a short training for contract employees on how to purchase a personal computer. Open the Word document named **PCBuyGuide.docx** and then use the information in the document to prepare your presentation. Make sure you keep the slides uncluttered and easy to read. Consider inserting clip art or other images in some of the slides. Insert custom animation effects to each slide in the presentation. Run the presentation and then make any necessary changes to the animation effects. Save the presentation and name it **P-C7-CS-PCBuyGuide**. Print the presentation as a handout.

Part 2

Some training sessions on purchasing a personal computer are only scheduled for 20 minutes. For these training sessions, you want to cover only the information about selecting computer hardware components. With the **P-C7-CS-PCBuyGuide.pptx** presentation open, create a custom show (you determine the name) that contains only the slides pertaining to selecting hardware components. Run the custom show and then print the custom show. Save **P-C7-CS-PCBuyGuide.pptx**.

Part 3

You would like to insert an audio file that plays at the end of the presentation and decide to find free audio files on the Internet. Log on to the Internet and then use a search engine to search for "free audio files" or "free audio clips." When you find a site, make sure that you can download and use the audio file without violating copyright laws. Download an audio file and then insert it in the last slide in your presentation. Set up the audio file to play after all of the elements display on the slide. Save and then close **P-C7-CS-PCBuyGuide.pptx**.

PowerPoint
Microsoft®

Integrating, Sharing, and Protecting Presentations

PERFORMANCE OBJECTIVES

Upon successful completion of Chapter 8, you will be able to:

- Import a Word outline into a presentation
- Save a presentation in different file formats
- Export a presentation to Word
- Copy and paste data using the Clipboard
- Link and embed objects
- Download designs
- Compare and combine presentations
- Insert, edit, and delete comments
- Manage presentation properties
- Protect a presentation
- Add a digital signature
- Inspect and check the accessibility and compatibility of a presentation
- Manage versions of presentations
- Customize PowerPoint options

Tutorials

8.1 Integrating, Sharing, and Protecting Presentations
8.2 Saving and Sending a Presentation
8.3 Importing, Embedding, and Linking Data
8.4 Preparing a Presentation for Sharing
8.5 Presentation Properties
8.6 Adding a Digital Signature
8.7 Inspecting a Presentation
8.8 Comparing and Combining Presentations; Customizing PowerPoint Options

Share data between programs in the Microsoft Office suite by importing and exporting data, copying and pasting data, copying and embedding data, or copying and linking data. The method you choose depends on how you use the data and whether the data is static or dynamic. Use options in the Save & Send tab Backstage view to send a presentation as an email attachment, save a presentation to a website or SharePoint, broadcast a presentation, and publish slides in a presentation. If you use PowerPoint in a collaborative environment, you may want to insert comments in a presentation and then share the presentation with others. Use options in the Info tab Backstage view to manage presentation properties, password-protect a presentation, insert a digital signature, inspect a presentation, and manage presentation versions. In this chapter, you will learn how to complete these tasks as well as how to download design templates from Office.com. Model answers for this chapter's projects appear on the following pages.

PowerPoint2010C8

Note: Before beginning the projects, copy to your storage medium the PowerPoint2010C8 subfolder from the PowerPoint2010 folder on the CD that accompanies this textbook and then make PowerPoint2010C8 the active folder.

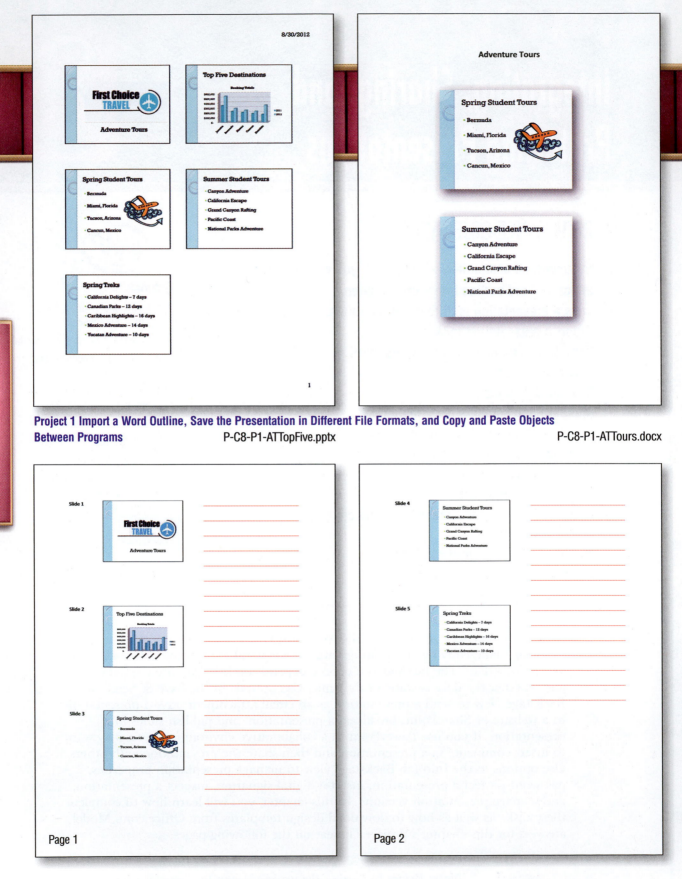

Project 1 Import a Word Outline, Save the Presentation in Different File Formats, and Copy and Paste Objects Between Programs

P-C8-P1-ATTopFive.pptx   P-C8-P1-ATTours.docx

P-C8-P1-ATTopTours.docx

Project 2 Embed and Link Excel Charts to a Presentation
P-C8-P2-FundsPres.pptx

Project 3 Download and Apply a Design Template to a Presentation and Prepare a Presentation for Sharing
P-C8-P3-ISPres.pptx

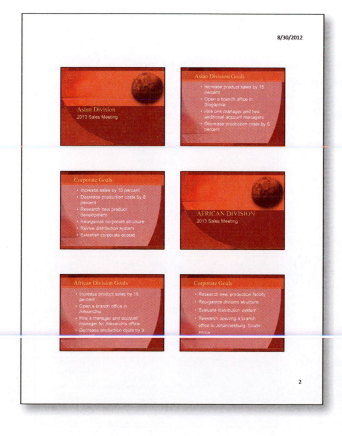

Project 1   **Import a Word Outline, Save the Presentation in**   **8 Parts**
                   Different File Formats, and Copy and Paste Objects
                   Between Programs

You will create a PowerPoint presentation using a Word document, save the
presentation in different file formats, and then copy and paste an Excel chart and
a Word table into slides in the presentation.

Importing a Word Outline

▼ Quick Steps

Import a Word Outline
1. Open blank presentation.
2. Click New Slide button arrow.
3. Click *Slides from Outline.*
4. Double-click desired document.

You can import a Word document containing text formatted with heading styles
into a PowerPoint presentation. Text formatted with a Heading 1 style becomes
the title of a new slide. Text formatted with a Heading 2 style becomes first level
text, paragraphs formatted with a Heading 3 style become second level text, and
so on. To import a Word outline, open a blank presentation, click the New Slide
button arrow in the Slides group in the Home tab, and then click *Slides from
Outline* at the drop-down list. At the Insert Outline dialog box, navigate to the
folder containing the Word document and then double-click the document. If text
in the Word document does not have heading styles applied, PowerPoint creates
an outline based on each paragraph of text in the document.

Project 1a   **Importing a Word Outline**   **Part 1 of 8**

1. At a blank presentation, click the New Slide button arrow in the Slides group in the Home
   tab and then click *Slides from Outline* at the drop-down list.
2. At the Insert Outline dialog box, navigate to
   the PowerPoint2010C8 folder on your storage
   medium and then double-click *ATTopFive.docx.*
3. Apply the *Solstice* design theme, apply
   the *Metro* theme colors, and apply the
   Foundry theme fonts.
4. Delete Slide 1.
5. Format the current Slide 1 by
   completing the following steps:
   a. Change the slide layout by clicking
      the Home tab, clicking the Layout
      button in the Slides group, and then
      clicking the *Title Only* layout at the
      drop-down list.
   b. Click the text *Adventure Tours* to select the
      placeholder and then drag the placeholder
      down toward the bottom of the slide and center
      the text horizontally. (Click the Center button
      in the Paragraph group in the Home tab.)

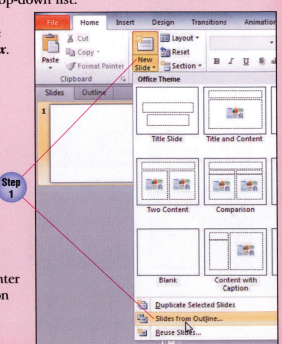

c. Insert the **FCTLogo.jpg** (do this with the Picture button in the Insert tab) and then increase the size of the logo so it fills a good portion of the upper part of the slide.

d. Set the color to transparent for the background of the logo by clicking the Picture Tools Format tab, clicking the Color button, clicking *Set Transparent Color* at the drop-down list, and then clicking just below the line below *First Choice Travel*.

6. Make Slide 2 active and then change the layout to *Title Only*.

7. Make Slide 3 active, change the line spacing to 2.0 for the bulleted text, and then insert a clip art image of your choosing related to *travel* or *sunshine*.

8. Make Slide 4 active and then change the line spacing to 1.5 for the bulleted text.

9. Save the presentation and name it **P-C8-P1-ATTopFive**.

Copying and Pasting Data ▪■■■■■■■■■■■■■■■■■■■

Use the Copy and Paste buttons in the Clipboard group in the Home tab to copy data such as text or an object from one program and then paste it into another program. For example, in Project 1b, you will copy an Excel chart and then paste it into a PowerPoint slide. You can move and size a copied object, such as a chart, like any other object.

Project 1b   **Copying an Excel Chart to a Slide**   **Part 2 of 8**

1. With **P-C8-P1-ATTopFive.pptx** open, make Slide 2 active.
2. Open Excel and then open the workbook named **Top5Tours.xlsx** located in the PowerPoint2010C8 folder on your storage medium.
3. Click the chart to select it. (Make sure you select the chart and not an element in the chart.)
4. Click the Copy button in the Clipboard group in the Home tab.
5. Close the **Top5Tours.xlsx** workbook and exit Excel.
6. In PowerPoint, with Slide 2 active, click the Paste button in the Clipboard group in the Home tab.
7. Resize and move the chart so it fills a good portion of the slide below the title and to the right of the slide design background.
8. Modify the chart by completing the following steps:

a. Make sure the chart is selected and then click the Chart Tools Design tab.

b. Click the More button at the right side of the chart styles thumbnails and then click *Style 38* at the drop-down gallery (sixth option from the left in the fifth row).

c. Click the Chart Tools Format tab.

d. Click the Shape Outline button arrow in the Shape Styles group and then click *No Outline* at the drop-down gallery.

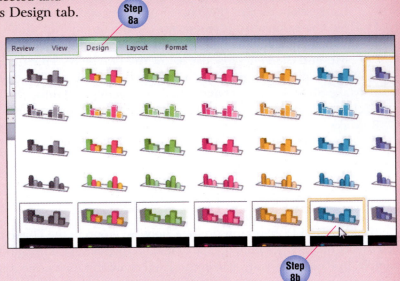

Step 8a

Step 8b

9. Display Slide 1 in the Slide pane and then run the presentation.

10. Print only Slide 2.

11. Save **P-C8-P1-ATTopFive.pptx**.

Click the Options button at the bottom of the Clipboard task pane to customize the display of the task pane.

Use the Clipboard task pane to collect and paste multiple items. You can collect up to 24 different items and then paste them in various locations. Turn on the display of the Clipboard task pane by clicking the Clipboard group dialog box launcher. The Clipboard task pane displays at the left side of the screen. Select data or an object you want to copy and then click the Copy button in the Clipboard group.

Continue selecting text or items and clicking the Copy button. To insert an item, position the insertion point in the desired location and then click the button in the Clipboard task pane representing the item. If the copied item is text, the first 50 characters display. When all desired items are inserted, click the Clear All button to remove any remaining items from the Clipboard task pane. If you want to paste all items from the Clipboard task pane at once, click the Paste All button.

Project 1c — Collecting and Pasting Text Between a Document and a Presentation   Part 3 of 8

1. With **P-C8-P1-ATTopFive.pptx** open, make Slide 4 active and then insert a new slide with the *Title and Content* layout.

2. Click the text *Click to add title* and then type Spring Treks. Select *Spring Treks* and then change the font color to black.

3. Copy text from Word by completing the following steps:

   a. Open Word and then open **AdvTreks.docx**.

   b. Click the Clipboard group dialog box launcher to display the Clipboard task pane.

   c. If any data displays in the Clipboard task pane, click the Clear All button located toward the top of the task pane.

    d. Select the text *Yucatan Adventure – 10 days* (including the paragraph mark following the text—consider turning on the display of nonprinting characters) and then click the Copy button in the Clipboard group.

    e. Select the text *Mexico Adventure – 14 days* and then click the Copy button.

    f. Select the text *Caribbean Highlights – 16 days* and then click the Copy button.

    g. Select the text *California Delights – 7 days* and then click the Copy button.

    h. Select the text *Canyon Adventure – 10 days* and then click the Copy button.

    i. Select the text *Canadian Parks – 12 days* and then click the Copy button.

    j. Select the text *Royal Canadian Adventure – 14 days* and then click the Copy button.

 4. Click the PowerPoint button on the Taskbar and then paste items from the Clipboard task pane by completing the following steps:

    a. With Slide 5 active, click the text *Click to add text*.

    b. Click the Clipboard group dialog box launcher to display the Clipboard task pane.

    c. Click the *California Delights* item in the Clipboard task pane.

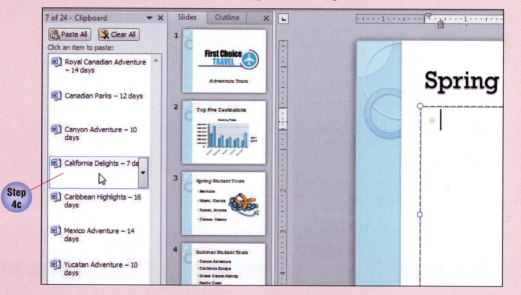

    d. Click the *Canadian Parks* item in the Clipboard task pane.

    e. Click the *Caribbean Highlights* item in the Clipboard task pane.

    f. Click the *Mexico Adventure* item in the Clipboard task pane

    g. Click the *Yucatan Adventure* item in the Clipboard task pane. (Press the Backspace key twice to remove the bullet below *Yucatan Adventure* and the blank line.)

 5. Select the bulleted text and then change the line spacing to 1.5.

 6. Clear the Clipboard task pane by clicking the Clear All button located in the upper right corner of the task pane.

 7. Close the Clipboard task pane by clicking the Close button (contains an *X*) located in the upper right corner of the task pane.

 8. Make Slide 1 the active slide and then run the presentation.

 9. Print the presentation as a handout with all slides printed horizontally on one page. (Make sure the first gallery in the Settings category displays as *Print All Slides*.)

10. Save **P-C8-P1-ATTopFive.pptx**.

11. Make Word the active program, close the Clipboard task pane, close **AdvTreks.docx**, and then exit Word.

Sharing Presentations ■■■■■■■■■■■■■■■■■■■■■■■■■

PowerPoint provides a number of options for sharing presentations between programs, sites on the Internet, other computers, and as attachments. Options for sending and sharing presentations are available at the Save & Send tab Backstage view shown in Figure 8.1. Display this view by clicking the File tab and then clicking the Save & Send tab.

Saving and Sending a Presentation

The Save & Send tab Backstage view contains the Save & Send section with options for sending a presentation as attachment to an email, saving a presentation to the Web or SharePoint, and broadcasting a presentation and publishing slides in a presentation.

With the *Send Using E-mail* option selected, options for sending a presentation display such as sending a copy of the presentation as an attachment to an email, creating an email that contains a link to the presentation, attaching a PDF or XPS copy of the open presentation to an email, and sending an email as an Internet fax. To send the presentation as an attachment, you need to set up an Outlook email account. If you want to create an email that contains a link to the presentation, you need to save the presentation to a web server. Use the last option, *Send as Internet Fax*, to fax the current presentation without using a fax machine. To use this button, you must be signed up with a fax service provider. If you have not previously signed up for a service, you will be prompted to do so.

Figure 8.1 Save & Send Tab Backstage View

With the *Send Using E-mail* option selected, this section displays options for sending the presentation as an email attachment, as a PDF or XPS attachment, or as an Internet fax.

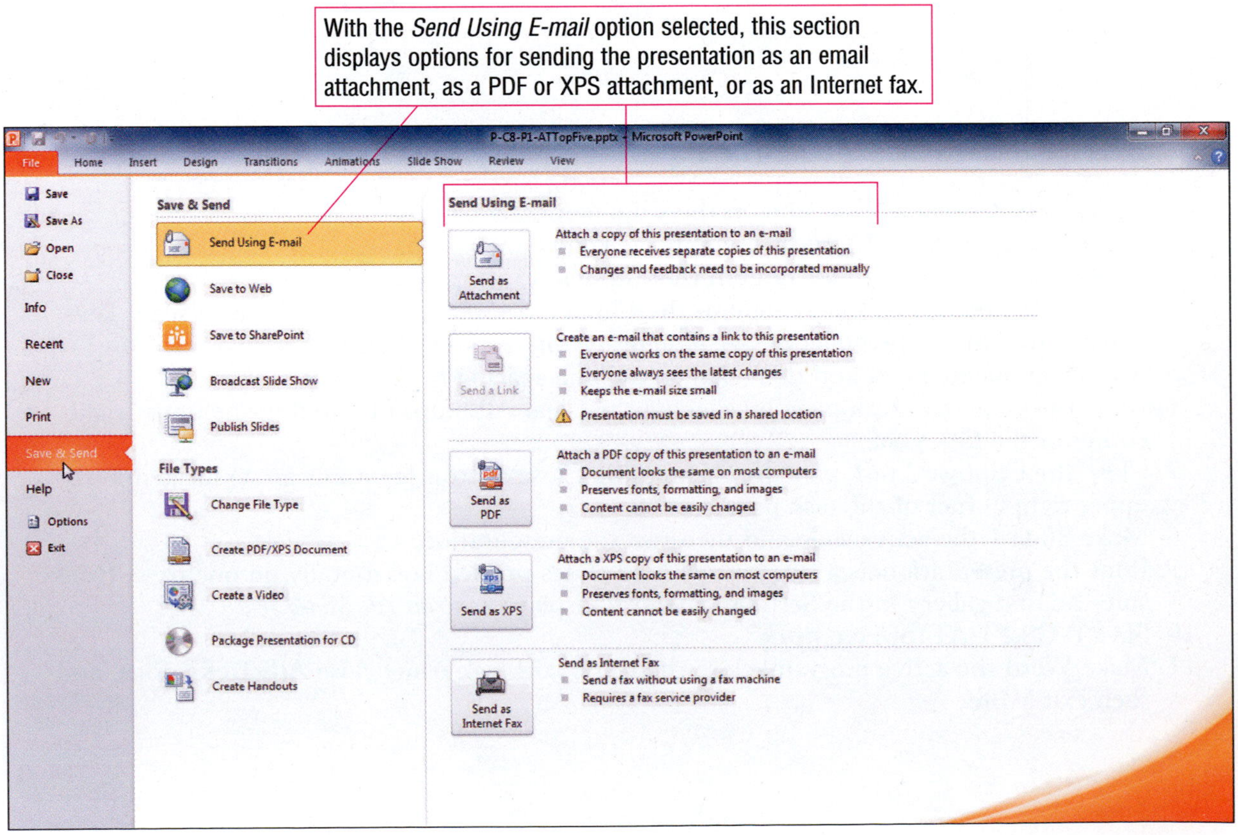

With the remaining two options in the Send Using E-mail category of the Save & Send tab Backstage view, you can send the presentation in PDF or XPS format. The letters PDF stand for *portable document format*, which is a file format developed by Adobe Systems® that captures all of the elements of a presentation as an electronic image. The XPS format is a Microsoft file format for publishing content in an easily viewable format. The letters XPS stand for *XML paper specification*, and the letters XML stand for *extensible markup language*, which is a set of rules for encoding presentations electronically. The options listed below *Attach a PDF copy of this presentation to an e-mail* and *Attach a XPS copy of this presentation to an e-mail* describe the format and the advantages of saving in the PDF or XPS format.

If you want to share presentations with others, consider saving presentations to Windows Live SkyDrive, which is a file storage and sharing service that allows you to upload files that can be accessed from a web browser. To save a presentation to SkyDrive, you need a Windows Live ID account. If you have a Hotmail, Messenger, or Xbox LIVE account, you have a Windows Live ID account.

Microsoft SharePoint is a collection of products and software that includes a number of components. If your company or organization uses SharePoint, you can save a presentation in a library on your organization's SharePoint site so you and your colleagues have a central location for accessing presentations. To save a presentation to a SharePoint library, open the presentation, click the File tab, click the Save & Send tab, and then click the Save to SharePoint button.

You can save a presentation as a blog post with the Publish as Blog Post button in the Save & Send tab Backstage view. To save a blog post, you must have a blog site established. Click the Publish as Blog Post button and information about supported blog sites displays at the right side of the Save & Send tab Backstage view.

Project 1d — Sending a Presentation as an Email Attachment — Part 4 of 8

Note: Before completing this optional exercise, check with your instructor to determine if you have Outlook set up as your email provider.

1. With **P-C8-P1-ATTopFive.pptx** open, click the File tab and then click the Save & Send tab.
2. At the Save & Send tab Backstage view, click the Send as Attachment button in the *Send Using E-mail* category.
3. At the Outlook window, type your instructor's email address in the *To* text box.
4. Click the Send button.

Saving a Presentation in a Different Format

▼ **Quick Steps**

Save Presentation in Different Format
1. Click File tab.
2. Click Save & Send tab.
3. Click *Change File Type* option in File Types category.
4. Click desired format in Change File Type category.
5. Click Save As button.

When you save a presentation, it is automatically saved as a PowerPoint presentation. If you need to share a presentation with someone who is using a different presentation program or a different version of PowerPoint, you may want to save the presentation in another format. At the Save & Send tab Backstage view, click the *Change File Type* option in the File Types category and the view displays as shown in Figure 8.2.

With options in the *Presentation File Types* section, you can choose to save a PowerPoint presentation with the default file format (.pptx) or to save a presentation in a previous version of PowerPoint. Use the *OpenDocument Presentation (*.odp)* option to save a presentation and make it available to open in other applications. The OpenDocument format enables files to be exchanged, retrieved, and edited with any OpenDocument-compliant software. Save a presentation as a template if you want to use the presentation as a basis for creating other presentations. If you save a presentation in the PowerPoint Show (*.pps) format, the presentation automatically starts when you open it. This might be useful, for example, in a situation where you email a presentation to a colleague or client and you want the presentation to automatically start when opened. Save a presentation using the *PowerPoint Picture Presentation* option and the contents of the presentation are flattened to a single picture per slide. A presentation saved in this format can be opened and viewed but not edited.

Figure 8.2 Save & Send Tab Backstage View with Change File Type Option Selected

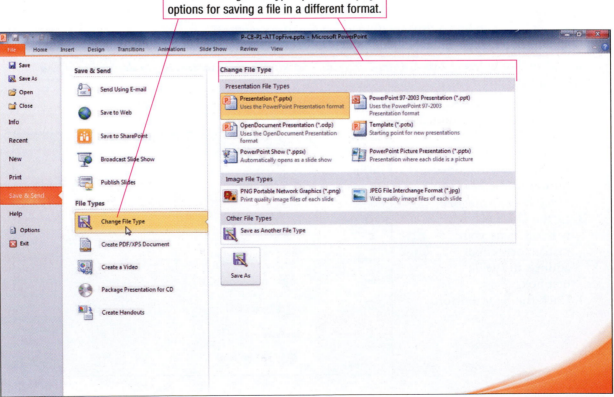

Click the *Change File Type* option to display options for saving a file in a different format.

1. Make sure that **P-C8-P1-ATTopFive.pptx** is open.
2. Save the presentation as a PowerPoint Show by completing the following steps:
   a. Click the File tab and then click the Save & Send tab.
   b. At the Save & Send tab Backstage view, click the *Change File Type* option in the File Types category.
   c. Click the *PowerPoint Show (*.ppsx)* option in the *Presentation File Types* section and then click the Save As button.

   d. At the Save As dialog box, click the Save button. (This saves the presentation with the file extension *.ppsx*.)
3. Close **P-C8-P1-ATTopFive.ppsx**.
4. Open the **P-C8-P1-ATTopFive.ppsx** file in Windows Explorer by completing the following steps:
   a. Click the Windows Explorer button (button containing yellow file folders) on the Taskbar.
   b. In Windows Explorer, double-click the drive representing your storage medium.
   c. Navigate to the PowerPoint2010C8 folder on your storage medium and then double-click **P-C8-P1-ATTopFive.ppsx**. (This starts the presentation in Slide Show view.)
   d. Run the presentation.
   e. When the presentation has ended, press the Esc key.
   f. Close Windows Explorer by clicking the Windows Explorer button on the Taskbar and then clicking the Close button located in the upper right corner of the window.
5. Open **P-C8-P1-ATTopFive.pptx** (make sure you open the file with the *.pptx* file extension) and then save the presentation in a previous version of PowerPoint by completing the following steps:

a. Click the File tab and then click the Save & Send tab.

b. Click the *Change File Type* option in the File Types category.

c. Click *PowerPoint 97-2003 Presentation (*.ppt)* in the *Presentation File Types* section and then click the Save As button.

d. At the Save As dialog box, type **P-C8-P1-ATTopFive-2003format** in the *File name* text box and then click the Save button.

e. At the Microsoft PowerPoint Compatibility Checker dialog box, click the Continue button.

f. At the presentation, notice that the file name at the top of the screen displays followed by the words [*Compatibility Mode*].

6. Close **P-C8-P1-ATTopFive-2003format.ppt**.

7. Open **P-C8-P1-ATTopFive.pptx** (make sure you open the file with the *.pptx* file extension) and then save the presentation in OpenDocument Presentation format by completing the following steps:

a. Click the File tab and then click the Save & Send tab.

b. Click the *Change File Type* option in the File Types category.

c. Click *OpenDocument Presentation (*.odp)* in the *Presentation File Types* section and then click the Save As button.

d. At the Save As dialog box, make sure *P-C8-P1-ATTopFive.odp* displays in the *File name* text box and then click the Save button.

e. At the message that displays telling you that the presentation may contain features that are not compatible with the format, click the Yes button.

f. Run the presentation and notice that formatting remained the same.

8. Close **P-C8-P1-ATTopFive.odp**.

9. Open **P-C8-P1-ATTopFive.pptx** (make sure you open the file with the *.pptx* file extension) and then save the presentation as a picture presentation by completing the following steps:

a. Click the File tab and then click the Save & Send tab.

b. Click the *Change File Type* option in the File Types category.

c. Click *PowerPoint Picture Presentation (*.pptx)* in the *Presentation File Types* section and then click the Save As button.

d. At the Save As dialog box, type **P-C8-P1-ATTopFive-Picture** in the *File name* text box and then click the Save button.

e. At a message telling you that a copy of the presentation has been saved, click OK.

f. Close **P-C8-P1-ATTopFive.pptx**.

g. Open **P-C8-P1-ATTopFive-Picture.pptx**.

h. Click Slide 1 in the Slide pane and notice how the entire slide is selected rather than a specific element in the slide. In this format, you cannot edit a slide.

10. Close **P-C8-P1-ATTopFive-Picture.pptx**.

With options in the *Image File Types* section, you can save slides in a presentation as graphic images as PNG or JPEG files. Save slides as PNG images if you want print quality and save slides as JPEG images if you are going to post the slide images to the Internet. To save a slide or all slides as graphic images, click either the *PNG Portable Network Graphics (*.png)* option or the *JPEG File Interchange Format (*.jpg)* option in the *Image File Types* section and then click the Save As button. At the Save As dialog box, type a name for the slide or presentation and then click the Save button. At the message that displays, click the Every Slide button if you want every slide in the presentation saved as a graphic image or click the Current Slide Only button if you want only the current slide saved as a graphic image. If you click the Every Slide button, a message displays telling you that all slides in the presentation were saved as separate files in a folder. The name of the folder is the name that you type in the *File name* text box in the Save As dialog box.

▼ Quick Steps

Save Presentation in PDF/XPS Format

1. Open presentation.
2. Click File tab.
3. Click Save & Send tab.
4. Click *Create PDF/XPS Document* option.
5. Click Create PDF/XPS button.
6. At Publish as PDF or XPS dialog box, specify if you want to save in PDF or XPS format.
7. Click Publish button.

Project 1f   **Saving Slides as Graphic Images**   **Part 6 of 8**

1. Open **P-C8-P1-ATTopFive.pptx**.
2. Click the File tab and then click the Save & Send tab.
3. At the Save & Send tab Backstage view, click the *Change File Type* option in the File Types category.
4. Click the *PNG Portable Network Graphics (*.png)* option in the *Image File Types* section and then click the Save As button.
5. At the Save As dialog box, make sure **P-C8-P1-ATTopFive.png** displays in the *File name* text box and then click the Save button.
6. At the message that displays, click the Every Slide button.
7. At the message telling you that each slide has been saved as a separate file in the P-C8-P1-ATTopFive.png folder, click OK.
8. Open Word.

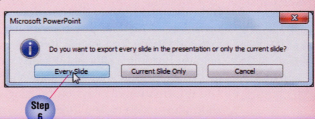

Step 6

9. At a blank document, change the font size to 18, turn on bold, change the alignment to center, and then type Adventure Tours.
10. Press the Enter key twice and then insert one of the slides saved in PNG format by completing the following steps:

a. Click the Insert tab and then click the Picture button in the Illustrations group.

b. At the Insert Picture dialog box, navigate to the P-C8-P1-ATTopFive folder in the PowerPoint2010C8 folder on your storage medium and then double-click *Slide3.PNG*.

11. Format the image in the document by completing the following steps:

   a. Click in the *Shape Height* measurement box in the Size group in the Picture Tools Format tab, type 2.8, and then press Enter.

   b. Click the *Drop Shadow Rectangle* option in the Picture Styles group.

12. Press Ctrl + End to move the insertion point to the end of the document, press the Enter key, and then complete steps similar to those in Steps 10 and 11 to insert and format the image *Slide4.PNG* in the document.

13. Save the document and name it **P-C8-P1-ATTours**.

14. Print and then close **P-C8-P1-ATTours.docx**.

15. Exit Word.

Step 10b

▼ **Quick Steps**

Save Presentation as Video
1. Open presentation.
2. Click File tab, Save & Send tab.
3. Click *Create a Video* option.
4. Click Create Video button.

Package Presentation for CD
1. Open presentation.
2. Click File tab, Save & Send tab.
3. Click *Package Presentation for CD* option.
4. Click Package for CD button.
5. Click Copy to CD button or Copy to Folder button.

As you learned earlier, the portable document format (PDF) captures all of the elements of a presentation as an electronic image, and the XPS format is used for publishing content in an easily viewable format. To save a presentation in PDF or XPS format, click the File tab, click the Save & Send tab, click the *Create PDF/XPS Document* option in the File Types category, and then click the Create PDF/XPS button in the Create a PDF/XPS Document category. This displays the Publish as PDF or XPS dialog box with the *PDF (*.pdf)* option selected in the *Save as type* option button. If you want to save the presentation in XPS format, click the *Save as type* option button and then click *XPS Document (*.xps)* at the drop-down list. At the Save As dialog box, type a name in the *File name* text box and then click the Publish button.

If you save the presentation in PDF format, the presentation opens in Adobe Reader and if you save the presentation in XPS format, the presentation opens the XPS Viewer window. You can open a PDF file in Adobe Reader or in your web browser, and you can open an XPS file in your web browser.

With the *Create a Video* option in the File Types category, you can create a video from the presentation that incorporates all of the recorded timings and narrations and preserves animations and transitions. The information at the right side of the Save & Send tab Backstage view describes creating a video and provides a hyperlink to get help on burning a slide show video to a DVD or uploading it to the Web. Click the Get help burning your slide show video to DVD or uploading it to the Web hyperlink and information displays on burning your slide show video to disc, publishing your slide show video to YouTube, and turning your presentation into a video.

Use the *Package Presentation for CD* option to copy a presentation including all of the linked files, embedded items, and fonts. This option will also save the PowerPoint Viewer program in case the destination computer does not have PowerPoint installed. Click the *Package Presentation for CD* option in the File Types category and then click the Package for CD button and the Package for CD dialog box displays. At this dialog box, type a name for the CD and specify the files you want copied. You can copy the presentation to a CD or to a specific folder.

1. With **P-C8-P1-ATTopFive.pptx** open, save the presentation in PDF format by completing the following steps:
   a. Click the File tab and then click the Save & Send tab.
   b. Click the *Create PDF/XPS Document* option in the File Types category.
   c. Click the Create PDF/XPS button.

   d. At the Publish as PDF or XPS dialog box, insert a check mark in the *Open file after publishing* check box and then click the Publish button. (In a few moments the presentation displays in PDF format in Adobe Reader.)
   e. Scroll through the presentation in Adobe Reader.
   f. Click the Close button located in the upper right corner of the window to close Adobe Reader.

2. Save the presentation in XPS format by completing the following steps:
   a. Click the File tab and then click the Save & Send tab.
   b. Click the *Create PDF/XPS Document* option in the File Types category.
   c. Click the Create PDF/XPS button.
   d. At the Publish as PDF or XPS dialog box, click the *Save as type* option box and then click *XPS Document (*.xps)* at the drop-down list.

   e. Make sure the *Open file after publishing* check box contains a check mark and then click the Publish button. (In a few moments the presentation displays in the XPS Viewer.)
   f. Scroll through the presentation in the XPS Viewer.
   g. Click the Close button located in the upper right corner of the window to close the XPS Viewer.

3. Save **P-C8-P1-ATTopFive.pptx** as a video by completing the following steps:
   a. Click the File tab and then click the Save & Send tab.
   b. Click the *Create a Video* option in the File Types category.
   c. Click the Create Video button in the *Create a Video* section.
   d. At the Save As dialog box, click the Save button. (Saving to video takes a minute or so. The Status bar displays the saving progress.)

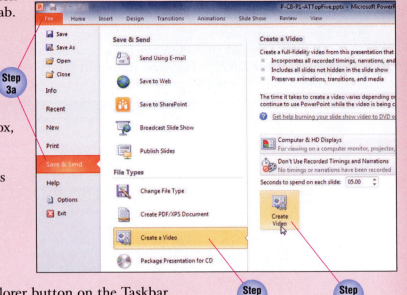

4. When the video has been saved, play the video by completing the following steps:
   a. Click the Windows Explorer button on the Taskbar.
   b. Navigate to the PowerPoint2010C8 folder on your storage medium and then double-click **P-C8-P1-ATTopFive.wmv**. (This opens the presentation video in a viewing window.)
   c. Watch the presentation video and, when it is finished, close the viewing window.
   d. Close Windows Explorer.

5. With **P-C8-P1-ATTopFive.pptx** open, package the presentation by completing the following steps:
   a. Click the File tab and then click the Save & Send tab.
   b. Click the *Package Presentation for CD* option in the File Types category.
   c. Click the Package for CD button.
   d. At the Package for CD dialog box, type **ATTopFiveforCD** in the *Name the CD* text box.
   e. Click the Copy to Folder button.
   f. At the Copy to Folder dialog box, click the Browse button.
   g. Navigate to your storage medium.
   h. Click the Select button.
   i. At the Copy to Folder dialog box, click OK.
   j. At the message asking if you want to include linked files in the presentation, click the Yes button.
   k. When a window displays with the folder name and files, close the window by clicking the Close button in the upper right corner of the window.
   l. Close the Package for CD dialog box by clicking the Close button.

HINT

Export a presentation to Word to allow more control in formatting handouts.

With the *Create Handouts* option in the File Types category at the Save & Send tab Backstage view, you can export a PowerPoint presentation to a Word document. You can print slides as handouts in PowerPoint; however, you may prefer to export the presentation to Word to have greater control over the formatting of the handouts. To export a presentation, open the presentation, click the File tab, click the Save & Send tab, and then click the *Create Handouts* option in the File Types category. This displays the Send To Microsoft Word dialog box shown in Figure 8.3. At this dialog box, select the page layout you want to use in Word and then click OK.

Figure 8.3 Send To Microsoft Word Dialog Box

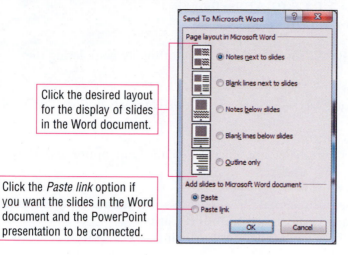

Click the desired layout for the display of slides in the Word document.

Click the *Paste link* option if you want the slides in the Word document and the PowerPoint presentation to be connected.

The first four page layout options will export slides as they appear in PowerPoint with lines to the right or below the slides. The last option will export the text only as an outline. If you select the *Paste link* option, the Word document will be automatically updated whenever changes are made to the PowerPoint presentation.

Project 1h   Exporting a Presentation to Word

1. Make sure **P-C8-P1-ATTopFive.pptx** is open, click the File tab, and then click the Save & Send tab.
2. At the Save & Send tab Backstage view, click the *Create Handouts* option in the File Types category.
3. Click the Create Handouts button.
4. At the Send To Microsoft Word dialog box, click the *Blank lines next to slides* option and then click OK.
5. Click the Word button on the Taskbar.
6. In Word, select the first column (the column that contains *Slide 1*, *Slide 2*, and so on) and then turn on bold. (The presentation was inserted in a table in Word.)
7. Select the third column (contains the lines) and then change the font color to red.

Step 4

Step 6

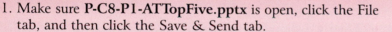

8. Save the document and name it **P-C8-P1-ATTopTours**.
9. Print and then close **P-C8-P1-ATTopTours.docx**.
10. Exit Word.
11. In PowerPoint, export **P-C8-P1-ATTopFive.pptx** as an outline by completing the following steps:
    a. Click the File tab and then click the Save & Send tab.
    b. At the Save & Send tab Backstage view, click the *Create Handouts* option in the File Types category.
    c. Click the Create Handouts button.
    d. At the Send To Microsoft Word dialog box, click the *Outline only* option and then click OK.
    e. Click the Word button on the Taskbar.
    f. In Word, scroll through the document and then exit Word without saving the document.
12. In PowerPoint, save and then close **P-C8-P1-ATTopFive.pptx**.
13. Capture an image of the Open dialog box and insert the image in a PowerPoint slide by completing the following steps:
    a. Press Ctrl + N to display a new blank presentation.
    b. Click the Layout button in the Slides group in the Home tab and then click the *Blank* layout at the drop-down list.
    c. Click the File tab and then click the Open button.
    d. At the Open dialog box, click the option button that displays to the right of the *File name* text box (option button that contains the text *All PowerPoint Presentations*) and then click *All Files (*.*)* at the drop-down list.
    e. Make sure that all of your project files display. You may need to scroll down the list box to display the files.
    f. Hold down the Alt key and then press the Print Screen button on your keyboard. (This captures an image of the Open dialog box.)
    g. Click the Cancel button to close the Open dialog box.
    h. Click the Paste button. (This inserts the image of the Open dialog box into the slide.)
14. Print the slide as a full page slide.
15. Close the presentation without saving it.

Project 2 Embed and Link Excel Charts to a Presentation   3 Parts

You will open a company funds presentation and then copy an Excel pie chart and embed it in a PowerPoint slide. You will also copy and link an Excel column chart to a slide and then update the chart in Excel.

Embedding and Linking Objects ■■■■■■■■■■■■■■■

One of the reasons the Microsoft Office suite is used extensively in business is because it allows data from an individual program to be seamlessly integrated into another program. For example, a chart depicting sales projections created in Excel can easily be added to a slide in a presentation to the company board of directors on the new budget forecast.

Integration is the process of completing a file by adding parts to it from other sources. Duplicating data that already exist in another program should be a rare instance. Copy and paste objects from one application to another when the content is not likely to change. If the content is dynamic, the copy and paste method becomes problematic and prone to error. To illustrate this point, assume one of the outcomes from the presentation to the board of directors is a revision to the sales projections. The chart that was originally created in Excel has to be updated to reflect the new projections. The existing chart in PowerPoint needs to be deleted and then the revised chart in Excel copied and pasted to the slide. Both Excel and PowerPoint need to be opened and edited to reflect this change in projection. In this case, copying and pasting the chart was not efficient.

To eliminate the inefficiency of the copy and paste method, you can integrate data between programs. An object can be text in a presentation, data in a table, a chart, a picture, a slide, or any combination of data that you would like to share between programs. The program that was used to create the object is called the *source* and the program the object is linked or embedded to is called the *destination*.

Embedding and linking are two methods you can use to integrate data in addition to the copy and paste method. When an object is embedded, the content in the object is stored in both the source and the destination programs. When you edit an embedded object in the destination program, the source program in which the program was created opens. If the content in the object is changed in the source program, the change is not reflected in the destination program and vice versa.

Linking inserts a code into the destination file connecting the destination to the name and location of the source object. The object itself is not stored within the destination file. When linking, if a change is made to the content in the source program, the destination program reflects the change automatically. Your decision to integrate data by embedding or linking will depend on whether the data is dynamic or static. If the data is dynamic, then linking the object is the most efficient method of integration.

HINT

Static data remains the same while dynamic data changes periodically or continually.

Embedding Objects

An object that is embedded will be stored in both the source *and* the destination programs. The content of the object can be edited in *either* the source or the destination; however, a change made in one will not be reflected in the other. The difference between copying and pasting and embedding is that embedded objects can be edited with the source program's editing tabs and options.

Since embedded objects are edited within the source program, the source program must reside on the computer when the presentation is opened for editing. If you are preparing a presentation that will be edited on another computer, you may want to check before embedding any objects to verify that the other computer has the same programs.

To embed an object, open both programs and both files. In the source program, click the desired object and then click the Copy button in the Clipboard group in the Home tab. Click the button on the Taskbar representing the destination program file and then position the insertion point at the location where you want the object embedded. Click the Paste button arrow in the Clipboard group and then click *Paste Special* at the drop-down list. At the Paste Special dialog box, click the source of the object in the *As* list box and then click OK.

▼ **Quick Steps**

Embed an Object
1. Open source program.
2. Select desired object.
3. Click Copy button.
4. Open destination program.
5. Click Paste button arrow.
6. Click *Paste Special.*
7. Click source of object.
8. Click OK.

You can edit an embedded object by double-clicking the object. This displays the object with the source program tabs and options. Make any desired changes and then click outside the object to exit the source program tabs and options. You can apply animation effects to an embedded object with the same techniques you learned in Chapter 7.

Project 2a **Embedding an Excel Chart in a Presentation** **Part 1 of 3**

1. Open **FundsPres.pptx** and then save the presentation with Save As and name it **P-C8-P2-FundsPres**.
2. Open Excel and then open the workbook named **Funds01.xlsx** located in the PowerPoint2010C8 folder on your storage medium.
3. Click the chart to select it. (Make sure the chart is selected and not an element in the chart.)
4. Click the Copy button in the Clipboard group in the Home tab.
5. Click the PowerPoint button on the Taskbar.
6. Make Slide 4 active.
7. Click the Paste button arrow and then click *Paste Special* at the drop-down list.
8. At the Paste Special dialog box, make sure *Microsoft Office Graphic Object* is selected in the *As* list box and then click OK.

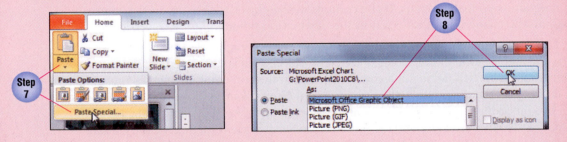

9. With the chart selected, click the Chart Tools Design tab.
10. Click the More button at the right side of the Chart Styles thumbnails and then click *Style 4* (fourth option from the left in the top row).
11. Click the Chart Tools Format tab.
12. Click in the *Shape Height* measurement box and then type 6.
13. Click in the *Shape Width* measurement box, type 9.5, and then press Enter.
14. Press Ctrl + B to bold the text in the pie.
15. Center the pie chart in the slide below the title.
16. Save **P-C8-P2-FundsPres.pptx**.
17. Click the Excel button on the Taskbar, close the workbook, and then exit Excel.

▼ **Quick Steps**

Link an Object
1. Open source program.
2. Select desired object.
3. Click Copy button.
4. Open destination program.
5. Click Paste button arrow.
6. Click *Paste Special*.
7. Click *Paste link* option.
8. Click OK.

Linking Objects

If the content of the object that you will integrate between programs is likely to change, then link the object from the source program to the destination program. Linking the object establishes a direct connection between the source and destination programs. The object is stored in the source program only. The destination program will have a code inserted into it that indicates the name and location of the source of the object. Whenever the presentation containing the link is opened, a message displays saying that the presentation contains links and the user is prompted to update the links.

To link an object, open both programs and open both program files. In the source program file, click the desired object and then click the Copy button in the Clipboard group in the Home tab. Click the button on the Taskbar representing the destination program file and then position the insertion point in the desired location. Click the Paste button arrow in the Clipboard group in the Home tab and then click *Paste Special* at the drop-down list. At the Paste Special dialog box, click the source program for the object in the *As* list box, click the *Paste link* option located at the left side of the *As* list box, and then click OK.

Project 2b   **Linking an Excel Chart to a Presentation**   **Part 2 of 3**

1. With **P-C8-P2-FundsPres.pptx** open, open Excel and then open **Funds02.xlsx** located in the PowerPoint2010C8 folder on your storage medium.
2. Save the workbook with Save As and name it **P-C8-P2-MMFunds**.
3. Copy and link the chart to a slide in the presentation by completing the following steps:
   a. Click the chart to select it.
   b. Click the Copy button in the Clipboard group in the Home tab.
   c. Click the PowerPoint button on the Taskbar.
   d. Make Slide 5 active.
   e. Click the Paste button arrow and then click *Paste Special* at the drop-down list.
   f. At the Paste Special dialog box, click the *Paste Link* option.
   g. Make sure *Microsoft Excel Chart Object* is selected in the *As* list box and then click OK.

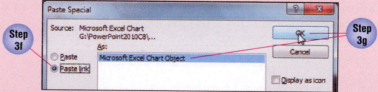

   h. Increase the size of the chart in the slide so it fills a good portion of the slide below the title. Move the chart so it appears balanced below the title.
4. Click the Excel button on the Taskbar, close **P-C8-P2-MMFunds.xlsx**, and then exit Excel.
5. Make Slide 1 active and then run the presentation.
6. Save and then close **P-C8-P2-FundsPres.pptx**.

Editing Linked Objects

Edit linked objects in the source program in which they were created. Open the document, workbook, or presentation containing the object, make the changes as required, and then save and close the file. If both the source and destination programs are open at the same time, the changed content is reflected immediately in both programs.

1. Open Excel and then open **P-C8-P2-MMFunds.xlsx**.
2. Make the following changes to data in the following cells:
   a. Change B2 from *13%* to *17%*.
   b. Change B3 from *9%* to *12%*.
   c. Change B6 from *10%* to *14%*.
3. Click the Save button on the Quick Access toolbar to save the edited workbook.
4. Close **P-C8-P2-MMFunds.xlsx** and then exit Excel.
5. In PowerPoint, open **P-C8-P2-FundsPres.pptx**.
6. At the message telling you that the presentation contains links, click the Update Links button.
7. Make Slide 5 active and then notice the changes in the chart data.
8. Print the presentation as a handout with six slides horizontally per page.
9. Save and then close **P-C8-P2-FundsPres.pptx**.

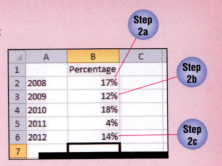

Project 3   Download and Apply a Design Template to a Presentation and Prepare a Presentation for Sharing   11 Parts

You will download a design template from Office.com and apply the template to a company presentation. You will insert, edit, and delete comments in the presentation; modify the presentation properties; inspect the presentation; and encrypt the presentation with a password.

Downloading Designs ▪▪▪▪▪▪▪▪▪▪▪▪▪▪▪▪▪▪▪▪▪

Quick Steps

Download a Design
1. Click File tab, New tab.
2. Click *Design slides* option.
3. Click desired category.
4. Click desired design.
5. Click Download button.

H I N T

Microsoft checks the validity of your Microsoft Office software when you download a template.

PowerPoint 2010 provides a number of design templates you can apply to a presentation. The Office.com website contains additional design templates you can download and apply to a presentation. To view the available design templates for downloading, click the File tab and then click the New tab. At the New tab Backstage view, click the *Design slides* option in the *Office.com Templates* section. This displays categories of design templates. Click a category and design templates in the category display in the *Office.com Templates* section and information about the design displays at the right side of the Backstage view.

Some design options in the middle panel may contain a small logo of shoulders and a head. This indicates that the design template was created by a member of the Microsoft Office Online Community and Microsoft cannot guarantee that the design will work or that the design template is free from viruses or defects.

To download a design template, click the desired template in the *Office.com Templates* section and then click the Download button located at the right side of the Backstage view. A message may display telling you that the templates are only available to customers running genuine Microsoft Office. If this message displays, click the Continue button. When the download is complete, the design template is applied to the open presentation and is also available in the Themes group in the Design tab.

Note: Check with your instructor before downloading a design template. To download a template you must have access to the Internet and access to the hard drive. If the Target the market design template is already downloaded, skip Steps 1 through 8 below. If you do not have access to the design template or cannot download it, open ISPres.pptx, save it with the name P-C8-P3-ISPres, apply a design theme of your choosing, and then continue with Step 10.

1. At a blank presentation, click the File tab and then click the New tab.
2. At the New tab Backstage view, click the *Design slides* option in the *Office.com Templates* section.

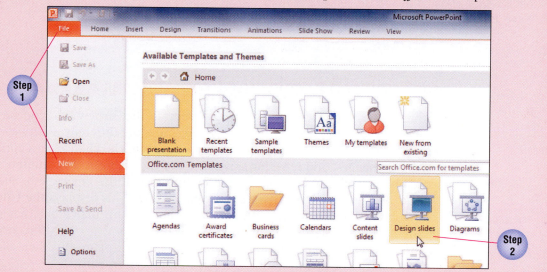

3. Click the *Business* folder in the *Office.com Templates* section.
4. Scroll down the list of design templates and then click the *Target the market design template* (shown below).
5. Click the Download button that displays at the right side of the Backstage view. (If a message displays telling you that the templates are only available to customers running genuine Microsoft Office, click the Continue button.) This applies the design template to the current blank presentation.

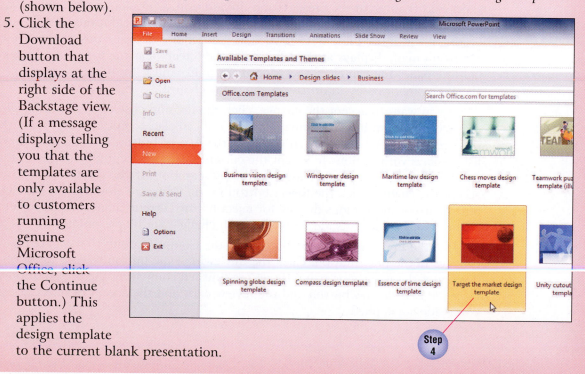

6. Close the presentation without saving it.
7. Open **ISPres.pptx** and then save the presentation with the name **P-C8-P3-ISPres**.
8. Apply the new design template by clicking the Design tab, clicking the More button at the right side of the theme thumbnails, and then clicking the *Target the market design template* theme that displays in the *Custom* section of the drop-down gallery.
9. Click the Colors button in the Themes group and then click *Office Theme 5* at the drop-down gallery.
10. Save **P-C8-P3-ISPres.pptx**.

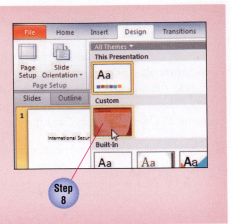

Step 8

Comparing and Combining Presentations ■■■■■■■■■■

Compare

With the Compare button in the Compare group in the Review tab, you can compare two PowerPoint presentations to determine the differences between the presentations. You have the options of combining all of the changes, accepting only specific changes, and rejecting some or all of the changes. To combine and compare presentations, open the first presentation, click the Review tab, and then click the Compare button in the Compare group. This displays the Choose File to Merge with Current Presentation dialog box. At this dialog box, navigate to the folder containing the presentation you want to compare with the current presentation, click the presentation name in the Content pane, and then click the Merge button. (You can also double-click the presentation name.)

When you click the Merge button (or double-click the presentation name), a Reviewing pane displays at the right side of the screen containing changes to slides and changes to the presentation. In addition, a revision mark displays in a slide indicating a difference between slides in the two presentations. If a difference occurs to the entire presentation, such as a difference between design themes, a revision mark displays at the left side of the screen near the top of the Slides/ Outline pane. You can click a revision mark to expand it to display a revision check box followed by information about the change.

If you want to accept the change, click the revision check box and then click the Accept button in the Compare group. You can also accept a change by clicking the Accept button arrow. When you click the Accept button arrow, a drop-down list displays with options to accept the current change, accept all changes to the current slide, or accept all changes to the presentation. If you do not want to accept the change, click the Reject button in the Compare group. Click the Reject button arrow and options display for rejecting the current change, rejecting all changes to the current slide, or rejecting all changes to the presentation.

Use the Previous and Next buttons in the Compare group to navigate to changes in the presentation. Click the Reviewing Pane button to turn on or off the display of the Reviewing pane. If you are finished comparing the presentations, click the End Review button and the review ends and the accept or reject decisions you made are applied.

1. With **P-C8-P3-ISPres.pptx** open, click the Review tab and then click the Compare button in the Compare group.

2. At the Choose File to Merge with Current Presentation dialog box, navigate to the PowerPoint2010C8 folder on your storage medium, click *ISSalesMeeting.pptx* in the Content pane, and then click the Merge button located toward the lower right corner of the dialog box. (This displays the presentation with the Reviewing pane at the right side of the screen.)

3. Click the revision check box that displays before the word *Theme* in the revision mark that displays near the top of the Slides/Outline pane. (When you insert a check mark in the check box, the design theme is removed from the presentation since the presentation you are comparing the current presentation to does not include a design theme.)

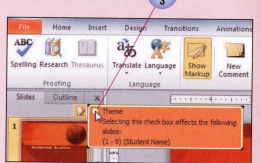

4. You decide that you want the design theme to remain so click the Reject button in the Compare group. (You could also click again the revision check box before the word *Theme* in the revision mark.)

5. Click the Next button in the Compare group to display the next change.

6. Click the revision check box to the left of the text *All changes to Content Placeholder 2* located in the upper right corner of the slide in the Slides pane.

7. Click the Reject button to reject this change.

8. Click the Next button.

9. Click the Accept button to accept the changes made to the subtitle in the slide.

10. Click the Next button.

11. Click the Accept button to accept the changes made to the placeholder text.

12. Click the Next button.

13. Click the revision check box to the left of the text *Table contents* located at the right side of the table in the slide. Notice the change to the amount for the West region.

14. Click the Reject button to reject the change made to the amount.

15. Click the Next button.

16. Click the revision check box to the left of the text *All changes to Content Placeholder 2* located in the upper right corner of the content placeholder in the slide and then click the Reject button.

17. Click the Next button.

18. Click the Accept button to accept the change to text in the content placeholder in Slide 9.

19. Click the Next button.

20. At the message that displays telling you that PowerPoint has reached the end of the changes and asking if you want to continue from the beginning of the change list, click the Cancel button.

21. Click the End Review button in the Compare group.

22. At the message that displays asking if you are sure you want to end the review, click the Yes button.

23. Save **P-C8-P3-ISPres.pptx**.

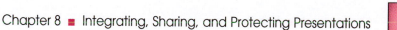

▼ **Quick Steps**

Insert a Comment
1. Click Review tab.
2. Click New Comment button.
3. Type comment text.

Using Comments ■■■■ ■■ ■■ ■ ■ ■■■ ■ ■

If you are sending out a presentation for review and want to ask reviewers specific questions or provide information about slides in a presentation, insert a comment. To insert a comment, display the desired slide and then position the insertion point where you want the comment to appear. Click the Review tab and then click the New Comment button in the Comments group. At the comment box that displays, type the desired comment. After typing the desired comment, click outside the comment box and a small yellow box displays with the user's initials and a comment number. Comments by individual users are numbered sequentially beginning with 1.

To print comments, display the Print tab Backstage view and then click the second gallery in the Settings category (this is the gallery containing the text *Full Page Slides*). At the drop-down list that displays, make sure the *Print Comments and Ink Markup* check box contains a check mark. Comments print on a separate page after the presentation is printed.

By default, the Show Markup button is active (displays with an orange background) in the Comments group in the Review tab. With this button active, comment boxes display in slides. If you want to hide comment boxes, click the Show Markup button to deactivate it. Use the Next button in the Comments group to display the next comment in a presentation and use the Previous button to display the previous comment. If you turn off the display of comment boxes, you can use the Next and Previous buttons to display comments.

New Comment   Next

Show Markup   Previous

Edit Comment   Delete

Project 3c   **Inserting Comments**   **Part 3 of 11**

1. With **P-C8-P3-ISPres.pptx** open, make Slide 2 active and then insert a comment by completing the following steps:
   a. Position the insertion point immediately right of the word *Australia*.
   b. Click the Review tab.
   c. Click the New Comment button in the Comments group.
   d. Type the following in the comment box: **Include information on New Zealand branch.**

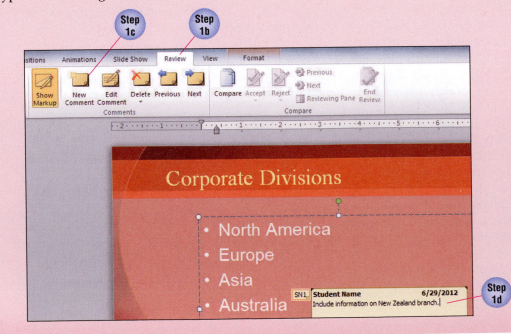

2. Make Slide 3 active and then insert a comment by completing the following steps:
   a. Click in the chart to select it. (Make sure you select the chart and not a chart element.)
   b. Click the New Comment button in the Comments group.
   c. Type the following in the comment box: **Include a chart showing profit amounts.**
3. Make Slide 5 active, position the insertion point immediately right of the word *line* at the end of the third bulleted item, and then insert the comment **Provide detailed information on how this goal will be accomplished.**
4. Make Slide 8 active, position the insertion point immediately right of the word *Singapore* in the second bulleted item, and then insert the comment **Who will be managing the Singapore office?**
5. Click the Previous button in the Comments group to display the comment box in Slide 5.
6. Click the Previous button to display the comment box in Slide 3.
7. Click the Show Markup button in the Comments group in the Review tab to turn off the display of comment boxes.
8. Click Slide 5 and notice that the comment box is not visible.
9. Click the Next button to display the comment box in Slide 2.
10. Click the Show Markup button to turn on the display of comment boxes.
11. Print the presentation and the comments by completing the following steps:
    a. Click the File tab and then click the Print tab.
    b. At the Print tab Backstage view, click the second gallery in the Settings category, make sure the *Print Comments and Ink Markup* option contains a check mark, and then click the *9 Slides Horizontal* option.
    c. Click the Print button.
12. Make Slide 1 active and then run the presentation beginning with Slide 1.
13. Save **P-C8-P3-ISPres.pptx**.

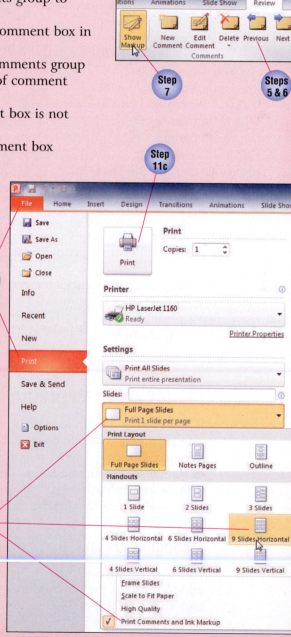

To edit text in a comment box, click the comment box you want to edit and then click the Edit Comment button in the Comments group in the Review tab. This expands the comment box and positions the insertion point inside the box. To delete a comment from a slide, click the small box containing the user's initials and comment number and then click the Delete button in the Comments group in the Review tab. You can also right-click the box containing the initials and then click *Delete* at the shortcut menu.

Move a comment by selecting the comment box and then dragging it to the desired location.

Project 3d   Editing and Deleting Comments   Part 4 of 11

1. With **P-C8-P3-ISPres.pptx** open, make Slide 8 active and then edit the comment by completing the following steps:
   a. Click the comment box containing the user's initials and comment number.
   b. Make sure the Review tab is active and then click the Edit Comment button in the Comments group.
   c. Select and delete the text in the comment box and then type **Check with Sandy Cates to determine who will be appointed branch manager.**

   ### Asian Division Goals
   - Increase product sales by 15 percent
   - Open a branch office in Singapore
   - Hire one man

   SN4 **Student Name**   6/29/2012
   Check with Sandy Cates to determine who will be appointed branch manager.

   Step 1c

2. Delete the comment in Slide 3 by completing the following steps:
   a. Click twice on the Previous button in the Comments group in the Review tab to display Slide 3 and the comment in the slide.
   b. Click the Delete button in the Comments group in the Review tab.
3. Print the presentation as a handout with nine slides horizontally per page and make sure the comments print.
4. Save **P-C8-P3-ISPres.pptx**.

Managing Presentation Information ■■■■■■■■■■■■

If you plan to distribute or share a presentation, you should check the presentation information and decide if you want to insert presentation properties in the presentation file, protect the presentation with a password, check the compatibility of the presentation, and access versions of the presentation. You can complete these tasks along with other tasks at the Info tab Backstage view shown in Figure 8.4. Display this view by clicking the File tab and then clicking the Info tab.

Managing Presentation Properties

Each presentation you create has properties associated with it such as the type and location of the presentation and when the presentation was created, modified, and accessed. You can view and modify presentation properties at the Info tab Backstage view and at the document panel.

Property information about a presentation displays at the right side of the Info tab Backstage view. You can add or update a presentation property

Figure 8.4 Info Tab Backstage View

Click this button to display a drop-down list of options for protecting your presentation.

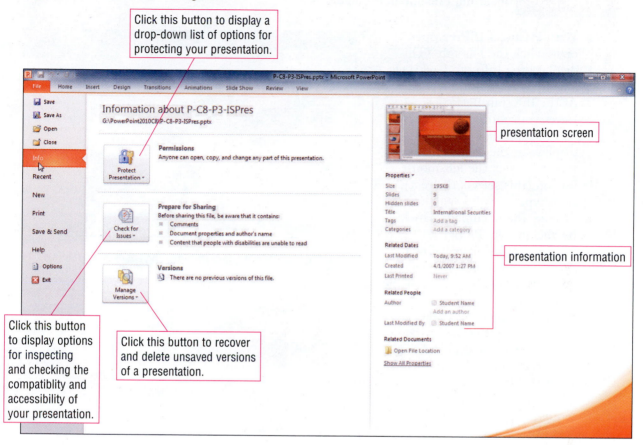

presentation screen

presentation information

Click this button to display options for inspecting and checking the compatiblity and accessibility of your presentation.

Click this button to recover and delete unsaved versions of a presentation.

by hovering your mouse over the information that displays at the right of the property (a rectanglular box with a light yellow border displays) and then typing the desired information. In the *Related Dates* section, dates display for when the presentation was created and when it was last modified and printed. The *Related People* section displays the name of the author of the presentation and also contains options for adding additional author names. Click the folder below the *Related Documents* section to display the folder contents where the current presentation is located.

You can display additional presentation properties by clicking the Show All Properties hyperlink. You can also manage presentation properties at the document panel shown in Figure 8.5. Display this panel by clicking the Properties button that displays below the thumbnail at the right side of the Info tab Backstage view and then clicking *Show Document Panel* at the drop-down list. Inserting text in some of the text boxes can help you organize and identify your presentations.

Figure 8.5 Document Panel

Document Properties ▾				Location: G:\PowerPoint2010C8\P-C8-P3-ISPres.pptx		* Required field ×
Author:	Title:	Subject:	Keywords:	Category:	Status:	
	IS Sales Meeting					
Comments:						

1. With **P-C8-P3-ISPres.pptx** open, click the File tab. (This displays the Info tab Backstage view.)

2. At the Info tab Backstage view, hover your mouse over the text *International Securities* that displays at the right of the *Title* property, click the left mouse button (this selects the text), and then type **IS Sales Meeting**.

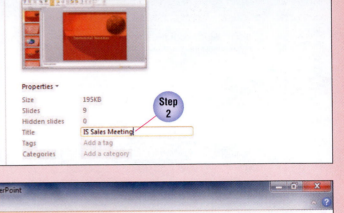

3. Display the document panel by clicking the Properties button that displays below the presentation thumbnail and then click *Show Document Panel* at the drop-down list.

4. At the document panel, press the Tab key twice (this makes the *Subject* text box active) and then type **IS Corporate Sales Meeting**.

5. Press the Tab key and then type the following words in the *Keywords* text box: **International Securities, sales, divisions**.

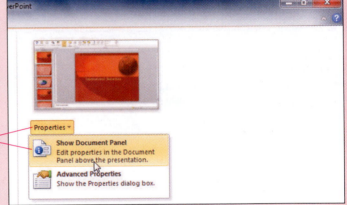

6. Press the Tab key and then type **sales meeting** in the *Category* text box.

7. Press the Tab key twice and then type the following in the *Comments* text box: **This is a presentation prepared for the corporate sales meeting**.

8. Close the document panel by clicking the Close button located in the upper right corner of the panel.

Author:	Title:	Subject:	Keywords:	Category:	Status:
Student Name	IS Sales Meeting	IS Corporate Sales Meeting	International Securities, sales,	sales meeting	

Comments:
This is a presentation prepared for the corporate sales meeting.

9. Save **P-C8-P3-ISPres.pptx**.

▼ **Quick Steps**

Mark a Presentation as Final
1. Click File tab.
2. Click Protect Presentation button.
3. Click *Mark as Final*.

Protecting a Presentation

Click the Protect Presentation button in the middle panel at the Info tab Backstage view and a drop-down list displays with the following options: *Mark as Final*, *Encrypt with Password*, and *Add a Digital Signature*. Click the *Mark as Final* option to save the presentation as a read-only presentation. When you click this option, a message displays telling you that the presentation will be marked and then saved. At this message, click OK. This displays another message telling you that the presentation has been marked as final to indicate that editing is complete and that it is the final version of the presentation. The message further indicates that when a presentation is marked as final, the status property is set to "Final"; typing, editing commands, and proofing marks are turned off; and that the presentation can be identified by the Mark As Final icon, which displays toward the left side of the Status bar. At this message, click OK. After a presentation is marked as final, the message "This presentation has been marked as final to discourage editing." displays to the right of the Protect Presentation button in the Info tab Backstage view.

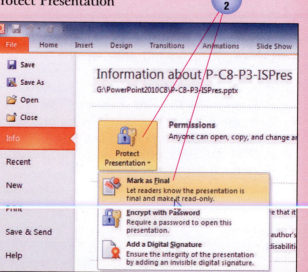

Protect
Presentation

Encrypting a Presentation

You can protect a presentation with a password by clicking the Protect Presentation button at the Info tab Backstage view and then clicking the *Encrypt with Password* option at the drop-down list. At the Encrypt Document dialog box that displays, type your password in the text box (the text will display as round bullets) and then press the Enter key (or click OK). At the Confirm Password dialog box, type your password again (the text will display as round bullets) and then press the Enter key (or click OK). When you apply a password, the message *A password is required to open this document displays* to the right of the Protect Presentation button.

If you encrypt a presentation with a password, make sure you keep a copy of the password in a safe place because Microsoft cannot retrieve lost or forgotten passwords. If you do not remember your password you will not be able to open the presentation. You can change a password by removing the original password and then creating a new one. To remove a password, open the password-protected presentation, display the Encrypt Document dialog box, and then remove the password (round bullets) in the *Password* text box.

▼ **Quick Steps**

Encrypt Presentation
1. Click File tab.
2. Click Protect Presentation button.
3. Click *Encrypt with Password*.
4. Type password, press Enter.
5. Type password again, press Enter.

Project 3f   **Marking a Presentation as Final**   **Part 6 of 11**

1. With **P-C8-P3-ISPres.pptx** open, click the File tab.
2. At the Info tab Backstage view, click the Protect Presentation button and then click *Mark as Final* at the drop-down list.
3. At the message telling you the presentation will be marked as final and saved, click OK.
4. At the next message that displays, click OK. (Notice the message that displays to the right of the Protect Presentation button.)
5. Click the File tab to return to the presentation.
6. At the presentation, notice the message bar that displays above the Ruler.
7. Close the presentation.

8. Open **P-C8-P3-ISPres.pptx**, click the Edit Anyway button on the yellow message bar, and then save the presentation.

9. Encrypt the presentation with a password by completing the following steps:

Step 8

Step 9b

a. Click the File tab, click the Protect Presentation button at the Info tab Backstage view, and then click *Encrypt with Password* at the drop-down list.

b. At the Encrypt Document dialog box, type your initials in uppercase letters. (Your text will display as round bullets.)

c. Press the Enter key.

d. At the Confirm Password dialog box, type your initials again in uppercase letters (your text will display as bullets) and then press the Enter key.

10. Click the File tab to return to the presentation.

11. Save and then close **P-C8-P3-ISPres.pptx**.

12. Open **P-C8-P3-ISPres.pptx**. At the Password dialog box, type your initials in uppercase letters and then press the Enter key.

13. Change the password by completing the following steps:
   a. Click the File tab.
   b. At the Info tab Backstage view, click the Protect Presentation button and then click *Encrypt with Password* at the drop-down list.
   c. At the Encrypt Document dialog box, delete the round bullets in the *Password* text box, type your first name in lowercase letters, and then press Enter.
   d. At the Confirm Password dialog box, type your first name again in lowercase letters and then press the Enter key.
   e. Click the File tab to return to the document.

14. Save and then close **P-C8-P3-ISPres.pptx**.

15. Open **P-C8-P3-ISPres.pptx**. At the Password dialog box, type your first name in lowercase letters and then press Enter.

16. Remove the password protection by completing the following steps:
   a. Click the File tab.
   b. At the Info tab Backstage view, click the Protect Presentation button and then click *Encrypt with Password* at the drop-down list.
   c. At the Encrypt Document dialog box, delete the round bullets in the *Password* text box and then press the Enter key.
   d. Click the File tab to return to the presentation.

17. Save **P-C8-P3-ISPres.pptx**.

Adding a Digital Signature

You can add a *digital signature*, which is an electronic stamp that vouches for a presentation's authenticity, to a presentation to authenticate it and indicate that you agree with its contents. When you add a digital signature, the presentation is locked so that it cannot be edited or changed unless you remove the digital signature. Before adding a digital signature, you must obtain one. You can obtain a digital signature from a commercial certification authority, or you can create your own digital signature. When you create a digital signature, it is saved on the hard drive or the network. Depending on how your system is set up, you might be prevented from using a digital signature. To add a digital signature, click the Protect Presentation button and then click the *Add a Digital Signature* option at the drop-down list. At the Microsoft PowerPoint digital signature information message, click OK. At the Get a Digital ID dialog box, click the *Create your own digital ID* option and then click OK. At the Create a Digital ID dialog box, insert information and then click Create.

You can remove a digital signature and the presentation is no longer authenticated. Remove the digital signature at the Signatures task pane. Display the Signatures task pane by clicking the Signatures button that displays toward the left side of the Status bar. This button indicates that a digital signature has been applied to the presentation. You can also display the Signatures task pane by clicking the File tab and then clicking the View Signatures button at the Info tab Backstage view. Remove the signature by hovering the mouse pointer over the name in the Signatures task pane, clicking the down-pointing arrow at the right of the name, and then clicking *Remove Signature* at the drop-down list. At the message asking if you want to permanently remove the signature, click Yes and then click OK at the message telling you that the signature has been removed.

Quick Steps

Create a Digital Signature
1. Click File tab.
2. Click Protect Presentation button.
3. Click *Add a Digital Signature*.
4. Click OK.
5. Click *Create your own digital ID*.
6. Click OK.
7. Type information.
8. Click Create button.
9. Type purpose at Sign dialog box.
10. Click Sign button.
11. Click OK.

View Signatures

Project 3g — **Creating, Adding, and Removing a Digital Signature**

Part 7 of 11

Note: Depending on your system setup, you may not be able to complete this project, or you may need to skip some steps in the project. Please check with your instructor before beginning this project.

1. With **P-C8-P3-ISPres.pptx** open, click the File tab.
2. At the Info tab Backstage view, click the Protect Presentation button and then click *Add a Digital Signature* at the drop-down list.
3. At the Microsoft PowerPoint digital signature information message, click OK.
4. At the Get a Digital ID dialog box, click the *Create your own digital ID* option and then click OK.
5. At the Create a Digital ID dialog box, insert the following information:
   a. Type your name in the *Name* text box.
   b. Type your actual email address or a fictitious email address in the *E-mail address* text box.
   c. Type your school's name in the *Organization* text box.
   d. Type the city in which your school is located in the *Location* text box.
   e. Click the Create button.

Step 4

---

6. At the Sign dialog box, type **Agreeing to the contents of the presentation.** in the *Purpose for signing this document* text box.

7. Click the Sign button.

8. At the message saying your signature has been successfully saved, click OK.

9. Click the File tab to return to the presentation and then click each of the ribbon tabs and notice the commands and buttons that are inactive or dimmed.

10. Display the Signatures task pane by clicking the File tab and then clicking the View Signatures button at the Info tab Backstage view.

11. View the invisible digital signature details by hovering the mouse pointer over your name in the Signatures task pane, clicking the down-pointing arrow that displays to the right of your name, and then clicking *Signature Details* at the drop-down list.

12. Notice the signature details, including the information on the inserted digital signature and the purpose of the signature.

13. Click the Close button to close the Signature Details dialog box.

14. Remove the digital signature by completing the following steps:
    a. Hover the mouse pointer over your name in the Signatures task pane, click the down-pointing arrow to the right of your name, and then click *Remove Signature* at the drop-down list.
    b. At the message asking if you want to permanently remove the signature, click Yes.
    c. At the message telling you the signature has been removed and the presentation has been saved, click OK.

15. Close the Signatures task pane.

16. Save **P-C8-P3-ISPres.pptx**.

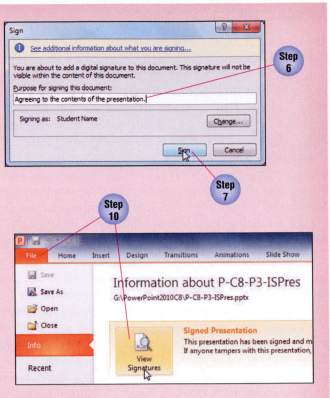

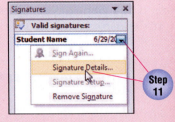

▼ **Quick Steps**

Inspect a Presentation
1. Click File tab.
2. Click Check for Issues button.
3. Click *Inspect Document*.
4. Remove check mark from items you do not want to inspect.
5. Click Inspect button.
6. Click Close button.

Inspecting a Presentation

Use options from the Check for Issues button drop-down list at the Info tab Backstage view to inspect a presentation for personal and hidden data and to check a presentation for compatibility and accessibility issues. When you click the Check for Issues button, a drop-down list displays with the options *Inspect Document*, *Check Accessibility*, and *Check Compatibility*.

PowerPoint includes a document inspector feature you can use to inspect your presentation for personal data, hidden data, and metadata. Metadata is data that describes other data, such as presentation properties. You may want to remove some personal or hidden data before you share a presentation with other people. To check your presentation for personal or hidden data, click the File tab, click the

Check for Issues button at the Info tab Backstage view, and then click the *Inspect Document* option at the drop-down list. This displays the Document Inspector dialog box.

Check for Issues

By default, the document inspector checks all of the items listed in the dialog box. If you do not want the inspector to check a specific item in your presentation, remove the check mark preceding the item. For example, if you know your presentation contains comments and/or annotations, click the *Comments and Annotations* check box to remove the check mark. Click the Inspect button located toward the bottom of the dialog box, and the document inspector scans the presentation to identify information.

When the inspection is complete, the results display in the dialog box. A check mark before an option indicates that the inspector did not find the specific items. If an exclamation point is inserted before an option, the inspector found items and displays a list of the items. If you want to remove the found items, click the Remove All button that displays at the right of the desired option. Click the Reinspect button to ensure that the specific items were removed and then click the Close button.

Project 3h   **Inspecting a Presentation**   **Part 8 of 11**

1. With **P-C8-P3-ISPres.pptx** open, click the File tab.
2. At the Info tab Backstage view, click the Check for Issues button and then click *Inspect Document* at the drop-down list.
3. At the Document Inspector dialog box, you decide that you do not want to check the presentation for XML data, so click the *Custom XML Data* check box to remove the check mark.

4. Click the Inspect button.

5. Read through the inspection results and then remove all comments by clicking the Remove All button that displays at the right side of the *Comments and Annotations* section.
6. Click the Close button to close the Document Inspector dialog box.
7. Click the File tab to return to the presentation.
8. Save **P-C8-P3-ISPres.pptx**.

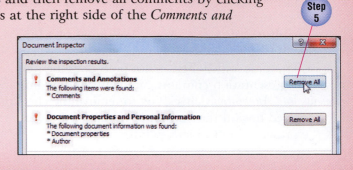

Step 5

Checking the Accessibility of a Presentation

▼ **Quick Steps**

Check Accessibility
1. Click File tab.
2. Click Check for Issues button.
3. Click *Check Accessibility*.

PowerPoint 2010 includes the accessibility checker feature, which checks a presentation for content that a person with disabilities, such as a visual impairment, might find difficult to read. Check the accessibility of a presentation by clicking the Check for Issues button at the Info tab Backstage view and then clicking *Check Accessibility*. The accessibility checker examines the presentation for the most common accessibility problems in PowerPoint presentations and groups them into three categories: errors—content that is unreadable to a person who is blind; warnings—content that is difficult to read; and tips—content that may or may not be difficult to read. The accessibility checker examines the presentation, closes the Info tab Backstage view, and displays the Accessibility Checker task pane.

At the Accessibility Checker task pane, unreadable errors are grouped in the *Errors* section, content that is difficult to read is grouped in the *Warnings* section, and content that may or may not be difficult to read is grouped in the *Tips* section. Select an issue in one of the sections, and an explanation of how to fix the issue and why displays at the bottom of the task pane.

Project 3i Completing an Accessibility Check   **Part 9 of 11**

1. With **P-C8-P3-ISPres.pptx** open, click the File tab.
2. At the Info tab Backstage view, click the Check for Issues button and then click *Check Accessibility* at the drop-down list.
3. Notice the Accessibility Checker task pane that displays at the right side of the screen. The task pane displays an *Errors* section. Click *Content Placeholder 3 (Slide 3)* in the *Errors* section and then read the information that displays toward the bottom of the task pane describing why you should fix the error and how to fix it.

Accessibility Checker

Inspection Results

❗ Errors

☐ Missing Alt Text
  Content Placeholder 3 (Slid...
  Content Placeholder 3 (Slid...

Step 3

4. Add alternative text (which is a text-based representation of the chart) to the chart by completing the following steps:
   a. With Slide 3 active, right-click immediately above the legend in the chart and then click *Format Chart Area* at the shortcut menu.
   b. At the Format Chart Area dialog box, click the *Alt Text* option located at the bottom of the left panel.
   c. Click in the *Title* text box and then type **Division Profit Chart**.
   d. Select and then delete any text that displays in the *Description* text box and then type **Profits: North America, 35%; Europe, 22%; Asia, 17%; Australia, 14%; and Africa, 12%.**
   e. Click the Close button.
5. Click the remaining item in the Accessibility Checker task pane and then read the information that displays toward the bottom of the task pane.
6. Close the Accessibility Checker task pane by clicking the Close button located in the upper right corner of the task pane.
7. Save **P-C8-P3-ISPres.pptx**.

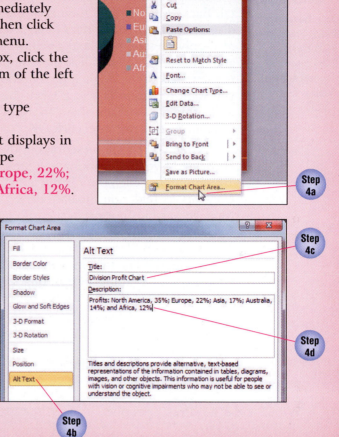

Checking the Compatibility of a Presentation

Use one of the Check for Issues button drop-down options, *Check Compatibility*, to check your presentation and identify elements that are either not supported or will act differently in previous versions of PowerPoint from PowerPoint 97 through PowerPoint 2007. To run the compatibility checker, open the desired presentation, click the Check for Issues button at the Info tab Backstage view, and then click *Check Compatibility* at the drop-down list. This displays the Microsoft PowerPoint Compatibility Checker dialog box that displays a summary of the elements in the presentation that are not compatible with previous versions of PowerPoint and indicates what will happen when the presentation is saved and then opened in a previous version.

▼ **Quick Steps**

Check Compatibility
1. Click File tab.
2. Click Check for Issues button.
3. Click *Check Compatibility*.
4. Click OK.

Managing Versions

As you are working in a presentation, PowerPoint is automatically saving your presentation every 10 minutes. This automatic backup feature can be very helpful if you accidentally close your presentation without saving it, or if the power to your computer is disrupted. As PowerPoint is automatically saving a backup of your currently open presentation, the saved presentations are listed to the right of the Manage Versions button in the Info tab Backstage view. Each autosave presentation displays with *Today*, followed by the time and *(autosave)*. When you save and then close your presentation, the autosave backup presentations are deleted.

▼ Quick Steps

Open Autosave Backup Presentation
1. Click File tab.
2. Click presentation name at right of Manage Versions button.

Manage Versions

To open an autosave backup presentation, click the File tab to display the Info tab Backstage view and then click the backup presentation you want to open that displays to the right of the Manage Versions button. The presentation opens as a read-only presentation, and a yellow message bar displays with a Compare button and a Restore button. Click the Compare button and the autosave presentation is compared to the original presentation. You can then decide which changes you want to accept or reject. Click the Restore button and a message displays indicating that you are about to overwrite the last saved version with the selected version. At this message, click OK.

When you save a presentation, the autosave backup presentations are deleted. However, if you are working in a presentation that you close without saving (after 10 minutes) or the power is disrupted, PowerPoint keeps the backup file in the *UnsavedFiles* folder on the hard drive. You can access this folder by clicking the Manage Versions button in the Info tab Backstage view and then clicking *Recover Unsaved Presentations*. At the Open dialog box that displays, double-click the desired backup file you want to open. You can also display the *UnsavedFiles* folder by clicking the File tab, clicking the Recent tab, and then clicking the Recover Unsaved Presentations button that displays toward the bottom of the screen below the *Recent Places* list box.

Project 3j   Checking the Compatibility of Elements in a Presentation and Managing Versions

Part 10 of 11

1. With **P-C8-P3-ISPres.pptx** open, click the File tab.
2. Click the Check for Issues button and then click *Check Compatibility* at the drop-down list.
3. At the Microsoft PowerPoint Compatibility Checker dialog box, read the information that displays in the *Summary* list box.
4. Click OK to close the dialog box.
5. Click the File tab and then check to see if any versions of your presentation display to the right of the Manage Versions button. If so, click the version (or the first version, if more than one displays). This opens the autosave presentation as read-only.
6. Close the read-only presentation.
7. Click the File tab, click the Manage Versions button, and then click *Recover Unsaved Presentations* at the drop-down list.

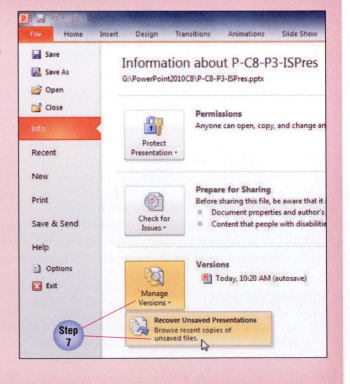

8. At the Open dialog box, check to see if recovered presentation file names display along with the date and time and then click the Cancel button to close the Open dialog box.
9. Save the presentation.

Customizing PowerPoint Options ■■■■■■■■■■■■■■

You can customize PowerPoint with options at the PowerPoint Options dialog box shown in Figure 8.6. Display this dialog box by clicking the File tab and then clicking the Options button that displays below the Help tab. The panel at the left side of the dialog box contains a number of options you can select to customize specific features in PowerPoint. For example, click the *General* option in the left panel and options display for turning on or off the display of the Mini toolbar when text is selected, enable or disable live preview, and change the user name and password.

Figure 8.6 PowerPoint Options Dialog Box

Click each of the options in this panel to display customization features and commands.

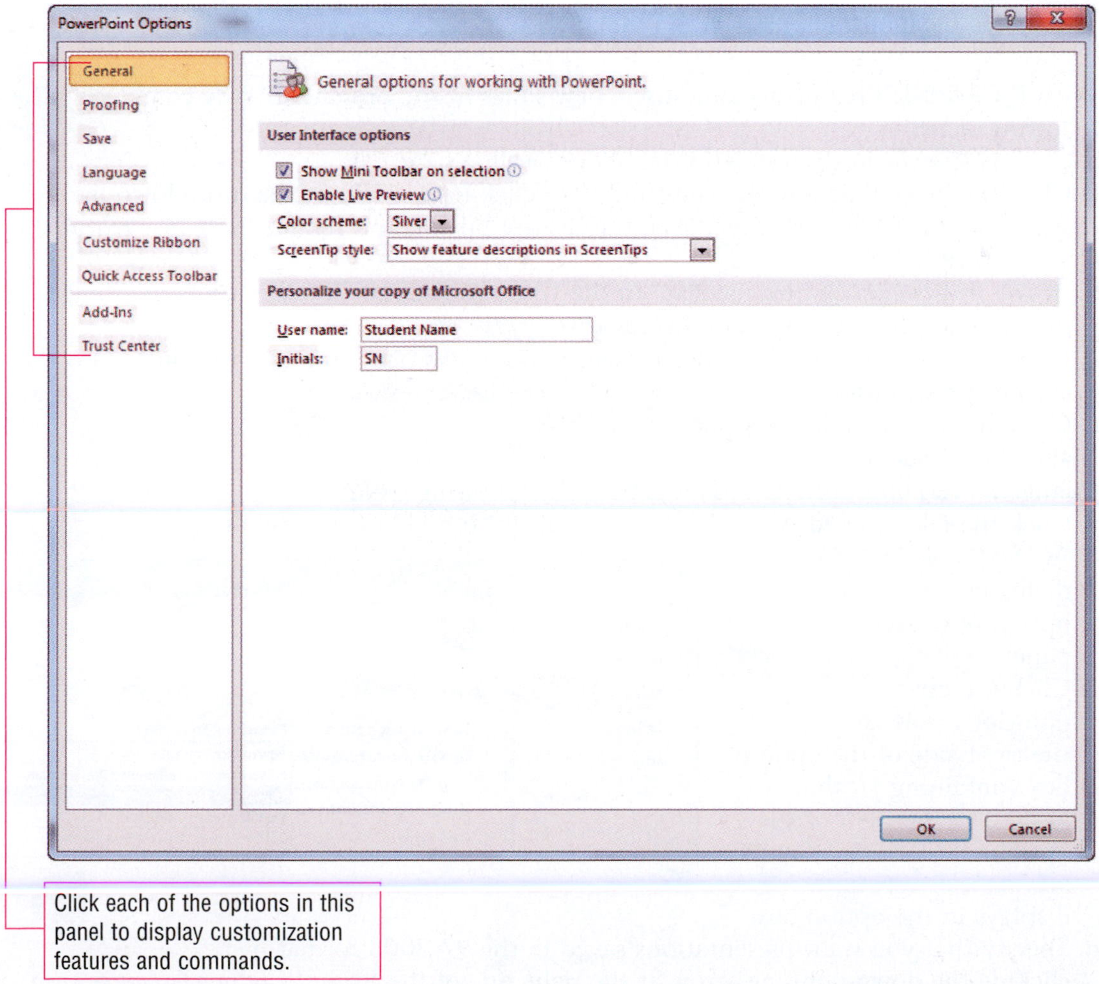

Click the *Save* option at the PowerPoint Options dialog box and the dialog box displays with options for customizing how presentations are saved. You can change the format in which files are saved from the default of *PowerPoint Presentation* to a macro-enabled PowerPoint presentation, a 97-2003 presentation, or an OpenDocument presentation. With other options you can specify, by minutes, how often you want PowerPoint to automatically save a presentation, specify whether or not you want an autosaved version of a presentation saved if you close a presentation without first saving it, and specify a default location for saving presentations.

Click the *Proofing* option at the PowerPoint Options dialog box and the dialog box displays with options for customizing spell checking. Click the AutoCorrect Options button and the AutoCorrect dialog box displays with options for changing how PowerPoint corrects and formats text as you type. With the other options in the PowerPoint Options dialog box with the *Proofing* option selected, you can specify what you want and do not want checked during a spelling check and you can create a custom spell checking dictionary.

Project 3k | **Customizing PowerPoint Options** | **Part 11 of 11**

1. With **P-C8-P3-ISPres.pptx** open, insert new slides in the presentation by completing the following steps:
   a. Click below the bottom slide in the Slides/Outline pane.
   b. Click the New Slide button arrow and then click *Reuse Slides* at the drop-down list.
   c. At the Reuse Slides task pane, click the Browse button and then click *Browse File* at the drop-down list.
   d. At the Browse dialog box, navigate to the PowerPoint2010C8 folder on your storage medium and then double-click **ISPresAfrica.pptx**.
   e. Click each of the three slides in the Reuse Slides task pane to insert the slides into the current presentation.
   f. Close the Reuse Slides task pane.
2. Make Slide 1 active.
3. Change PowerPoint options by completing the following steps:
   a. Click the File tab and then click the Options button below the Help tab.
   b. At the PowerPoint Options dialog box, click the *Save* option in the left panel.
   c. Click the down-pointing arrow at the right side of the option box containing *10* that is located to the right of the option text *Save AutoRecover information every*, until *1* displays in the option box.
   d. Specify that you want presentations saved in the 97-2003 format by clicking the down-pointing arrow at the right side of the *Save files in this format* option box and then clicking *PowerPoint Presentation 97-2003* at the drop-down list.

e. Click the *Proofing* option in the left panel of the PowerPoint Options dialog box.

f. Click the *Ignore words in UPPERCASE* check box to remove the check mark.

g. Click the *Ignore words that contain numbers* check box to remove the check mark.

h. Click OK to close the PowerPoint Options dialog box.

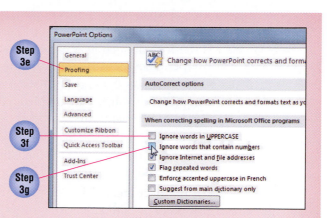

4. Complete a spelling check of the presentation and make changes as needed.

5. Save the presentation, print six slides horizontally per page, and then close the presentation.

6. Press Ctrl + N to open a new blank presentation.

7. Click the File tab and then click Save As.

8. At the Save As dialog box, notice that the *Save as type* option is set at *PowerPoint 97-2003 Presentation (*.ppt)* because you changed the default format at the PowerPoint Options dialog box.

9. Display the PowerPoint Options dialog box and make the following changes:

a. Click the *Save* option in the left panel.

b. Change the number to *10* in the option box that is located to the right of the option text *AutoRecover information every*.

c. Click the down-pointing arrow at the right side of the *Save files in this format* option box and then click *PowerPoint Presentation* at the drop-down list.

d. Click the *Proofing* option in the left panel of the PowerPoint Options dialog box.

e. Click the *Ignore words in UPPERCASE* check box to remove the check mark.

f. Click the *Ignore words that contain numbers* check box to remove the check mark.

g. Click OK to close the PowerPoint Options dialog box.

h. At the message that displays telling you that you are changing the default file format to Office Open XML and asking if you want to change this setting for all Microsoft Office applications, click the No button.

10. Close the blank presentation.

Chapter Summary

- Create a PowerPoint presentation by importing a Word document containing text with heading styles applied using the *Slides from Outline* option at the New Slides drop-down list.

- With options at the Save & Send tab Backstage view, you can send a presentation as an email attachment or fax, save your presentation to the Web, SharePoint, or in a different file format, and post your presentation to a special location such as a blog.

- With options in the Send Using E-mail category at the Save & Send tab Backstage view, you can send a presentation in PDF or XPS format.

- Click the *Change File Type* option in the File Types category at the Save & Send tab Backstage view, and options display for saving a presentation in a different file format such as a previous version of PowerPoint, a PowerPoint show, an OpenDocument presentation, and as graphic images.

- At the Save & Send tab Backstage view, you can create a PDF or XPS file with a presentation, create a video, package the presentation in a folder or on a CD, and create handouts.

- Use the Copy and Paste buttons in the Clipboard group to copy data from one program to another. Use the Clipboard task pane to collect and paste up to 24 items and paste the items into a presentation or other program files.

- An object created in one program in the Microsoft Office suite can be copied, linked, or embedded to another program in the suite. The program containing the original object is called the source program and the program the object is pasted to is called the destination program.

- An embedded object is stored in both the source and the destination programs. A linked object is stored in the source program only. Link an object if you want the contents in the destination program to reflect any changes made to the object stored in the source program.

- Download designs from Office.com by displaying the New tab Backstage view and then clicking the *Design slides* option in the *Office.com Templates* section.

- Use the Compare button in the Compare group in the Review tab to compare two presentations to determine the differences between the presentations. Use options in the Compare group to accept or reject differences and display the next or previous change.

- Insert, edit, and delete comments with buttons in the Comments group in the Review tab.

- View and modify presentation properties at the Info tab Backstage view and at the document panel. Display this panel by clicking the Properties button and then clicking *Show Document Panel* at the drop-down list.

- With options from the Protect Presentation button drop-down list at the Info tab Backstage view, you can mark a presentation as final, encrypt the presentation with a password, and add a digital signature.

- With options from the Check for Issues button drop-down list at the Info tab Backstage view, you can inspect a document for personal and hidden data, check a presentation for content that a person with disabilities, such as a visual impairment, might find difficult to read, and check the compatibility of the presentation with previous versions of PowerPoint.

- PowerPoint automatically saves a presentation every 10 minutes. When you save a presentation, the autosave backup presentation(s) are deleted. Use the Manage Versions button at the Info tab Backstage view to open an autosave backup presentation.

- Customize PowerPoint with options at the PowerPoint Options dialog box. Display this dialog box by clicking the File tab and then clicking the Options button.

Commands Review

FEATURE	RIBBON TAB, GROUP	BUTTON, OPTION
Insert Outline dialog box	Home, Slides	, Slides from Outline
Clipboard task pane	Home, Clipboard	
Save & Send tab Backstage view	File, Save & Send	
Publish as PDF or XPS dialog box	File, Save & Send	
Package for CD dialog box	File, Save & Send	
Send To Microsoft Word dialog box	File, Save & Send	
Paste Special dialog box	Home, Clipboard	, Paste Special
Compare presentations	Review, Compare	
Encrypt Document dialog box	File, Info	, Encrypt with Password
Document Inspector dialog box	File, Info	, Inspect Document
Accessibility Checker task pane	File, Info	, Check Accessibility
Microsoft PowerPoint Compatibility Checker dialog box	File, Info	, Check Compatibility

Concepts Check   Test Your Knowledge

Completion: In the space provided at the right, indicate the correct term, symbol, or command.

1. Display the Insert Outline dialog box by clicking the New Slide button arrow and then clicking this option.

2. Click this option at the Save & Send tab Backstage view to display options for sending a copy of a presentation as an attachment to an email.

3. Use this task pane to collect and paste multiple items.

4. A presentation you save as a PowerPoint show will display with this file extension.

5. With options in the *Image File Types* section of the Save & Send tab Backstage view in the Change File Type category, you can save slides in a presentation as graphic images as JPEG files or this type of file. _____

6. If you save the presentation in PDF format, the presentation opens in this. _____

7. With this option in the File Types category at the Save & Send tab Backstage view, you can export a PowerPoint presentation to a Word document. _____

8. Do this to an object if you want the contents in the destination program to reflect any changes made to the object stored in the source program. _____

9. Download a design template with options at this Backstage view. _____

10. The New Comment button is located in the Comments group in this tab. _____

11. Display additional presentation properties at the Info tab Backstage view by clicking this hyperlink. _____

12. Display the Encrypt Document dialog box by clicking the File tab, clicking the Protect Presentation button at the Info tab Backstage view, and then clicking this option at the drop-down list. _____

13. Apply this to a presentation to vouch for the authenticity of the presentation. _____

14. Use this feature to inspect your presentation for personal data, hidden data, and metadata. _____

15. Use this feature to check a presentation for content that a person with a visual impairment might find difficult to read. _____

16. Customize PowerPoint with options at this dialog box. _____

Skills Check Assess Your Performance

Assessment

1 COPY WORD AND EXCEL DATA INTO A SALES CONFERENCE PRESENTATION

1. Open **NWPres.pptx** and then save the presentation with Save As and name it **P-C8-A1-NWPres**.
2. Make Slide 2 active and then complete the following steps:
   a. Open Excel and then open the workbook named **SalesProj.xlsx** (located in the PowerPoint2010C8 folder on your storage medium).
   b. Copy the chart and paste it into Slide 2.
   c. Resize the chart so it fills most of the slide below the title.
   d. Close the workbook and exit Excel.
3. Make Slide 4 active and then complete the following steps:
   a. Draw a text box in the slide.
   b. Open Word and then open the document named **HerbRemedies.docx**.
   c. Copy the first three terms and the paragraph below each term in the document to the text box in Slide 4.
   d. Select the text in the placeholder, change the font to Rockwell, and then change the font size to 24.
   e. Move and/or resize the placeholder so it fills most of the slide below the title.
4. Make Slide 5 active and then complete the following steps:
   a. Draw a text box in the slide.
   b. Make active the **HerbRemedies.docx** Word document.
   c. Copy the last two terms and the paragraph below each term in the document and paste them into Slide 5 in the text box.
   d. Select the text in the text box, change the font to Rockwell, and then change the font size to 24.
   e. Move and/or size the text box so it fills most of the slide below the title.
5. Make Word active, close **HerbRemedies.docx**, and then exit Word.
6. With PowerPoint active, apply animation effects to each item on each slide.
7. Run the presentation.
8. Save **P-C8-A1-NWPres.pptx**.
9. Print the presentation as a handout with six slides horizontally per page.
10. Export the presentation to a Word document that prints blank lines next to slides.
11. Save the Word document and name it **P-C8-A1-NWPresHandout**.
12. Print and then close **P-C8-A1-NWPresHandout.docx** and then exit Word.
13. In PowerPoint, close **P-C8-A1-NWPres.pptx**.

Assessment

2   COPY AND LINK WORD AND EXCEL DATA INTO A COMMUNICATIONS PRESENTATION

1. Open **CommPres.pptx** and then save the presentation with Save As and name it **P-C8-A2-CommPres**.
2. Open Word and then open the document named **VerbalSkills.docx** (located in the PowerPoint2010C8 folder on your storage medium).
3. Copy the table and embed it (use the Paste Special dialog box and click Microsoft Word Document Object in the *As* list box) into Slide 5.
4. Resize the table so it better fills the slide.
5. Make Word active, close the **VerbalSkills.docx** document, and then exit Word.
6. Open Excel and then open the workbook named **NVCues.xlsx** (located in the PowerPoint2010C8 folder on your storage medium).
7. Copy the chart and link it to Slide 6. Resize the chart so it fills a majority of the slide below the title.
8. Save and then close **P-C8-A2-CommPres.pptx**.
9. Make the following changes to the chart in **NVCues.xlsx**:
   a. Select the chart and then apply the *Style 18* chart style. ***Hint: Do this in the Chart Tools Design tab***.
   b. Apply the *Gradient Fill – Purple, Accent 4, Reflection* WordArt style. ***Hint: Do this in the Chart Tools Format tab***.
   c. Change the shape outline to *No Outline*.
   d. Change the amount in B2 from *35%* to *38%*.
   e. Change the amount in B3 from *25%* to *22%*.
10. Save and then close **NVCues.xlsx** and then exit Excel.
11. In PowerPoint, open **P-C8-A2-CommPress.pptx**. (At the message that displays when you open the presentation, click the Update Links button.)
12. Make Slide 2 active and then insert the following comment after the second bulleted item: **Ask Lauren to provide a specific communication example.**
13. Make Slide 4 active and then insert the following comment after the third bulleted item: **Insert a link here to the writing presentation prepared by Sylvia.**
14. Make Slide 8 active and then insert the following comment after the third bulleted item: **Distribute evaluation forms to audience.**
15. Run the presentation.
16. Save the presentation and then print the presentation as a handout with four slides horizontally per page and make sure the comments print.
17. Run the Document Inspector and remove comments.
18. Run the accessibility checker and then create the following alt text (right-click chart, click *Format Object*, click *Alt Text* option) for the chart in Slide 6 with the title *Top Five Nonverbal Cues* and the description *Eye contact, 35%; Smiling, 25%; Posture, 15%; Position, 15%; Gestures, 10%*.
19. Close the Accessibility Checker task pane.
20. Save and then close **P-C8-A2-CommPres.pptx**.

Assessment

3   SAVE A SALES CONFERENCE PRESENTATION IN VARIOUS FORMATS

1. Open **P-C8-A1-NWPres.pptx** and then save the presentation in the PowerPoint 97-2003 Presentation (*.ppt) file format and name the presentation **P-C8-A3-NWPres-2003format**. (At the compatibility checker dialog box, click Continue.)
2. Close **P-C8-A3-NWPres-2003format.ppt**.
3. Open **P-C8-A1-NWPres.pptx** and then save each slide in the presentation as a JPEG image file.
4. Close **P-C8-A1-NWPres.pptx** without saving the changes.
5. Open Word and at a blank document, complete the following steps:
   a. Change the font to Rockwell, change the font size to 24 points, change the alignment to center, and then type **Nature's Way**.
   b. Press the Enter key and then insert the **Slide4.JPG** slide. (Use the Picture button to insert this slide. The slide is located in the **P-C8-A1-NWPres** folder in the PowerPoint2010C8 folder on your storage medium.)
   c. Change the height of the slide to 2.8 inches.
   d. Press Ctrl + End, press the Enter key, and then insert the **Slide5.JPG** slide.
   e. Change the height of the slide to 2.8 inches.
   f. Save the word document and name it **P-C8-A3-Herbs**.
   g. Print and then close **P-C8-A3-Herbs.docx** and then exit Word.
6. Open **P-C8-A1-NWPres.pptx** and then save the presentation in PDF file format. When the presentation displays in Adobe Reader, scroll through the presentation and then close Adobe Reader.
7. In PowerPoint, close **P-C8-A1-NWPres.pptx**.
8. Capture an image of the Open dialog box and insert the image in a PowerPoint slide by completing the following steps:
   a. Press Ctrl + N to display a new blank presentation.
   b. Click the Layout button in the Slides group in the Home tab and then click the *Blank* layout at the drop-down list.
   c. Click the File tab and then click the Open button.
   d. At the Open dialog box, click the option button that displays to the right of the *File name* text box (option button that contains the text *All PowerPoint Presentations*) and then click *All Files (*.*)* at the drop-down list.
   e. Make sure that all of your project and assessment files display. You may need to resize the dialog box to display the files.
   f. Hold down the Alt key and then press the Print Screen button on your keyboard. (This captures an image of the Open dialog box.)
   g. Click the Cancel button to close the Open dialog box.
   h. Click the Paste button. (This inserts the image of the Open dialog box into the slide.)
9. Print the slide as a full page slide.
10. Close the presentation without saving it.

Assessment

4 DOWNLOAD AND FILL IN A COURSE COMPLETION CERTIFICATE

1. Create the certificate shown in Figure 8.6 with the following specifications:
   a. In PowerPoint, display the New tab Backstage view, click the *Award certificates* option, click the Business folder, and then search for and download the *Excellence award (with eagle)* template.
   b. Type the company name as shown in Figure 8.7, type your name in place of *Student Name*, (the certificate will automatically insert the current date below your name), and type the name and title of the president/CEO as shown in the figure.
2. Save the certificate and name it **P-C8-A4-Certificate**.
3. Print and then close **P-C8-A4-Certificate.pptx**.

Figure 8.7 Assessment 4

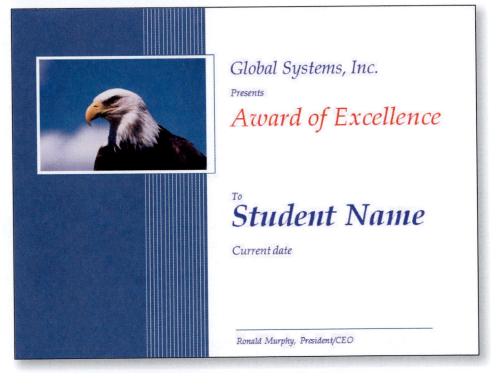

Global Systems, Inc.

Presents

Award of Excellence

To

Student Name

Current date

Ronald Murphy, President/CEO

Visual Benchmark Demonstrate Your Proficiency

1 CREATE JPEG IMAGE FILES AND CREATE A WORD DOCUMENT

1. Open **FCTTours.pptx**, save all of the slides in the presentation in the JPEG graphic format, and then close **FCTTours.pptx** without saving the changes.
2. Open Word and, at a blank document, create the document shown in Figure 8.8 with the following specifications:
    a. Set the two lines of text in 24-point Calibri bold.
    b. Insert each slide and change the height of each slide to 2.5 inches, change the text wrapping to *Tight*, and size and position the slides as shown in Figure 8.8.
3. Save the completed Word document and name it **P-C8-VB1-FCTCovers**.
4. Print and then close **P-C8-VB1-FCTCovers.docx** and then exit Word.

2 CREATE A TRAVEL COMPANY PRESENTATION

1. Create the presentation shown in Figure 8.9 with the following specifications:
    a. In PowerPoint, download the design template named *Photo journal design template*. (Find this design template by clicking the *Design slides* option at the New tab Backstage view and then clicking the Travel folder.)
    b. Close the presentation.
    c. At a blank presentation, use the **FCTQtrlyMtg.docx** Word outline document to create the presentation. ***Hint: Use the* Slides from Outline *option at the New Slide button drop-down list.***
    d. Apply to the presentation the Photo journal design template you downloaded.
    e. Change the layout of Slide 1 to *Blank* and then insert the **FCTLogo.jpg** image. Make the white background of the logo transparent. (Do this with the *Set Transparent Color* option from the Color button drop-down gallery at the Picture Tools Format tab.) Size and position the logo as shown in Figure 8.8.
    f. Make Slide 5 active, change the layout to *Title Only* and then copy and link the Excel chart in **Bookings.xlsx** to the slide. Size and position the chart as shown in Figure 8.9. (Close Excel after inserting the chart.)
    g. Insert the clip art in Slide 2 (use the search word *travel* at the Clip Art task pane) and then make any other formatting changes so your slides appear similar to the slides in Figure 8.9.
2. Save the presentation and name it **P-C8-VB2-FCTQtrlyMtgPres**.
3. Print the presentation as a handout with six slides horizontally per page.
4. Close **P-C8-VB2-FCTQtrlyMtgPres.pptx**.
5. Open Excel, open **Bookings.xlsx**, and then make the following changes to the data in the specified cells:
    - C2: Change *45* to *52*
    - C3: Change *36* to *41*
    - C4: Change *24* to *33*
    - C5: Change *19* to *25*
6. After making the changes, save and then close **Bookings.xlsx** and then exit Excel.
7. Open **P-C8-VB2-FCTQtrlyMtgPres.pptx** and update the links.
8. Print the presentation as a handout with six slides horizontally per page.
9. Save and then close **P-C8-VB2-FCTQtrlyMtgPres.pptx**.

Figure 8.8 Visual Benchmark 1

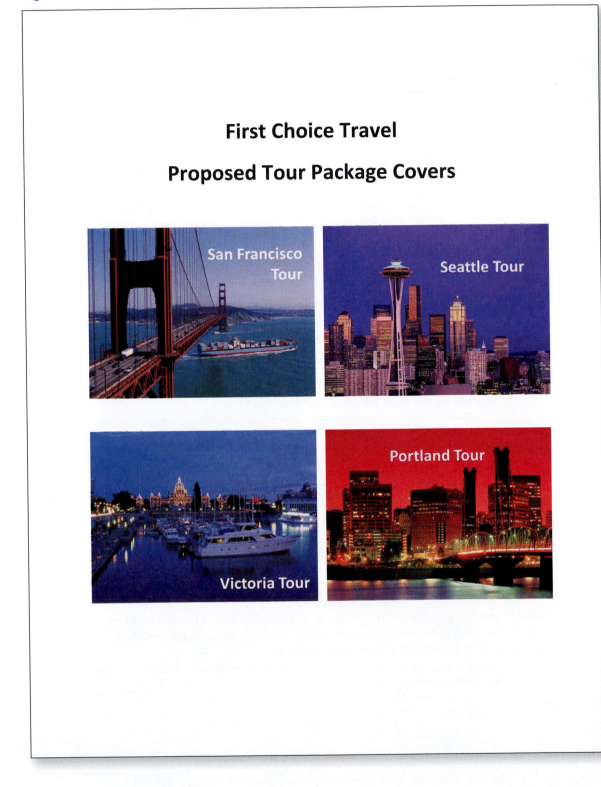

Figure 8.9 Visual Benchmark 2

Figure 8.9 Visual Benchmark 2—*continued*

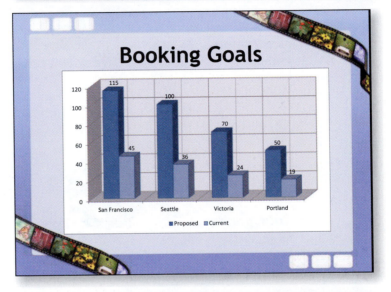

Case Study   Apply Your Skills

Part 1

You work for Rocky Mountain Family Medicine and are responsible for preparing education and training materials and publications for the center. You want to be able to insert the center logo in publications so you decide to save the logo as a graphic image. To do this, open the presentation (one slide) named **RMFMLogo.pptx** and then save the slide as a JPEG graphic image.

Part 2

You are responsible for presenting information on childhood diseases at an education class at a local community center. Open the Word document named **ChildDiseases.docx** and then use the information to create a presentation with the following specifications:

- Apply the *Flow* design theme.
- Change the layout for the first slide to *Title Only*, type an appropriate title for the presentation, and then move the title to the bottom of the slide. Insert the **RMFMLogo.jpg** graphic image in the first slide and then size and position the logo attractively on the slide. (Consider setting transparent color to the background of the logo graphic image. Do this with the *Set Transparent Color* option in the Color button drop-down list in the Picture Tools Format tab.)
- Create additional slides with the information in the **ChildDiseases.docx** Word document.
- Apply any additional enhancements to improve the presentation.

Run the presentation and then save the presentation with the name **P-C8-CS-RMFMDiseases**. Print the presentation as a handout with six slides horizontally per page and then close the presentation.

Part 3

You need to prepare a presentation for an upcoming education and training meeting. Import the Word outline document named **RMFMOutline.docx** into a PowerPoint presentation and then make the following changes:

- Apply the *Flow* design theme.
- Create the first slide with the *Title Only* layout, insert the **RMFMLogo.jpg** graphic image, and then size and position the logo in the same manner as the first slide in **P-C8-CS-RMFMDiseases.pptx**. Insert the title *Education and Training* in the title placeholder.
- Change the layout to *Title Only* for the Community Contacts slide and then copy the table from the Word document **RMFMContacts.docx** and paste it into the Community Contacts slide. Increase the size of the table so it better fills the slide.
- Change the layout to *Title Only* for the Current Enrollment slide and then copy the chart from the Excel workbook **RMFMEnroll.xlsx** and link it to the Current Enrollment slide.
- Apply any additional enhancements to improve the presentation.

Run the presentation and then save the presentation with the name **P-C8-CS-RMFMClasses**. Print the presentation as a handout with six slides horizontally per page and then close the presentation. You check the enrollments for classes and realize that more people have enrolled so you need to update the numbers in the Excel workbook. Open the **RMFMEnroll.xlsx** Excel workbook and then change *46* to *52*, *38* to *40*, and *24* to *27*. Save and then close the workbook. Open the **P-C8-CS-RMFMClasses.pptx** presentation and then update the links. Print only the Current Enrollment slide and then close the presentation.

Part 4

You decide that you want to include information in the **P-C8-CS-RMFMClasses.pptx** presentation on measles. Using the Internet, search for information on measles such as symptoms, complications, transmission, and prevention. Include this information in new slides in the **P-C8-CS-RMFMClasses.pptx** presentation. Run the presentation and then print only the new slides. Save and then close the presentation.

PowerPoint

Microsoft®

Performance Assessment

PowerPoint2010U2

Note: Before beginning unit assessments, copy to your storage medium the PowerPoint2010U2 folder from the PowerPoint2010 folder on the CD that accompanies this textbook and then make PowerPoint2010U2 the active folder.

Assessing Proficiency ▪▪▪▪▪▪▪▪▪▪▪

In this unit, you have learned to add visual elements to presentations such as tables, charts, and SmartArt graphics; create a photo album; apply formatting in Slide Master view; insert action buttons; apply custom animation effects; and set up slide shows. You also learned how to copy, embed, and link data between programs; how to insert comments; and how to protect and prepare a presentation.

Assessment 1 Save a Slide in JPEG Format and Copy and Link Objects in a Presentation

1. Open **GreenSpaceLogo.pptx**, save the only slide in the presentation as a JPEG graphic image, and then close **GreenSpaceLogo.pptx**.
2. Open **GreenSpacePres.pptx** and then save the presentation with the name **P-U2-A1-GreenSpacePres**.
3. Display the presentation in Slide Master view and then make the following changes:
   a. Click the top slide master thumbnail.
   b. Select the text *CLICK TO EDIT MASTER TITLE STYLE* and then change the font color to *Green*.
   c. Select the text *Click to edit Master text styles*, change the font color to *Gold, Accent 3, Darker 50%*, and then change the bullet color to *Green*.
   d. Close Slide Master view.
4. Make Slide 1 active and then make the following changes:
   a. Insert the **GreenSpaceLogo.jpg** graphic image.
   b. Set transparent color for the logo background (the white background). (Do this with the *Set Transparent Color* option at the Color button drop-down gallery in the Picture Tools Format tab.)
   c. Size and position the logo so it is positioned attractively on the slide. (Consider offsetting the image slightly to the right to balance it with the slide title.)
5. Make Slide 6 active and then insert the following data in a table. You determine the formatting of the table and the formatting of the data in the table:

Project	Contact	Completion Date
Moyer-Sylvan Complex	Barry MacDonald	07/31/2013
Waterfront Headquarters	Jasmine Jefferson	02/15/2014
Linden Square	Marion Van Horn	09/30/2014
Village Green	Parker Alderton	12/31/2014
Cedar Place Market	Gerry Halderman	03/31/2015

6. Make Slide 7 active and then insert the following data in a SmartArt organizational chart. You determine the organization and formatting of the chart:

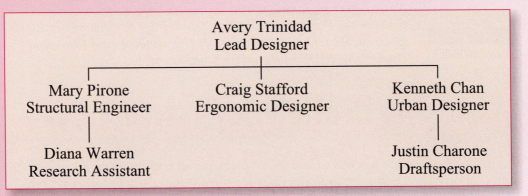

7. Make Slide 5 active and then create a column chart with the following data. Delete the chart title and chart legend. You determine the formatting and layout of the chart.

	Revenues
1st Qtr.	$25,250,000
2nd Qtr.	$34,000,000
3rd Qtr.	$22,750,000
4th Qtr.	$20,500,000

8. Make Slide 8 active and then insert a SmartArt diagram with the *Repeating Bending Process* diagram (found in the *Process* group) with the following information (insert the information in the slides from left to right). You determine the design and formatting of the SmartArt diagram.

    Mission Analysis
    Requirements Analysis
    Function Allocation
    Design
    Verification

9. Check each slide and make any changes that improve the visual appeal of the slide.

10. Make Slide 1 active and then run the presentation.

11. Make Slide 3 active, click immediately right of the slide title, and then insert the comment **Check with Marilyn about adding River View Mall to this list.**

12. Make Slide 4 active, click immediately right of the word *Australia* in the bulleted text, and then insert the comment **What happened to the plans to open an office in Sydney?**

13. Print the presentation as a handout with four slides horizontally per page and make sure the comments print.

14. Save and then close **P-U2-A1-GreenSpacePres.pptx**.

Assessment 2 **Copy and Paste Data between Programs and Insert Action Buttons in a Telecommunications Presentation**

1. Open **TelecomPres.pptx** and then save the presentation with the name **P-U2-A2-TelecomPres**.
2. Make Slide 6 active and then create a new Slide 7 (with the Title and Content layout) with the following specifications:
   a. Insert the title *APPLICATION* in the slide.
   b. Open Word and then open **WordConcepts.docx**.
   c. Display the Clipboard task pane. (Make sure the task pane is empty. If not, click the Clear All button.)
   d. Select and then copy *RECEIVING* and the paragraph below it.
   e. Select and then copy *STORING* and the paragraph below it.
   f. Select and then copy *TRANSMITTING* and the paragraph below it.
   g. Display the **P-U2-A2-TelecomPres.pptx** presentation.
   h. Click in the bulleted text *Click to add text*.
   i. Turn on the display of the Clipboard task pane.
   j. Paste the *TRANSMITTING* item in the slide.
   k. Paste the *RECEIVING* item in the slide.
   l. Clear and then close the Clipboard.
   m. Select all of the bulleted text and then change the font size to 28. Delete the bullet below the last paragraph.
   n. Make the **WordConcepts.docx** document active, close the Clipboard task pane, close the document, and then exit Word.
3. Make Slide 1 active and then insert an action button with the following specifications:
   a. Use the *Action Button: Forward or Next* option to draw the button.
   b. Draw the button in the lower right corner of the slide and make it approximately one-half inch in size.
   c. Change the shape fill of the button to *Blue, Accent 2, Lighter 40%*.
4. Display the presentation in Slide Master view and then make the following changes:
   a. Click the top slide master thumbnail.
   b. Insert an action button in the lower right corner of the slide with the same specifications as those in Step 3.
   c. Close Slide Master view.
5. Run the presentation. (Use the action buttons to advance slides. At the last slide, press the Esc key.)
6. Create a footer that prints your first and last names at the bottom of each slide, create a footer for handouts that prints the presentation title *Telecommunications Technology*, and insert the date in the upper right corner.
7. Print the presentation as a handout with four slides horizontally per page.
8. Save and then close **P-U2-A2-TelecomPres.pptx**

Assessment 3 **Save a Template Presentation and Copy, Embed, and Link Objects between Programs**

1. Display a blank presentation, click the View tab, and then click the Slide Master button.
2. Click the top slide master thumbnail in the slides thumbnail pane.
3. Apply the *Technic* theme and change the theme colors to *Median*.
4. Apply the *Style 8* background style.

5. Insert **ISLogo.jpg** in the master slide (use the Picture button in the Insert tab), change the height of the logo to one inch, and drag the logo to the lower right corner of the slide master. Set transparent color for the logo background (the white background). (Do this with the *Set Transparent Color* option at the Color button drop-down list in the Picture Tools Format tab.)

6. Close Slide Master view.

7. Save the presentation as a template to the PowerPoint2010U2 folder on your storage medium and name the template **XXXISTemplate** (use your initials in place of the *XXX*).

8. Close **XXXISTemplate.potx**.

9. Open **XXXISTemplate.potx**. (To do this, display the New tab Backstage view and then click *New from existing*. At the New from Existing Presentation dialog box, navigate to the PowerPoint2010U2 folder on your storage medium and then double-click ***XXXISTemplate.potx***.)

10. Save the presentation and name it **P-U2-A3-ISMtg**.

11. Format the first slide with the following specifications:
    a. Change to the *Blank* layout.
    b. Use WordArt to create the text *International Securities*. (You determine the shape and formatting of the WordArt text.)

12. Create the second slide with the following specifications:
    a. Choose the *Title Slide* layout.
    b. Type **European Division** as the subtitle.
    c. Type **2012 SALES MEETING** as the title.

13. Create the third slide with the following specifications:
    a. Choose the *Title Only* layout.
    b. Type **REGIONAL SALES** as the title.
    c. Open Excel and then open **ISWorkbook01.xlsx**.
    d. Save the workbook with Save As and name it **ISSalesWorkbook**.
    e. Select cells A1 through D5 (the cells containing data) and then copy and embed the cells in Slide 3.
    f. Increase the size of the cells so they better fill the slide.

14. Create the fourth slide with the following specifications:
    a. Choose the *Title and Content* layout.
    b. Type **2013 GOALS** as the title.
    c. Type the following as the bulleted items:
       ♦ **Increase product sales by 15 percent**
       ♦ **Open a branch office in Spain**
       ♦ **Hire one manager and two additional account managers**
       ♦ **Decrease production costs by 6 percent**

15. Create the fifth slide with the following specifications:
    a. Choose the *Title and Content* layout.
    b. Type **HIRING TIMELINE** as the title.
    c. Create a table with two columns and five rows and then type the following text in the cells in the table. (You determine the formatting of the cells.)

Task	Date
Advertise positions	03/01/2012 to 04/30/2012
Review resumes	05/15/2012 to 06/01/2012
Conduct interviews	06/15/2012 to 07/15/2012
Hire personnel	08/01/2012

16. Create the sixth slide with the following specifications:
    a. Choose the *Title Only* layout.
    b. Type **PRODUCTION EXPENSES** as the title.
    c. Make Excel the active program and then close **ISSalesWorkbook.xlsx**.
    d. Open **ISWorkbook02.xlsx**.
    e. Save the workbook with Save As and name it **ISExpensesWorkbook**.
    f. Copy and then link the pie chart in **ISExpensesWorkbook.xlsx** to Slide 6.
    g. Increase the size of the pie chart so it better fills the slide.
    h. Make Excel active, close **ISExpensesWorkbook.xlsx**, and then exit Excel.
17. Run the presentation.
18. Create a footer that prints your first and last names at the bottom of each slide, create a footer for handouts that prints the presentation title *2012 Sales Meeting*, and insert the date in the upper right corner.
19. Print the presentation as a handout with six slides horizontally per page.
20. Save and then close **P-U2-A3-ISMtg.pptx**.
21. Open Excel and then open **ISExpensesWorkbook.xlsx**.
22. Make the following changes:
    a. B2: Change *38% to 41%*
    b. B3: Change *35% to 32%*
    c. B4: Change *18% to 21%*
    d. B5: Change *9% to 6%*
23. Save, print, and close **ISExpensesWorkbook.xlsx** and then exit Excel.
24. With PowerPoint the active program, open **P-U2-A3-ISMtg.pptx**. (At the message that displays, click the Update Links button.)
25. Display Slide 3, double-click the cells, and then make the following changes to the data in the embedded cells:
    a. C2: Change *2678450* to *2857300*
    b. C3: Change *1753405* to *1598970*
    c. C4: Change *1452540* to *1635400*
26. Run the presentation.
27. Print the slides as a handout with six slides horizontally per page.
28. Save **P-U2-A3-ISMtg.pptx**.
29. Apply a transition and sound of your choosing to all slides in the presentation.
30. Use the Rehearse Timings feature to set the following times for the slides to display during a slide show (your actual time will display with an extra second for each slide):

    Slide 1 = 3 seconds
    Slide 2 = 3 seconds
    Slide 3 = 6 seconds
    Slide 4 = 5 seconds
    Slide 5 = 6 seconds
    Slide 6 = 5 seconds
31. Set up the slide show to run continuously.
32. Run the presentation beginning with Slide 1. Watch the slide show until the presentation has started for the second time and then end the show.
33. Save and then close the presentation.

Assessment 4 Apply Custom Animation Effects to a Travel Presentation

1. Open **AustraliaTour.pptx** and then save the presentation with the name **P-U2-A4-AustraliaTour**.
2. With Slide 1 active, apply a *Fly In* entrance animation effect to the title *Australia Tour* that has the title fly in from the bottom.
3. Display the presentation in Slide Master view and then make the following changes:
   a. Click the third slide master thumbnail.
   b. Apply a *Fly In* entrance animation effect to the title that has the title fly in from the top.
   c. Apply a *Fly In* entrance animation effect to the bulleted text that has the text fly in from the left and then dims to a color of your choosing when the next bullet displays.
   d. Close Slide Master view.
4. Make Slide 5 active, select the sun shape that displays above *Sydney*, and then draw a freeform motion path from Sydney to Melbourne, Tasmania, Adelaide, Perth, Derby, Darwin, Cairns, and then back to Sydney. Change the duration to *04.00*.
5. Make Slide 6 active and then make the following changes:
   a. Click the bottom shape to select it. (You may want to move the top two shapes out of the way.)
   b. Apply the *Grow & Turn* entrance effect.
   c. Click the Add Animation button and then click the *Shrink & Turn* exit effect.
   d. Click the middle shape to select it and then apply the *Grow & Turn* entrance effect.
   e. Click the Add Animation button and then click the *Shrink & Turn* exit effect.
   f. Click the top shape to select it and then apply the *Grow & Turn* entrance effect.
   g. Position the shapes so they are stacked on top of each other so you do not see a portion of the shapes behind.
6. Save **P-U2-A4-AustraliaTour.pptx**.
7. Make Slide 1 active, run the presentation, and make sure the animation effects play correctly.
8. Print the presentation as a handout with all slides printed horizontally on one page.
9. Close **P-U2-A4-AustraliaTour.pptx**.

Assessment 5 Inspect a Presentation and Save a Presentation in Different Formats

1. Open **P-U2-A1-GreenSpacePres.pptx** and then save the presentation with the name **P-U2-A5-GreenSpacePres**.
2. Inspect the presentation using the Document Inspector dialog box and remove comments from the presentation.
3. Run the compatibility checker. (Click OK at the Microsoft Compatibility Checker dialog box.)
4. Save the presentation in *PowerPoint 97-2003* format and name it **P-U2-A5-GreenSpacePres-2003format**. (Click the Continue button at the compatibility checker message.)
5. Close **P-U2-A5-GreenSpacePres-2003format.ppt**.

6. Open **P-U2-A5-GreenSpacePres.pptx** and then save the presentation as a PDF document.

7. View the presentation in Adobe Reader.

8. After viewing all of the slides, close Adobe Reader.

9. Close **P-U2-A5-GreenSpacePres.pptx** without saving the changes.

10. Capture an image of the Open dialog box and insert the image in a PowerPoint slide by completing the following steps:

    a. Press Ctrl + N to display a new blank presentation.

    b. Click the Layout button in the Slides group in the Home tab and then click the *Blank* layout at the drop-down list.

    c. Click the File tab and then click the Open button.

    d. At the Open dialog box, click the option button that displays to the right of the *File name* text box (option button that contains the text *All PowerPoint Presentations*) and then click *All Files (*.*)* at the drop-down list.

    e. Scroll down the Open dialog box list box to display your assessment files.

    f. Hold down the Alt key and then press the Print Screen button on your keyboard. (This captures an image of your Open dialog box.)

    g. Click the Cancel button to close the Open dialog box.

    h. Click the Paste button. (This inserts the image of your Open dialog box into the slide.)

11. Print the slide as a full page slide.

12. Close the presentation without saving it.

Writing Activities ■■■■■■■■■■■■■■■■■■

The following activities give you the opportunity to practice your writing skills along with demonstrating an understanding of some of the important PowerPoint features you have mastered in this unit. Use correct grammar, appropriate word choices, and clear sentence structure.

Activity 1 Prepare and Format a Travel Presentation

You work for First Choice Travel and you are responsible for preparing a presentation on travel vacations. Open the Word document named **TravelVacs.docx** and then print the document. Close the document and then exit Word. Using the information in the document, prepare a PowerPoint presentation with the following specifications:

1. Create a presentation that presents the main points of the document.

2. Rehearse and set times for the slides to display during a slide show. You determine the number of seconds for each slide.

3. Insert a song into the first slide from the Clip Art task pane. At the Clip Art task pane, change the *Results should be* option to only *Audio*.

4. Set up the presentation to run on an endless loop and the audio to play across all slides and continuously as long as the presentation is running.

5. Run the presentation. (The slide show will start and run continuously.) Watch the presentation until it has started for the second time and then end the show by pressing the Esc key.

6. Save the presentation and name it **P-U2-Act1-TravelVacs**.

7. Print the presentation as a handout with six slides horizontally per page.

8. Close **P-U2-Act1-TravelVacs.pptx**.

Activity 2 Prepare and Format a Presentation on Media Files

Using PowerPoint's Help feature, learn more about audio and video file formats compatible with PowerPoint 2010. (Search specifically for *compatible audio and video file formats*.) Using the information you find in the Help files, create a presentation with *at least* the following specifications:

- Slide containing the title of the presentation and your name
- Create at least three slides each containing information on a compatible audio file format including the file format, extension, and a brief description of the format.
- Create at least three slides each containing information on a compatible video file format including the file format, extension, and a brief description of the format.
- Optional: If you are connected to the Internet, search for websites where you can download free audio clips and then include this information in a slide as well as a hyperlink to the site.

Save the completed presentation and name it **P-U2-Act2-AudioVideo**. Run the presentation and then print the presentation as a handout with six slides horizontally per page. Close **P-U2-Act2-AudioVideo.pptx**.

Internet Research ━━━━━━━━━━━

Presenting Office 2010

Make sure you are connected to the Internet and then explore the Microsoft website at www.microsoft.com. Browse the various categories and links on the website to familiarize yourself with how information is organized.

Create a PowerPoint presentation that could be delivered to someone who has just purchased Office 2010 and wants to know how to find more information about the software from the Microsoft website. Include points or tips on where to find product release information and technical support. Include hyperlinks to important pages at the Microsoft website. Add formatting and enhancements to make the presentation as dynamic as possible. Save the presentation and name it **P-U2-Int-Office2010**. Run the presentation and then print the presentation as a handout with six slides per page. Close **P-U2-Int-Office2010.pptx**.

Job Study

Creating a Skills Presentation

You are preparing a presentation that you will use when presenting information on jobs at your local job fair. Open the Word document named **JobDescriptions.docx**, print the document, and then close the document and exit Word. Use the information in the document to prepare slides that describe each job (do not include the starting salary). Using the Internet, locate information on two other jobs that interest you and then create a slide for each job that provides information on job responsibilities. Determine the starting salary for the two jobs and then use that information along with the starting salary information for the jobs in the Word document to create a chart that displays the salary amounts. Locate at least two online job search websites and then include them in your presentation along with hyperlinks to the sites. Insert action buttons to move to the next page for the first slide through the second from the end. On your final slide, create an action button to return to the first slide.

Save the presentation and name it **P-U2-JobStudy**. Run the presentation and then print the presentation as a handout with six slides horizontally per page. Close **P-U2-JobStudy.pptx**.

Index

PowerPoint 2010 Feature	Ribbon Tab, Group	Button	Shortcut
Align text left	Home, Paragraph		Ctrl + L
Align text right	Home, Paragraph		Ctrl + R
Align text vertically	Home, Paragraph		
Audio clip	Insert, Media		
Bold text	Home, Font	B	Ctrl + B
Bullets	Home, Paragraph		
Center	Home, Paragraph		Ctrl + E
Chart	Insert, Illustrations		
Clip Art	Insert, Images		
Close presentation	File		Ctrl + F4
Copy	Home, Clipboard		Ctrl + C
Cut	Home, Clipboard		Ctrl + X
Font	Home, Font	Calibri	
Font color	Home, Font		
Font size	Home, Font	32	
Format Painter	Home, Clipboard		
Help	File		F1
Hyperlink	Insert, Links		Ctrl + K
Italicize text	Home, Font	I	Ctrl + I
Justify	Home, Paragraph		
Layout	Home, Slides		

PowerPoint 2010 Feature	Ribbon Tab, Group	Button	Shortcut
Line spacing	Home, Paragraph		
New slide	Home, Slides		Ctrl + M
Numbering	Home, Paragraph		
Paste	Home, Clipboard		Ctrl + V
Photo album	Insert, Images		
Picture	Insert, Images		
Print tab Backstage view	File, Print		Ctrl + P
Run presentation from beginning	Slide Show, Start Slide Show		F5
Save	File		Ctrl + S
Save As dialog box	File		F12
Screenshot	Insert, Images		
Shapes	Insert, Illustrations		
Slide Master view	View, Master Views		
SmartArt	Insert, Illustrations		
Spelling	Review, Proofing		F7
Table	Insert, Tables		
Text box	Insert, Text		
Themes	Design, Themes		
Underline text	Home, Font	U	Ctrl + U
Video clip	Insert, Media		
WordArt	Insert, Text		